GUIDE

POWER OF...
PC TOOLS
DELUXE™

THROUGH VERSION
7.1

2ND EDITION

CHARLES ACKERMAN

First Edition—1990
Second Edition—1991
ISBN 1-55828-181-9

Printed in the United States of America

To Rudolph Langer, Ph.D.,

whose daily moil proves that the best writers don't become authors.

ACKNOWLEDGMENTS

First, I would like to thank all the people at Central Point Software for being so courteous, enthusiastic, and helpful with this project. I've heard there's a tonic in the Pacific Northwest climate, and now I believe it.

When I started writing this book, there wasn't a single one on PC Tools Deluxe, the best-selling collection of DOS shell, desktop applications, and utility programs. Before this book was finished, Central Point Software had to set up a separate department simply to support all the books in progress. Through it all, they have been unfailing in their support, and this during an intense period of Beta product development.

CONTENTS

P C Tools Deluxe is a family of programs for the IBM PC. When you start to work with them, they are helpful; once you get used to them, they become necessary. This book is all about PC Tools Deluxe.

This Introduction is all about the book. It will help if you understand beforehand how I organized the book, and the way certain features are set up throughout.

I've written this book with many audiences in mind. Those who have never used PC Tools Deluxe need introductory information. Others want to know a lot about certain aspects of the program. Finally, some people will be familiar with most features, and simply need more advanced instruction.

Here's how I've presented the various parts of this book:

The first part contains three chapters, and teaches you how to use PC Shell. Chapter 1 describes the program and takes you on a quick tour of both the Desktop Manager and the PC Shell.

> This presumes that you have already installed the PC Tools program. If you haven't, begin with the Appendix.

Chapter 2 lets you get used to the PC Shell interface and basic commands. Chapter 3 describes the menu interface in detail (except for launching applications), and different ways of configuring the PC Shell screen. Chapter 4 is devoted to the Program List menu, and how to use it to launch programs. Only a minority of readers will use the PC Shell to this degree.

The second part of this book contains chapters that describe the components of Desktop Manager. These modules—including the Notepads, Outlines, and Databases editors—provide an integrated education about what you can do in Desktop Manager. The Notepads module comes first because most people will spend most of their time in the Notepads editor screen. The Clipboard and Outlines modules follow because they share much of the appearance and behavior of the Notepads editor.

The third section of this book contains chapters describing the various PC Tools utility programs. This section includes a description of the Windows-based PC Tools programs.

There is a method to this organization. On one hand, there is a flow from the general to the specific. On the other hand, the chapters are modular. You can read them in almost any order and still understand them, just as the PC Tools Deluxe programs can be used in any order.

This is a hands-on book. Examples are integrated into the text for every significant command in every PC Tools program. These examples are connected to one another with text and illustrations, but most of our time will be spent learning how to use the various features. You can follow the examples that interest you and skip over the ones that don't.

I am writing this book out of a real affection for PC Tools Deluxe. It is the best implementation of a DOS Shell and Desktop applications programs presently on the market, and Central Point Software, the maker of PC Tools, continues to keep its product current.

Terminology

Keyboard operations are represented throughout this book in brackets. For example, [Enter] refers to the Enter key, [F1] to the first function key, [Ctrl} to the Control key, and [A] to the letter A key.

DOS is not case-sensitive, so you can enter either uppercase or lowercase characters after the DOS prompt. For example, typing CHKDSK, chkdsk, or CHkdSk and pressing [Enter] all have the same effect. But to eliminate confusion, this book presents commands in uppercase. For example, if I ask you to experiment with the DOS command CHKDSK, I will present it like this:

Type: CHKDSK

Press: [Enter]

When a program responds with a message, I will present the text in typewriter typeface (also called Courier):

```
This text appears in Courier.
```

Notes and helpful hints are boxed with a shaded rule around them. Good luck and good reading.

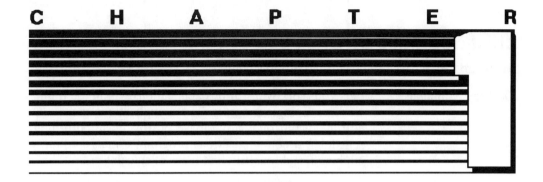

A TOUR OF PC TOOLS DELUXE

T his chapter is a quick tour of PC Tools Deluxe. On this tour you will gain experience using PC Tools by loading the Desktop Manager and learning how to use the basic program controls. Subsequent chapters will describe the Desktop Manager in detail and explore the other programs of PC Tools.

1

THE PROGRAMS OF PC TOOLS DELUXE

There are twenty-five principal programs that comprise PC Tools Deluxe:

Desktop Manager
Lets you work with various applications within the framework of a single program. These applications include an editor, an outliner, a database editor, an appointment scheduler, a communications program, a macro editor, a clipboard, and four different types of calculators.

PC Shell
Displays your disk contents in windows, in filename list, and in tree directory form. Also lets you perform all sorts of procedures on your disk files and memory configuration.

Compress
Maximizes disk performance by defragmenting file sections and making more efficient use of disk space.

DiskFix
Analyzes your disks, locates and fixes errors. Also revives corrupted or damaged floppy disks.

File Fix
Fixes damaged and corrupted files for dBASE, Lotus 1-2-3, and Symphony.

Mirror
Protects against data loss. This program saves filename information and recreates lost data.

Unformat
Formats disks in various ways. Designed to replace the DOS program FORMAT.COM.

Recovery Disk
Creates a recovery floppy disk that helps you to recover from a disastrous hard disk failure in which FAT (file allocation table) and system data were lost.

Undelete
Undeletes files and directories that have been deleted and not written over. There is both a DOS and a Windows version of this program.

Data Monitor
Protects your files in several ways, operating as a TSR (terminate-and-stay-resident) program monitoring your disk activity. You can find a list of files that cooperate to protect your data after this action.

Wipe
Wipes data off disks.

PC Secure	Protects your files by encrypting, compressing, and hiding files from view.
VDefend	Protects your files against several hundred viruses, and prevents the unauthorized formatting of your disks.
PC Format	Central Point Software's proprietary version of a disk formatting program (designed to replace the DOS command FORMAT.COM).
PC Cache	Disk caching program that speeds up access to your frequently used data.
System Information	Displays information about your current computer hardware configuration.
Memory Information	Displays information about the way your computer is currently using its memory.
FileFind	Locates individual files or groups of files across directories and drives.
Directory Maintenance	Helps you navigate through and maintain directories on different drives.
View	Lets you view the contents of data files,without having to load the program that wrote the file.
Commute	A communications program that lets you work with files on another computer by remote control.
Backup	Lets you backup file data from your hard disk to floppy disks or tape. There is both a DOS and a Windows version of this program.
TSR Monitor	Lets you monitor the status of TSR programs loaded in DOS when you work in Windows. This is a Windows program.
Program Launcher	Lets you launch DOS programs while working in Windows. This is a Windows program.
Scheduler	Lets you control the schedules of Backup, Commute, Email, and DiskFix while working in Windows. There is both a DOS and a Windows version of this program.

There are five PC Tools programs that are designed to protect your data. They are Data Monitor, Mirror, Wipe, PC Secure, VDefend, and PC Format. There are also five programs that run under Windows: Backup, Undelete, Program Launcher, TSR Monitor, and Scheduler.

Some of these are new programs, such as VDefend and Data Monitor. Others, such as Directory Maintenance, FileFind, and Undelete, are utilities that were available in previous version of PC Tools but now serve as stand-alone programs. These were a part of the PC Shell but have been enhanced and moved into separate programs of their own.

The programs added to Version 7 of PC Tools Deluxe that run under DOS include Commute, File Fix, Recover Disk, Unformat, Data Monitor, Wipe, VDefend, System Information, Memory Information, File Find, Directory Maintenance, and View.

> PC Tools Deluxe should be installed on your computer before you proceed with this chapter. If you haven't installed the program, read the appendix for more information.

All of these programs can work together or separately, depending upon what you want to do. They can be called programs, applications, or modules, and these names are used interchangeably throughout the book.

WAYS OF LOADING THE PROGRAMS

You can load the Desktop Manager and PC Shell programs two ways: as standard programs or as resident programs. If you use the programs often while you're working with other programs, then you'll probably want to run them in *resident mode*. This is a nickname for TSR, or terminate-and-stay-resident. This means that the program is first loaded into RAM (random access memory), and then terminated, but a portion remains in RAM. Resident mode allows you to interrupt your work in another program, pop the Desktop Manager or PC Shell up, work with it, then pop it back down again to resume your work.

However, running programs in resident mode causes computer conflicts, so the *standard mode* is also provided. Standard mode is how most programs for the IBM PC are designed to run: you load them from the DOS prompt. Running the Desktop Manager or PC Shell in standard mode should give you no conflicts, but you don't have the flexibility of popping in and out of the programs.

Running as a Standard Program

To load the Desktop Manager as a standard program:

Type: DESKTOP

Press: [Enter]

When you load the program in standard mode, you might see a copyright screen. If it appears, press any key to remove it. Then press [Enter] to open the main menu. Your screen should look like Figure 1.1.

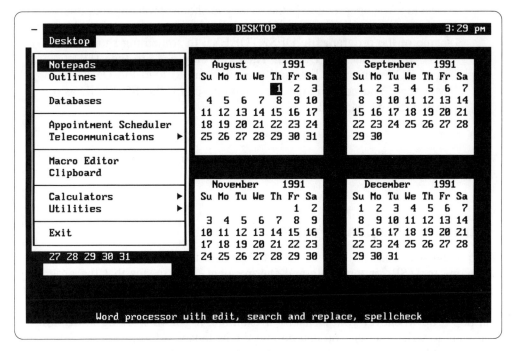

Figure 1.1. The Desktop main menu

This screen is fairly simple. The top line shows you're working in PC TOOLS, and the name of the only menu shows that you're working in the Desktop. This is the Desktop Manager main menu, which contains ten selections. The top selection, Notepads, should be highlighted. The bottom line on the screen shows the message: WORD PROCESSOR WITH EDIT, SEARCH AND REPLACE, SPELLCHECK. It defines the activities you can perform in Notepads.

You can check the activities provided in the other Desktop menu selections by pressing [⇓] and viewing the messages that appear on the bottom line for each selection. When you get to Telecommunications, you'll notice that another menu appears. This is called a *nested menu*. The nested menu under Telecommunications lets you select the type of communications you want to work with. In addition to Telecommunications, there are two other nested menus off of the Desktop menu, each denoted by an arrow to the right of the Desktop menu selection.

> You may occasionally need to use a program other than the Desktop Manager. If this is the case, you should probably load the program in standard mode. You might also want to change the name of the program file DESKTOP.EXE to something short and easy to type, such as D.EXE. Then you only need to type [D] at your DOS command line and press [Enter] to load the Desktop Manager. You can change the filename using the PC Shell, as explained in Chapter 2.

When you've reached the bottom of the Desktop menu, pressing [⇓] or [Home] will return you to Notepads.

Running as a Resident Program

The second way you can load PC Tools Deluxe is as a *resident* program. This is a nickname for TSR, or terminate-and-stay-resident. This means that the program is first loaded into RAM (random access memory) and then terminated, but a portion still resides in RAM. The beauty of running a program in resident mode is that you can pop it up whenever you need it. For example, if you're working in dBASE and you want to write a letter, you can pop up the Notepads Editor, write the letter, then pop Notepads down again and return to your work in dBASE.

The ability for the PC Tools programs to go resident is one of their most marvelous features. I run both the Desktop Manager and the PC Shell in resident mode most of the time. That way, they're always at hand when I need them.

Watch out when you have PC Tools programs and other programs loaded as resident. Running several TSRs at the same time can cause memory conflict, which leads to problems. If this happens, you should juggle the order in which the programs are loaded to determine what combination lets them cooperate the best.

If you run any PC Tools programs in resident mode and you also want to run SideKick or SideKick Plus, you must load the PC Tools programs first. The SideKick programs insist on being loaded last. If you try to load any PC Tools programs resident after loading SideKick or SideKick Plus, you'll get an error message. To clear the conflict, you'll have to unload the SideKick program first, load the PC Tools programs, and then reload SideKick or SideKick Plus.

To load the Desktop Manager in resident mode:

> **Type:** DESKTOP /R

> **Press:** [Enter]

The last part of this command, /R, is called the */R switch*, and means *load as resident*. In addition to the /R switch, there are other switches you can use for the Desktop Manager that let you customize the way the program looks or behaves. You will learn about these later in this book.

When the Desktop Manager is fully loaded as a resident program, it will display a message window on the screen and return to the DOS prompt (See Figure 1.2).

```
C:\>desktop /r


          PCTOOLS Desktop (tm)
               Version 7
          Copyright (c) 1988-1991
        Central Point Software, Inc.
        523 Kbytes free, 15 windows
            Hotkey: <CTRL><SPACE>

    ██████████████████████████████

C:\>
```

Figure 1.2. The Desktop Manager loaded as a resident program

The bottom two lines of this screen provide valuable information that is not shown when you load the program in the standard mode. The line above the bottom line shows how much memory remains in your computer and how many windows you can open. The bottom line shows which keys are configured as the hotkeys. Hotkeys are keys that you press to activate a command. The Desktop Manager shows <CTRL><SPACE> as a hotkey (if the hotkeys haven't been reconfigured). This means that when you press [Ctrl]-[Spacebar] at the same time, the Desktop Manager is activated, or popped up, regardless of what else you're doing:

Press: [Ctrl]-[Spacebar]

As the Desktop Manager pops up, you'll see the following message:

LOADING DESKTOP OVERLAYS. PLEASE WAIT.

In a few moments, your screen should again look just like Figure 1.1. You can explore some of the menu selections if you want to. Program control doesn't vary between modes of operation.

In resident mode, you can exit the Desktop Manager in three ways:

1. Press [Esc] to back out of whatever you've loaded onto your screen.

2. Return to the Desktop menu and select Exit.

3. Press [Ctrl]-[Spacebar], which pops down the program. When you do this, you've terminated only your use of the program; it still lies in memory waiting for you to pop it back up.

You cannot load the Desktop Manager, or any other PC Tools program that can go resident, in both resident and standard modes at the same time. If you forget, and try to load the program a second time, either in the same or different mode, you'll get an error message (if you're lucky) or a conflict (if you're not). When your programs conflict, you'll probably have to reboot the computer.

SWITCHING BETWEEN STANDARD AND RESIDENT MODES

Switching from standard mode to resident mode is not difficult. All you have to do is exit the program in standard mode and reload it with the /R switch.

If you want to switch from resident mode to standard mode, you'll first have to unload the program from memory. You can either use a menu selection or run the KILL.BAT program.

To remove the Desktop Manager from your computer's memory, first pop up the program:

Press: [Ctrl]-[Spacebar]

To open the Utilities menu:

Press: [U]

To select and execute the *Unload PCTOOLS Desktop Menu* command:

Press: [U]

In a moment, the program will be unloaded from your computer's memory. To perform this procedure more quickly, you can press [Alt]-[Spacebar] at the same time and then press [U] twice.

If you get a message that the program can't unload because other TSR programs have blocked its exit, you'll have to pop down the Desktop Manager, unload the other programs, and then unload the Desktop Manager..

You can also unload the Desktop Manager program from memory using a batch file program supplied on the PC Tools program disks. This program is called KILL.BAT, and it runs a program called INKILL.BAT that unloads all PC Tools programs currently resident in memory. When the Desktop Manager is loaded as resident and the DOS prompt is displayed, implement this program as follows:

Type: KILL

Press: [Enter]

FUNCTION-KEY ASSIGNMENTS

When function keys have assignments in various PC Tools Deluxe screens, the assignments usually are noted at the bottom of the screen. The Desktop menu screen is the exception; the following three function keys work, but none of them are noted:

[F1] **Help**   Opens the general Help screen.

[F2] **Index**   Opens the Help index.

[F3] **Exit**   Exits the Desktop menu screen and returns you to your previous work.

You should explore the two functions that access help, [F1] and [F2], before you go further into the program.

HELP

There are four major sources of help when using PC Tools programs: the manuals that come with the disks, outside sources (such as this book), the online help (accessible with the function keys), and the designers of the PC Tools program, who can be contacted at Central Point Software by phone or by accessing their technical support bulletin board. This chapter describes how to access the online help. Chapter 13, "Using Telecommunications," describes how to contact the CPS bulletin board.

When you access help from a specific operation in a PC Tools program, the program senses where you are and what you're doing and presents help information specific to the operation. This is known as *context-sensitive* help.

Regardless of where you are in any of the PC Tools programs, you can access context-sensitive and interactive help at any time by pressing [F1]. For example, while you're viewing the Desktop menu (shown in Figure 1.1), call up its Help screen, which is shown in Figure 1.3.

Press: [F1]

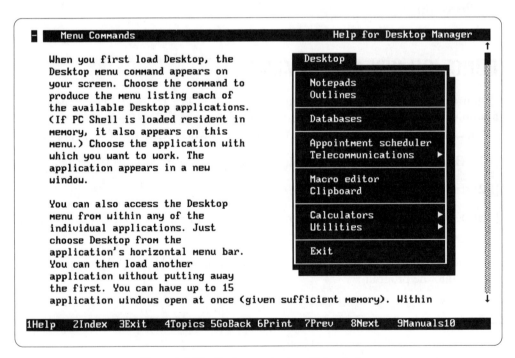

Figure 1.3. The Desktop main menu Help window

The information on this screen tells you how to use help while working in Desktop. You'll find the Notepads selection in the menu on the right side of your screen highlighted. If you wish to find out more about the Notepads module:

Press: [Enter]

This opens a more detailed screen, shown in Figure 1.4, that provides help on Notepads.

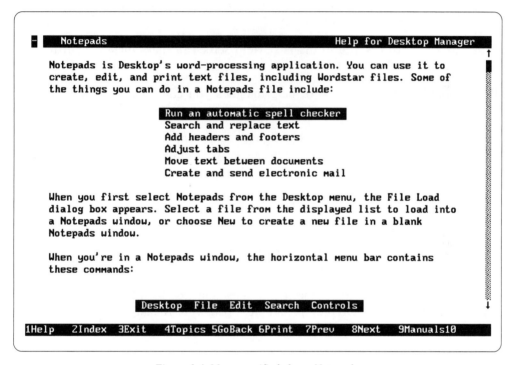

```
 ■  Notepads                                    Help for Desktop Manager
                                                                        ↑
     Notepads is Desktop's word-processing application. You can use it to  ■
     create, edit, and print text files, including Wordstar files. Some of
     the things you can do in a Notepads file include:

                    Run an automatic spell checker
                    Search and replace text
                    Add headers and footers
                    Adjust tabs
                    Move text between documents
                    Create and send electronic mail

     When you first select Notepads from the Desktop menu, the File Load
     dialog box appears. Select a file from the displayed list to load into
     a Notepads window, or choose New to create a new file in a blank
     Notepads window.

     When you're in a Notepads window, the horizontal menu bar contains
     these commands:

                  Desktop  File  Edit  Search  Controls                 ↓
 1Help   2Index  3Exit    4Topics 5GoBack 6Print  7Prev    8Next    9Manuals10
```

Figure 1.4. More specific help on Notepads

To return to the main Help screen:

Press: [F5]

The commands assigned to the function keys appear at the bottom of the screen.

[F1] Help   Opens up help on help.

[F2] Index   Displays a complete index list of help items.

[F3] Exit   Exits help and returns you to your previous place.

[F4] Topics   Displays a list of help topics you can view to access more specific information.

[F5] GoBack   Moves you one step back in your sequence of commands.

[F6] Print   Prints the current Help screen.

[F7] Prev   Moves you to the previous Help screen in the sequence built into the PC Tools help system.

[F8] Next   Moves you to the next Help screen in the sequence built into the help system.

[F9] Manuals   Displays a list of help manuals you can access for more specific information.

To view specific help on an entry, highlight the entry and:

    Press: [Enter]

To close any Help window:

    Press: [Esc]

Pressing [Esc] is the most common way for backing out of something. You can press [Esc] to close help, exit a module, and even quit the Desktop Manager.

If you accidentally press [Esc] too many times and exit the Desktop Manager, just type DESKTOP at the DOS prompt and press [Enter] to reload the program. To continue the tour, you should be looking at the Desktop main menu (shown in Figure 1.1).

ENTERING COMMANDS

Desktop Manager and PC Shell provide you with three ways to enter commands:

Key commands   Pressing keyboard and function keys. This is easier for people who have memorized frequently used commands and who are good typists.

Mouse controls   Pointing to a menu selection and clicking the mouse button. This is easier for people who are accustomed to working with a mouse and who prefer visual control over their activities.

Pull-down menus Highlighting a menu item and pressing [Enter]. This is easier for new users.

There are five Windows-based programs that operate under the Windows GUI (graphical user interface). These are described in Chapter 18, "Windows Programs."

Working with Key Commands

In all PC Tools programs, you can move screens and menus and select commands using cursor keys ([⇐], [⇒], [PgUp], [PgDn], [End], and [Home]), letter keys, and function keys. [Tab] will move you forward, and [Ctrl]-[Tab] will move you backward. You used cursor keys earlier to scrol! through selections on the Desktop menu.

One way to use keys to open a menu item is to press the letter key that appears in a different color or in reverse video on the monitor. To open Notepads:

> **Press:** [N]

This opens the Notepads dialog box, shown in Figure 1.5.

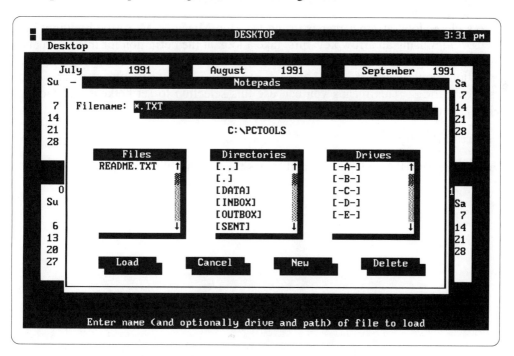

Figure 1.5. The Notepads dialog box

A dialog box is so named because it carries on a dialog with you; it asks what file you want to use and what you want to do with the file. You then reply. In this example, when you select Notepads on the Desktop menu, the dialog box asks you to select the file you want to check or edit.

You will work with Notepads in Chapter 6. For this quick tour, however, you should close the Notepads dialog box:

Press: [Esc]

Only two commands on the Desktop Manager main menu are activated by a key other than the first letter of the command. The first is the Clipboard, which uses B, and the second is Exit, which uses [X].

You'll find that pressing letter keys to move around menus can be very helpful. You might have to memorize a few irregular commands, such as [B] for Clipboard, but after using them a few times, they'll become habit. Menus respond quickly. After you become familiar with the menu structure of PC Tools, you'll go whizzing through menus to the exact command you want to use.

Take a closer look at other menus in the Desktop Manager. Move the highlight bar over *Utilities* using an arrow key. First take a look at the definition for this command on the bottom line of your screen. When the Utilities selection is highlighted, the definition should read: `Utilities to adjust Desktop operation and performance`. This means you can use this selection to set hotkeys and view a representation of the ASCII table. Now open the nested menu:

Press: [Enter]

Figure 1.6 shows the dialog box that displays the three utilities you can use.

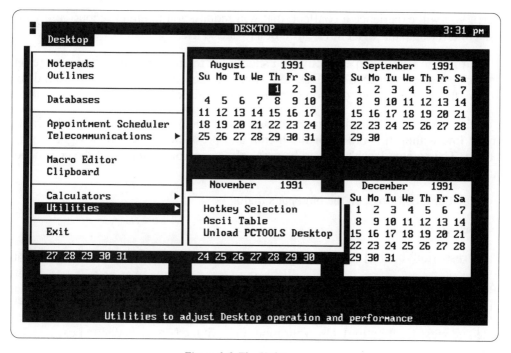

Figure 1.6. The Utilities menu

The first command on the Utility Programs, *Hotkey Selection,* should be highlighted. To select this command:

Press: [Enter]

This opens a third menu, which lets you reset hotkeys. Hotkeys will be explained later in this book. For now, press [Esc] until you return to the Desktop menu.

Using a Mouse

A mouse, track ball, or similar device can provide you with excellent control over Desktop Manager and most other PC Tools programs. Of course, to be able to use a mouse, your computer must be installed with a mouse and a mouse driver. The latter is a disk file that comes with the mouse you purchase.

The mouse cable is connected to a serial port, and the mouse driver is activated every time you boot your computer. Occasionally, when you've installed a mouse and you try to use modem communications (which also must be connected to a serial port), you will experience a conflect. that will require you to either reconfigure your system or disable the serial device you don't want to use.

If your mouse is installed correctly, you should see the mouse pointer somewhere on the screen when you load the Desktop Manager. You move the pointer around by sliding the mouse on your desktop or by rolling the track ball.

To select a menu command using the mouse, place the pointer anywhere on the command line within the borders of the menu, and press either the left or right mouse button. The pointer doesn't have to be precisely on any of the letters of the command name.

To use your mouse to open the Notepads dialog box:

Select: Notepads

Press: [Left button]

When the Notepads dialog box appears, four commands specific to mouse control appear on the right side of the dialog box: Load, New, Cancel, and Delete. To select any of these, place the pointer on the box containing the command you want to execute and press [Left button]. Use your mouse to exit the Notepads dialog box:

Select: Cancel

Press: [Left button]

This returns you to the Desktop menu. Another good example to work with is the Help index you looked at earlier (Figure 1.3):

Press: [F1]

You can use your mouse to scroll down through the index by placing your pointer on the down-arrow at the bottom of the scroll bar on the right side of the window and pressing [Left button]. Similarly, you can scroll back up by placing your pointer on the up arrow and pressing [Left button].

You'll find scroll bars throughout the Desktop Manager modules, as well as arrows and other features you can use with your mouse to open, close, and resize windows.

To initiate commands, this book will use only keyboard and menu commands because most PC users do not have a mouse, although those who do will find using one simple.

Using Pull-down Menus

The PC Tools Deluxe programs are intensively menu driven. You've seen the Desktop menu and menus nested in the Desktop menu. For a more detailed example, take a look at the Clipboard menu system (shown in Figure 1.7). When you're viewing the main menu, open your Clipboard module window:

Press: [B]

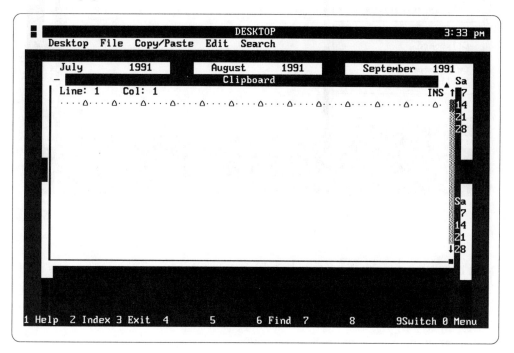

Figure 1.7. The Clipboard window

When the Clipboard window appears, you'll find the names of five pull-down menus you can use in the Clipboard: Desktop, File, Copy/Paste, Edit, Search, and Window. To open a pull-down menu, press [Alt] or [F10] and the key that matches the first letter of the menu you want to open.

For instance, to open the Desktop menu:

Press: [Alt]-[D]

When the menu is open, it will look like Figure 1.8.

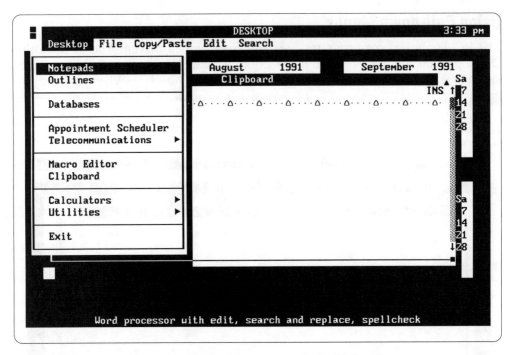

Figure 1.8. The Desktop menu open in the Clipboard

Don't be concerned with the details on this or any of the other Clipboard menus until you start working with this module in Chapter 7. To close any pull-down menu:

Press: [Esc]

Another example is to open the Search menu:

Press: [Alt]-[S]

This provides you with two commands: Find and Replace. If you wish to open the Find menu:

Press: [Enter]

To close that menu and return to the Clipboard screen:

Press: [Esc]

> You can press either [Alt] or [F10] to activate the top menu bar. You'll notice the first letters of each pull-down menu name change color or shade. I prefer to use [Alt] because I can hold it down with my thumb.

The Desktop and Window pull-down menus are available in the nine applications you can access from the Desktop menu. Each module then provides other menus unique to the work you can do in the module. First, return to the Desktop menu:

Press: [Esc]

Press: [Alt]-[D]

Then open one of the calculators:

Press: [C]

Press: [Enter]

Now open a second module.

Press: [Alt]-[D]

This opens the Desktop menu. Select the Clipboard again (so that you don't have to go through a dialog box):

Press: [B]

Now open the Edit menu in the Clipboard:

Press: [Alt]-[E]

Your screen should resemble Figure 1.9.

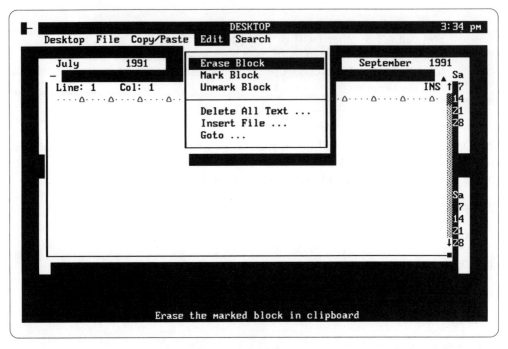

Figure 1.9. The Edit Menu

What you've done is open the algebraic calculator, overlay it with the Clipboard, then open the Edit pull-down menu.

Before moving on, close the Edit menu:

Press: [Esc]

Press: [F9]

Notice that the calculator switches with the Clipboard screen. Press [F9] again to return to the Clipboard.

Now open the Control menu, which is similar in appearance and behavior to the Control menu in Windows applications (see Chapter 18):

Press: [Alt]-[Spacebar]

The Control menu is shown in Figure 1.10.

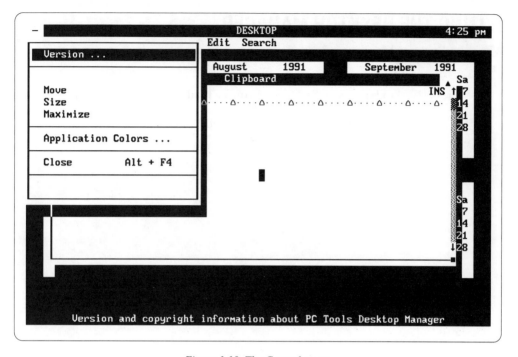

Figure 1.10. The Control menu

Using the Control menu, you can change the way your current window appears and behaves using these commands:

Version	Displays the current name and number of the version of PC Tools you're using.
Restore	Restores the current window to its default size.
Move	Lets you move the current window around your screen.
Size	Lets you change the size of the current window.
Maximize	Expands the current window to full size.
Application Colors	Lets you select colors for features on your screen.
Close	Closes the current window and moves you to the next window underneath.
Switch To	Lets you switch to another open window.

EXITING THE DESKTOP MANAGER

When the Desktop Manager is loaded as a standard program; you can exit it in two ways:

1. Press [Esc] to back out of whatever you've loaded onto your screen.

2. Return to the Desktop menu and select *Exit.*

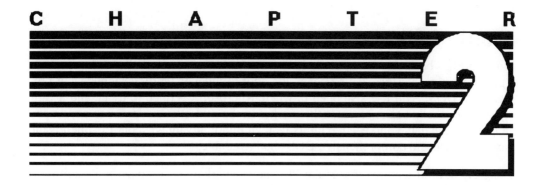

USING PC SHELL

A *shell* is a tool that gives you a graphical view of your work environment and increased functionality, which provides greater control over DOS, Microsoft's disk operating system for the IBM PC family of computers. The basic purpose of a shell is to make working with an operating system easier.

ABOUT PC SHELL

Microsoft has been slow to upgrade its DOS. Only with version 4.0 did they include a graphical user interface. This opened the door to independently designed shell programs for DOS. Avid users stepped in where Microsoft declined to tread, and a variety of DOS shells began to enter the market in the mid-1980s. There are now many DOS shells available and each exhibits its own minor advantages, but PC Shell is the most complete and comprehensive DOS shell available.

There are several features that make PC Shell remarkable. Foremost is its ability to go resident, which lets you work with DOS without leaving another program.

PC Shell also provides an extensive range of commands you can use to manage and work with your disk files.

While working in PC Shell, you can:

- Work in a graphic-windowed environment
- Change the user level to suit your skills and needs
- Use all popular DOS commands more easily, use the original commands on the DOS command line, and use more commands than are provided in DOS
- Use keyboard and mouse controls
- Recover inadvertently deleted files
- View a wide variety of file contents in their original format
- Launch outside applications, such as WordPerfect, dBASE, Lotus, and the PC Tools utility programs
- Access Desktop Telecommunications to send and receive e-mail and fax transmissions
- Work with standard network-compatible DOS functions on Novell's NetWare and IBM's Token-Ring networks
- Customize and configure the shell environment to your own needs, either temporarily or permanently
- View information about your current computer system configuration
- View the location of specific files on a screen map
- View a display of current memory usage

Believe it or not, a complete list would be much longer than this. However, don't be intimidated; everything will be explained in the next three chapters.

LOADING AND QUITTING PC SHELL

PC Shell can be loaded in both standard and resident mode. The mode you use determines the way you enter and exit the program.

Standard Mode

Standard mode refers to the way most programs are loaded. They can be accessed only from the DOS prompt. To load another standard program, you must quit the first program and load the second.

If you want to load PC Shell in standard mode, you use the following command at the DOS prompt:

Type: PCSHELL

Press: [Enter]

You'll see messages indicating that the system area and disk tree are being read. The screen then appears with the copyright notice overlaying it. To begin working in PC Shell, press any key.

> You can insert the command PCSHELL in your AUTO-EXEC.BAT file if you want PC Shell to appear each time you boot your computer.

When you load PC Shell in standard mode, you use the maximum amount of memory for the program, which means that you'll have the quickest program response. To exit PC Shell when it has been loaded in standard mode:

Press: [Esc]

You'll be prompted to confirm whether you really want to exit. To confirm and return to the DOS prompt:

Press: [Esc]

You should use PC Shell in standard mode only when you will be using it for an extended period of time, such as when you copy files from the hard disk to a floppy or tape backup, compress files, and do other routine DOS housekeeping chores.

Resident Mode

Resident mode refers to the ability of PC Shell to reside in your computer's memory and to be called up whenever you need it. You can pop up the shell using hotkeys, work in PC Shell, then pop it down and return to your previous work. PC Shell will reside in your computer's memory, ready to be popped up the next time it is needed. As explained in Chapter 1, this type of program is called a TSR program.

To load PC Shell into memory:

Type: PCSHELL /R

Press: [Enter]

In resident mode, PC Shell displays a sign-on screen that looks like Figure 2.1.

```
C:\>pcshell /r


       PCTOOLS PC Shell (TM)
             Version 7
    Copyright (c) 1985-1991
  Central Point Software, Inc.
        536 Kbytes free
      Hotkey: <CTRL> <ESC>

  ████████████████████████


C:\>
```

Figure 2.1. PC Shell sign-on screen

This message remains on screen when the system returns to the DOS prompt. It gives you the name and version number of the program you're working with, copyright information, and the amount of memory that remains free after loading PC Shell. It also tells you the hotkeys you would use to pop the program up and down, which ensures that you will always be able to find the meanings of your hotkeys.

Once PC Shell has been loaded into memory, you can pop it up and use it, or load another program in standard or resident mode. (If you load the Desktop Manager in resident mode after PC Shell, you'll be able to access PC Shell from a command on the Desktop main menu.) To pop up PC Shell:

Press: [Ctrl]-[Esc]

PC Shell reads the system area and tree structure just as when you loaded the program in standard mode. It takes a little longer than usual the first time you load it, because it has to read the current data and setup.

Even though you can pop up PC Shell over another program, you shouldn't do this when the other program is in the middle of an operation, such as saving a file. TSR programs override whatever else is going on, and if you're saving a file, the save operation is stopped immediately. In most cases, saving will resume when you pop the TSR program back down, but it is possible that the operation will go haywire. You could lose some or all of the data in the file.

To exit PC Shell when in resident mode:

Press: [Ctrl]-[Esc]

You can also press [Esc] twice, or [Esc] once and [X] once to exit PC Shell. Once the PC Shell is popped down, you return to whatever you were doing before you loaded it—the DOS prompt, another program, or the Desktop main menu.

> You can insert the commands for loading PC Shell in resident mode into your AUTOEXEC.BAT file, which automatically executes programs when you turn on your computer. If you want to load the Desktop Manager and PC Shell each time you start to work, you may insert the following series of commands into your AUTOEXEC.BAT.
>
> ```
> @echo off
> pcshell/rl
> desktop/rs
> cls
> ```
>
> The /rl and /rs switches define memory use. You'll learn about them in the next section.

Tradeoffs in Resident Mode

Using PC Shell in resident mode involves some tradeoffs in memory and load precedence. PC Shell is sensitive to other resident programs, so you can use it with other TSRs, but there are exceptions. You can't install PC Shell after loading SideKick or SideKick Plus. These insist on being loaded last.

In some cases, two TSR programs will use the same hotkeys. When you press the hotkeys, both programs try to grab the controls, and you'll probably end up with a memory conflict that requires you to reboot. PC Shell allows you to reconfigure the hotkeys that control it, but you should avoid using conflicting TSR programs.

Precedence in loading also applies to precedence in unloading. Since DOS can't tolerate a hole in memory, you have to unload resident programs in precisely the opposite order that you loaded them. This subscribes to the LIFO rule: last in, first out. You can always remove all resident PC Tools programs by running KILL.BAT.

Since every program you run uses some RAM, DOS can be severely constrained by the 640-kilobyte limit for RAM. It's easy to run into *RAM cram*—running out of RAM and having to unload a program to make room for another. PC Shell isn't immune to this, but you can adjust the amount of memory it uses by loading the program using various switches. You can use as few as ten or as many as 255 kilobytes.

Using Switches

There are seventeen switches that can change the appearance or behavior of PC Shell. Some are available only in resident mode, others can be used in both modes. Some switches can be used together, while others are mutually exclusive. Most use letters that serve as a reminder for what action the switch performs.

Switches available in PC Tools are:

drive: A letter designating the active drive. It specifies which drive becomes active when PC Shell is popped up. For example, typing PCSHELL D: [Enter] makes the D drive active. Once working within PC Shell, you can switch active drives using shell commands. This switch can be used for both standard and resident modes and with other switches.

/A### Determines the *active memory size* for PC Shell above 225 kilobytes, letting you fine-tune the amount of computer memory and squeeze in other programs. The amount of resident memory used by the shell when it is not active equals the setting you specify (in kilobytes). For example, /A245 would use 245 kilobytes of RAM.

/BW Sets the *black-and-white video mode,* which provides a better screen display when using a color card with a monochrome monitor.

/DQ Saves the current memory map for an application when PC Shell pops up. DQ stands for *Disable Quickload.* Loading PC Shell with this switch takes extra time, but ensures that nothing will be lost when you return to your previous application. You should use this switch only if you experience problems exiting PC Shell to return to your previous work.

/FF   On CGA (color graphics adaptor) display monitors, this switch (for *Free Flicker*) disables screen-snow suppression, which can slow down screen movement, particularly when you scroll through data or move through screens by pressing [PgDn].

/F#   Lets you assign a specific function key to serve as the second hotkey. For example, /F1 makes the hotkeys [Ctrl]-[F1], and [F2] makes them [Ctrl]-[F2]. You can use this switch only when in resident mode.

/LE   This switch stands for *Left Exchange*. It is designed to accommodate left-handed mouse users by exchanging the functions on the left side of your mouse with those on the right side.

/IM   Stands for *Ignore Mouse,* and can be used to disable the mouse if it is an early model or is otherwise incompatible with PC Shell.

/IN   This switch stands for the *INColor card*. It runs PC Shell in color mode if your computer uses the Hercules InColor video card. If you use an InColor card and load PC Shell resident without activating this switch, PC Shell will be displayed in black-and-white. If you load PC Shell standard, its normal colors will be displayed without using this switch.

/Odrive*:* Determines in which drive to store the temporary swap files PC Shell uses to store information on disk and conserve RAM, whether the program has been loaded as resident or standard. If you don't specify a drive, the default drive containing the PC Tools program files is used. Use this switch if you've created a RAM drive with enough room to accommodate the files. For example, if your RAM drive is D, use the switch /OD. The more RAM you use, the less disk space you need. The disk space required for the four memory variables in resident mode are:

> **/RT**   *Tiny* mode: uses 439 kilobytes of disk space for the three files if PC Shell is hotkeyed from DOS. If hotkeyed from another application, it uses 653 kilobytes.
>
> **/RS**   *Small* mode: uses 505 kilobytes for the three files if hotkeyed from DOS; otherwise 371 kilobytes.
>
> **/RM**   *Medium* mode: uses 338 kilobytes for the three files if hotkeyed from DOS; otherwise 434 kilobytes.

/RL *Large* mode: uses 234 kilobytes for the three files regardless of where you hotkey it.

/PS2 Reconfigures your mouse setting, if necessary, when you are working with Microsoft Windows or on an IBM PS/2 computer.

/350 Configures your display for VGA mode with 350 lines on your screen. The results you see vary, depending upon your type of display monitor.

/R Loads PC Shell in resident mode and lets you specify one of four memory usages. The less memory you use for PC Shell, the more you have for other uses; the more memory you use, the quicker PC Shell responds.

    /RT Loads PC Shell into *tiny* use of memory (approximately 10 kilobytes of RAM). This is the default setting (same as /R) if you don't specify another value.

    /RS Loads PC Shell into *small* use of memory (approximately 88 kilobytes of RAM).

    /RM Loads PC Shell into *medium* use of memory (approximately 120 kilobytes of RAM).

    /RL Loads PC Shell into *large* use of memory (approximately 225 kilobytes of RAM). Refer to the /A### switch for more information about how you can fine-tune memory usage in the large setting.

/TR# This switch stands for *Tree Read.* It determines how often PC Shell should read the current tree structure on disk. PC Shell uses the information to display the tree structure in the *Tree List* window. /TR0 tells PC Shell to read the disk tree structure each time the program is loaded. Other numbers serve as the number of days between reads; for example, /TR1 reads the disk every day, /TR7 reads it once a week.

Switch characters are not case-sensitive.

> I load the Desktop Manager using the small memory setting and I load PC Shell using the large memory setting, because quick access to DOS is important to me. Rarely, I have to unload PC Shell and reload it using less memory, but this is easy to do.

Depending upon your computer configuration, some switches might be necessary, others recommended, and others will have no effect at all. When you use mutually exclusive switches, only the last switch takes effect. For example, if you load PC Shell using the command *PCSHELL /RL /RS /RM,* PC Shell will be installed resident using the medium amount of memory. The /RM switch was the first memory allocation switch to be parsed, and fixed memory allocation. The /RS switch was the second to be parsed, and the /RL switch was the third, but the feature they both work with had already been allocated.

If you use PC Shell in resident mode—and I strongly recommend that you do—the most crucial switches are those that control memory size, the /R and /A### switches. The four /R switches allow you to load the program conveniently using one of four preset memory configurations. The /A### switch lets you adjust how much memory PC Shell occupies in the large setting.

THE PC SHELL SCREEN

When PC Shell is loaded and active, it looks like Figure 2.2.

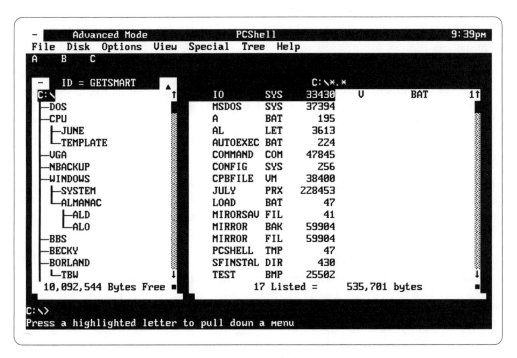

Figure 2.2. The PC Shell screen

The default level of operation is Advanced, indicated in the upper-right corner of your screen. In default, this screen has five primary groups of features:

Top menu bar   The top line displays the name of the program (PC Shell), six pull-down menus, and the current time.

Drive line   The second line from the top shows the letters of installed drives detected by PC Shell, with the active drive highlighted.

Two windows   Taking up the largest part of your screen, the left window shows the current tree structure. The right window shows the current directory file contents.

DOS command line   The second line from the bottom shows the familiar DOS prompt, which allows you to type DOS commands when you prefer.

Function key bar   All ten function keys have assignments in PC Shell.

The Tree and File-List Windows

PC Shell presents you with a graphical user interface (GUI) driven by key and menu commands.

Two windows show on the default PC Shell screen. The *Tree List* window, on the left, shows the directories on the current drive in a tree-like structure. The bottom line of this window shows the amount of unused space on the current drive. The *File List* window, on the right, shows the list of files in the directory highlighted in the Tree List window. The bottom line of the File List window shows the number of files in the current directory and how much space they occupy.

Only one window can be active at a time. The active window appears with a double-highlighted border. To toggle back and forth between the left and right window, use the tab key. To move around within a single window, use arrow keys, [PgDn], and [PgUp].

To select a different directory and its file contents on the current disk, make the left window active. Then press [⇓] or [PgDn] to highlight the directory you want to use.

When you press [PgDn] in the File List window, you'll move to the bottom of a short list of files (if they only form one column). If the list is longer, you'll move to the filename at the top of the second column. Pressing [PgDn] again moves you to the top of the third column. Pressing [PgDn] a fourth time begins to move you through screenfuls of filenames. This can be a little disconcerting at first, but soon you find it helpful. The [PgUp] key moves you upward in the same manner.

Viewing Different Disk Drives

The drive line is the second line from the top of your screen. This shows the label *Drive* and the letters of installed drives PC Shell detects on your computer. On my computer, drives A, B, and C are available (see Figure 2.3), but if you use many different drives, the letters can stretch across most of this line.

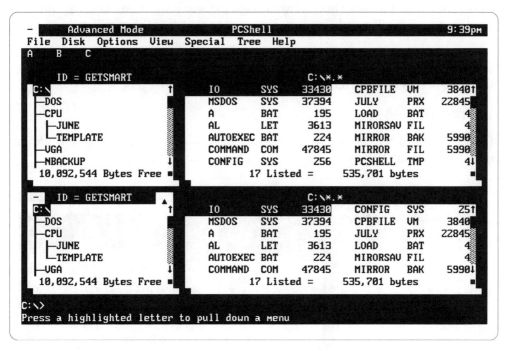

Figure 2.3. PC Shell showing two sets of windows

You can view the file structure on other disks by pressing [Ctrl] and the letter key that matches the drive letter you want to use. For example, to view the file structure on disk A:

Press: [Ctrl]-[A]

For this command to work, there must be a disk in the drive you want to switch to.

Notice that the drive letter A changes to reflect the new disk drive being viewed. Notice also that the disk file information beneath the window changes. You can also view the file structure of two disks simultaneously on this screen.

Press: [Ins]

This should open a set of left and right windows, one set above the other, as shown in Figure 2.3. You switch between pairs of drive windows the same way you switch between windows for one drive, by pressing [Tab].

Press [Shift]-[Tab] to walk backward through the windows. This way, regardless of which window is active, only one key is needed to switch to the other windows.

You can see the usefulness of viewing two pairs of windows when viewing the contents of two different drives. First, make the lower pair of windows active. Next, display the contents of the disk in drive A in this set:

Press: [Ctrl]-[A]

The lower set of windows displays the contents of the disk in drive A while the upper set continues to display the C-drive contents. See Figure 2.4.

```
 -       Advanced Mode            PCShell                       9:41PM
 File  Disk  Options  View  Special  Tree  Help
A    B    C
      ID = GETSMART                        C:\*.*
C:\                     t   IO       SYS    33430   CPBFILE  VM    38401
 ─DOS                       MSDOS    SYS    37394   JULY     PRX   22845
 ─CPU                       A        BAT      195   LOAD     BAT       4
   ─JUNE                    AL       LET     3613   MIRORSAV FIL       4
   ─TEMPLATE                AUTOEXEC BAT      224   MIRROR   BAK    5990
 ─VGA                       COMMAND  COM    47845   MIRROR   FIL    5990
 ─NBACKUP                ↓  CONFIG   SYS      256   PCSHELL  TMP      4↓
  10,092,544 Bytes Free ■      17 Listed =    535,701 bytes        ■

 -       ID = None          ▲                      A:\*.*
A:\                     t   FINSTALL EXE   350868                     t
                            README   COM     8038

                        ↓                                            ↓
     3,072 Bytes Free ■        2 Listed =     358,906 bytes          ■

A:\>
Press a highlighted letter to pull down a menu
```

Figure 2.4. PC Shell showing contents of two different disks

You can press [Tab] or [Shift]-[Tab] to switch back and forth between the upper- and lower-disk displays. Two things change when you do this: the active-disk letter for the drive, and the directory-contents information.

You can close and open the inactive set of windows using the [Ins] and [Del] keys. To close the inactive set of windows:

Press: [Del]

To open the closed display:

Press: [Ins]

If you don't want to close a display, but just want to take a better look at the contents in the active window:

Press: [F8]

This zooms the active window to full-screen size. Pressing [F8] a second time returns you to the previous display. Working within a single window, you should practice pressing [Tab], [Shift]-[Tab], [Ins], [Del], and [F8], as well as your cursor keys, [PgDn], and [PgUp]. You will often use these keys; the sooner you memorize them, the more comfortable you'll be working in PC Shell.

The DOS Command Line

You're given direct access to the DOS command line on the second line from the bottom of your screen. The cursor will be blinking after the DOS prompt when the PC Shell screen appears in the default configuration. The current path that shows in the active window will always be reflected in the DOS prompt.

When the DOS command line is showing and you type character keys, the characters will appear next to the DOS prompt. This lets you access familiar DOS commands.

Try this DOS command:

Type: VER

Press: [Enter]

PC Shell will tell you it is freeing memory to run the command, then it will run VER, the DOS command that checks the current version of DOS. The PC Shell screen will disappear, the version number will be displayed, and then the PC Shell screen will reappear. You might want to try this with the DOS command DIR, too.

If you don't see a DOS reply, check the current setting for Background Mat.

Press: [Alt]-[V]-[C]

Make sure the setting for the command *Background Mat* is turned off.

If you intend to use commands on the DOS line frequently and read responses from the screen, you'll want to close the left window so you can view the replies from DOS.

Press: [Alt]-[V]-[C]

This opens the View/Custom List Configure pull-down menu. Don't pay too much attention to this menu right now, just select the *Tree List Window* command:

Press: [T]

The left window should disappear. Now you're ready to run some commands and view DOS replies.

If you leave PC Shell while the Tree List window is turned off, you'll be asked whether you want to save this change to the configuration or cancel it. You shouldn't change the default configuration of PC Shell until you've become familiar with its default appearance:

Press: [C]

Configuring the DOS Command Line

If you find you don't need the DOS command line, you can turn it off and use that extra line to display one more line of information in the windows. To do this:

Press: [Alt]-[V]

This opens the View pull-down menu. To select Custom List Configure:

Press: [C]

The arrow to the right of this command shows that the command leads to another menu.

Press: [D]

This selects the DOS Command Line and toggles the feature off. The extra line is added to the bottom of the closest window or windows.

You can also replace the DOS command line with a list of shortcut key assignments. These commands comprise the second tier of the most popular commands in PC Shell. (The first tier is assigned to the function keys.) You'll find out more about shortcut keys in the next chapter.

Command History

An internal record is kept of the previous fifteen commands you've typed and executed at the DOS command line. This lets you access previous commands and reinsert them on the DOS command line. This way you won't have to retype often-used commands.

After you've typed several commands, you can move back and forth through the list to the command you want. To move backward through the list, press [Ctrl]-[⇐]. To move forward through the list, press [Ctrl]-[⇒]. Practice using this feature now:

Type: DIR

Press: [Enter]

Type: VER

Press: [Enter]

Type: CHKDSK

Press: [Enter]

When the last command has finished running, you can re-enter the CHKDSK command this way:

Press: [Ctrl]-[⇐]

You don't execute the command until you press [Enter]. To access a command you executed before CHKDSK:

Press: [Ctrl]-[⇐]

You'll see VER appear. If this is the command you want:

Press: [Enter]

The VER command is executed just as if you had typed it in.

To repeat the CHKDSK command:

Press: [Ctrl]-[⇒]

When CHKDSK appears on the DOS command line, you can execute it, look for other commands, or type a new command.

The Function Keys

The fifth and last feature in the PC Shell screen is the display of ten function keys and the commands assigned to them:

[F1] Help   Called PCSHELL.HLP, this opens the first Help screen for PC Shell.

[F2] QView   Opens the Quick viewer showing the contents of the selected file. You can view and move through file contents using viewer, but you cannot edit the file.

[F3] Exit   Exits PC Shell, returning you to the previous screen and application.

[F4] Unsel   Unselects all selected files.

[F5] Copy   Opens the File Copy box, which begins the process of copying a file to a different location.

[F6] Display   Opens the Display Options menu, which lets you select various ways to display filenames in the File List window.

[F7] Locate   Opens the File Locate box, which lets you specify the parameters for the filename you're looking for. You can use DOS wildcards, * and ?, which replace combinations of characters in the filenames.

[F8] Zoom   Toggles the active window between full screen and the current size.

[F9] Select   Opens the File Select window, which lets you select a range of file-names in the File List window based upon some common character-istic of their filenames.

[F10] Menu   Moves you into the Program List mode. Pressing [F10] when view-ing the Program List moves you back into PC Shell. Note that only the function key number appears on the bottom line of your screen: *1 Help, 2Q View,* and so on. F10 appears as *0 Menu.*

You can reassign commands to most of your function keys if you want to customize them for your own use. This is described in the next chapter.

Using the Default Function Key Assignments

The ten commands assigned to the displayed function keys are most frequently used when working with DOS files in PC Shell. The Copy key [F5] is the only function key that corresponds to an actual DOS command; it does the same thing as the commands DOS COPY, XCOPY, and DISKCOPY. The other function keys are only available in PC Shell; they help you to work with DOS commands on a refined basis. Learning these commands will make working in PC Shell many times more effective than working directly with DOS..

Help

The [F1] key lets you access context-sensitive help in all the PC Tools programs. To view its effect in PC Shell, make the Tree List window active. Then:

Press: [F1]

Press: [Enter]

This shows you help in the Tree List window, as shown in Figure 2.5.

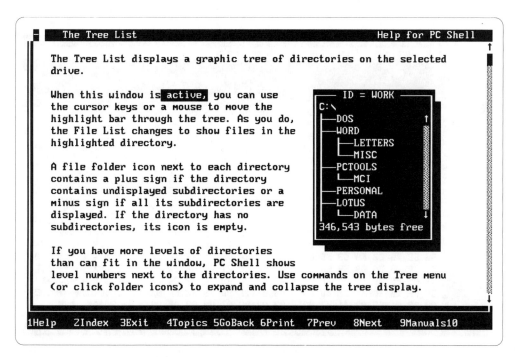

Figure 2.5. The Help window popped open when the Tree List is active

To see more information:

> **Press:** [PgDn]

To access help information about any aspect of PC Shell, press [F9]. To view help information specific to a certain item, highlight that item and press [Enter]. Close any Help screen by pressing [F3] for EXIT, or by pressing [Esc].

Taking a Quick View

Viewing file contents quickly is handy when you want to refer to a file without loading it into the program that created it (such as dBASE, WordPerfect, or Lotus 1-2-3).

To view the contents of a file quickly, highlight the filename and press [F2]. You can view the contents of a wide variety of file types in their native formats. PC Shell has four types of generic viewers that display text, spreadsheet, database, and binary data on your screen.

For example, highlighting in my root directory the command .COM file and pressing [F2] makes my screen look like Figure 2.6.

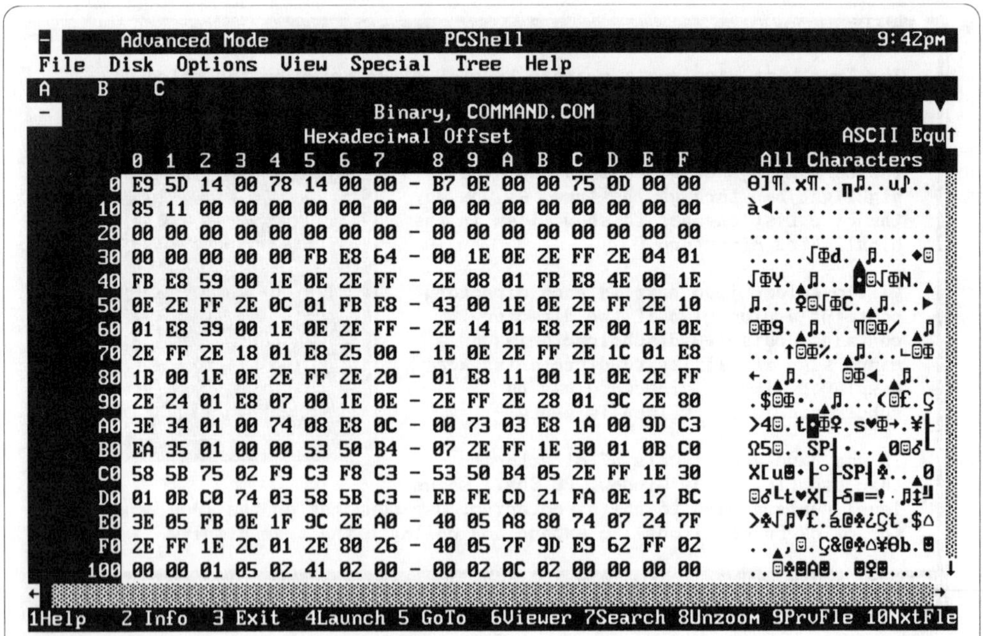

Figure 2.6. COMMAND.COM displayed in the Binary Viewer

If I highlight my dBASE database file on publishers and press [F2], my screen looks
like Figure 2.7.

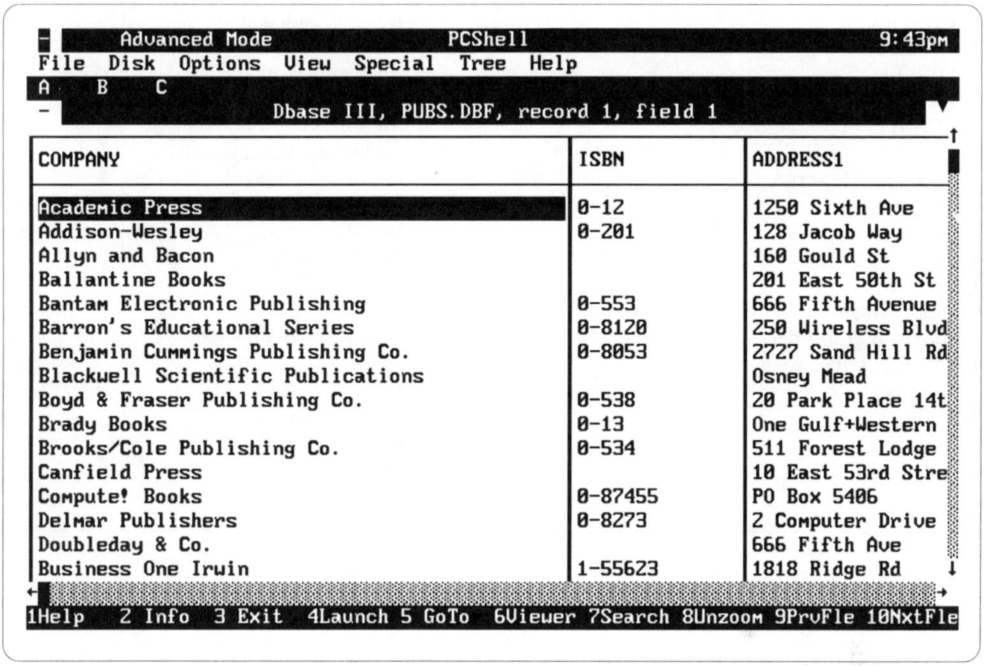

```
─  Advanced Mode              PCShell                      9:43pm
 File  Disk  Options  View  Special  Tree  Help
A   B    C
 ─            Dbase III, PUBS.DBF, record 1, field 1

┌──────────────────────────────────┬───────────┬─────────────────┐
│ COMPANY                          │ ISBN      │ ADDRESS1        │
├──────────────────────────────────┼───────────┼─────────────────┤
│ Academic Press                   │ 0-12      │ 1250 Sixth Ave  │
│ Addison-Wesley                   │ 0-201     │ 128 Jacob Way   │
│ Allyn and Bacon                  │           │ 160 Gould St    │
│ Ballantine Books                 │           │ 201 East 50th St│
│ Bantam Electronic Publishing     │ 0-553     │ 666 Fifth Avenue│
│ Barron's Educational Series      │ 0-8120    │ 250 Wireless Blvd│
│ Benjamin Cummings Publishing Co. │ 0-8053    │ 2727 Sand Hill Rd│
│ Blackwell Scientific Publications│           │ Osney Mead      │
│ Boyd & Fraser Publishing Co.     │ 0-538     │ 20 Park Place 14t│
│ Brady Books                      │ 0-13      │ One Gulf+Western│
│ Brooks/Cole Publishing Co.       │ 0-534     │ 511 Forest Lodge│
│ Canfield Press                   │           │ 10 East 53rd Stre│
│ Compute! Books                   │ 0-87455   │ PO Box 5406     │
│ Delmar Publishers                │ 0-8273    │ 2 Computer Drive│
│ Doubleday & Co.                  │           │ 666 Fifth Ave   │
│ Business One Irwin               │ 1-55623   │ 1818 Ridge Rd   │
└──────────────────────────────────┴───────────┴─────────────────┘
1Help   2 Info  3 Exit  4Launch 5 GoTo  6Viewer 7Search 8Unzoom 9PrvFle 10NxtFle
```

Figure 2.7. A dBASE database file in the Data Base Viewer

If the file you're viewing contains more characters than can fit onto one screen, press
[PgDn] or [PgUp].

Table 2.1 shows the four viewers and the types of files you can display in them.

Binary Viewers	Text Viewers
.ARC files	ASCII files
.BIN files	.BAT files
.COM files	Desktop Notepad
.EXE files	DisplayWrite
.OVL files	Microsoft Word
.PAK files	Microsoft Works
.PCX files	Multimate
	Multimate Advantage
Database Viewers	Lotus Symphony
Clipper	WordPerfect 4.2
dBASE	WordPerfect 5
dBXL	WordStar (all)
Foxbase	XyWrite
Lotus Symphony	
Microsoft Works data	**Spreadsheet Viewers**
Notepads Database	Excel
Paradox	Lotus 1-2-3 (all)
R:Base	Lotus Symphony
	Microsoft Works
	Mosaic Twin
	Quattro

Table 2.1. Four quick viewers and associated files

SELECTING AND UNSELECTING FILES

Selecting files lets you work with a group of files at the same time, for instance to copy or delete more than one file in the current directory. You can select one file at a time or select a group based upon some common characteristic of their filenames. To select one file at a time, move your cursor over the filename in the File List window and press [Enter]. This places the filename in reverse video (or a different color, depending upon your screen) and inserts a number to the left of the filename.

As an example, when I mark my AUTOEXEC.BAT and CONFIG.SYS files in my root directory, my screen looks like Figure 2.8.

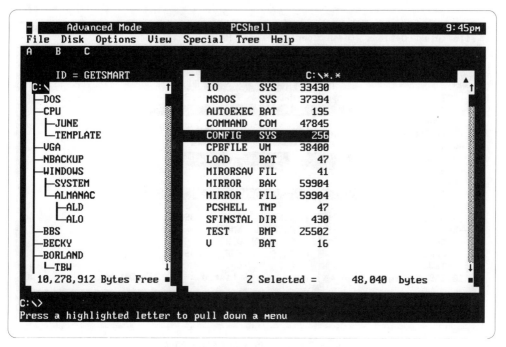

Figure 2.8. My AUTOEXEC.BAT and CONFIG.SYS selected in that order

As soon as you select a file, your cursor moves down one filename. You can continue selecting files in this way.

Use [F9] to select files that share a common characteristic in their filenames. Any of the DOS wildcards can by used when specifying selection criteria. For example, to specify the criteria:

Press: [F9]

This opens the File Select Filter window, which looks Figure 2.9.

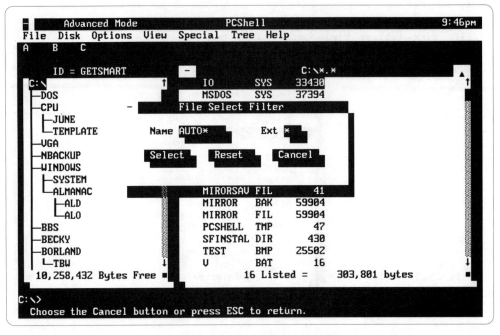

Figure 2.9. The File Select Filter window

When this window first appears, asterisks will show in the fields for both Name and Ext. In Figure 2.9, I've already typed in AUTO*. I will use these characteristics to select all the files in the current directory (in this case, my root directory) that begin with AUTO.

You type the common characteristics of the filename in the Name field and the characteristics for the file extension in the Ext field. Once you've entered the characteristics you want to use, begin the selection process:

Press: [Enter] twice

Notice that SELECT is highlighted; it then executes. In a moment, the selected files appear in the File List window, as shown in Figure 2.10.

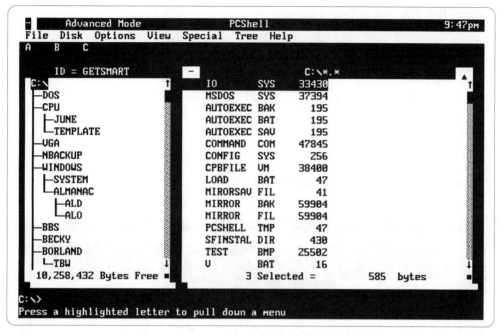

Figure 2.10. A group of filenames beginning with AUTO* selected

You can reselect a group of filenames by pressing [F9], then pressing [Tab] to high-light RESET, and then entering a new group of characters.

You can unselect a group of currently selected files by pressing [F4].

Copying Files

You can copy a file two ways:

1. To a different directory or disk using the same filename

2. To the same directory using a different filename

An example of the first method is copying a file from your hard disk to a floppy disk. An example of the second is making a backup copy of the original file in the same directory.

The basic procedure for copying files is to select the file or files you want to copy, press [F5] to begin the copy process, select the destination, then complete the copy. If you're copying a file to the same directory, you must also rename it.

Copying One File to a Different Location

To copy a file to a different location using the same filename, first highlight or select the filename you want to copy. Then, select the destination drive and directory. Finally, execute the copy.

For this example, to move your AUTOEXEC.BAT file to another directory:

Highlight: AUTOEXEC.BAT

Press: [F5]

This opens the File Copy box, which looks like Figure 2.11.

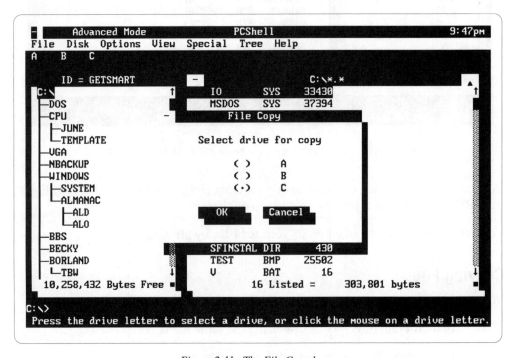

Figure 2.11. The File Copy box

Select the A-drive. To copy the AUTOEXEC.BAT file from the root directory on hard-drive C to the DOS directory:

Press: [Enter] twice

You can do this if your C drive is selected by default. Otherwise, you can press the arrow keys to select C, then press [Enter] to enter your selection.

To move the highlighting over your DOS directory name in the Tree List window:

Highlight: DOS

Press: [Enter]

This selects the directory that will receive the file copy. The contents of DOS (or whatever directory you use) are displayed after the copy, so that you can double check.

If a file with the same name already exists in the destination, you'll be warned and asked what to do. A second File Copy box will appear, as shown in Figure 2.12.

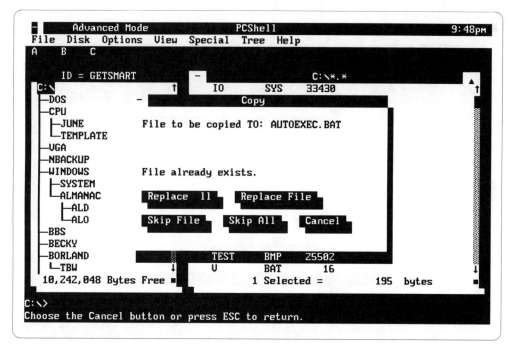

Figure 2.12. A warning prompt for File Copy

In Figure 2.12, the *Replace All* option is highlighted by default, which assumes that you want to update the filename presented at the top of the box. To replace the existing file with the new copy:

Press: [Enter]

Copying One File to the Same Directory

You can also copy a file to the same directory as long as you change the filename. To make a backup of AUTOEXEC.BAT in the root directory and call it AUTOEXEC.BAK:

> **Highlight:** AUTOEXEC.BAT

> **Press:** [F5]

> **Press:** [Enter] twice

This begins the copying process and selects the current directory as the destination. PC Shell will display the box shown in Figure 2.13.

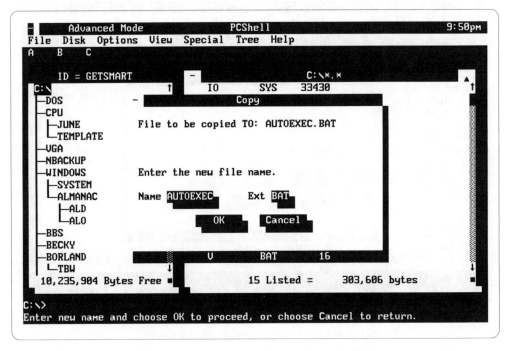

Figure 2.13. The File Copy box making a backup

You need to change at least one character in either the filename or its extension. After deciding which character to change:

> **Press:** [Enter]

Type: BAK

Press: [Enter]

As a precaution, you'll be asked to confirm the new filename.

To complete the copy:

Press: [Enter]

You could also press [C] or point at COPY to complete the copying.

You should now have two files with the same name in your root directory: the original (AUTOEXEC.BAT) and the new copy (AUTOEXEC.BAK).

Copying Several Files

If you want to copy more than one file at a time, select the files you want to copy and press [F5]. For example, to copy AUTOEXEC.BAT and CONFIG.SYS and their backups to the DOS subdirectory, highlight all four files. Then:

Press: [F5]

Press: [C]

Press: [Enter]

Select: DOS

Press: [Enter]

When copying more than one file at a time, a window monitors the progress of the series. When you copy more than one file, the options in this box become important:

Replace All   Replaces all files selected for copying and copies over any same-named files in the destination.

Replace File   Replaces the single file whose name appears at the top of the box.

Skip file   Ignores the current file and moves to the next selected filename in the sequence.

Skip All   Skips all remaining selected filenames and returns you to the PC Shell screen.

Cancel   Exits the file copy procedure.

If you start copying files using a single window zoomed to full-screen size, each window you work in will appear in full-screen size.

If you start the copying while in the Tree List window, you can move only the currently highlighted file from the current directory.

If you start File Copy while you're using a four-window display, that is, you're viewing the Tree List and the File List for two different directories or disks, you'll be asked to confirm whether the second, or inactive, set of windows should serve as the target destination, as shown in Figure 2.14.

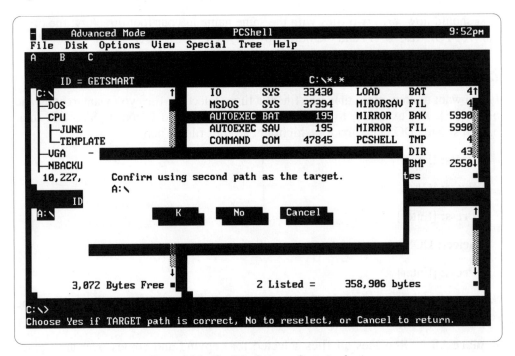

Figure 2.14. The File Copy confirmation box

You don't have to use the second path as the target, although it might make the copying process easier to follow.

REARRANGING THE DISPLAY OF FILENAMES

The arrangement of individual filenames in the File List window can often be crucial to your work with the files. To rearrange the display of the filenames:

Press: [F6]

This opens the Display Options box, shown in Figure 2.15.

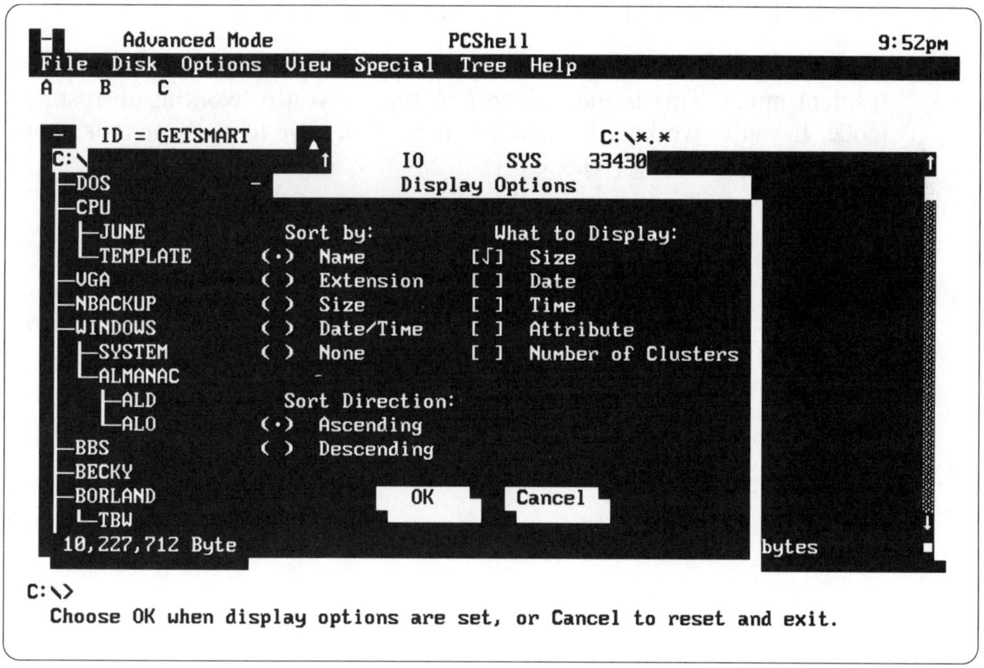

```
 ┌─┐    Advanced Mode            PCShell                        9:52pm
 └─┘ File  Disk  Options  View  Special  Tree  Help
     A     B     C
      ─  ID = GETSMART        ▲              C:\*.*
    C:\                      ↑     IO      SYS     33430                  ↑
      ─DOS             ─              Display Options
      ─CPU
        ─JUNE            Sort by:            What to Display:
        ─TEMPLATE      (·)  Name          [√]  Size
      ─VGA             ( )  Extension     [ ]  Date
      ─NBACKUP         ( )  Size          [ ]  Time
      ─WINDOWS         ( )  Date/Time     [ ]  Attribute
        ─SYSTEM        ( )  None          [ ]  Number of Clusters
        ─ALMANAC        ─
          ─ALD         Sort Direction:
          ─ALO       (·)  Ascending
      ─BBS             ( )  Descending
      ─BECKY
      ─BORLAND              ┌──────┐    ┌────────┐
        ─TBW               │  OK  │    │ Cancel │
      10,227,712 Byte       └──────┘    └────────┘              bytes  ▪

 C:\>
   Choose OK when display options are set, or Cancel to reset and exit.
```

Figure 2.15. The Display Options box

Press the number corresponding to the type of arrangement you want to view. Some settings work well together, such as Name/Ascending or Date/Descending. Others don't, such as Name/Ascending and Ext/Descending.

Once you pick the sort order you want to use, the option names will show on this screen and *OK* will brighten up. Pressing [Enter] accepts the new order and closes this screen. You'll see the filenames in the current File List window displayed in the new order.

You'll find it gets easier to work with the PC Shell as you spend more time with the program. You'll memorize the keys and commands you use most often in very little time.

EXITING PC SHELL

You can exit PC Shell in three ways:

1. Press [F3] and then [X] to confirm your intention to exit.

2. Press [Ctrl]-[Esc], the same two keys you pressed to pop open PC Shell in resident mode. This is the quickest method if you're working in resident mode. If you're working in standard mode, you have to confirm your intention to exit by pressing [X].

3. Press [Esc] and then [X].

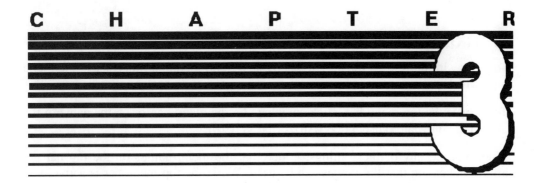

THE MENU INTERFACE OF PC SHELL

Menus are one of the easiest ways of working with data that is presented visually. You can access most of the commands in the various PC Tools Deluxe programs through pull-down and pop-up menus. Pull-down menus appear under menu labels on the top menu bar. Pop-up menus appear when you select certain menu commands or press other keys—such as function keys or hot keys—to activate commands.

WORKING WITH MENUS

To work with pull-down menus, first activate the top menu bar, then select the menu with which you want to work.

To activate the top menu bar, click anywhere on the menu bar, or on the name of the menu bar you want to use, press [Alt], or press [F10].

When you do any of these things, notice that the menu names on the top bar get bright, indicating that the menus can be used. While the top menu bar is active, you cannot use any other command in PC Shell.

Once the top menu bar is active, you can pull down any menu either by pressing the letter key corresponding to its name or by highlighting the menu name using the arrow keys and then pressing [Enter]. Once a menu is open, you can scroll through the entire selection by pressing [⇑] or [⇓].

Once you've opened a menu, you select a command the same way you selected the menu: either highlight the command and press [Enter], or press the letter key assigned to the command, which appears in bold. If you use PC Shell often, you will soon find that pressing letter keys is the fastest way to move.

There are seven pull-down menus in PC Shell, as shown in Figure 3.1:

File	Lets you work with files in various ways.
Disk	Lets you work with disks in various ways.
Options	Lets you change the way PC Shell looks and behaves.
View	Lets you change the way you view elements in the PC Shell screens.
Special	Displays special information about aspects of your computer.
Tree	Lets you manipulate the tree structure as displayed in the Tree List window.
Help	Lets you view the Help screen specific to the active feature or the procedure you're using, or open the Help index. You can also open specific Help screens by pressing [F1].

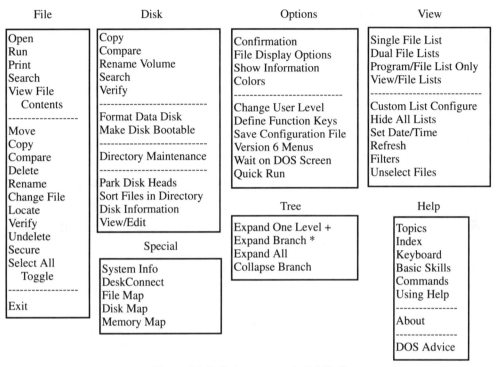

File	Disk	Options	View
Open	Copy	Confirmation	Single File List
Run	Compare	File Display Options	Dual File Lists
Print	Rename Volume	Show Information	Program/File List Only
Search	Search	Colors	View/File Lists
View File	Verify	----------	----------
Contents	----------	Change User Level	Custom List Configure
----------	Format Data Disk	Define Function Keys	Hide All Lists
Move	Make Disk Bootable	Save Configuration File	Set Date/Time
Copy	----------	Version 6 Menus	Refresh
Compare	Directory Maintenance	Wait on DOS Screen	Filters
Delete	----------	Quick Run	Unselect Files
Rename	Park Disk Heads		
Change File	Sort Files in Directory	**Tree**	**Help**
Locate	Disk Information	Expand One Level +	Topics
Verify	View/Edit	Expand Branch *	Index
Undelete		Expand All	Keyboard
Secure	**Special**	Collapse Branch	Basic Skills
Select All	System Info		Commands
Toggle	DeskConnect		Using Help
----------	File Map		----------
Exit	Disk Map		About
	Memory Map		----------
			DOS Advice

Figure 3.1. Pull-down menus in PC Shell

THE FILE MENU

The File pull-down menu lets you work with disk files in a variety of ways. In some cases, you can only work with individually highlighted files. With other commands, you can work with both single files or groups of files. The File pull-down menu contains seventeen commands, three of which open submenus of their own with more commands:

Open   Opens a file that already exists.

Run   Runs an application.

Print   Opens the Print menu, which lets you print a file in any of several ways.

Search   Lets you search for text in files in various ways.

View	Displays the contents of the selected file.
Move	Lets you move one or more files.
Copy	Lets you copy one or more files.
Compare	Lets you compare two or more files.
Delete	Lets you delete files.
Rename	Lets you rename files.
Change File	Opens the Change File menu, which lets you change a file four different ways.
Locate	Lets you locate a single file or a group of files with similar characteristics.
Verify	Verifies the integrity of files.
Undelete	Moves you into the Undelete program.
Secure	Opens the Secure menu, which lets you encrypt or decrypt files, or change settings you use for encryption.
Secure All Toggle	Selects all files for securing.
Exit	Lets you exit the PC Shell. You'll be asked first whether you really want to exit, and whether you want to save the current configuration of PC Shell.

Most of these commands are self-explanatory. Highlight the file or files you want to work with, open the File pull-down menu, select the command you want to use, and PC Shell will walk you through a simple list of instructional windows that tell you what to do. However, six of the commands on the File pull-down menu require a bit more elaboration.

The PC Shell Editor

PC Shell has a simple editor that lets you view and edit the contents of various types of files. It is a modified form of the Desktop Notepads module, which you'll learn about in Chapter 6. We'll save most of the details for editing files for that chapter. Once you become familiar with Notepads, you'll find working with PC Shell a snap.

To use the editor, highlight or select a filename in the File List window, then open the File/Change submenu and select the *Edit File* command. For example, to view and edit the AUTOEXEC.BAT file:

Highlight: AUTOEXEC.BAT

Press: [Alt]-[F]-[G]-[E]

This selects the command *Change File*.

Press: [Enter] three times

This accepts the two commands *Change File* and *Edit File,* as well as the filename AUTOEXEC.BAT. PC Shell will tell you to wait while it loads the Editor. It might take a moment or two for the PC Shell Editor to appear. When the PC Shell Editor is loaded, it should resemble Figure 3.2.

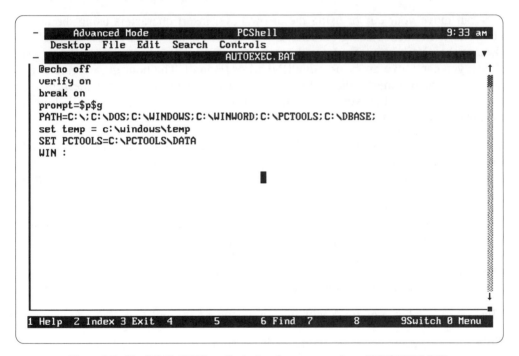

Figure 3.2. The PC Shell Editor displaying the contents of my AUTOEXEC.BAT

> If you are operating in resident mode, you'll see your screen go blank and your DOS prompt reappear. After the DOS prompt, a string of commands appears that looks something looks something like this:
>
> ```
> c:\PCTOOLS\DESKTOP.EXE C:\AUTOEXEC.BAT /25
> /N/SR=21,78,2,0,F0
> ```
>
> This loads the Desktop, selects the file AUTOEXEC.BAT to view, and then adds various switches that configure the Notepads module depending upon your system and preferences.

You can move your cursor using the arrow keys, insert characters using the arrow keys, insert characters using the character keys, and delete text by pressing [Del] or [Backspace]. You can move down through screenfuls of text by pressing [PgDn] and [End]; you can move up by pressing [PgUp] or [Home]. The hour-glass figure at the bottom of the file marks the end of the file. You can work in either the *insert* or *overwrite* modes. When you're working in insert mode, the label INS will show in the upper-right corner and your cursor will change to a block shape.

The *Cut, Copy,* and *Paste* commands use a clipboard available only to the PC Shell Editor. It is different from the Desktop clipboard or the hotkey clipboard (which can accessed throughout the PC Tools programs by pressing [Ctrl]-[Del]). The Editor clipboard works only for the current file; when you exit the Editor, the contents of the clipboard are lost. This means you *cannot* use it to transfer characters from one file to another. You can, however, use the hotkey clipboard to transfer character between files. You can access five menus at the top of the PC Shell Editor screen:

Desktop   Lets you access the *Exit* command on the Desktop main menu. This lets you exit the PC Shell Editor and return to the PC Shell screen.

File   Lets you work with two commands: *Save* and *Exit Without Saving.*

Edit   Lets you work with all editing commands except spell-checking.

Search   Lets you search for words or phrases.

Controls   Lets you work with all commands controlling page layout and aspects of the Editor screen.

To open any of these menus, hold down [Alt] while you press the letter key that matches the first letter of the menu name. For example, to open the File pull-down menu, press [Alt]-[F]. You can activate the menu bar, which contains the menu names, by pressing [F10].

Commands have been assigned to six function keys arranged on the bottom of the PC Shell Editor screen:

[F1] Help   Lets you access help information.

[F2] Index   Opens an index of subjects you can browse through for more help.

[F3] Exit   Closes the PC Shell Editor and returns you to your previous work.

[F6] Find   Opens the Search and Replace window, which lets you specify which text to search for.

[F9] Switch   Lets you switch between open screens (if you've opened any others, such as a Notepads window).

[F10] Menu   Activates the PC Shell Editor menu bar.

The PC Shell Editor is handy, but you shouldn't plan to use it to do extensive editing. You can use QuickView in the PC Shell (press[F2]) to view the contents of a file, but you should save heavy editing for the Desktop Notepads module.

To exit the PC Shell Editor:

Press: [Esc]

If you've made changes that weren't saved to disk, you'll be asked if you want to save or abandon them; otherwise, you'll return to the PC Shell screen.

Printing Files

The *File Print* command uses the DOS redirection command, so your printer must have the capability to handle DOS ASCII files directly. If you're using a PostScript printer, you'll have to print the file to a separate printed disk file first, then read the disk file into a PostScript Editor that supports your printer.

To begin the print:

    Press: [Alt]-[F]-[P]

    Press: [Enter]

This opens the File Print box, which looks like Figure 3.3.

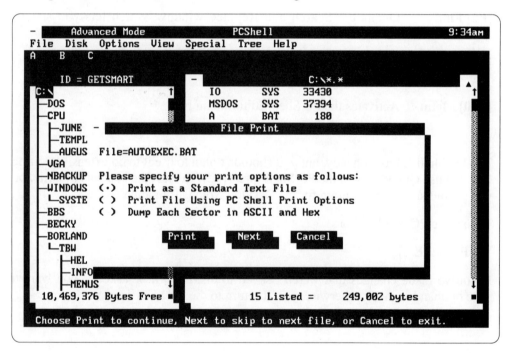

Figure 3.3. The File Print box

If the file you're trying to print has one of four extensions: .$$$, .BAK, .COM, or .EXE, you'll be given an error message. You can print files with all other extensions.

Select the option you want to use by pressing the appropriate letter key: [P] for printing as a standard text file, [O] for using printing options, and [D] for dumping the file as hexadecimal and ASCII code. Then, begin the print:

Select: Print

Press: [Enter]

The highlighted file or selected files will begin to print immediately, unless you've selected the second option. If you want to print according to special options, you'll have to set them in a second File Print menu, which looks like Figure 3.4.

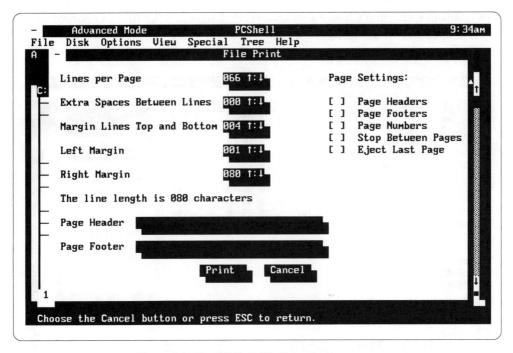

Figure 3.4. The PC Shell File Print Options menu

These are the same options you can use in the Page Layout menu of the Desktop Manager. Each format setting will be defined as it is highlighted (more information about printing text files is given in Chapter 6). When all the settings are as you want them:

Select: PRINT

Press: [Enter]

Printing begins. If you're printing more than one file, move to the next one by selecting NEXT. You can exit printing by pressing [X].

Changing File Attributes

You can change one to four file attributes using the *Attribute Change* command on the File/Change submenu. Just highlight or select the file or files whose attributes you want to change, then:

Press: [Alt]-[F]-[G]-[A]

This opens the Attribute Change window. When I select all the files in my root directory and open this window, my screen looks like Figure 3.5.

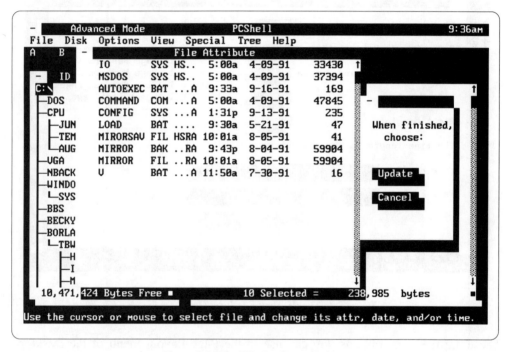

Figure 3.5. The File Attribute window

You're given the usual file information in this window, including file size and time and date of last change. The four attributes, or bits, you can change are:

H The hidden bit hides the filename from the standard DOS command DIR. However, you can still see hidden filenames in the PC Shell File List window.

S The system bit shows whether the file is necessary to run your disk operating system (DOS).

R The read-only bit shows that you can only read the file contents; you can't write over the file with changes.

A The archive bit shows if the file has been changed since the last time it was backed up. This bit is switched off whenever you backup the file using DOS BACKUP, PC Backup, or another backup program.

To change one or more attributes, open the Attribute Change window. You'll find your cursor blinking under the space reserved for the first attribute H. To switch any attribute on or off, just press the letter of the attribute. For example, if A is on and you want to switch it off, press [A]. To switch it back on, press [A] a second time. You can only change attributes when the two commands on the right side of the window, UPDATE and EXIT, are not highlighted.

Once you've made the changes you want to save, press [Tab] to select UPDATE, and then press [Enter]. To cancel changes, highlight EXIT and press [Enter].

Using the Hex Editor

The PC Shell Hex Editor displays file contents in two modes at the same time: hexadecimal and ASCII codes. If you know what you're doing, you can change the contents of a file by making changes to either the hexadecimal or ASCII displays.

> The only difference between the PC Shell Hex Editor and the PC Shell Text Editor is the way each displays data. In fact, on both editors the data is stored on disk in binary form, a series of ones and zeros. The editors must first translate this binary data to the form they've been designed to display.

You can select several files in a group and view their contents sequentially. To view the contents of a file in hex format, highlight or select the filename, open the File/Change submenu, and select the command *Hex Edit*. For example, to view the contents of COMMAND.COM in hex:

Highlight: COMMAND.COM

Press: [Alt]-[F]-[G]-[H]

My screen changes look like Figure 3.6. If the function key [F6] has been assigned to hex, press it to make your screen look like Figure 3.6.

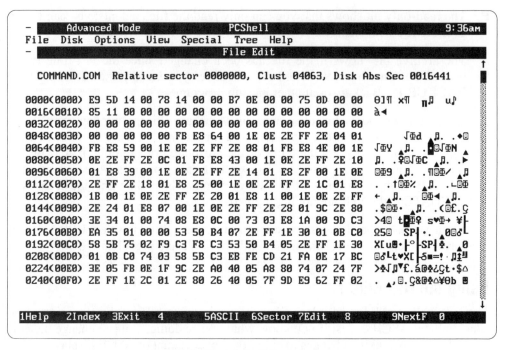

Figure 3.6. The PC Shell Hex Editor screen

You can't use any menus in this screen, but you can use these function keys:

[F1] Help Opens the Help screen specific to the Hex Editor.

[F2] Index Opens the Help index specific to the Hex Editor.

[F3] Exit Closes the Hex Edit screen and returns you to the PC Shell screen.

[F5] ASCII Displays the data in ASCII code in a full-screen window.

[F6] Sector Lets you move to a specific sector for the file.

[F7] Edit Lets you edit the data on screen. Make sure you know what effects your changes will have before you make them.

[F9] NextF Displays the contents of the next file in the selected group.

To switch to the full-screen ASCII display, which resembles Figure 3.7:

> **Press:** [F5]

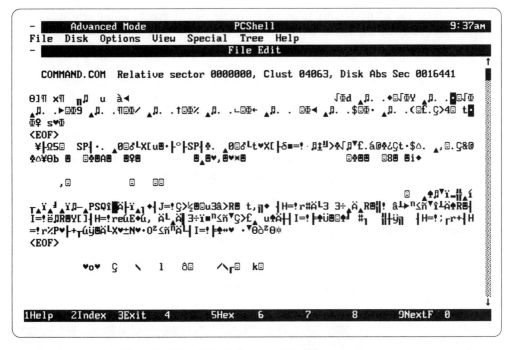

Figure 3.7. Full-screen ASCII display

This screen removes the hex code display and shows a little more file information in decipherable language. You can switch back and forth between these two views of a file by pressing [F5].

Deleting Files

New files are created and old files are deleted on a regular basis by even the most casual user. You can delete files and subdirectories in PC Shell in four ways:

1. Highlight a single filename (or select a group of filenames), press [Alt]-[F]-[D], then walk through the steps for deleting files. This executes the *Delete File* command on the File pull-down menu.

2. If the shortcut keys are showing, highlight the file (or select the group of files you want to delete), press [T], and walk through the deletion process.

3. If the DOS command line is showing, type DEL followed by the filename, then press [Enter]. If the path of the file to be deleted is not the current path, specify its path or switch to that directory before you execute the delete.

4. To delete a subdirectory, use the *Delete Subdirectory* command under the Directory Maintenance submenu off of the Disk pull-down menu.

> When you delete a file, only the first character is stripped from the filename. The data still remain on disk and can be recovered, as described in the section, "Undeleting Files and Directories."

The most common way to delete files in PC Shell is to highlight a single file or select multiple files, press [Alt]-[F]-[D], and delete the files.

For example, if you want to delete AUTOEXEC.BAK:

Highlight: AUTOEXEC.BAK

Press: [Alt]-[F]-[D]

This opens the File Delete box, shown in Figure 3.8.

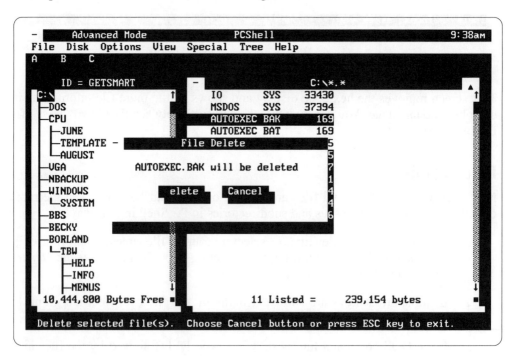

Figure 3.8. The File Delete Box

The name of the file you're going to delete should appear in the box. If it doesn't, press [C] to cancel the delete. If the correct name appears:

Press: [Enter]

This selects the default reply *Delete*. Filenames in the File List window will move up to take the place of the deleted file.

To delete a group of files, select each filename first, then begin the delete process. This opens a more detailed version of the File Delete box, as shown in Figure 3.9.

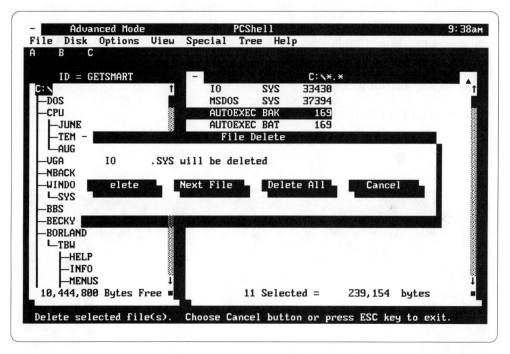

Figure 3.9. The File Delete box for a group of files

The name of the first file in the group will appear in the box, along with four options:

Delete   Deletes the displayed file.

Next File   Does not delete the displayed file and moves on to the next filename in sequence.

Cancel   Cancels the group delete and returns you to the PC Shell screen.

67

Delete All   Rapidly deletes all selected filenames. If the series is a long one, you can stop the process by pressing [Esc], but all files deleted up to that point will remain deleted unless you undelete them.

When you delete a file by mistake, PC Shell allows you to undelete it. Since this is a complicated utility, a full section in Chapter 17 is devoted to it.

Clearing Files

Clearing a file means wiping all the file data from the disk, so that there is no residual data that someone else might try to recover. To clear a file, use the *Clear File* command on the File/Change submenu. For example, to clear the file AUTOEXEC.BAK from your root directory:

Highlight: AUTOEXEC.BAK

Press: [Alt]-[F]-[G]-[C]

This opens the Wipe window, as shown in Figure 3.10.

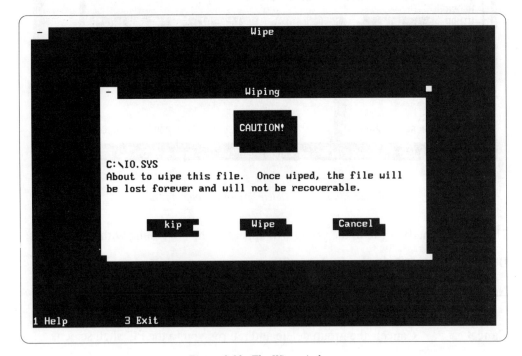

Figure 3.10. The Wipe window

There are three settings in this window you can change. The hex value refers to the hex character that will overwrite the file data. The hex character F6 shows up as a colon with a dash through the middle. You can use another character by typing it in.

There are three selections in this window:

Skip   Skips clearing the file.

Wipe   Wipes the file you've selected from the disk.

Cancel   Cancels the clearing process and returns you to PC Shell.

You can use two function keys when this window is open:

[F1] Help   Opens the Help screen for clearing files.

[F3] Exit   Closes the Wipe window and returns you to the PC Shell screen.

THE DISK MENU

The Disk pull-down menu lets you work with the following commands:

Copy   Copies a floppy disk. Same as the DOS command DISKCOPY. Select the source and target drives, insert the appropriate disks in the selected drives, and copy.

Compare   Compares two floppy disks and reports back on any mismatched data. You select the source and target drives, insert the disks, and execute the command.

Rename Volume   Lets you change the volume name on a disk.

Search   Opens the Disk Search window, which lets you search for text in disk files. Searching for ASCII characters is not case-specific. You can also search for hex characters by pressing [F9].

Verify   Verifies that all data on the current disk is readable. PC Shell will display its progress through the data portion of the disk it is verifying and alert you to bad data.

Format Data Disk   Formats a floppy disk as a data-only disk. No system files will be placed on the disk.

Make Disk Bootable	Formats a floppy disk as a system disk, which means you can boot your computer from the disk.
Directory Maintenance	Opens the Directory Maintenance module, which lets you work with disks and directories. See the following section for more detail..
Park Disk Heads	Parks your hard disk read/write heads over a useless track on the disk to minimize disk damage.
Sort Files in Directory	Sorts the list of displayed filenames in various ways.
Disk Information	Displays information about a specific disk.
View/Edit Disk	Lets you view and edit any sector of the current disk. You can find more information on this command below.

Directory Maintenance

The Directory Maintenance module lets you view and change various aspects of your disk directory structure. You can enter the module from one of two locations: the PC Shell or DOS. To enter from PC Shell:

Press: [Alt]-[D]-[M]

This opens the Disk pull-down menu and selects the *Directory Maintenance* command. It can take a moment or two to load the module from PC Shell.

To enter the module from DOS:

Type: DM

Press: [Enter]

This loads the file DM.EXE.

When the Directory Maintenance module is loaded, the screen looks like Figure 3.11.

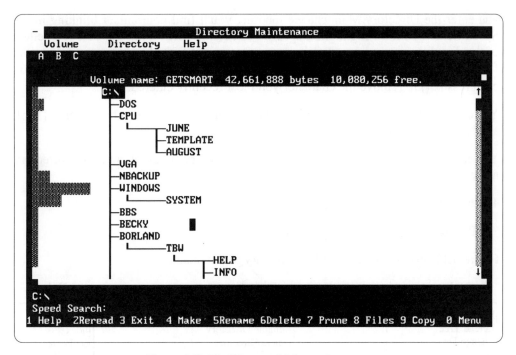

```
 -                      Directory Maintenance
    Volume       Directory      Help
   A   B   C

          Volume name: GETSMART   42,661,888 bytes   10,080,256 free.      ■
                    C:\                                                       ↑
                      ─DOS
                      ─CPU
                          L      ─JUNE
                                 ─TEMPLATE
                                 └AUGUST
                      ─UGA
                      ─NBACKUP
                      ─WINDOWS
                          L       ─SYSTEM
                      ─BBS
                      ─BECKY          ■
                      ─BORLAND
                          L       ─TBW
                                    L      ─HELP
                                           ─INFO                             ↓

 C:\
 Speed Search:
 1 Help  2Reread 3 Exit   4 Make  5Rename 6Delete 7 Prune 8 Files 9 Copy  0 Menu
```

Figure 3.11. The Directory Maintenance screen

This screen displays the names of three pull-down menus across the top (Volume, Directory, and Help); a list of available disks; a graphic display of the directory structure of the current disk, including a tree diagram; the DOS command line; a Speed Search box; and, finally, the ten function-key assignments.

You'll find out how to use the commands in this module in just a moment. For now, familiarize yourself with the details displayed in the center portion of this screen. The top bar of the center section displays the Volume name (GETSMART in Figure 3.11), the number of bytes occupied by files, and free bytes. Running down the left side is a graphical display of the size of each directory. You can change the way the size is depicted using the *Tree Data* command on the Volume pull-down menu.

The bulk of the center portion is occupied by a tree display. This shows the name of each file directory, as well as the subdirectories within each. You can move up and down this display using the cursor keys. The arrow keys move one directory at a time. Pressing [PgDn] or [PgUp] moves the cursor in larger jumps.

You can use the Speed Search function to go directly to a specific directory—if you know the name of the directory, or at least the first few characters in its name. When you enter the Directory Maintenance module, you'll find your cursor blinking in the Speed Search box. To highlight a specific directory, start typing the first few letters of the directory name. Immediately upon entering the first character, you'll go to the first directory that begins with that letter. Adding more letters refines the search. You can press [⇐] to remove the character you most recently entered.

You can move your cursor forward to other features on the screen by pressing [Tab], and backward by pressing [Ctrl]-[Tab].

You can display individual filenames in each directory by highlighting the directory name, then pressing [F8].

To remove a file list display:

> **Press:** [Esc]

Figure 3.12 shows a menu map for Directory Maintenance

Volume	Directory	Help
Rename Volume	Make Directory	Topics
Reread Tree	Rename Directory	Index
Change Drive	Delete Directory	Keyboard
Print Tree	Copy Tree	Basic Skills
Tree Data Display	Prune & Graft	Commands
------------------------	Branch Size	Using Help
Exit	Modify Attributes	----------------
	Show Files	About
	Network Rights	

Figure 3.12. Menu map of Directory Maintenance

The Volume Menu

The Volume menu lets you work with commands that control diskwide aspects, such as the volume name and tree display.

Rename Volume   Lets you change the name of an existing directory. Just highlight the directory, select this command, enter a new name, and press [Enter] twice.

Reread Tree   Rereads the current disk and displays an updated tree diagram of the directory structure.

Change Drive	Lets you change to another active drive.
Print Tree	Opens the Print Tree box, which lets you print the current tree structure to a port of your choosing, and lets you use graphics or nongraphics characters (depending upon your printer).
Tree Data	Opens the Tree Data Display window, which lets you select the way data is displayed along the left side of the center portion of the screen.
Exit	Exits the Directory Maintenance module and returns you to your previous location, either PC Shell or DOS.

The Directory Menu

The Directory menu works with commands that affect individual directories.

Make Directory	Lets you insert a new directory at the cursor location on the directory tree.
Rename Directory	Lets you change the name of an existing directory.
Delete Directory	Lets you delete a directory. You'll be prompted if the directory contains data.
Copy Tree	Lets you copy the tree.
Prune & Graft	Lets you "prune" (cut), then "graft" (attach) existing directories and their files to new locations.
Branch Size	Opens the Branch Size window, which displays the total number of files, size of all the files, and disk space allocated to these files within the current branch.
Modify Attributes	Opens the Modify Attributes window, which lets you change the attribute settings *Hidden* and *System* for the current directory.
Show Files	Opens the list of filenames displayed on the right side of the center portion of the screen, as shown in Figure 3.13. Same as pressing [F9]. To close, press [Esc].

Network Rights   Displays your network rights if you're using PC Tools over a network, and the program has been installed for that network.

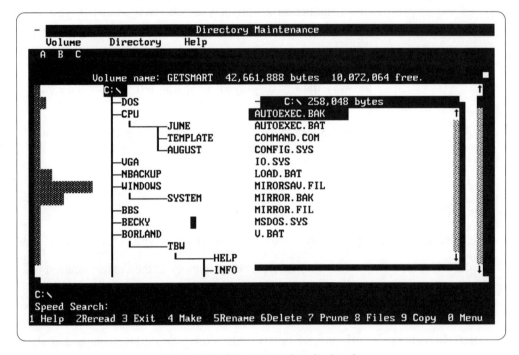

Figure 3.13. Files List window displayed

The ten function keys are given the following commands in the Directory Maintenance module:

[F1] Help   Opens on-line context-sensitive help.

[F2] Reread   Rereads the current disk directory structure and displays updated directory tree on screen.

[F3] Exit   Exits the Directory Maintenance module.

[F4] Make   Makes a new directory in the current cursor location.

[F5] Rename   Renames the currently selected directory.

[F6] Delete   Deletes the currently selected directory.

[F7] Prune   Lets you prune and graft directories.

[F8] Files   Displays a list of filenames in the current directory.

[F9] Copy   Lets you copy one directory to a new location.

[F10] Menu   Activates the top menu bar.

Exit Directory Maintenance by pressing [Esc]. You'll return to PC Shell or DOS, depending on where you started.

Viewing and Editing a Disk

You can use the *View/Edit Disk* command on the Disk pull-down menu to view and edit any portion of a disk. To open the Disk Edit screen:

    Press: [Alt]-[D]-[E]

Your screen should change to look like Figure 3.14.

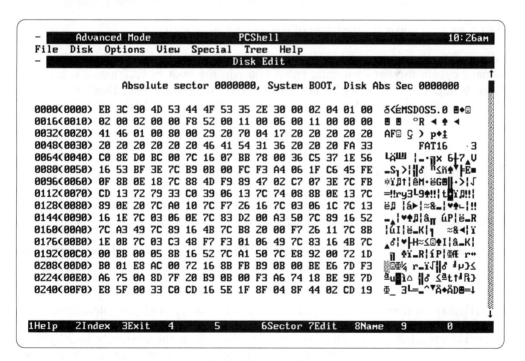

Figure 3.14. The Disk Edit screen

The top of the screen shows the disk location you're viewing in absolute sector and area. You can view half a sector, or 256 bytes of data, in the Disk Edit screen.

You can see three columns of data in this screen. The left column shows the *offset location* within each sector. The middle column shows the disk data in hexadecimal notation. The right column shows the disk data in ASCII.

You can use six function keys shown at the bottom of this screen:

[F1] Help   Opens the Help screen specific to the Disk Edit screen.

[F2] Index   Opens the Help index specific to the Disk Edit screen.

[F3] Exit   Closes the Disk Edit screen and returns you to the PC Shell screen. Same as pressing [Esc].

[F6] Sector   Lets you select a precise sector to view and edit.

[F7] Edit   Lets you edit the displayed data. [F5] saves changes you make them, and [F8] switches between the hexadecimal and ASCII displays.

[F8] Name   Displays the name of the sector you've viewing.

Editing data directly to disk has its risks. When you edit file data, you can't do much damage except to your own data; but if you edit the boot or FAT areas, you could destroy important data DOS needs for working with your disk. Don't make any changes to those areas, unless you know exactly what you are doing.

THE OPTIONS MENU

The Options pull-down menu provides the following ten commands, which let you change the way PC Shell looks and behaves:

Confirmation   Lets you tell PC Shell whether you want the program to confirm certain actions, such as when you delete or replace a file.

File Display Options   Lets you select in which order to display filenames.

Show Information   Displays information about the currently highlighted file, including filename, extension, path, attributes, and other file aspects.

Colors   Opens the Install program, which lets you select which colors should adorn various features displayed in the PC Shell.

Change User Level   Selects one of three user levels to work with—beginning, intermediate, and advanced—each of which contains its own arrangement of menu commands. A more detailed explanation of changing user levels follows.

Define Function Keys   Lets you redefine the function key command assignments displayed at the bottom of the PC Shell screen. A more detailed explanation of this function follows.

Save Configuration File   Saves the current configuration to a disk file.

Version 6 Menus   Lets you view and work with pull-down menu commands that were available in Version 6.

Wait on DOS Screen   Toggles on and off the delay it takes to redisplay your current DOS screen.

Quick Run   Toggles on and off your ability to quick-run a DOS command from within the PC Shell.

Changing User Levels

You can select one of three levels to work with: beginning, intermediate, and advanced. The level you select determines how many commands will appear on the File, Disk, and Special pull-down menus. You can use a menu command only when it appears; the higher the level you use, the more commands available.

> I suggest you base the level on your confidence level and not on your skill level. I preferred starting out in the Advanced Mode, even though I wasn't familiar with all the commands in PC Shell. I don't like being limited in what I can do, and I enjoy exploring commands I'm not familiar with.

Regardless of which level you select, all commands on the Applications menu are always available. You can, however, lock out all other menus, if you want PC Shell to be used only as an Applications launcher.

To switch between user levels:

Press: [Alt]-[O]-[U]

This opens the Change User Level box, which looks like Figure 3.15.

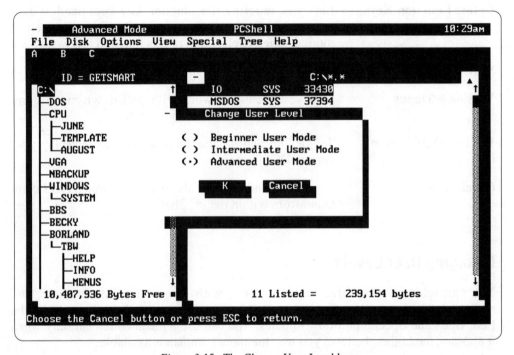

Figure 3.15. The Change User Level box

You can select a new level by pressing the key that matches the first letter of the level. For example, if you're using the default Advanced User Mode and want to switch to Beginner User Mode:

Press: [B]

To implement this selection:

Press: [O]

The new level becomes effective immediately. Check this by opening the File menu. In the Beginner's level, you should see only seven commands on the File menu.

After making any change to PC Shell, the Beginner's level will remain effective until you change it again or until you try to exit PC Shell. That's when you'll be asked whether you want to make the change permanent. Saving the change copies it to PCSHELL.CFG on disk.

If you're operating in standard mode and quit the program without saving changes, they won't be effective the next time you load the program. If you're operating in resident mode, changes remain in effect the next time you pop open PC Shell, but you'll get the same request to save or cancel changes the next time you try to quit PC Shell. This will continue to happen until you actually quit PC Shell.

Canceling changes removes them from PC Shell in both resident and standard modes. Each time you load PC Shell into memory, it will display the configuration as recorded in PCSHELL.CFG.

Defining Function Keys

Function keys are usually assigned to the most frequently performed functions within a program. In PC Shell, there are ten default assignments.

You can configure seven of the ten function keys in PC Shell to access different commands if you find you use them more frequently than the default commands. For example, you may move files more often than you copy them, in which case you may wish to substitute file move for file copy, or for file select.

To redefine one or more of your function keys:

Press: [Alt]-[O]-[K]

This opens the Define Function Keys box, shown in Figure 3.16.

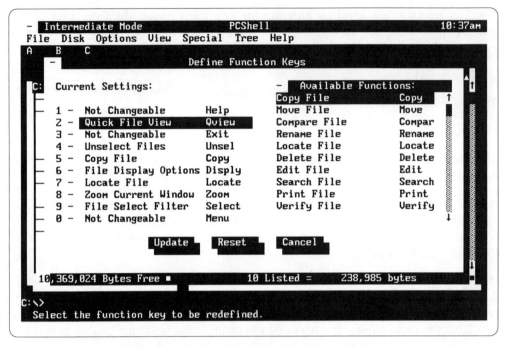

```
 -  Intermediate Mode                  PCShell                    10:37am
 File  Disk  Options  View  Special  Tree  Help
 A     B    C
       -
                          Define Function Keys
 C:    Current Settings:              -   Available Functions:
                                      Copy File            Copy
        1 -  Not Changeable      Help    Move File            Move
        2 -  Quick File View     Qview   Compare File         Compar
        3 -  Not Changeable      Exit    Rename File          Rename
        4 -  Unselect Files      Unsel   Locate File          Locate
        5 -  Copy File           Copy    Delete File          Delete
        6 -  File Display Options Disply Edit File            Edit
        7 -  Locate File         Locate  Search File          Search
        8 -  Zoom Current Window  Zoom   Print File           Print
        9 -  File Select Filter  Select  Verify File          Verify
        0 -  Not Changeable      Menu

                    Update      Reset       Cancel

     10,369,024 Bytes Free  ■            10 Listed  =      238,985 bytes

 C:\>
    Select the function key to be redefined.
```

Figure 3.16. The Define Function Keys box

Current Settings, on the left side, shows three columns: the ten function keys, their current assignments as displayed on your screen, and the actual command that has been assigned to each one.

Highlight the function key you want to reassign on the left side, then scroll through commands on the right side and pick the one you want to use.

Use the Update, Cancel, and Reset keys—shown on the bottom line—for shortcuts when you begin to reassign keys often.

Available Functions, on the right side, shows the top eight descriptions and matching commands from a list of sixty-eight functions that you can assign to seven of your ten function keys.)

The three keys you can't reconfigure are [F1] for help, [F3] for exit, and [F10] for menu. You'll find them marked as Not Changeable, followed by the command permanently attached to them. You can, however, assign these commands to other function keys if you wish. Also, you cannot assign [F11] and [F12], because these keys make peculiar calls to the BIOS (Basic Input-Output System).

When the Define Function Keys box first appears, you'll see the following line high-lighted:

```
F2 Quick File View     QView
```

You can select which function key you want to reassign by highlighting it using the [⇑] and [⇓] keys.

For this example, change the assignment for [F4] from Unselect Files to Undelete Files:

>   **Highlight:** F4—Unselect Files   Unsel

>   **Press:** [Tab]

This highlights the border of the Available Functions window. Now scroll through the list of commands:

>   **Press:** [PgDn]

Because there are many command choices, you might want to page down through the list for a quick first look. Eight presses will take you to the bottom of the list. Unfortunately, this list is not arranged in alphabetical order, but follows the order of the commands on the PC Shell menus. To insert the new menu description and command for [F4]:

>   **Highlight:** Undelete Files   Undel

>   **Press:** [Enter]

This switches you back to the Current Settings window. When you return to the PC Shell screen, you'll see the new command, *Undelete Files*, assigned to [F4].

To exit the Define Function Keys box:

>   **Press:** [Esc]

To make your changes permanent:

>   **Press:** [U]

Now you'll return automatically to the PC Shell screen. You should be able to see the new assignment after F4—Undel. You can always change this assignment back, assign the command to another key, or assign another function to [F4]. When you exit PC Shell, you'll be asked again if you want to save or cancel the changes you

You can assign any of the sixty-two commands listed alphabetically in Table 3.1 to any of the seven configurable function keys in PC Shell.

Command	Code	Command	Code
Active List Switch	Switch	Make System Disk	System
All Windows Toggle	AllWin	Memory Map	MMap
Attribute Change	Attrib	Modify Display	ModDsp
Background Mat	MatBak	More File Info	Info
Change Drive	ChgDrv	Move File	Move
Change User Level	Level	One Tree/File List	1list
Compare Disk	DComp	Park Disk	Park
Compare File	Compar	Print Directory	PrintD
Copy Disk	DCopy	Print File	Print
Copy File	Copy	Quick File View	Qview
Date/Time	DatTim	Re-read the Tree	TreeRd
Default Viewer	DfView	Rename Volume	DRenam
Define Function Keys	Fkeys	Rename File	Rename
Delete File	Delete	Screen Colors	Color
Directory Maint	DMaint	Search Disk	DSrch
Directory Sort	DSort	Search File	Search
Disk Info	DInfo	Setup Configuration	Config
Disk Map	DMap	Short Cut Keys	SCutKy
DOS Command Line	DOSCmd	Size/Move Window	SizMov
Edit File	Edit	Switch Tree/File	Tab
Exit PC Shell	Exit	System Info	SysInf
File Display Options	Disply	Tree List Window	TreeW
File List Filter	Limit	Two Tree/File List	2list
File List Window	FileW	Undelete Files	Undel
File Map	FMap	Unselect Files	Unsel
File Select Filter	Select	Verify Disk	DVerfy
Format Disk	Format	Verify File	Verify
Help Index	Index	View/Edit Disk	DEdit
Hex Edit File	HedEdt	View Window	ViewW
Launch	Launch	Viewer Configuration	ViewCg
Locate File	Locate	Zoom Current Window	Zoom

Table 3.1. All assignments for function keys

THE VIEW MENU

The View menu provides eleven commands that let you control the way you view windows in PC Shell. Two of these commands open submenus that provide more specific commands.

Single File List   Displays a single tree list and directory file list.

Dual File Lists	Displays dual tree lists and directory file lists. This is the best way to copy or move files from one disk to another, or to compare files on different disks.
Program/File Lists	Displays a single tree and directory file list along with a program window list.
Program List Only	Displays a program window list only.
Viewer/File Lists	Displays a single tree and directory file list, along with a View window.
Custom List Configure	Opens a submenu that lets you control the appearance of windows in PC Shell. You can find out more about this command below.
Hide All Lists	Hides all list windows from view, leaving you the top menu bar and bottom function key assignments.
Set Date/Time	Lets you reset the current date and time.
Refresh	Rereads the directory tree and refreshes the displayed tree list and directory filenames.
Filters	Opens a submenu that lets you select whether you want to list or select files.
Unselect Files	Unselects all selected files.

Using and Configuring Viewers

To view a file, just highlight its name and press [F2]. For example, to view the contents of your AUTOEXEC.BAT:

> **Highlight:** AUTOEXEC.BAT

> **Press:** [F2]

My screen changes to look like Figure 3.17.

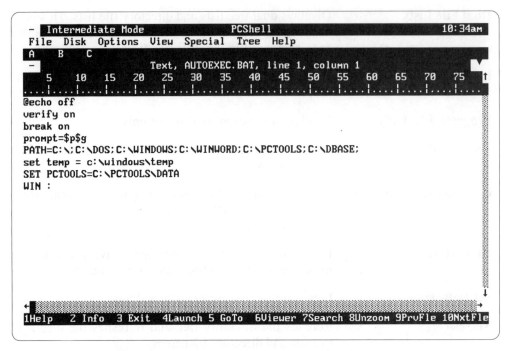

Figure 3.17. Text Viewer displaying my AUTOEXEC.BAT

This file uses the Text Viewer, which appears at the top of the View screen. The name of the file you're viewing appears on the right side of the same line. The function key assignments for the Text Viewer are:

[F1] Help   Opens the Help screen specific to the Text Viewer.

[F2] Index   Opens the Help index for the Text Viewer.

[F3] Exit   Closes the current viewer and returns you to the PC Shell screen.

[F4] Launch   Loads (launches) the file you're viewing, if it's a program file. Launching files is described in Chapter 4.

[F5] GoTo   Lets you go to a specific line or column.

[F6] Viewer   Lets you select a viewer.

[F7] Search   Opens a box that lets you search for a character string.

[F8] Unzoom   Switches the viewer to half screen. The [F8] key function then becomes Zoom, which you press if you want the viewer to switch back to full-screen.

84

[F9] PrevFle   Displays the contents of the top of the previous file.

[F10] NextF   Displays the contents of the top of the next file.

You can reconfigure the default viewer that appears on your screen when PC Shell can't figure out the type of file you want to view.

The Custom List Configure Menu

The Custom List Configure menu appears when you select the *Custom List Configure* command on the View pull-down menu. It lets you toggle on or off eight features in your PC Shell screen.

Tree List   Toggles the Tree List window (usually on the left side of your PC Shell screen).

File List   Toggles the File List window (usually on the right side of your PC Shell screen).

Program List   Toggles the Program List window (usually on the bottom half of your PC Shell screen.

View Window   Toggles the View window.

Background Mat   Toggles the matting behind your PC Shell windows.

DOS Command Line   Toggles the DOS command line near the bottom of your screen.

Viewer Config   Lets you configure your viewer window to appear horizontally or vertically.

Window Style   Lets you toggle the window style between tile and cascade. Tiled windows fit next to one another like tiles. Cascaded windows can slide over one another.

To display a list of filenames with similar characters, use the File List Filter.

Press: [Alt]-[V]-[L]-[L]

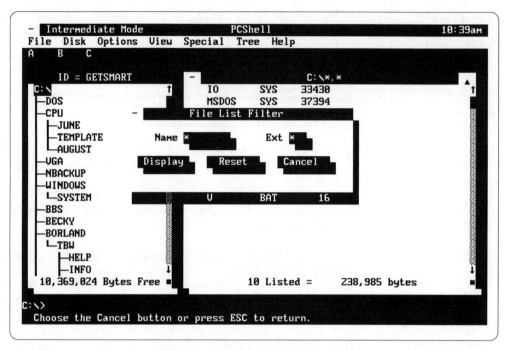

Figure 3.18. The File List Filter box

In this example, I've specified AUTO as the first four characters of all the filenames I want to display. You can use the DOS wildcards * and ? to modify the filename selection. When I select this list, my screen changes to look like Figure 3.19.

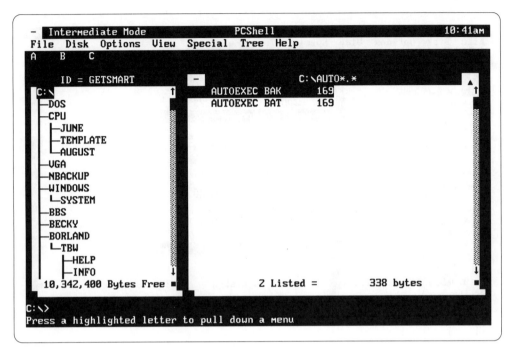

Figure 3.19. All AUTO* files displayed in my File List window

Changing Date and Time

You can change the time displayed in the PC Shell window and in other applications running in your computer, including the Desktop Manager.

To open the Set Date and Time box, shown in Figure 3.20:

Press: [Alt]-[V]-[T]

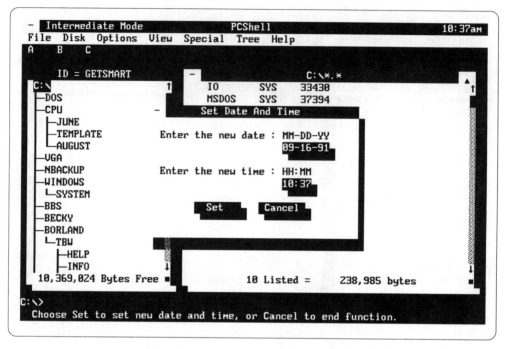

Figure 3.20 The Set Date and Time window

To change the date, type in the new digits, making sure to enter zeros where appropriate. Press [Enter] to set the date, then type in the new time. To set the changes, press [Enter] or [S].

THE SPECIAL MENU

The Special pull-down menu provides five commands that reveal information about your computer.

System Info Opens the System Information module, which displays a wide variety of information about your computer system.

DeskConnect Displays information about your connection to another computer through REMOTE.EXE. You must load REMOTE and connect to another computer before this command will display anything.

File Map Displays a map of file usage.

Disk Map   Displays a map of disk usage.

Memory Map   Displays a map of memory usage.

The last four commands are simple and self-explanatory. The first command, *System Information,* deserves more explanation.

The System Information Module

The System Information module provides a wide variety of commands to check the way your computer system is currently configured and operating. You can enter the System Information module in two ways: Select the *System Information* command on the Special pull-down menu, or type *SI* at the DOS prompt and press [Enter].

When the program starts to load, it will take a moment or two to read all the information it needs to know to display data. When the System Information screen appears, it will look like Figure 3.21.

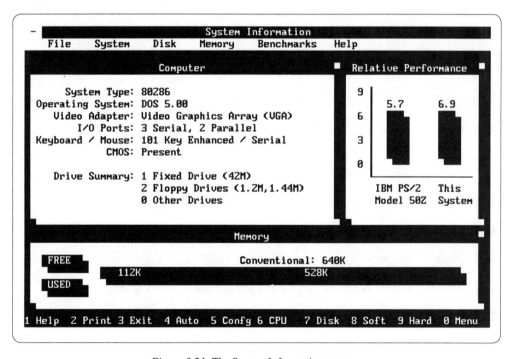

Figure 3.21. The System Information screen

The middle of the screen shows basic information about your current computer hardware configuration. There are six pull-down menus at the top. Figure 3.22 shows a menu map for the System Information module.

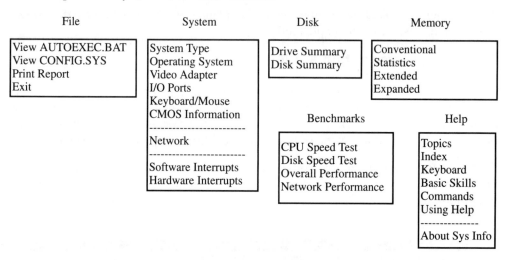

Figure 3.22. Menu map of System Information

The ten function keys have the following assignments:

[F1] Help   Displays context-sensitive on-line help.

[F2] Print   Opens the Reporting Options screen, as shown in Figure 3.23, which lets you select how to print a report of your computer configuration.

[F3] Exit   Lets you exit the System Information screen.

[F4] Auto   Displays the contents of your AUTOEXEC.BAT file

[F5] Confg   Displays the contents of your CONFIG.SYS file

[F6] CPU   Displays the Relative CPU Performance Index screen.

[F7] Disk   Displays the Measuring Disk Drive Performance screen.

[F8] Soft   Displays the Software Interrupt Information screen.

[F9] Hard   Displays the Hardware Interrupt Information screen.

[F10] Menu   Activates the top menu bar.

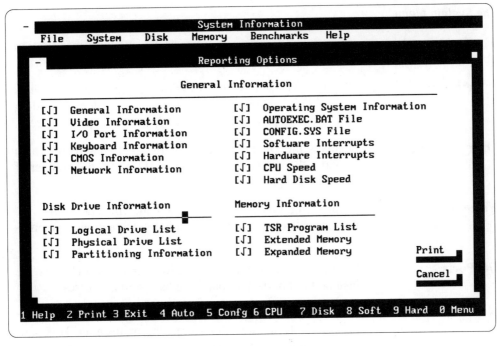

Figure 3.23. The Reporting Options screen

You should review the following menu commands so you're familiar with the various ways to obtain information about your computer configuration.

The File Menu

The File pull-down menu gives you four commands that work with files.

View AUTOEXEC.BAT   Lets you view the contents of your AUTOEXEC.BAT file. Same as pressing [F4].

View CONFIG.SYS   Lets you view the contents of your CONFIG.SYS file. Same as pressing [F5].

Print Report   Lets you print a report of various aspects of your computer configuration.

Exit   Lets you exit System Information. Same as pressing [F3].

The System Menu

The System pull-down menu provides nine commands for viewing information about your system.

System Type	Displays the General Information screen, which provides general information about your computer system, including CPU type, co-processor if installed, and bus type and size.
Operating System	Displays the Operating System Information screen, which provides the version number, OEM ID, and serial number of your operating system.
Video Adapter	Displays the *Video* Information screen, which describes various aspects of the type of installed video and video memory usage.
I/O Ports	Displays the I/O Port Information screen, which lists the installed I/O ports and matching base port addresses.
Keyboard/Mouse	Displays the Keyboard/Mouse Information screen, which provides information about the type of installed keyboard and its functionality, as well as information about any installed mouse.
CMOS Information	Displays the CMOS Information screen, which lists information about floppy and hard drives, and about installed memory and CMOS status.
Network	Displays the Network Information screen, which describes aspects of any installed active network.
Software Interrupts	Displays the Software Interrupt Information screen, which lists all memory addresses with software interrupts, including the interrupt name and software-program owner. Same as pressing [F8].
Hardware Interrupts	Displays the Hardware Interrupt Information screen, which lists all memory addresses with hardware interrupts, including the interrupt name and software program that controls a piece of hardware. Same as pressing [F9].

The Disk Menu

The Disk pull-down menu displays two commands that display disk-drive information:

Drive Summary   Displays the Logical Drive Information screen, which identifies the installed drives, type size, and current default directory. Same as pressing [F7].

Disk Details   Displays the Logical Drive Detailed Information screen, which describes many features on a selected disk drive.

The Memory Menu

The Memory pull-down menu provides four commands for viewing aspects of memory:

Conventional   Displays the Conventional Memory Information screen, which lists your current memory usage in the area of memory below one megabyte.

Statistics   Displays the Conventional Memory Statistics screen, which shows how much total and conventional memory you have, and the largest free block of memory.

Extended   Displays the Extended Memory Information screen, which lists your current memory usage for extended memory.

Expanded   Displays the Extended Memory Information screen, which lists your current memory usage for expanded memory.

The Benchmarks Menu

The Benchmarks pull-down menu provides four commands for viewing computer performance benchmark information:

CPU Speed Test   Same as pressing [F6].

Disk Speed Test   Displays the Measuring Disk Drive Performance screen, which reports back on aspects of the current drive.

Overall Performance   Displays the Relative Overall Performance Index screen, which provides statistical averages for four different performance categories.

Network Performance   Displays the Network Performance screen, which reports on performance characteristics of an installed and active network system.

The Help Menu

The Help pull-down menu displays various help subjects you can access regarding System Information.

To close the System Information module

      Press: [Esc]

      Press: [Enter]

This returns you to PC Shell or DOS, depending on where you loaded the System Information module.

THE TREE MENU

The Tree pull-down menu provides four commands that let you control the way the tree graph is displayed in the Tree List window.

Expand One Level   Expands the level of subdirectories by one.

Expand Branch   Expands the current branch to all levels.

Expand All   Expands all levels.

Collapse Branch   Collapses the current branch by one level.

You should experiment with these commands to see how you want to configure your tree structure.

THE HELP MENU

The Help pull-down menu displays various help subjects you can access regarding PC Shell.

Topics   Lists eleven general topics on which you can find more detailed help.

Index   Lists an alphabetical index of specific items on which you can find help.

Keyboard   Displays help information about working with your keyboard.

Basic Skills   Lists eleven general topics on which you can find more detailed help.

Commands   Lets you select a specific pull-down command, then find out what it does.

Using Help   Describes how to use help.

About   Displays general information about working in PC Shell.

DOS Advice   Displays eleven subjects about DOS on which you can find more specific information.

You can find out how to maneuver around Help screens by reading the section on help in Chapter 1.

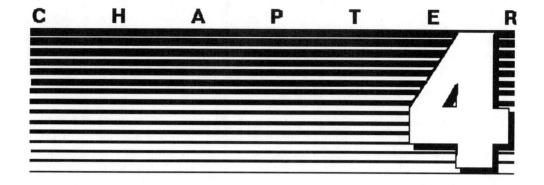

C H A P T E R

4

USING APPLICATIONS IN PC SHELL

Y ou can use the Program List menu to start—or launch—other programs while working in PC Shell. But before we get into the details of the PC Shell Program List menu, you should know a few things about applications.

Application programs are those that apply themselves to a specific task. Both PC Shell and Desktop Manager are application programs: PC Shell applies itself to management of your DOS environment, and Desktop Manager applies itself to routine business chores, such as writing letters, arranging your schedule, making calls, and calculating figures.

For PC Shell, the term *application* means any program that runs in DOS and ends with the file extension .EXE, .COM, or .BAT. These refer, respectively, to executable, command, and batch files. Most application programs, such as those for Lotus 1-2-3 and WordPerfect, run from .EXE or .COM files. These files contain machine code instructions compiled by the manufacturer of the program. Batch files are simple ASCII text files that DOS processes as commands.

WAYS OF LOADING APPLICATION PROGRAMS

You can load application programs four ways while working in PC Shell:

1. From the Program List menu.

2. From the File List window, either by highlighting a filename and pressing [Ctrl]-[Enter], by selecting Launch on the File pull-down menu, or by double-clicking Launch with your mouse. To load the application, you can load the *original* program file, or you can load a file *created* in the application program.

3. From the Binary Viewer while viewing the program file, or from another viewer while viewing a file created by the program.

4. From the DOS command line. (This method was described in Chapter 2, when you worked with the DOS command line in PC Shell).

If you've never used PC Shell before, then you probably should use the fourth method: entering the command from the DOS command line. The first three methods are specific to PC Shell, and will be discussed in this chapter in turn.

THE PROGRAM LIST MENU

The Program List menu in PC Shell is a window that can appear as part of the PC Shell user interface. You can open this window using one of two commands on the View pull-down menu: *Program/File Lists* ([Alt]-[V]-[F]) and *Program List Only* ([Alt]-[V]-[P]). The first command opens the Program List menu on the bottom half of your screen, as shown in Figure 4.1.

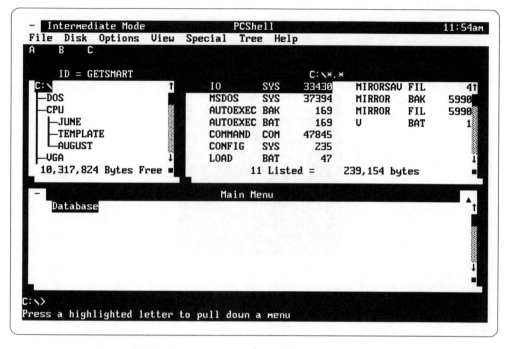

Figure 4.1. The Program List menu on the bottom half of the screen

When the Program List window appears, you must make it active if you want to use any commands in its menu. Press [Tab] until the window becomes active.

The command *Program List Only* makes the Program List window the only window showing, as shown in Figure 4.2.

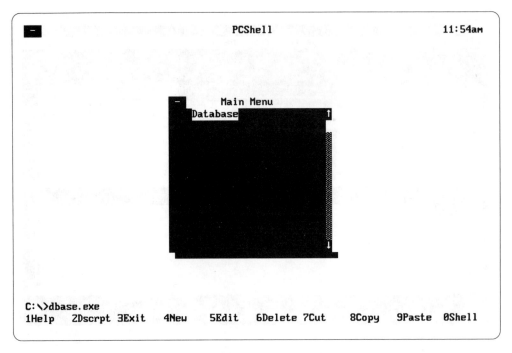

Figure 4.2. The Program List as the only window showing

We'll use this type of display for the rest of the chapter, which describes how you work with the Program List.

When the Program List Menu is active, you'll see the following ten commands assigned to the function keys at the bottom of your screen.

[F1] Help   Opens context-sensitive interactive help.

[F2] Dscrpt   Opens an area to the right of the main menu, where you can insert descriptions for various menu entries.

[F3] Exit   Closes the Program List Menu window.

[F4] New   Opens the New Menu Item box, which lets you declare whether you want to insert a new item in the current group, or insert a new group altogether.

[F5] Edit   Opens the Program Item Information window, which lets you edit the highlighted menu entry.

[F6] Delete   Asks if you want to delete the currently highlighted menu item.

[F7] Cut   Deletes the currently highlighted menu item without prompting you first.

[F8] Copy   Lets you copy the currently highlighted menu entry to a new location on the menu.

[F9] Paste   Lets you paste a menu entry to a new location.

[F10] Shell   Activates the top menu bar for PC Shell, letting you use all commands in PC Shell as you work in the Program List menu window.

RUNNING A PROGRAM

To run an application program, it has to be installed in your Program List menu. Then all you have to do is highlight the menu entry and press [Enter]. PC Shell will automatically load the program and let you work in it, then will return when you exit the program.

> You might run across some memory constraints when you launch applications from PC Shell. PC Shell disappears from your screen while you're working with the other program, and it might look like PC Shell is completely gone—but it's not. Part of PC Shell remains in your computer memory. This is what enables PC Shell to return when you exit the program. Your success in running another program, as well as in working with large files, depends upon how much memory your computer contains and the way the memory is configured.

Once you insert a program item into the Program List menu, you should check to make sure it runs correctly. For example, to run dBASE III PLUS, you would:

    Highlight: dBASE3

    Press: [Enter]

The PC Shell Program List window should disappear from your screen. In a moment, the copyright screen for dBASE III PLUS should appear. (Naturally, if you've loaded a different program, you'll see that program's copyright screen.)

CUSTOMIZING THE APPLICATIONS MENU

The best way to get started is to insert a program item into the Program List menu, then launch the program. You can add an item or a group to a menu. An item is the command to load a specific program. A group is a collection of similar items. For example, you might use Paradox, dBASE III PLUS, or dBASE IV for your database management program. Each program will need its own item in the Program List menu. But they can all appear under the same group, called *Databases*.

Adding New Applications

You can install an entry into the Program List menu for any DOS application program. To add a new program name:

> **Press:** [F4]

This opens the New Menu Item window, which asks whether you want to create a new group or a new item. A new group contains a series of items. A new item is inserted in the current group. For this example, let's first create a new group, then insert a new item into it.

> **Highlight:** Group

> **Press:** [Enter] twice

This opens the Program Group Information box, as shown in Figure 4.3.

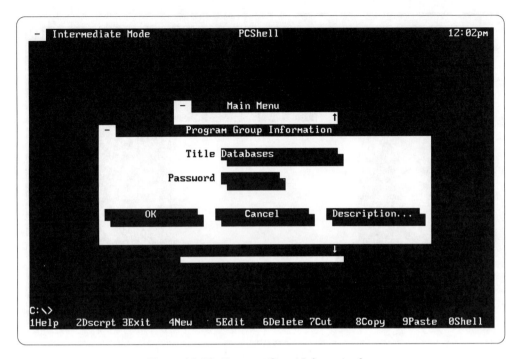

Figure 4.3. The Program Group Information box

This is where you type the name of the group that will appear on the menu. You can also enter a password if you want to restrict access to the applications in this group. Three commands at the bottom of the box let you accept and insert the information you've typed, cancel the information, or proceed to enter a description for the group. For our example:

> **Type:** Databases

> **Press:** [Enter] three times

When the Program Group Information box closes, you should see the new group name in the menu.

To open the group name and prepare to enter an item into the group, highlight the group name and press [Enter]. For our example:

> **Highlight:** Databases

> **Press:** [Enter]

Your screen should change to look like Figure 4.4

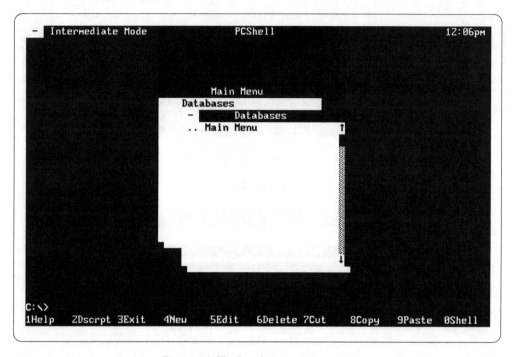

Figure 4.4. The Databases group menu

What you've done is create a submenu of the main menu. This is the menu that will hold your various database program names.

Our next step is to insert a program item name.

> **Press:** [F4]
>
> **Highlight:** Item
>
> **Press:** [Enter] twice

This opens the Program Item Information box, as shown in Figure 4.5.

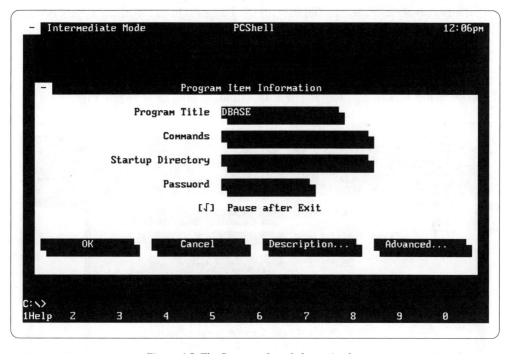

```
─ ▌Intermediate Mode              PCShell                      12:06pm
  ▌
  ▌
  ▌
  ▌        ─                  Program Item Information
  ▌
  ▌               Program Title  DBASE
  ▌
  ▌                   Commands  ████████████████████████
  ▌
  ▌          Startup Directory  ████████████████████████
  ▌
  ▌                  Password   ███████████████
  ▌
  ▌                      [√]   Pause after Exit
  ▌
  ▌       ████OK████      ████Cancel████   ███Description...███  ███Advanced...███
  ▌
  ▌
C:\>
1Help   2      3      4      5      6      7      8      9      0
```

Figure 4.5. The Program Item Information box

This box provides four fields into which you can enter information, plus four commands, which appear at the bottom of the box.

Program Title   The name of the program as you want it to appear on the menu.

Commands   The command you use to start up the program.

Startup Directory   The directory that contains the program startup filename.

Password   Lets you add a password to control access to the program.

The first three of the four commands along the bottom of this box are identical to their counterparts in the Program Group Information box. The fourth command lets you control certain advanced features that control the loading of programs.

Using Advanced Features

You can select the *Advanced Features* command at the bottom of the Program Item Information box to fine-tune the way the program will run when you launch it from the Program List menu.

To set any Advanced Features, begin with the Program Item Information box open:

> **Highlight:** Advanced
>
> **Press:** [Enter]

This opens the Advanced Program Item Information box, as shown in Figure 4.6.

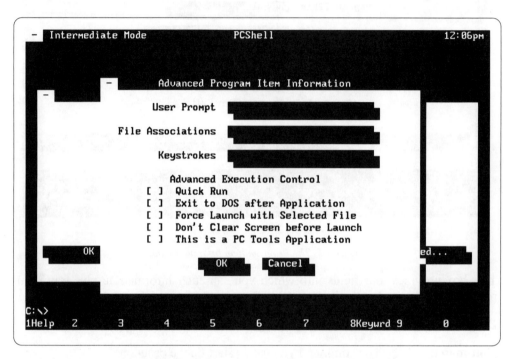

Figure 4.6. The Advanced Program Item Information box

This box provides three fields into which you can enter specific information, as well as five control options. The three fields are:

User Prompt   Lets you insert text that will appear on your screen before the program is run.

File Associations   Lets you declare specific files or groups of files that you can run with the program. For example, you might want to declare all DOC files to be associated with Microsoft Word, or you might want to declare all .WK? files to be associated with Lotus 1-2-3. You can use the DOS wildcards, ? and *, in the standard way.

106

Keystrokes   Lets you enter keystrokes that will be played back after the program is loaded. For example, you might want to load a specific file or template into a word processing program. You can enter keys three ways: by pressing the actual key, by typing the key name surrounded by brackets, or by choosing *Keywrd* on the message bar and then selecting an individual keyword.

The five control options are:

Quick Run   Runs the program without freeing memory used by PC Shell.

Exit to DOS after Application   When you exit the program, you'll return to DOS, not PC Shell.

Force Launch with Selected File   Forces the first selected filename to the program.

Don't Clear Screen before Launch   Doesn't clear your screen before loading the program.

This is a PC Tools Application   Declares the program as a PC Tools application program.

You don't need to set any of these control options to launch a program successfully. You can, however, fine-tune the launching with some of these options for some programs. You should probably experiment with these features so that you can understand how they behave.

Adding a Description

Once the Program List Menu contains an entry, you can add a description to the entry if you think it will help you identify the entry. For example, Figure 4.7 shows a description added to the menu entry DBASE so you know which database management program will be loaded when you execute the DBASE command.

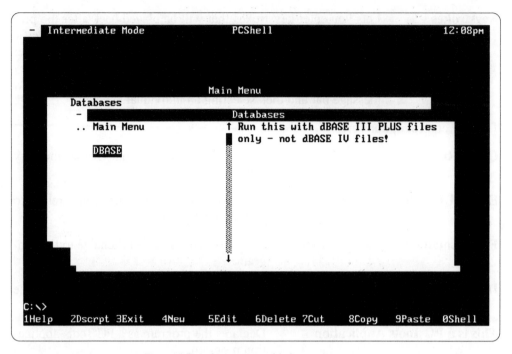

Figure 4.7. A description added to a menu entry

To open the Description window, highlight any Program List menu entry:

> **Press:** [F2].

If you haven't yet added any descriptions, then the right side of the window will be blank. To close the Description window:

> **Press:** [F2]

You can add a description to both group and item names. You can add a description two ways: when you first insert an entry, or when you edit an entry.

To add a description, select the *Description* command at the bottom of either the Group Information box or Item Information box. This moves you into a reduced version of the Notepads module. Your screen will look like Figure 4.8.

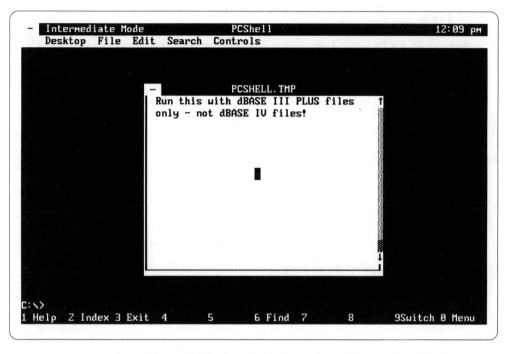

Figure 4.8. The Description Notepads screen

The filename by default is PCSHELL.TMP. This file contains the description information for the Program List menu. Some of the commands on the pull-down menus are disabled. For example, when you open the File pull-down menu, the only two commands you can use are *Save the File* and *Exit Without Saving*. You can use all the other editing commands, such as *Find*, *Search and Replace*, *Cut*, and *Paste* from the clipboard.

It helps to turn on Wordwrap, so that the text you type won't run off the right edge of the Description window:

Press: [Alt]-[C]-[W]

Next, type in the text you want to appear for the description. You can use the example of dBASE III PLUS shown above, or you can type in text any other program you want to launch.

Once the description text has been entered, save the file:

Press: [Alt]-[F]-[S]

109

>   **Press:** [Enter] twice

You'll return to the Program List menu. To view the description you've just added:

>   **Highlight:** DBASE

>   **Press:** [F2]

Your screen should change to look something like Figure 4.3.

You can change descriptions any time you want to:

1. Highlight the program name whose description you want to change.

2. Press [F5].

3. Highlight the *Description* command option and press [Enter].

4. Once the file PCSHELL.TMP opens, edit the text as you want to.

5. Save the changes.

Deleting Program Names

After awhile, you'll find that you switch to new programs,and no longer use old ones. When this happens, you'll probably want to delete the program item names from your Program List menu.

When you delete an item, you'll be asked whether you want to proceed with the deletion.

To delete an item or group name, just highlight the name and press [F6]. The program will ask whether you want to confirm the deletion. Press [Enter] to continue the deletion, or press [Esc] to abandon the deletion. If you continue to delete, the name will disappear from the menu.

Copying and Pasting

If you use the Program List menu often, you'll find you'll want to change it from time to time. You can copy program names and groups from one location to another, and cut names to paste in at another location.

To copy and paste an item

1. Highlight the name you want to copy.

2. Press [F8]. This begins the copying procedure.

3. Place your cursor where you want the name to appear. This can be in another group if you want.

4. Press [F9]. This pastes the name into the new location.

To cut and paste an item

1. Highlight the name you want to cut.

2. Press [F7]. This begins the cutting procedure.

3. Place your cursor where you want the cut name to appear.

4. Press [F9]. This pastes the name into the new location.

You can delete an item by cutting it and then never pasting it into a new location. This is quicker than deleting the name, but it removes the warning prompt you get with the deletion process.

Working with the Program List menu might seem a bit complicated at first, but if you use it at all, you'll soon get a feel for it.

LAUNCHING PROGRAMS

Launching means loading a program directly from the File List window in PC Shell.

There are two ways you can launch a program. The first is to launch the program filename; for example, you might launch WordPerfect using the filename WP.EXE in the File List window. The second way to launch a program is to an associated filename, for example, launching a document created with WordPerfect.

Launching a Program by Filename

To launch a program using its filename, just highlight or select the proper filename and press [Ctrl]-[Enter]. For example, to launch the WordPerfect program using the filename WP.EXE, move to the *Word* directory in the Tree List window. Then press [Tab] to move to the File List window and highlight WP.EXE. To launch:

Press: [Ctrl]-[Enter]

PC Shell will display a window that lets you specify and program parameters you wish to run with the file.

You'll find your cursor in the first position of the Run Parameter(s) field. You can type a filename or any switches that configure the program the way you want to use it.

Once you've typed the parameters, or if you want to skip over the parameters entirely:

Press: [Enter] twice

This highlights and accepts the *Run* command. The PC Shell screen disappears and the selected drive and pathway appear after the DOS prompt, followed by the program path name. After a few moments, the WordPerfect screen will appear.

The beauty of launching programs from the PC Shell screen is that when you exit the program, the PC Shell screen returns to your display. This lets you launch another program or perform some DOS housekeeping chores without having to pop the shell up again.

> If you've loaded PC Shell as a resident program and you pop it open at the DOS prompt to launch various programs, you can still pop open PC Shell while you're working in any one of the programs. This gives you the full use of PC Shell. Just be careful not to launch another program when you are doing this.

Launching a Program with an Associated File

You can also launch programs using filenames associated with the program. To do this, you first have to insert the program as an entry in the Applications pull-down menu.

For this example, I'll assume you have inserted an entry for WordPerfect. To launch this program using associated files, you should edit the File Specs field. For this example, move your cursor to this field and:

Type: *.DOC

This is the default extension created by WordPerfect if you don't declare another extension. Now, whenever you highlight or select a filename ending in .DOC and then launch that file, WordPerfect will load automatically.

You should watch out when using the .DOC extension. Other word-processing programs also use this extension by default, including MultiMate Advantage and Microsoft Word. This means that every filename ending in .DOC, regardless of whether it was created in WordPerfect or another program, will launch the WordPerfect program.

Once you've configured the WordPerfect entry this way, exit PC Shell and see if it works. For this example, I'll use a file named CHAP02.DOC, but you can use any text file ending in .DOC.

Highlight: CHAP02.DOC

Press: [Ctrl]-[Enter]

You won't be given the option of entering parameters. The PC Shell screen will disappear, the command for loading WordPerfect will be passed to your DOS command line, and the WordPerfect screen will appear. The file you used to launch WordPerfect will *not* appear in your WordPerfect screen. You'll have to load that yourself, specify the file in the Run with Selected File field for the WordPerfect Applications menu entry, or launch the WordPerfect program file WP.EXE and enter the file as a parameter.

When you exit a program launched from PC Shell, you will return to PC Shell. You can always access PC Shell from within a program if it has been installed as resident.

Using a Viewer

You can also launch a program while viewing the program file or an associated file in any one of the viewers provided as part of PC Shell. As with launching programs in general:

• You don't need to install the program on the Applications menu if you're viewing a program file (.BAT, .COM, or .EXE) in the Binary Viewer.

• You do have to install the program and associate file specifications if you want to launch the program while viewing an associated file in a viewer.

For example, take a quick view of the WordPerfect program WP.EXE in the Binary Viewer:

Highlight: WP.EXE

Press: [F2]

This opens the highlighted file. Because it is a binary file it is displayed in the binary viewer. To launch this program file, notice that the [F4] function key at the bottom of your screen will launch the file.

Press: [F4]

You'll be shown the Run File window, which lets you specify any parameters.

Press: [Enter] twice

WordPerfect will be loaded and you'll see the WordPerfect editing screen. When you exit WordPerfect, you'll return to the Binary Viewer still displaying the contents of WP.EXE.

You can load WordPerfect while viewing a file ending in .DOC, as long as the *.DOC specific has been entered in the File Specs field for the WordPerfect entry on the Applications menu. For instance:

Highlight: CHAP02.DOC

You'll move directly into the WordPerfect editing screen.

USING PC SHELL AS AN APPLICATIONS LAUNCHER ONLY

Launching applications from PC Shell is such a useful procedure, it's possible to configure your version of PC Shell to only launch applications. This locks out all the other commands and procedures, and keeps other users from working with the full capabilities of PC Shell.

To use PC Shell as an Applications Launcher, open the Change User Level submenu screen:

Press: [Alt]-[O]-[C]-[U]

To toggle on *Application List*:

Press: [L]

When an *X* appears next to that selection:

Press: [Enter] twice

This returns you to a highly modified version of the PC Shell screen.

This limits most of your work in PC Shell to launching applications. Five function keys are active in this version of PC Shell. The only important ones are [F7] Locate, which help you to locate files throughout your system, and [F10] Menu. You can't activate any menu by pressing [Alt], but you can access your previous version of PC Shell by pressing [F10].

Press: [F10]

Your previous version of PC Shell reappears. You can open up menus in this screen as before, but you can only access commands using hotkeys. You can't access a command by highlighting it and pressing [Enter].

When you exit PC Shell after reconfiguring it to become an applications launcher, you'll be asked to save or discard this change. If you save it, PC Shell will always appear as it did after you loaded it.

To return the full use of PC Shell, reopen the Change User Level submenu and toggle off *Application List*, then exit PC Shell and save the new configuration.

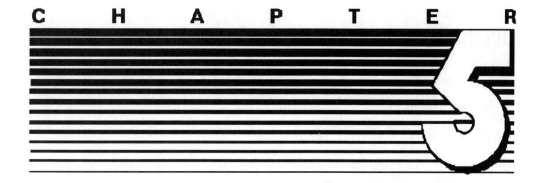

THE DESKTOP
MANAGER

In Chapter 1 you took a quick tour of some of the Desktop Manager features.
This chapter provides a more thorough explanation of the ways you can load the
Desktop Manager and use its features.

OPENING THE DESKTOP MANAGER

As explained in Chapter 1, you can load the Desktop Manager two ways: as a standard program and as a resident program. To load it as a standard program:

Type: DESKTOP

Press: [Enter]

This presumes either that your PC Tools directory is part of your path, or that you are logged into your PC Tools directory.

To run the Desktop Manager as a resident program, you must first load it into memory:

Type: DESKTOP/R

Press: [Enter]

Use the hotkeys to pop up the program:

Press: [Ctrl]-[Spacebar]

The first thing that appears is a screenful of calendars. Notice the pull-down menu name in the top left corner of your screen: *Desktop.* To open the Desktop main menu:

Press: [Enter]

When the Desktop main menu appears, your screen should look like Figure 5.1.

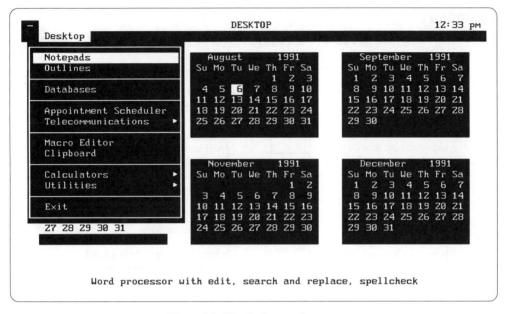

Figure 5.1. The Desktop main menu

The top line shows you're working in the Desktop Manager. If you loaded the PC Shell resident before loading the Desktop Manager, you should see eleven commands on the Desktop menu, as shown in Figure 5.1. If you didn't load the PC Shell as resident, you'll see only ten: the command *PC Shell* will not appear.

> Loading the PC Shell resident first lets you access PC Shell from the Desktop main menu, but I find this superfluous. When I want to open the PC Shell over any screen in the Desktop Manager, I just press [Ctrl]-[Esc], and as long as PC Shell has been loaded resident, it will pop up, regardless of whether I loaded it before or after the Desktop Manager.

Submenus

There are three submenus under the Desktop main menu, as shown in Figure 5.2.

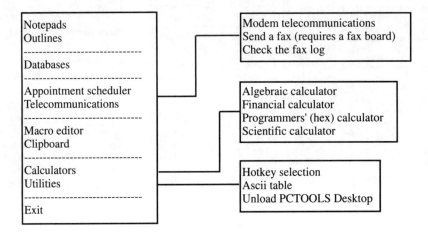

Figure 5.2. Three submenus under the Desktop main menu

Three function keys have assignments in this screen that aren't shown:

[F1] Help   Opens context-sensitive interactive help for the highlighted menu selection or the module you're working in.

[F2] Index   Opens the general Help index.

[F3] Exit   Quits the Desktop Manager and returns you to your previous work.

When you load the Desktop Manager as a standard program, the various module files will be called into play as you select them from the Desktop menu. This keeps your memory usage to a minimum.

Switches

When you load the Desktop Manager, particularly as a resident program, you can use various switches that change its appearance and behavior.

You can use the following switches when loading the Desktop Manager.

/350   The *VGA switch.* Displays features in the program in 350 lines if you have VGA display screen. This means you can see more things on your screen, such as more text files in the Notepads window. However, the tradeoff is that everything appears smaller and often harder to see.

/C#   The *communications port switch,* also called *base port address switch.* You use this switch, followed by the number 3 or 4, to specify COM3 or COM4 for IBM PCs with serial ports installed. These two serial ports are standard on PS/2 computers but not on IBM PCs, including XTs and ATs.

/CS   The *clear screen switch.* Clears the screen of whatever was showing before loading the Desktop Manager in resident mode (if you load the program in standard mode, the screen is cleared automatically). You're given the option of not clearing the screen in resident mode, because you might want to keep your eyes on what you were working with.

/DQ   The *Desktop quick switch.* Lets you load the Desktop Manager faster from your DOS prompt because whatever was showing on your screen before it loaded is not saved. When using the Desktop quick switch, you will *not* be able to pop the Desktop Manager back down again to resume your previous work.

/IN   The *Hercules InColor card switch.* Lets you run the program in color if you're using a Hercules InColor card. If you don't use this switch, the program will be displayed in black and white because resident programs can cause some conflict with Hercules InColor card displays.

/IM   The *disabling mouse switch.* Disables any mouse you have installed. This prevents input conflicts if you use an older mouse.

/LE   The *exchange left for right mouse switch.* Switches control behavior of the left and right buttons on a mouse.

/LCD   The *liquid crystal display switch.* Configures your screen display for a laptop LCD screen.

/MM   The *minus modules switch.* Lets you run the Desktop Manager without using any of the modules that were in the stack the last time you used the Desktop Manager in resident mode. If you don't use this switch, the modules that were saved in currently active windows will be made active again.

/Odrive   The *other drive switch.* Lets you move data to a drive other than the default drive by specifying the drive letter after the switch (for example, /OD moves data to the D drive). The default drive is the one that's current when you load the program in standard mode or pop up the program in resident mode.

Periodically, the Desktop Manager moves data to the DESKTOP.OVL, DESKTOP.IMG, and DESKTOP.THM files. The program needs to know where these files are, or else it won't work. You can use the /O switch to place these files on a RAM drive or in extended memory for more rapid performance. Since these can grow in size as you use the program, you must make sure enough space is available on the drive you specify, or the default drive will be used regardless of your instructions.

/R   The *resident switch.* Loads the program in TSR mode. Without this switch, the Desktop Manager is loaded as a standard program.

/RA   The *resident appointment switch.* Loads the program in resident mode and automatically pops open the Appointment Scheduler module. This way, you can see what is on your to-do list before you begin any other work.

/RL   The *large memory switch.* Loads Desktop Manager resident in the large mode, occupying 241 kilobytes of memory. This is the default setting.

/RM   The *medium memory switch.* Loads Desktop Manager resident in the medium mode, occupying 158 kilobytes of memory.

/RS   The *small memory switch.* Loads Desktop Manager resident in the small mode, occupying 119 kilobytes of memory.

/RT   The *tiny memory switch.* Loads Desktop Manager resident in the tiny mode, occupying 11 kilobytes of RAM.

You can use several switches at the same time, as long as they don't contradict one another. If your switches are contradictory, only the rightmost switch will have an effect because parsing is done from right to left. For example, the first switch read in the command DESKTOP/R/T/M is /M, which allocates memory usage. The /T switch, which also allocates memory usage, will be disregarded.

When setting memory size with a memory-usage switch, you do not have to separate the resident switch and the memory-usage switch with a slash. For example, you can load the program as resident and specify that it occupies the medium resident mode by typing either /R/M or /RM.

You can place switches adjacent to one another or separate them with one or more spaces. I prefer a single space between each switch; it helps me to keep track of them. For example, I sometimes load the Desktop Manager using DESKTOP /R /S. The characters for each switch must always appear together, however; / R is not a valid switch.

Examples For Using Switches

If you want to become adept at using the Desktop Manager, you should experiment with a few of the examples that follow. They demonstrate the effects of loading the Desktop Manager using the most common switches. Begin at your DOS prompt:

Type: DESKTOP /DQ

Press: [Enter]

This loads the program more quickly that usual, because the previous screen display is not saved.

Before you try another switch, you must first unload the Desktop Manager program from memory. A switch won't affect the program unless it's loaded along with the program.

Type: KILL

Press: [Enter]

This runs a small PC Tools batch file program, called KILL.BAT, that removes the resident-loaded Desktop Manager from memory. It will also remove the PC Shell if that's been loaded as resident.

If you have a VGA monitor, load the Desktop Manager in VGA mode:

Type: DESKTOP /350

Press: [Enter]

If your screen is not configured for VGA, this command will have no effect or it will blank out your screen, in which case you'll probably have to reboot your computer.

If you want to see how the clear screen switch works, first load the Desktop Manager in resident mode using the /CS switch:

Type: DESKTOP /R /CS

Press: [Enter]

Now load a standard program, such as a word processor, database, or spreadsheet program, that fills your screen. Next, pop up the Desktop Manager:

Press: [Ctrl]-[Spacebar]

You'll notice that only the main menu and top menu bar appear. Most of what you were looking at before remains on your screen. This is helpful when you want to use the Notepads Editor to copy information to or from the program you were working with before you popped up the Notepads.

USING THE UTILITIES COMMAND

The *Utilities* command does not lead you into a module like the other commands on the Desktop menu. Instead, you're given a menu of four additional commands that let you play with features in the program, including unloading the Desktop Manager from memory.

Before exploring the *Utilities* command, kill the Desktop Manager if you've loaded it as resident.

When the Desktop menu is showing:

Press: [U]

This opens the Utilities submenu, which lets you select one of the following items:

Hotkey selection	Opens a menu with four features of the Desktop Manager that have been assigned to hotkeys.
Ascii table	Opens a representation of the ASCII character table including the 256 characters and their equivalents in decimal and hexadecimal notation.
Unload PCTOOLS Desktop	Unloads the PC Tools Desktop Manager program when it is installed as resident. You'll be given a warning message reminding you of the conditions under which you can unload the programs.

Resetting Hotkeys

The Desktop Manager comes loaded with four features that can be accessed by pressing hotkeys.

Four features in the Desktop Manager program have been assigned hotkeys, and you can see these by opening the PCTOOLS Desktop Hotkey Selection box, shown in Figure 5.3. From the Desktop menu:

Press: [U]-[H]

```
┌──────────────────────────────────────────────────┐
│           PCTOOLS Desktop Hotkey Selection         │
│                                                    │
│     DESKTOP HOTKEY:        <CTRL><SPACE>           │
│     CLIPBOARD PASTE:       <CTRL><INS>             │
│     CLIPBOARD COPY:        <CTRL><DEL>             │
│     SCREEN AUTODIAL:       <CTRL><0>               │
└──────────────────────────────────────────────────┘
```

Figure 5.3. The PCTOOLS Desktop Hotkey selection box

There are four hotkey assignments:

Desktop Hotkey   Pops the Desktop main menu up or down.

Clipboard Paste   Pastes whatever is in the Clipboard to your current screen. This can be a PC Tools module screen or an outside application screen, such as WordPerfect or Lotus 1-2-3.

Clipboard Copy   Prepares to copy whatever is showing on your screen to the Clipboard, within the limits of the Clipboard.

Screen Autodial   Automatically dials the first number the program finds on your screen. A modem must be connected and turned on.

To change any of these hotkey assignments, highlight the feature whose keys you want to change, then press the new hotkeys you want to use. For example, if you use WordStar, you might want to change autodial from [Ctrl]-[O] to [Ctrl]-[Z]. This is a more sensible selection because WordStar (and programs that emulate it) use [Ctrl]-[O] to adjust the margins. If you do not change the autodial hotkey, you might not be able to use autodial.

To reset the autodial hotkey:

Highlight: SCREEN AUTODIAL

Press: [Ctrl]-[Z]

The bottom hotkeys selection should now look like this:

```
SCREEN AUTODIAL:  <CTRL><Z>
```

The new keys work as soon as you assign them, and they are saved when you close the window.

If you reassign the hotkeys that pop open the Desktop main menu, you may find that you can't pop the program open or closed. If this happens, exit to DOS (reboot if you have to), kill all PC Tools programs, then load the Desktop as a standard program and reset the hotkeys to their original settings.

To open either pull-down menu available in the Hotkeys Selection box, first press [Alt] (or [F10]) and then press [D] (for the Desktop pull-down menu) or [W] (for the Window pull-down menu). The top menu bar will remain highlighted.

> Do not try to open the Desktop or Window pull-down menus while working in this screen, because you might accidentally reassign their hotkeys to another feature, since one of the four hotkey selections remains highlighted at all times.

If you inadvertently change a hotkey assignment while trying to pull down a menu, reset the hotkeys immediately, or the change will become permanent.

Using Hotkeys to Pop the Program Up and Down

If the Desktop Manager program is loaded into your computer's memory as a TSR program, you can pop the Desktop main menu up or down at any time by pressing [Ctrl]-[Spacebar].

If you've already worked with the Desktop Manager program and popped it down using the hotkeys, pressing those keys again to pop it back up returns you to the screen you were looking at when you popped it down. This lets you move into and out of a specific feature quickly and easily.

Using Hotkeys for Autodialing

You can use hotkeys to dial phone numbers from the Desktop Manager. Dialing numbers automatically can be helpful if you frequently use your computer. to make calls. Although the Telecommunications module lets you dial numbers in a phone book, there may be times when you want to make a quick call and continue looking at your current screen.

To do this, type anywhere on your screen the number you want to dial, and press [Ctrl]-[O]. The Desktop Manager will load its overlay programs and display a box containing the number you've just typed. It will then ask whether you want to proceed with the call, search for another number, or cancel the autodial.

For example, type in a phone number.

> **Press:** [Ctrl]-[O]

When the Autodial box appears:

> **Press:** [Enter]

This accepts the default answer *Dial,* and dials the displayed number.

When you autodial a number, the program begins searching for numbers in the top-left corner of the screen and proceeds to scan each line until it either finds a number or scans the entire screen without finding a number. It displays the first number it runs across. If you want to dial a number that appears further down the screen:

> **Press:** [N]

You can try to dial any number. PC Tools will display whatever number it runs across in its Autodial box; it won't filter for valid or invalid numbers.

Viewing the ASCII Table

The ASCII character set is used by IBM and compatible personal computers for screen display. There are 256 characters in each set, and there are various sets. The first 128 characters are usually the same in all sets, the second 128 characters are graphic characters that can vary from set to set. Just because you see ASCII characters on screen doesn't mean you can print them; that depends on which ASCII sets have been installed in the printer.

If you want to insert ASCII characters into a Notepads file, you can open an ASCII Table from the Utilities submenu by selecting *Ascii table* on that menu. When you do this, the table appears as shown in Figure 5.4.

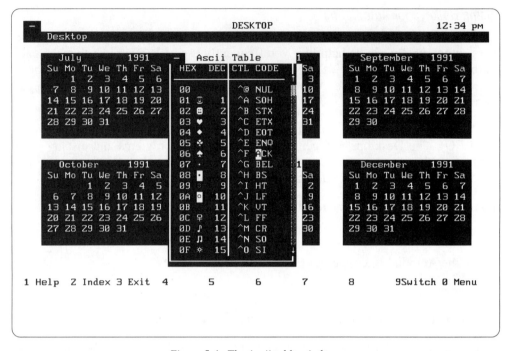

Figure 5.4. The Ascii table window

The hexadecimal and decimal values for each character are displayed on either side of the ASCII graphic symbol for the character. You can move up or down one screen by pressing the arrow keys, [PgDn], or [PgUp]. Your relative position in the numerical sequence of characters is shown on the horizontal scroll bar below the window. You can keep on cycling through the table as long as you want to. If you resize the window, the distance of your movements in screens and on the scroll bar will change.

The Control Menu

All Desktop modules include a menu that mimics the Windows control menu. Windows is the programwide screen controls that appear whenever you click on the icon in the upper-left corner of almost every Windows screen. When you're working in PC Tools Desktop, you can click on the same icon to open the Control menu. When it appears, it looks like Figure 5.5.

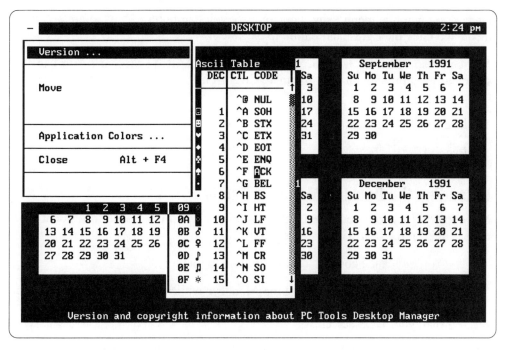

Figure 5.5. The PC Tools Desktop Control menu.

The Control menu provides the following eight commands:

Version   Displays the number of the PC Tools Desktop version you're using.

Restore   Restores your current screen to its previous size and position.

Move   Lets you move the current window to a new location on screen.

Size   Lets you change the size of the current window.

Maximize   Expands the current window to fill your entire screen.

Colors   Lets you change the colors of features on your screen.

Close   Closes the current window and returns you to the previous window.

Switch To   Lets you switch to another open window.

Not all of these commands will be enabled every time you open this menu. For example, when you've maximized a window to full-screen size, the *Maximize* command will be disabled. A disabled command will appear lighter.

Once you open this menu using your mouse, you can point to any command on the menu and click the right-hand button to execute it.

You can also open the Control menu by pressing [Alt]-[Spacebar]. You can then select any command on this menu by highlighting the command and pressing [Enter].

To close the Control menu:

Press: [Esc]

Unloading the Desktop Manager Safely

You shouldn't try to unload the Desktop Manager when it's loaded in resident mode under either of the following two conditions:

1. You've loaded another TSR program into memory.

2. You've popped up the Desktop Manager while working in another application; that is, you've popped up the Desktop Manager from a screen other than your DOS screen.

DOS will go crazy if you leave a hole in its memory. You have to unload programs in the *reverse* order in which they were loaded. In most cases, you'll get a warning message if you try to leave a hole in DOS. In some cases, though, no message will appear and you'll have to reboot the computer.

When I began using PC Tools, I found that the program-management setup caused lockups in my system and forced me to reboot too often. Every time I rebooted, the operation took awhile for all the PC Tools programs to load themselves. To correct this, I removed the commands inserted into my AUTOEXEC.BAT file by the PC Setup program and placed them in a separate batch file called LOAD.BAT.

With LOAD.BAT, I can wait until my DOS prompt appears, then type LOAD and press [Enter]. That's when the PC Tools programs load themselves into my computer's memory.

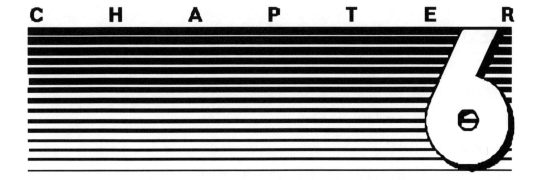

WORKING WITH NOTEPADS

The Notepads module is an abbreviated form of word processor that lets you create text files, edit text in a variety of ways, and print files. You can also insert headers and footers, and change the margins and line spacing to customize the printed format. You can open up to fifteen different text files at the same time and move between them.

The Notepads Editor has two limitations. First, it is not a full-featured word processor, although you can create more complex formats than most other editors allow. Second, you can work only with files containing 60,000 or fewer bytes.

Most of the time you spend in Notepads will probably be for creating simple text files, such as notes, brief descriptions, and letters.

OPENING THE EDITOR SCREEN

To access the Notepads module from the main menu:

Press: [N]

If you're working in another module:

Press: [Alt]-[D]-[N]

This opens the Notepads dialog box, which looks like Figure 6.1.

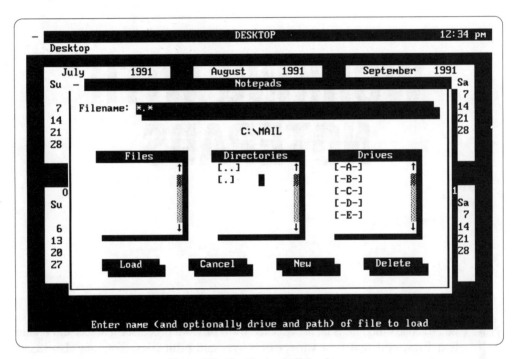

Figure 6.1. The Notepads dialog box

Your current directory appears beneath the filename line. Beneath the directory name is the Filename window, which shows all files ending in .TXT, as well as a list of other drive letters you might want to access. The program scans for all drives. I don't use any drive letters below C, though they show in my dialog box.

Four command buttons show on the bottom of the dialog box:

Load Loads the specified filename into the Notepads Editor screen.

Cancel Cancels your work in Notepads and returns you to the main menu or the module you were working in previously.

New Creates a new file. You can also create a new file by typing in a new file-name, pressing [Enter], and then selecting the command *Create*.

Delete Deletes the file highlighted in the List window.

You can use any of these four commands by pointing at them with your mouse cursor and pressing a key. Another way is to press [Tab] as many times as necessary to highlight the desired command, then press [Enter].

Take a look at the README.TXT file provided as part of the PC Tools program files. This file contains last-minute information about the programs that didn't make it into the manuals. With the Notepads dialog box showing:

Press: [Enter]

This moves your cursor down to the first filename at the top of the list, which is in alphabetical order. Move through most of the filenames by pressing [PgDn] several times. As you get close to the filename README.TXT, press [⇓]. When you've highlighted the filename README.TXT:

Press: [Enter]

When the contents of README.TXT are fully loaded into the Notepads Editor screen, it should look like Figure 6.2.

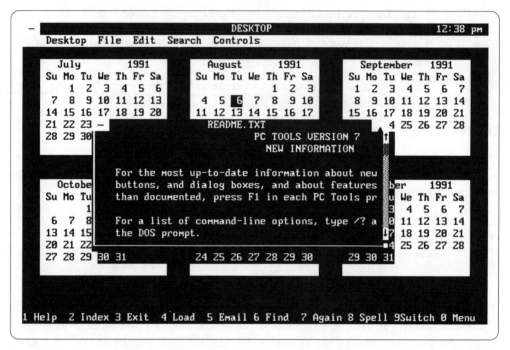

Figure 6.2. The Notepads Editor screen

To view the next screen:

Press: [PgDn]

To expand the window to full-screen size, open the Control menu:

Press: [Alt]-[Spacebar]

Now select the *Maximize* command:

Press: [X]

Your screen should now look like Figure 6.3.

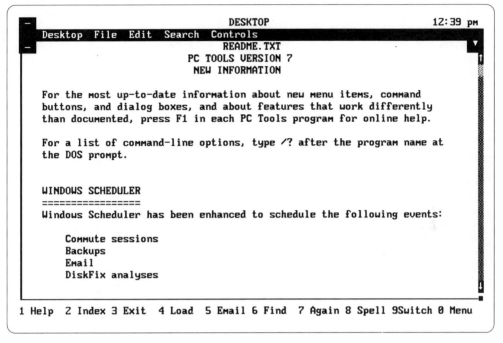

Figure 6.3. The Notepads Editor screen zoomed to fill your screen

Key Activities

The standard cursor control keys, including [PgDn] and [PgUp], control cursor movement.

The name of the file, README.TXT, appears in the top menu bar. You'll find the current time in the upper-right corner of the screen. To see more of the text in README.TXT:

Press: [PgDn]

The keys you can use in the Notepads Editor screen are shown in Table 6.1.

Function	Keys
Right one character	[⇒]
Right one word	[Ctrl]-[⇒]
End of line	[End]
Down one line	[⇓]
Down one line fixing cursor	[Ctrl]-[PgDn]
End of screen	[End]-[End]
Down one screenful	[PgDn]
End of file	[Ctrl]-[End]
Left one character	[⇐]
Left one word	[Ctrl]-[⇐]
Beginning of line	[Home]
Up one line	[⇑]
Up one line fixing cursor	[Ctrl]-[PgUp]
Beginning of screen	[Home]-[Home]
Up one screenful	[PgUp]
Beginning of file	[Ctrl]-[Home]
Insert character	Press character key
Insert space	[Spacebar]
Insert control character	[Ctrl]-character key
Insert tab stop	[Tab]
Delete hard carriage return	[Enter]
Delete current character	[Del]

Table 6.1. Key activities in the Notepads screen

Experiment with these keys now so you can get the feel of how they behave. While you're doing this, read the README.TXT file.

Document Control

The format of a text file is crucial if you want to view the contents in a recognizable form on your screen. It's important, therefore, that you understand a few things about how text characters appear on screen, and the various ways different programs display text characters.

There are two formats to which you can save Notepads files:

ASCII   This is the simplest format. It includes text characters, plus rudimentary formatting, such as tab stops and hard carriage returns.

PC Tools   Saves the file and includes the page layout features as defined in the Page Layout menu, which you'll learn about later in this chapter.

Most of the time, you'll view files in ASCII format and save them in PC Tools format. These are the default settings.When you save a file, you'll be given the choice of saving it in PC Tools format or ASCII format. ASCII doesn't include even the minimal format controls provided on the Page Layout menu.

NOTEPADS MENUS

There are five pull-down menus available in the Notepads module. You should already be familiar with one of the them, Desktop, which was described in Chapter 5. The remaining four are:

File   Loads, saves, and prints files. Also, you can set an autosave time period and quit a file without saving it.

Edit   Cuts, pastes, and copies text using the clipboard. This menu also lets you work with blocks of text, delete all text and insert text from another file, go to specific lines, and check spelling in the current file.

Search   Finds and replaces characters.

Control   Controls the appearance of a text file both on screen and when it's printed. This is where you work with page layout.

To open the Edit menu:

   Press: [Alt]-[E]

You can scroll through all five pull-down menus by pressing [⇐] or [⇒].

A NOTEPADS TUTORIAL

For the rest of this chapter, you'll work with the primary commands on these menus in a tutorial that leads you through creating, editing, and then printing a new file.

To exit the Notepads module:

> **Press:** [Esc]

This should close the Editor screen and return you to the Desktop main menu, or whatever screen you were working in when you opened the Notepads module.

Function Key Assignments

On the bottom line, you can see nine function-key assignments:

[F1] Help	Opens the general Help screen for the Notepads module.
[F2] Index	Opens the Help List index.
[F3] Exit	Closes the current Notepads screen and returns to your previous work.
[F4] Load	Opens the Notepads dialog box and lets you load a new or existing file into the Editor screen.
[F5] E-mail	Lets you send the current file as e-mail or schedule a time to send it.
[F6] Find	Opens the Find and Replace box, letting you specify search and replacement conditions.
[F7] Again	Lets you repeat the *Find* command.
[F8] Spell	Begins to spell-check the current file.
[F9] Switch	Switches you to another active window if one is available.
[F10] Menu	Activates the pull-down menu bar.

Creating a File

In this section, you will use Notepads to create a new file by declaring the filename in the Notepads dialog box. To open the Notepads dialog box at the Desktop menu:

Press: [N]

Type: TEST

The default characters *.TXT disappear from the Filename field and are replaced by the characters you type. Don't worry. The default extension will be added to this filename. Now, to actually create the file:

Press: [Enter]

This sends the program looking for the file. When it doesn't find the file, the program asks whether you want to create the file or cancel the creation.

Press: [Enter]

This tells the program to create the file. You could also press [O] for OK. If you want to cancel, press either [C] or [Esc].

When the Notepads screen appears, expand it to full size.

Press: [Alt]-[Spacebar]

Press: [X]

Insert and Overtype

You can find the label INS on the right end of the top line. This means *insert* mode is active. When you type a character inside existing text, it will move characters to the right of your cursor farther to the right. To switch off the insert mode:

Press: [Ins]

This switches you to *overtype* mode, shown by the absence of the INS indicator. This means anything you type will write over existing characters.

You can also switch between insert and overtype modes using the Controls pulldown menu:

Press: [Alt]-[C]-[O]

> If you want to declare a different default extension, such as .ASC, you should:
>
> **Type:** *.ASC
> **Press:** [Enter]
>
> This is the extension considered most appropriate for ASCII files. You can declare any three-letter extension you want, but I don't recommend the use of .EXE, .COM, .SYS, or .OVL. Files with these extensions could get confused with DOS program files. You should use .BAT when you create DOS batch files.

The Tab Line

A tab line appears as the second line in the Notepads Editor window, marking every fifth tab stop with a triangle. To switch the tab line off:

Press: [Alt]-[C]-[T]

This switch acts as a toggle. Just repeat it to turn the tab line back on.

You can change the tab stops easily. First, make sure the ruler line is showing on your screen:

Press: [Alt]-[C]-[R]

To delete a tab stop, first move to the one you want to delete:

Press: [Tab]

Press: [Del]

To insert a new stop, move to the location where you want a tab stop; use the cursor control keys to position your cursor:

Press: [Ins]

A triangular tab-stop marker should appear in your cursor position. when you are finished editing the tab line:

Press: [Esc]

This returns the cursor to where it was when you started to edit the tab line. Sometimes, you'll find you can't delete tab stops you've just inserted. If this happens, press [Esc] to exit the tab line and start the edit again.

Inserting Text

You can write any text you want to for the sample file in this chapter.

First, you must check three settings:

Press: [Alt]-[C]

Make sure that check marks appear to the left of the bottom two settings on this menu, *Wordwrap* and *Auto Indent*. When a musical note appears, it means that the setting is turned on. Make sure there isn't one next to the command *Control Char Display*. These are the default settings for these three commands.

Now begin your work in the Notepads Editor window. First, press [Tab] to move the cursor right five spaces. Type in words just as if you were using a typewriter.

Notice that the text drops down to the next line. This is called *Wordwrap*. Notepads automatically wraps text lines in column 75. Also notice that the next line begins directly beneath the first character of the first line. This is called *Auto Indent*, and it lets you keep typing without worrying about the position of the right margin.

Type several lines of text so you can see how these features work.

Pressing [Enter] inserts a hard carriage return. This moves your cursor down to the left margin of the next line. If Auto Indent is on, the cursor will move to the left margin as defined by the previous line. If Auto Indent is off, you'll move to the left edge of the screen.

To turn off Wordwrap:

Press: [Alt]-[C]-[W]

Notice that several lines of text disappear from your screen, and only characters up to Column 75 remain on screen. Turning Wordwrap off places all text on the same line until a hard-carriage return is encountered. The single lines of text scroll off the right side of your screen. Toggle Wordwrap back on:

Press: [Alt]-[C]-[W]

If your screen looks a bit different when you toggle Wordwrap back on, press [PgUp] or [Home] to reposition the text.

To turn off Auto Indent:

Press: [Alt]-[C]-[A]

Notice how the second and subsequent text lines move over to the left edge of the Editor window. Toggle Auto indent back on:

Press: [Alt]-[C]-[A]

Saving Files

Now that you've entered text into TEST.TXT, save your work:

Press: [Alt]-[F]-[S]

When told to save a file, Notepads will open the Save File to Disk box, shown in Figure 6.4

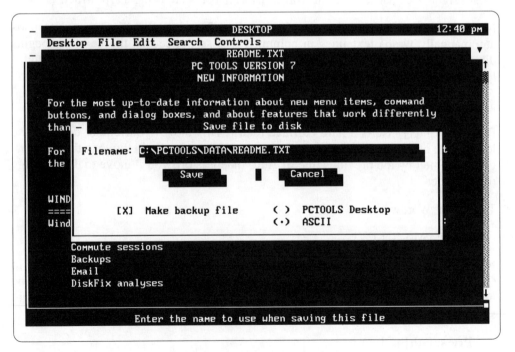

Figure 6.4. The Save File to Disk box

This box lets you specify three save conditions:

1. The name of the file being saved. The current filename will appear as the default, but you can change the name to any other filename acceptable to DOS.

2. Whether or not you want to create a backup file. This lets you protect your work by creating two identical files, but it also uses up twice as much disk space.

3. The file-save format. You can save the file in pure ASCII, which is the default, or in PC TOOLS Desktop format; the settings are defined in your current Page Layout submenu, under the Controls menu.

Autosave

Your work in the Notepads Editor screen is saved automatically every five minutes by a feature called *Autosave*. However, I never feel very comfortable with a five-minute interval. If the power to my computer fails before five minutes is up, I'll lose quite a bit of work.

To change the interval to one minute:

Press: [Alt]-[F]

Press: [A]

This opens the Automatic File Save box, displaying your cursor under the time setting. You specify the new time interval in minutes simply by typing in the new number:

Type: 1

To make this the new setting:

Press: [O]

There's a trade-off when you shorten the interval. When your computer saves a file, it suspends all other work on the computer until it is finished. In most cases, this doesn't amount to much of a delay, but if the file is particularly large and you're in an impatient mood, you might find yourself typing while nothing appears on your screen. Your computer has a keyboard buffer that should hold at least fifteen characters. This memory will be displayed on your screen when the saving is complete.

Saving Your Setup

Now that you've learned how to control the way the Notepads Editor screen appears and behaves, you might want to save the settings you'd like to use most frequently.

> **Press:** [Alt]-[C]-[S]

This selects the *Save Setup* command on the Controls menu and records the settings to a file called NOTEPADS.CFG. You can change the settings any time you want to and then save that configuration.

For my work, I turn off the tab line and Auto Indent, but leave Wordwrap on.

Control Codes

In a previous section we referred to hard-carriage returns, which are control codes. Control codes control the way text appears on the screen and when printed. You insert control characters into text when you press [Tab] and [Enter]. The first inserts a tab, the second a hard carriage return.

You can see these two symbols displayed graphically by turning on the display of control characters:

> **Press:** [Alt]-[C]-[C]

Notice how a small arrow appears before the first line. This is a tab control code symbol. Notice the arrows at the end of each line where you pressed [Enter]. These are hard carriage return control codes.

As a general rule, you don't need to worry about control codes. If you start viewing text files created in other editors or word processors, switching on the display of control characters is a good way to search for unwanted control codes: you'll end up with some problems if you try to print text files that contain strange control codes, or to send files through electronic mail.

If you want to use the Notepads Editor to create files you want to put in another program, you can insert control codes specific to that program. Simply hold down [Ctrl] and press the letter key that matches the control code you want to insert.

For example, ^I is the letter code for a tab stop (the caret symbol ^ stands for *Control*). You might want to insert this code as an experiment. Place your cursor before some characters.

Press: [Ctrl]-[I]

Notice how the characters following your cursor move to the right five spaces, which also happens when you press [Tab]. You can do the same thing with the hard carriage return control code, which is ^J.

Press: [Ctrl]-[J]

This moves all characters after your cursor down to the next line, which also happens when you press [Enter].

If you try to insert a control code that has no effect in the Notepads Editor, you'll see the ASCII character instead. For example, you can see standard and reverse video funny faces, if you press [Ctrl]-[A] and [Ctrl]-[B]. You can see the complete list of control codes at the top of the ASCII table.

Press: [Alt]-[D]-[U]-[A]

This pops open the ASCII table over the Notepads Editor screen, seen in Figure 6.5.

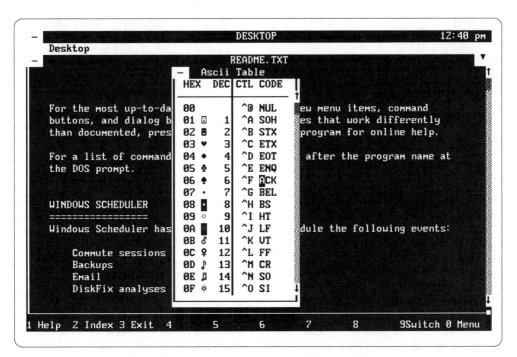

Figure 6.5. The ASCII Table overlaying the Notepads Editor screen

You can create fancier formats for files you print in the Notepads module, as long as you know what effects the control codes will have in the printer you're using. You can customize the printing of Notepads files to your printer by creating and loading specific printer macro files. You can find sample printer macro files in SAMPLE.PRO, which is provided as a file in the PC Tools Deluxe program. You can find out more about this file in Chapter 15.

EDITING A FILE

Once you've inserted text into a Notepads file, you can edit and change the text using a variety of editing tools. These involve simple text inserting and deleting, deleting all text in the file, inserting text from another file, handling text in blocks, copying to and from the Clipboard, and spell-checking your work.

The first thing to do is view the scroll bars tracking your cursor position in the file. Place your cursor on any text line. Notice how the marker on the right side scroll bar matches the line your cursor is on. Move your cursor down one line:

Press: [⇓]

Notice how the marker also moves down one line.

Look at the bottom scroll bar. Move your cursor to the beginning of the current line:

Press: [Home]

Notice how the bottom scroll bar marker moves to the left end of the bar. Next, move your cursor to the right end of the text line:

Press: [End]

Now, back the cursor up a word at a time:

Press: [Ctrl]-[⇐]

Press these two keys a few more times to move your cursor back several words. Notice how the marker moves back with your cursor. Now move your cursor back one letter at a time:

Press: [⇐]

Experiment with the cursor and scroll-bar marker movements on several different text lines. The interesting effect is that the scroll bar adjusts to each text line. If there are only a few words on a line, the marker will move in bigger jumps since there are fewer letters to fill out the line. When a text line is full of characters, the marker movements are smaller.

Working With Blocks

You work with blocks of text when you want to copy or move several lines from one location to another. You can copy or move text within a single file or between two or more files. Use the Clipboard to hold the text while you move to the new location.

There are four steps for copying or moving text:

1. Highlight the block of text.

2. Copy or cut it to the Clipboard.

3. Move to the new location where you want the block of text to appear.

4. Paste the block into the new location.

Whenever you want to work with a section of text, you must first select the text you want to work with by highlighting it. To select text, position your cursor before the first character of the block you want to highlight:

Press: [Alt]-[E]-[M]

Now move your cursor to the last character in the block. Highlighting will follow the progress of your cursor. Once you've highlighted all the text you want to work with, select the operation you want to use.

An alternative way to highlight text is to use the [Shift] key in conjunction with the cursor control keys, but first you must make sure that the Num Lock light is turned on:

Press: [Num Lock]

To extend highlighting to the right one character at a time, press [Shift]-[⇒]. Hold down both keys until you've highlighted all the text you want. To extend highlighting to the end of the line, press [Shift]-[End]. To highlight an entire line, press [Shift]-[⇓].

Once you've highlighted the text, just press [Alt]-[E]-[T].

You can extend highlighting in jumps by holding down [Shift] while pressing [Ctrl]-[⇓] to move the cursor. It can be difficult to hold down three keys at the same time, but if you do a lot of cutting and pasting, then you'll soon find this a matter of habit.

While highlighting a block, if you decide you don't want to copy or cut the text, press [Esc] to turn the highlighting off, or press [Alt]-[E]-[U].

To *copy* the block you've highlighted:

    Press: [Alt]-[E]-[C]

The highlighting will disappear. The block has now been copied into the Clipboard, while remaining in the original file. To see the contents of your Clipboard:

    Press: [Alt]-[D]-[B]

This opens the Desktop main menu, selects Clipboard, and opens the Clipboard screen over the Notepads Editor screen, as shown in Figure 6.6.

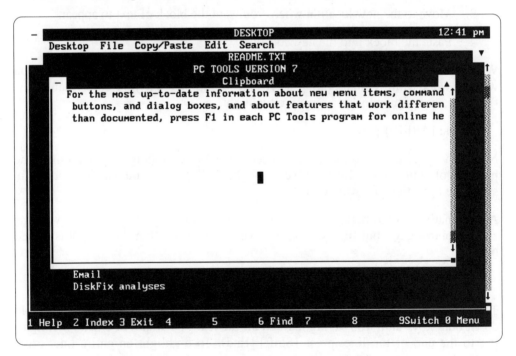

Figure 6.6. The Clipboards window over the Notepads Editor screen

The Clipboard can only hold two kilobytes worth of characters, which is about sixty lines of text. If the block you've selected exceeds that amount, you'll get an error message, in which case you should reduce the size of the block you're copying. If you need to copy more than two kilobytes of text, you should complete the copy by repeating these steps for each block of about sixty lines.

To move the block, erasing it from the original file, first *cut* it, by highlight the text, then:

Press: [Alt]-[E]-[T]

This cuts the text from the file and puts it into the Clipboard. The letter *T* is used to make you think twice about what you are doing. When you cut text, you may lose it if you forget to paste it back out from the Clipboard or if the power to your computer fails before you paste it back out.

To *paste* the block, or place it in another section of text, move your cursor to where you want the text to appear. Then:

Press: [Alt]-[E]-[P]

The text you copied into the Clipboard (see Figure 6.7) should appear at your cursor position. It might take a few moments for all the text to appear because the Editor window has to format the text for its new location.

The DIG Commands

Three commands on the Edit pull-down menus let you delete all the text in the file you're viewing, insert all the text from another file, and go to a specific line in the current file. These three appear in the same group of commands and are activated respectively by the letter keys [D], [I], and [G].

Delete

To delete all text in the current file:

Press: [Alt]-[E]-[D]

You'll be given a warning, just in case you don't want to delete all the text. To continue:

Press: [Enter]

All characters will disappear from the current file.

> As long as a file hasn't been save to disk (either by you or by Autosave), you can resurrect the file text that you have deleted by reloading the disk file into the Notepads Editor screen.

Insert

To insert all text from another file into the current file, first place your cursor where you want the text to begin appearing:

Press: [Alt]-[E]-[I]

Type: name of file to insert

Press: [Enter]

As long as you've specified the filename correctly, and the path if necessary, the text from the other file will appear.

Go to

To go to a specific line in the file:

Press: [Alt]-[E]-[G]

Type: line number

Press: [Enter]

The line you've specified will become the top line in the current window.

Checking Spelling

The Notepads module comes with a dictionary containing approximately 70,000 words that can be used to spell-check.

You can use three commands on the Edit menu to check the spelling of a single word, all the text displayed on your screen, or the entire file. Since checking the spelling of an entire file is the most usual method, it has been assigned to the [F8] key.

To spell-check an entire file, you can begin anywhere in the file:

Press: [F8]

The Editor will start the spell-check at the first word in the file and compare every word against entries in the PC Tools dictionary. While it does this, a message near the top of the Editor window tells you that spell-checking is in progress. As long as a match is found for each word in sequence, the check progresses smoothly. This procedure is a bit slow if you're used to working in a sophisticated word processor, but it's a pleasure to have a spell-checker at all in a TSR Editor.

When the program finds a word that isn't in its dictionary, the word will be highlighted and the Word Misspelled box appears. For example, when I spell-check README.TXT, the first word flagged is *e-mail*, as shown in Figure 6.7.

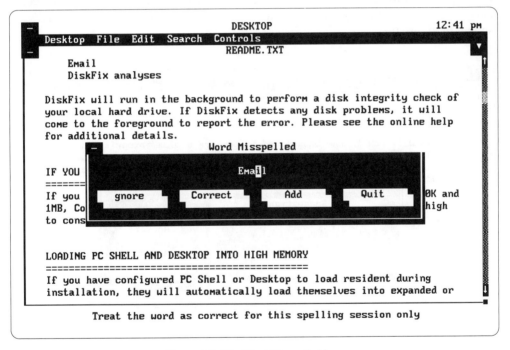

Figure 6.7. The Word Misspelled box

This box displays the flagged word and gives you four options:

Ignore   Ignores the word for the rest of the spell-check and continues the spell-check. Pressing [Esc] also ignores the flagged word, closes the box, and continues the spell-check.

Correct   Opens a list of possible substitutes for the flagged word.

Add   Adds the flagged word to your dictionary so it won't be flagged again.

Quit   Closes the window, ends the spell-check, and returns you to your work in the file.

If you press [C] to select Correct, the Editor will try to find a list of words that come closest to what it thinks you want to use. The possible substitutes for "e-mail" are shown in Figure 6.8.

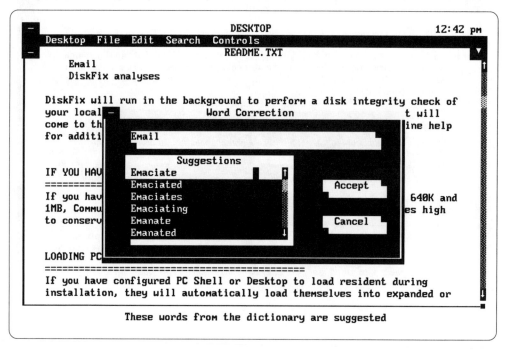

Figure 6.8. List of suggested corrections

The closest match to the misspelled word appears at the top of the list and is high-lighted. If this is the correct spelling of the word you want:

Press: [Enter]

If the highlighted word is not the one you want, but there's another on the list that might be more suitable, use the arrow keys to highlight the correct word and then press [Enter].

You can cancel the spell-checking any time by pressing [Esc]. You can cancel the spell-check when the Word Misspelled box appears by pressing [C], or highlighting Cancel and pressing [Enter].

A word is flagged when a match is not found in the dictionary, but this doesn't nec-essarily mean the word is misspelled. Because of the 70,000-word limit in the PC Tools dictionary and certain limitations in the spell-check procedure, a word might be flagged when it is not really misspelled.

When this happens, you can either ignore the word for the rest of the spell-check or add the word to the dictionary so future checks in other documents will not flag the word. When you add a word to your dictionary, it becomes a permanent entry. You can't remove words. You can't even edit DICT.SPL using the *FileEdit* command in PC Shell.

Searching and Replacing

Searching for text lets you find a string of text quickly. Replacing text lets you search for a specific string of characters and replace it with something else. You can use the Search menu for both finding and replacing text. Since replacing text is such a com-mon procedure in writing, you can also use the [F6] function key for replacement.

Finding Text

If all you want to do is find text:

Press: [Alt]-[S]-[F]

This opens the Search menu and then the Find box, which look like Figure 6.9.

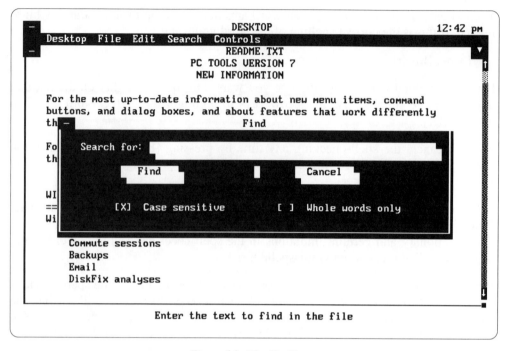

Figure 6.9. The Find box

You can find your cursor blinking in the Search for field, which is where you type the text you want to search for. For example, if you want to search for *I love you dearly*:

Type: I love you dearly

Press: [Enter] twice

This highlights and then executes the *Find* command. The program will move you to the first occurrence of this string of text, place your blinking cursor under the first letter of the string, and reopen the Find box. If you want to find the next occurrence of the text:

Press: [Enter]

You can search for more occurrences of the same text by continuing to press [Enter] after each find. When the Editor can't find another occurrence, it will beep. Searching always begins in the current cursor position and proceeds toward the end of the file.

You can narrow down the search criteria by turning on one or the other of two conditions at the bottom of the Find box.

Case Sensitive   When Case Sensitive is on, the Editor will search for text exactly as you type it. For example, if you don't turn on *Case Sensitive* and specify "me" as the text to search for, the Editor will flag all occurrences of *ME, Me, mE,* and *me.* If you turn on *Case Sensitive*, the Editor will only flag *me.*

Whole Words Only   When Whole Words Only is on, the Editor will search for text that corresponds to the words you've specified. The Editor assumes that you're entering whole words. For example, if Whole Words Only isn't on and you specify "men" as the text to search for, the Editor will flag all occurrences of men, including *mentor, amen,* and any other words that contain the three letters m-e-n. If you turn on Whole words Only, the Editor will flag only the word *men,* with a space on both sides.

The default settings for both of these conditions is off. To toggle either on or off, press [Tab], which highlights the condition, and then press [Enter]. The letter X will appear next to a condition when it is turned on.

Replacing Text

If you want to search for text and replace it, you must tell the Editor a few more things:

Press: [F6]

This opens the Find and Replace box, which looks like Figure 6.10.

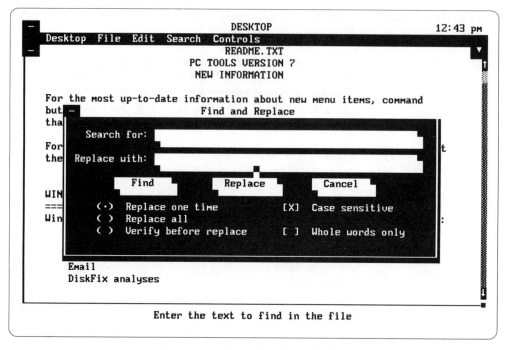

Figure 6.10. The Find and Replace box

As before, you'll find your cursor in the Search For field. Type the text you want to search for and press [Enter]. This moves you to the Replace With field. Type the text you want to use as a replacement and press [Enter]. When the first occurrence is found, the Find and Replace box reappears. Pressing [Enter] finds the next occurrence. Thus you can change the way replacement works by replacing one word at a time, or by pressing [Enter] repeatedly.

You can specify text to search for, case sensitivity, and whole words in this window just as you did in the Find box. You also specify the text you want substitute as a replacement.

You can refine the replacement process with three additional commands:

Replace one time   Substitutes the second string for the first and proceeds to the next occurrence.

Replace all   Substitutes the second string for the first in all occurrences in the current file.

Verify before replace   Finds the next occurrence of the first string and displays on the bottom line of your screen the words:

```
ENTER:make change   ESC:abort   SPACE:skip
```

If you want to replace the string, press [Enter]. If you want to cancel the replacement procedure, press [Esc]. If you want to skip this occurrence and proceed to the next one, press [Spacebar].

Searching and replacing text is one of the more powerful editing features available in the Notepads module.

CHANGING THE FORMAT

Even though the Notepads module is just an Editor, you're given a basic amount of format control within the program with the Page Layout and Header/Footer selections and printer macros.

Working with Page Layout

You can work with seven format settings using the *Page Layout* selection under the Controls pull-down menu.

Press: [Alt]-[C]-[P]

When the Page Layout box appears, it should look Figure 6.11.

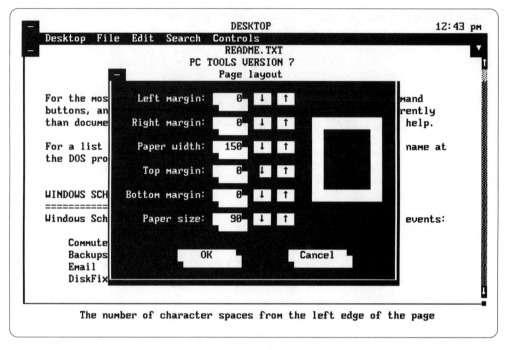

Figure 6.11. The Page Layout box

The default settings show when the menu first appears.

You might want to experiment with different values for these settings to see which appeals to you the most.

You can move among the seven settings by pressing [Tab] or [Enter] and typing in new values. If you change a value and then issue the *OK* command (highlight OK and press [Enter]), the values will remain in effect until you change them again.

I use the default six lines for my top and bottom margins, but I prefer a left margin in column 0 and a right margin in column 65. The *Starting Page* number is 1, which you'll want to use most of the time. If you want to print part of a longer document, you should adjust the starting page number to the number of the page where your printing begins. Page numbers will be printed by default in a blank footer. To display page numbers, you must use a header or footer.

Headers and Footers

A header is text that appears at the top of every printed page, and a footer is text that appears at the bottom. Some word processors let you select odd or even pages of headers and footers, but you can't do this in the Notepads module.

To declare headers and footers:

Press: [Alt]-[C]-[H]

This opens the Page Header & Footer box, shown in Figure 6.12.

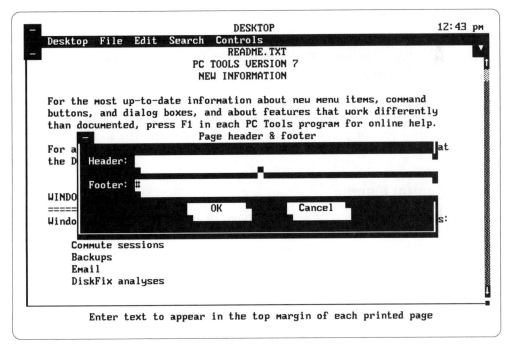

Figure 6.12. Page Header & Footer box

You can find your cursor in the first position of the Header field. You're given space for fifty characters maximum in the header and footer. This limits you to one line of text even if you've set your margins to create a text line of less than fifty characters. Headers and footers appear in the top and bottom margins and remain unaffected by your margin settings.

Notice the number character (#) in the Footer field. This is the symbol you use to declare where the page number should appear. If you insert the same symbol in the Header field, you'll get page numbers in both the header and footer of every page.

If you want the page number to appear in the header only:

> **Type:** #
>
> **Press:** [Enter]
>
> **Press:** [Backspace]
>
> **Press:** [Enter] twice

This changes the field entries, issues the *OK* command, and closes the Page Header & Footer box. These settings will remain in effect for the next printing, or until you exit the Notepads module.

You can see header and footer text only when you print the file. You can use headers and footers not only to print page numbers, but also to print the name of the file, the time and date of printing, and other information that helps you to organize your work.

Printer Control Macros

You can insert fancier formats for several types of printers using macro commands supplied in SAMPLE.PRO. These files contain a variety of commands that let you enter special format commands—such as near-letter-quality, boldface, and italics—into a Notepads file that will yield the formatting features when printed.

To make these commands work, you have to activate the printer control macro file for your printer by using the Macros module and its associated commands.

For example, to make the HPLJF.PRO file active:

> **Press:** [Alt]-[D]-[M]
>
> **Type:** HPLJF
>
> **Press:** [Enter]

When the contents of the file appear on screen:

> **Press:** [F8]

Press: [⇓]

This should highlight *Active* when you are in PC Tools Desktop

Press: [Enter] twice

Now exit the Macros module (macros are fully explained in Chapter 15):

Press: [Esc]

You can now use some of the macros in HPLJF.PRO. For instance, to create bold-face text when you want to print a file, place your cursor where you want the bold-face to begin. Let's print the title of README.TXT in boldface. Place your cursor in front of the text *PC Tools Version 7* at the top of the file, above the line *New Information.*

Press: [Ctrl]-[B]

This turns on boldface printing. Now, move your cursor to the end of the line:

Press: [End]

Insert the command that turns on boldface printing:

Press: [Ctrl]-[H]

On screen, the commands and text look like Figure 6.13.

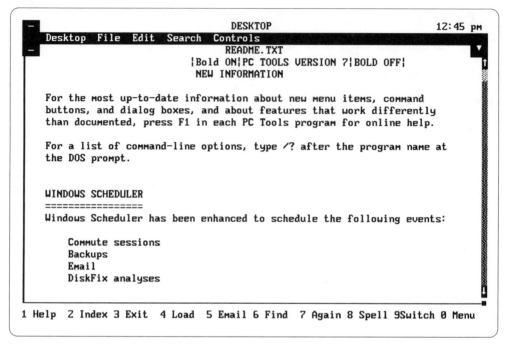

Figure 6.13. Bold on and off commands inserted into text

PRINTING A FILE

To print a file, you must be viewing it.

Press: [Alt]-[F]-[P]

This opens the Print box, which looks like Figure 6.14.

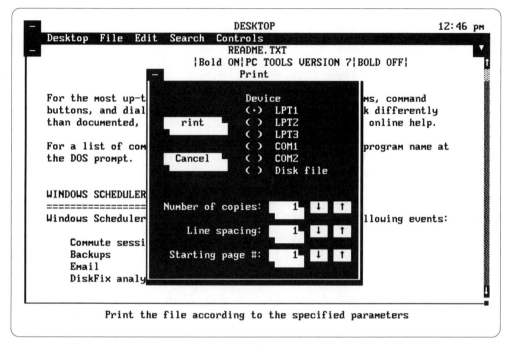

Figure 6.14. The Print box

Before you begin printing something, make sure your *Number of Copies* and *Device* settings are correct. With the Print window open, press [Tab] to highlight the six choices you have under *Device*.

When you've highlighted the current device setting, press [⇓] or [⇑] to highlight the device you want to use. LPT ports are parallel ports, and COM ports are serial ports. The sixth setting, *Disk File,* lets you print a text file to disk.

For example, print the file README.TXT using a header that identifies the file.

First, load the README.TXT file into the Notepads Editor.

> **Press:** [Alt]-[F]-[L]
>
> **Type:** README
>
> **Press:** [Enter]

When the text appears, insert the header text:

Press: [Alt]-[C]-[H]

Type: Contents of PC Tools README.TXT

Press: [Enter] three times

Now open the Page Layout box:

Press: [Alt]-[C]-[P]

Make the left margin begin in column 5, the right margin in column 65, and leave the top and bottom margins at 6.

Now begin the printing. Make sure your printer is turned on, has enough paper, and is connected to your computer. When you're all set:

Press: [Alt]-[F]-[P]

Press: [Enter]

In a few moments, your printer should start to give you the printed output.

Printing to a Disk File

One of the options you're given as a device is Disk File. This means you print the file to disk. This includes all the printing characteristics of the Page Layout and Header/Footer settings. When you print a file to disk, the disk file is given the same name as the file, but the extension is changed to .PRT.

There are three reasons why you might want to print a file to disk:

1. You can view the results of printing in the Notepads Editor to see if they're what you want.

2. You can send the printed file by electronic mail, changing it to a format that might be more acceptable to your e-mail service.

3. You can print the file using the DOS redirection command: TYPE FILE-NAME >PRN.

To print the README.TXT to a disk file, begin by viewing the file:

Press: [Alt]-[F]-P]

Press [Tab] to select Disk File

Press: [Enter] twice

When the printing is finished, you can view the results:

Press: [Alt]-[D]-[N]

Type: README.PRT

Press: [Enter]

Your screen will look like Figure 6.15.

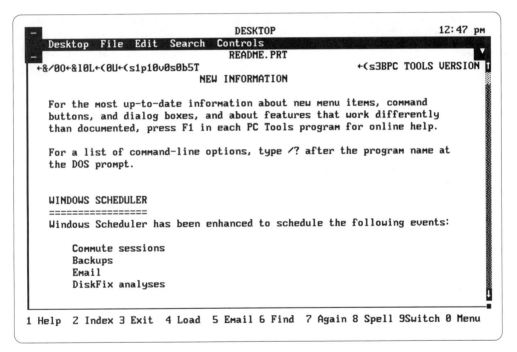

Figure 6.15. Viewing README.PRT

Notice how the header and page layout margin settings appear. These can be crucial when you send text messages via MCI Mail, which occasionally gives a line-length-format error when lines exceed 65 characters. Setting the right margin to column 65 and printing the file before you send it makes sure you won't get that error.

If you send disk files via e-mail, you should watch out for one more item. When you print a text file to disk, the program inserts a lot of useless hard-carriage-return symbols at the end of the file. As an example, Figure 6.16 shows the end of a file I printed to disk and plan to send by MCI Mail.

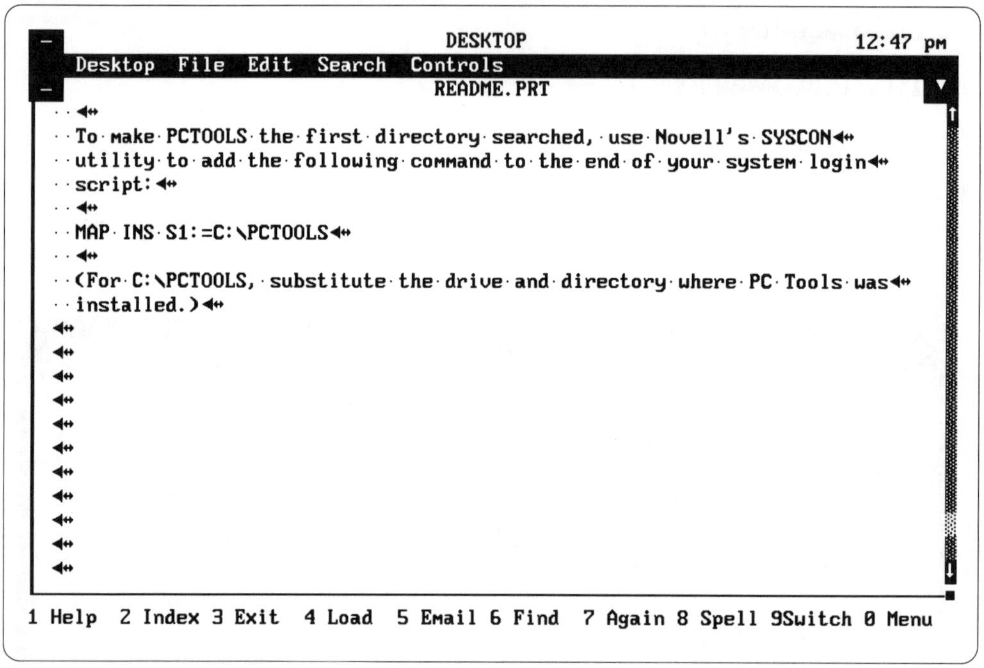

Figure 6.16. The end of a file printed to disk

Notice all those hard carriage returns after the slash mark. The slash mark tells MCI Mail it has come to the end of my text. It will keep asking for an answer until the hard-carriage-return symbols play out. This doesn't prevent you from finally telling MCI Mail to send the message, but it does waste your time.

If you plan to send a disk file over e-mail and, after printing the file, view it in the Notepads Editor, turn on control-character display, move to the end of the file, and delete all the hard-carriage-return symbols after the slash. Then save the file. Now you're ready to send it.

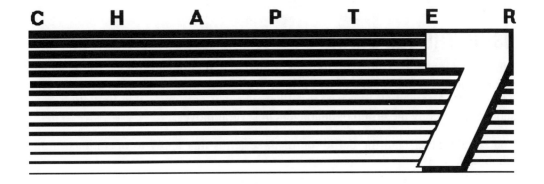

C H A P T E R

7

WORKING WITH THE CLIPBOARD

T he Clipboard is a specialized form of the Notepads Editor screen that lets you store, edit, and transfer character text from one application to another, either inside or outside the Desktop Manager.

USING THE CLIPBOARD

While working in the Clipboard, you're limited to two kilobytes of characters, which amounts to about half a page of text printed with single-line spacing, or about 60 text lines of the Notepads Editor screen. Whenever you encounter this limitation, you should cut or copy the group of characters in several moves.

You should understand the definition of three terms that apply to operations in the Clipboard.

Copy   Leaves the original text in place and duplicates it in a new location.

Cut   Removes text from one location and inserts it into another.

Paste   Places text from the Clipboard into another application or file.

You'll use the Clipboard to perform all three of these procedures.

You should view the Clipboard only as a temporary storage area. You can edit text there, but you cannot save text there except by printing it to a disk or to paper. Whenever you cut or copy text to the Clipboard, any text it previously held is replaced.

The Clipboard Screen

To open the Clipboard screen from the Desktop menu:

> **Press:** [B]

If you're working in another Desktop application:

> **Press:** [Alt]-[D]-[B]

The Clipboard screen appears immediately.

Your screen should now look like Figure 7.1.

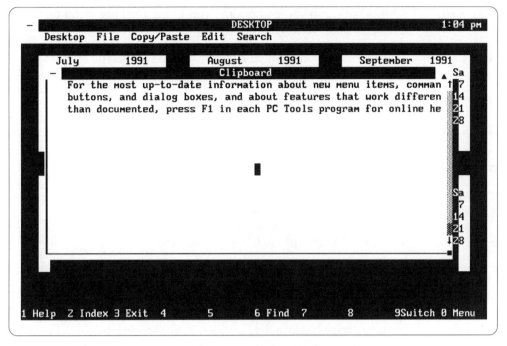

Figure 7.1. The Clipboard screen showing most recent copy

When the Clipboard screen appears, expand it to full-screen size:

Press: [Alt]-[W]-[Z]

In this case, you're looking at the text you copied from a Notepads Editor screen in the previous chapter. The Clipboard will display the text you've most recently cut or copied. If you have not yet cut or copied anything into it, nothing will be displayed.

The top of the screen shows that you're working in the Clipboard. The Line and Column markers are the same as in Notepads, as is the INS reminder. Notice how no filename appears in the upper-right corner—only the label CLIPBOARD.

The Clipboard is an abbreviated implementation of the Notepads Editor screen. Only six function keys have assignments in the Clipboard Editor screen:

[F1] Help Displays general information about the Clipboard and lets you move to the index.

[F2] Index Displays index items.

[F3] Exit   Closes the Clipboard and returns you to the Desktop menu or whatever you were working in previously. Same as pressing [Esc].

[F6] Find   Opens the Find box, which lets you search for specific text the same way you search in Notepads.

[F9] Switch   Switches you between active windows.

[F10] Menu   Activates the top menu bar.

Pull-down Menus

The menu map of the Clipboard is an abbreviated version of the Notepads screen. There are four menus designed for the Clipboard:

File   Prints the contents of the Clipboard screen.

Copy/Paste   Copies or pastes the Clipboard screen contents to another application, and sets the rate of playback.

Edit   Erases text and marks or removes the mark from a text block to paste or copy. Also deletes all the text showing in the Clipboard screen, inserts text from another file (up to the two-kilobyte limit), and goes to a specific line number in the Clipboard.

Search   Finds text or searches for and replaces text the same way as in the Notepads Editor screen. Use [F6] and [F7] respectively for quicker response.

Most of these menus are similar to the menus in the Notepads Editor screen. However, the Clipboard has no Controls menu and the Clipboard Copy/Paste and Edit menus contain subsets of the Notepads Edit menu. Figure 7.2 is the complete Clipboard menu map.

File	Copy/Paste	Edit	Search

```
Print
```

```
Paste from Clipboard
Copy to Clipboard
-------------------------
Set Playback Delay
```

```
Erase Block
Mark Block
Unmark Block
----------------------
Delete All Text
Insert File
Goto
```

```
Find
Find Again
---------------
Replace
```

Figure 7.2. The Clipboard menu map

These controls all behave as described for the Notepads. You can enter characters in either insert or overtype mode.

Saving and Printing the Clipboard Contents

There are two ways to save the contents of the Clipboard screen:

1. Print them to paper or to a disk file.

2. Paste them into another file and save that file

To print the contents to paper or a disk file:

Press: [Alt]-[F]-[P]

This opens the Print box, which lets you select the output device and the number of copies to print. All Clipboard files, when printed to disk, are saved as CLIPBOAR.PRT. If you intend to copy more than one Clipboard file to disk, you should change the name of each file after it's been printed. If you don't, the newer file will overlay the older file. You'll be given a warning if this is about to happen.

Saving the contents of the Clipboard by pasting them into another file will be explained in the following sections.

COPYING AND PASTING

In Chapter 6, you used specific Clipboard commands in Notepads. You can also use commands on the Clipboard Copy/Paste pull-down menu with other Desktop modules, outside applications, and even your DOS screen.

You can copy and paste between other Desktop modules when the program is run in both resident and standard mode, but you can only use the Clipboard with outside applications (including your DOS screen) in resident mode. You must first pop open the Clipboard screen over the outside application.

Copy and Paste Hotkeys

Two commands on the Copy/Paste pull-down menu, Paste from Clipboard and Copy to Clipboard, can be activated by hotkeys. This lets you Copy and Paste any time you're working with your computer, not just when you're working in the Clipboard screen or even in the Desktop Manager. You can use the menu commands, but the hotkeys work more quickly.

The hotkey assignments are:

[Ctrl]-[Del]   Begins the copy procedure. You then have to highlight the block you want to copy and then press [Enter] to copy it to the clipboard.

[Ctrl]-[Ins]   Executes the paste.

You can view these two hotkey assignments and change the keys assigned to them:

    Press: [Alt]-[D]-[U]-[H]

This accesses the PCTOOLS Desktop Hotkey Selection box, shown in Figure 7.3

```
        PCTOOLS Desktop Hotkey Selection

    DESKTOP HOTKEY:      <CTRL><SPACE>
    CLIPBOARD PASTE:     <CTRL><INS>
    CLIPBOARD COPY:      <CTRL><DEL>
    SCREEN AUTODIAL:     <CTRL><0>
```

Figure 7.3. The PC TOOLS Desktop Hotkey Selection box

If you want to change any of these assignments, highlight its command and press the two new keys you want to assign it. However, the [Ctrl]-[Ins] and [Ctrl]-[Del] key combinations are practically universal for cut and paste routines in DOS utility programs.

The third command on the Copy/Paste menu, *Set Playback Delay*, is described at the end of this chapter.

Copying and Pasting Within the Desktop Manager

You can copy characters from any Desktop Module and paste them into the editing portion of any other module within the Desktop Manager. The term *editing portion* refers to the fact that some modules allow you only a small area in which to enter characters. For example, in the Telecommunications screen, you can insert text into individual phone-book entries; and in Calculators screens, you can insert characters only into the display registers. But you probably won't want to paste any characters into these modules anyway.

Here are the basic steps for copying:

1. Open the screen from which you want to copy

2. Press [Ctrl]-[Del]

3. Highlight the first character you want to copy

4. Press [Enter]

5. Press the arrow keys to extend the block to cover the last character you want to copy

6. Press [Enter]

That's all there is to it. The text is now in the Clipboard.

For example, to copy the entire Algebraic calculator and save this image as a file, first open the Algebraic calculator:

Press: [Alt]-[C]-[A]

Now toggle on the narrow display:

Press: [Alt]-[O]-[W]

Now initiate copying. You should see a block-shaped cursor in the middle of your screen, as shown in Figure 7.4.

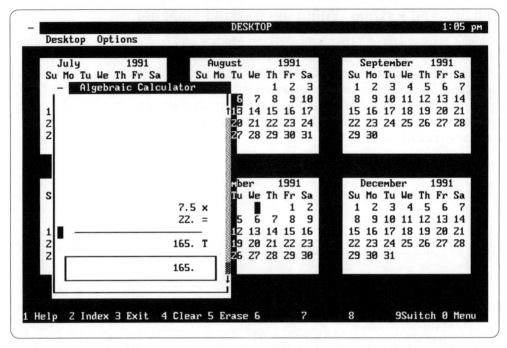

Figure 7.4. The copy cursor to the right of the Algebraic calculator

Move the cursor over the first character you want to copy, in this case the upper-left corner of the Algebraic clipboard. You can only use the arrow keys to move the cursor; the other cursor-control keys, such as [Home] and [PgUp], have no effect. Once your cursor is in position:

Press: [Enter]

Now, move the cursor over the last character you want to copy, again using the arrow keys. This would be the lower-right corner of the calculator. As your cursor moves, you'll notice that the highlighted area expands. This is the area that will be copied to the clipboard. As you expand the highlighting, notice that you have free control over what part of the screen you want to highlight. You can even highlight the border area. Unfortunately, you can only copy characters that are in the current screen—you can't scroll the screen up or down to copy characters that aren't showing. Figure 7.5 shows a substantial part of the Algebraic calculator highlighted.

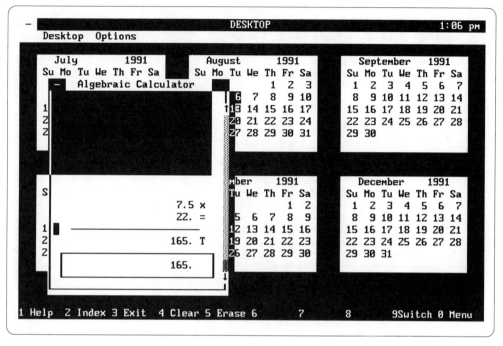

Figure 7.5. Highlighting extending over the Algebraic calculator

You can highlight a box of any shape. All you're doing is marking a section of the screen to copy. This lets you select whatever characters are showing, including data in a spreadsheet and text in a word processor. Once all the characters you want to copy have been highlighted:

Press: [Enter]

The highlighting will disappear. Check the Clipboard to see how successful you were:

Press: [Alt]-[D]-[B]

Figure 7.6 shows the result.

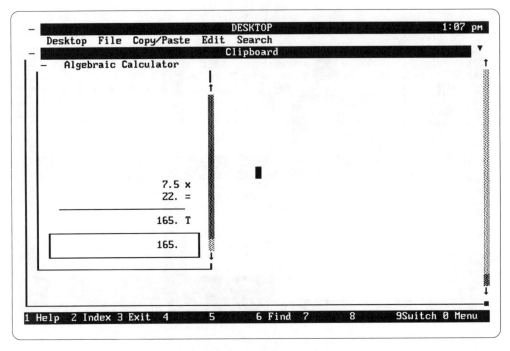

Figure 7.6. The Algebraic calculator copied into the Clipboard

Now save this as a separate file that will be needed later in this book:

Press: [Alt]-[F]-[P]

Select: Disk file

Press: [Enter] twice

Copying and Pasting Outside the Desktop Manager

When you use the Clipboard with an outside application—such as WordPerfect, dBASE, or Lotus 1-2-3—you can copy characters from the Application screen to the Clipboard, and vice versa. To copy characters from an outside application, Desktop must be loaded as a resident program. The steps are substantially the same as in copying within Desktop.

Work through an example of copying text from a WordPerfect word processing screen. First, move to the screen that contains the text you want to copy. Make sure all the text you want to copy appears on your screen, since you can't scroll up or down once you've activated *Clipboard Copy.*

Press: [Ctrl]-[Del]

You'll see the message that the Desktop overlays are being loaded. When they're loaded, no menu or module screen will appear. Instead, the block cursor will appear. Place the cursor on the first character you want to copy:

Press: [Enter]

Move the cursor to the last character and make sure the highlighted box includes all the text you want to copy. Do not press [Enter] again yet.

Once you're sure the block is complete:

Press: [Enter]

Highlighting will disappear, and you'll see a message that the system is being restored. This means that the text is being pasted into the Clipboard, and the Desktop program is being popped down. The application screen will remain, and you can continue to work in it.

Now, paste the example you've just cut into another part of the WordPerfect file. Then paste the same characters into a Notepads file. First, open the Desktop menu and look at the current contents of the Clipboard:

Press: [Ctrl]-[Spacebar]

Open the Clipboard:

Press: [B]

My Clipboard looks like Figure 7.8.

Figure 7.8. My Clipboard containing text copied from WordPerfect

Now, move this text to a Notepads file:

Press: [Alt]-[D]-[N]

Type: CLIP.TXT

Press: [Enter] three times

This creates a text file called CLIP.TXT and moves you into the file.

Press: [Ctrl]-[Ins]

This pastes the current contents of the Clipboard into the Notepads screen. After doing this, my screen looks like Figure 7.9.

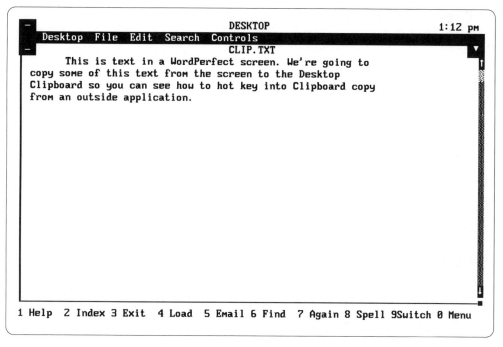

Figure 7.9. A Notepads file containing application text

Copying from the Clipboard to an Application

You can work in the reverse and copy Clipboard characters to an outside application. If you're working from the previous example, just exit the Notepads Editor screen:

Press: [Esc]

This returns you to the Clipboard screen shown in Figure 7.1. To copy this text to the outside and underlying application:

Press: [Alt]-[C]-[P]

This exits the Clipboard, restores the system, and returns you to the application screen, where the characters will begin to appear at the cursor location. When the characters have been pasted in, the application remains.

If you're working in the application when you want to paste the current Clipboard characters, and you already know what characters are in the Clipboard, position your cursor to where you want the characters to appear:

Press: [Ctrl]-[Ins]

Again, the characters will appear, starting at the cursor position.

Adjusting Playback Delay

You can adjust the amount of time-delay between the pasting of each character using a menu selection in the Clipboard. In most cases, you will not need to adjust this factor. Whether characters should be delayed depends upon what applications you're working with. Most word processors don't need a delay; however, it's wise to delay pasting into spreadsheets and databases a few clock ticks.

To increase the delay, begin in the Clipboard screen and:

Press: [Alt]-[C]-[S]

This opens the Set Playback Delay box, which looks like Figure 7.10.

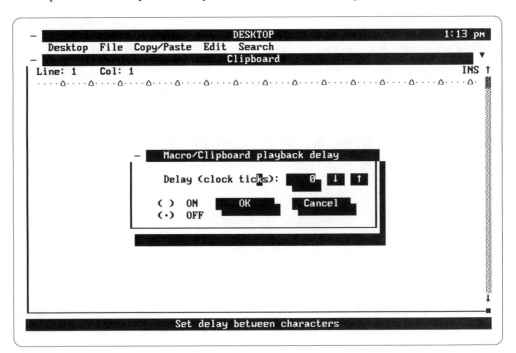

Figure 7.10. The Macro/Clipboard Playback Delay box

There are eighteen clock ticks per second. To set a delay of a third of a second:

Type: 6

Press: [Enter]

Notice that the *off* button is highlighted.

To highlight the *on* button:

Press: [⇑]

Press: [Enter]

With ON highlighted, select OK and then accept it:

Press: [Enter] twice

What you've done is insert a 1/3-second delay between the pasting of each character. You can adjust this figure if it's too slow or too fast.

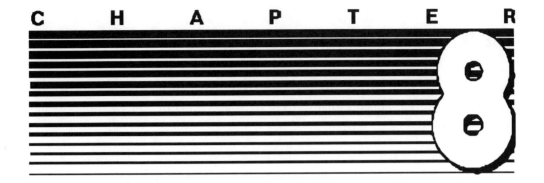

C H A P T E R

8

WORKING WITH OUTLINES

O utlines are lists of individual text lines organized according to a specific structure. They are ideal for organizing the contents of a text file. For example, a *To-Do* list is a simple outline that gets more complicated when you organize hierarchically the things you have to do.

Pseudocode for software programs is a more complex example of an outline. Although most computer users don't write computer programs, they do write text. The text can have various effects on a reader, depending upon the way its contents are organized.

THE OUTLINES EDITOR

The Outlines Editor is a specialized form of text editor. It lets you arrange lines of text in an organized sequence that reflects your perception of how each line should relate to the others.

> It has been my experience that not many people use outliners because they feel little urgency to be so organized. For them, the Appointment Scheduler will be sufficient. You can create a to-do list in the Appointment Scheduler and not worry about such arcane terms as headlines, collapsing and expanding, and promoting and demoting.
>
> Still, there is a solid core of users whose activities are well-served by outlining. Programmers, project planners, and other individuals need to keep track of a variety of activities, relating each one to the others. For them, an outliner is a godsend, and it's these users who will benefit the most from this chapter.

The Outlines Editor screen is an expanded version of the Notepads Editor screen, described in Chapter 6. All the commands in the Notepads screen are available in the Outline screen except for two on the Controls pull-down menu: Wordwrap and Auto Indent. In the Outlines Editor, these two features are set in specific ways and can't be changed: Wordwrap is always off, and Auto indent is always on. You'll see what effects these have when you begin working with an outline.

There's one additional pull-down menu in the Outlines screen that you can't find in Notepads; it's called Headlines. You can find this menu after the Controls menu. To see it:

Press: [Alt]-[H]

It should look like Figure 8.1.

Headlines

```
┌──────────────────────────┐
│ Expand Current           │
│ Expand All               │
│ -------------------------│
│ Show Level               │
│ -------------------------│
│ Collapse Current         │
│ Main Headline Only       │
│ -------------------------│
│ Promote                  │
│ Demote                   │
└──────────────────────────┘
```

Figure 8.1. The Headlines menu

What Are Headlines?

Headlines are the distinctive feature that make outlines different from text files created in the Notepads Editor. Once you understand the concept of headlines, you'll have no trouble creating outlines.

A headline is a single line of text that extends from the left margin to the end of the line, which is always marked by a hard carriage return. Since Wordwrap doesn't work in the Outlines Editor screen, a line of text containing more than 80 characters will continue beyond the right edge of your screen.

Understanding headlines may seem difficult at first because a line of text can serve as both a headline and a heading. Although it's easy to confuse these two terms, it's not so easy to clarify them without looking at an outline. The distinction should become clearer as you read the section "Working With Headlines" in this chapter.

OPENING THE OUTLINES MODULE

To open the Outlines module from the Desktop menu:

> **Press:** [O]

To open it from any other Desktop module:

> **Press:** [Alt]-[D]-[O]

Both of these move you to the Outlines dialog box, which looks like Figure 8.2.

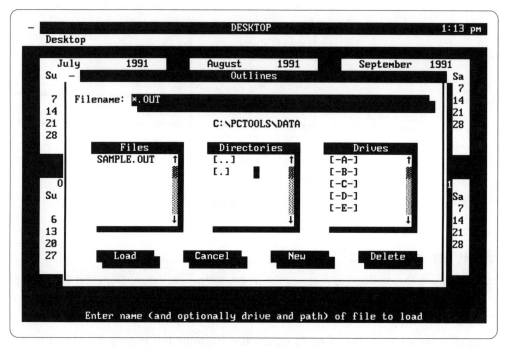

Figure 8.2. The Outlines dialog box

This box behaves identically to the Notepads dialog box, with one exception. In the default configuration, the Outlines dialog box displays only filenames that end in .OUT, which stands for outline. You can view a complete list of files in the current directory this way:

Type: *.*

Press: [Enter]

You can filter for any other arrangement of filenamess using the DOS wild-card characters ? and *.

If no other outline files have been created, only one file should show in the default display of the Outlines box: SAMPLE.OUT. This is a sample outline file provided as part of the PC Tools program

To open SAMPLE.OUT:

Press: [Enter] twice

If for any reason the file SAMPLE.OUT is not available to you, its contents are provided in the section "Creating an Outline" at the end of this chapter. This file makes understanding outlines easier, since it lets you see one. Many readers will have access to SAMPLE.OUT.

This highlights and then selects the top file. When your Outlines screen first appears, it might be in the small size. If it is, you should expand it to full-screen size:

Press: [Alt]-[Spacebar]

Press: [X]

Your screen should look like Figure 8.3.

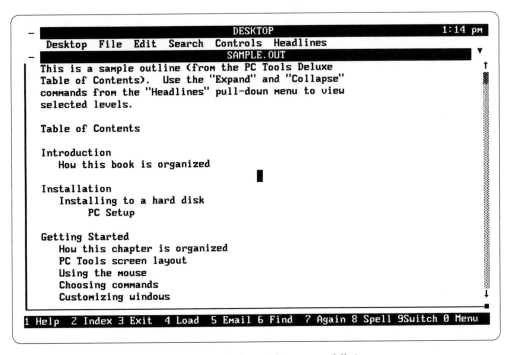

Figure 8.3. The Outlines Editor screen full size

The features on the Outlines Editor screen, excluding the text and filename, are identical to those on the Notepads screen, except for one item. The additional pull-down menu name *Headlines* appears on the right side of the top menu bar.

The line and column markers, tab line, the insert label, scroll bars, and time in the upper-right corner are the same features that appear in the Notepads Editor screen.

There are ten function-key assignments:

[F1] Help   Opens the general Help screen.

[F2] Index   Opens the Help index.

[F3] Exit   Closes the Outline Editor screen and returns you either to the Desktop menu or to your previous work.

[F4] Load   Opens the Outlines dialog box so you can load another outline.

[F5] E-mail   Lets you send outlines as e-mail.

[F6] Find   Opens the Find box, which lets you specify text to find.

[F7] Again   Lets you repeat a search for text in an outline.

[F8] Spell   Lets you spell-check an outline.

[F9] Switch   Switches between active PC Tools windows.

[F10] Menu   Activates the top menu bar. Same as pressing [Alt] and holding it down.

The complete menu map for the Outlines Editor screen is shown in Figure 8.4.

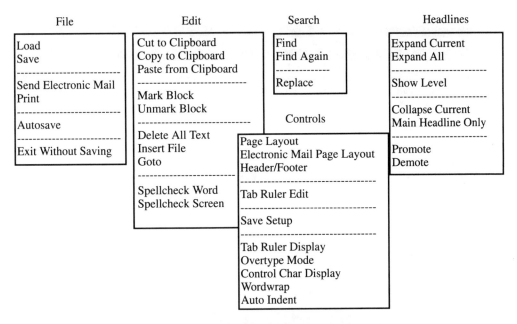

File	Edit	Search	Headlines
Load	Cut to Clipboard	Find	Expand Current
Save	Copy to Clipboard	Find Again	Expand All
------------------	Paste from Clipboard	--------------	------------------
Send Electronic Mail	------------------------	Replace	Show Level
Print	Mark Block		------------------
------------------	Unmark Block		Collapse Current
Autosave	------------------------	**Controls**	Main Headline Only
------------------	Delete All Text	Page Layout	------------------
Exit Without Saving	Insert File	Electronic Mail Page Layout	Promote
	Goto	Header/Footer	Demote
	------------------------	------------------------------	
	Spellcheck Word	Tab Ruler Edit	
	Spellcheck Screen	------------------------------	
		Save Setup	

		Tab Ruler Display	
		Overtype Mode	
		Control Char Display	
		Wordwrap	
		Auto Indent	

Figure 8.4. Menu map for the Outlines Editor screen

Take a closer look at the text as shown in Figure 8.3. The first four lines describe the file and how you expand and collapse headlines. Each text line, beginning with the line *Table of Contents* and ending with the line *Choosing Commands,* is a headline. To see more of the file:

Press: [PgDn]

WORKING WITH HEADLINES

The best way to start working with headlines is to follow the instructions at the top of the SAMPLE.OUT file. In its default appearance, all headlines are expanded in the file, so you should collapse them first. The meanings of these terms will become clearer as you work through the following example.

Press: [Alt]-[H]-[M]

Notice how the outline shrinks to show just four headlines, as shown in Figure 8.5.

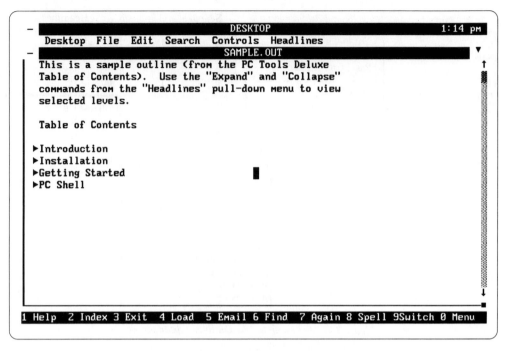

Figure 8.5. All headlines below main collapsed

Selecting *Main Headline Only* collapses all headlines but the main ones.

Commands on the Headlines menu are defined as follows:

Expand Current	Expands and displays the current level of headlines. The current level is the one below your current cursor position.
Expand All	Expands and displays all levels of headlines.
Show Level	Displays first-level headlines only.
Collapse Current	Collapses and hides all headlines at the current level.
Main Headline Only	Collapses the outline so that only the main headlines show. Main headlines are the text lines that begin at the left margin.
Promote	Moves the current headline up one level. The level of a headline is determined by its level of indentation.
Demote	Moves the current headline down one level.

The question of current level is an important one, so expand the outline back to its original appearance.

   Press: [Alt]-[H]-[A]

This expands all levels of the current outline, regardless of what was collapsed before. Notice that there are two levels of indentation on your screen when you're looking at the top of the SAMPLE.OUT file, (Figure 8.3). This means there are three levels of headlines. The main level always begins at the left margin. Pressing [Tab] once moves your cursor to the second level. Pressing [Tab] a second time moves your cursor to the third level.

You can change the column position of each tab stop using the *Tab Ruler Edit* command on the Controls pull-down menu. Changing the position of tab stops doesn't change the levels of headlines.

Collapsing and Expanding Headlines

One advantage of working with outlines is that you can hide and then display selected headlines. *Collapse* means "hide displayed headlines," and *expand* means "display hidden headlines."

> Don't worry about making changes to the SAMPLE.OUT file. As long as you don't save the changes, they won't become permanent. If for any reason you can't back out of a change you're making, just exit from the Outlines Editor, return to the main menu, and reload SAMPLE.OUT. The contents and structure of the original disk file will appear.

Collapsing or redisplaying headlines lets you view an abbreviated or expanded version of an outline to obtain different visual readings of the outline's organization. This might not be appropriate when working with a small outline; but when an outline grows to exceed the viewing capacity of your computer screen, you'll find that collapsing part of the outline to see only the major features can be very helpful.

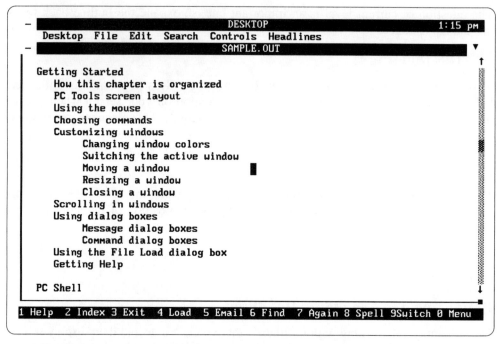

Figure 8.6. Viewing a section of SAMPLE.OUT

The *current headline* is at the level below your current cursor position. In Figure 8.6, for example, the current headline in the SAMPLE.OUT file is *Getting Started.* You may choose a new current headline by moving the cursor down the file contents and repositioning the text. To choose *Customizing Windows,* for instance, place your cursor anywhere on that line. You can press [PgDn] until you find the text, or press [F6], type "customizing window," and let the program search for the text. This makes the text lines indented beneath your cursor the current level, and collapses, or hides them.

Press: [Alt]-[H]-[C]

The effects are shown in Figure 8.7.

Figure 8.7. Collapsing current headlines

Notice that as the five subordinate lines disappear, the next headline, on the same level as the current headline, moves up to fill the gap. And a right-facing arrow appears next to the headline marked by the current cursor. This symbol indicates that there are hidden headlines beneath the line.

To redisplay, or expand, the hidden (or collapsed) headlines:

Press: [Alt]-[H]-[E]

Collapsing headlines can be somewhat tricky until you learn how to select the appropriate level. Now move your cursor around the SAMPLE.OUT file and practice collapsing other current levels. You'll soon get a feel for how this works. You can always expand hidden levels this way:

Set the cursor at a headline marked with a right-facing arrow, then:

Press: [Alt]-[H]-[A]

Showing Headlines

Show Headlines displays all headlines at the cursor level and hides those below it This lets you pick the bottom level of an outline, which can be useful when you're working with a particularly intricate outline, and you want to see how the various sublevels line up with one another.

Promoting and Demoting Headlines

Promoting and demoting headlines means changing the apparent headline level. You can only promote and demote headlines at and below the current level. For instance, in Figure 8.6, place your cursor on the line *Changing Window Colors*. To promote this headline one level, as shown in Figure 8.8:

Press: [Alt]-[H]-[P]

Figure 8.8. A headline promoted

To demote the same headline, leave your cursor where it is:

Press: [Alt]-[H]-[D]

Notice the changes in Figure 8.9; they're quite dramatic.

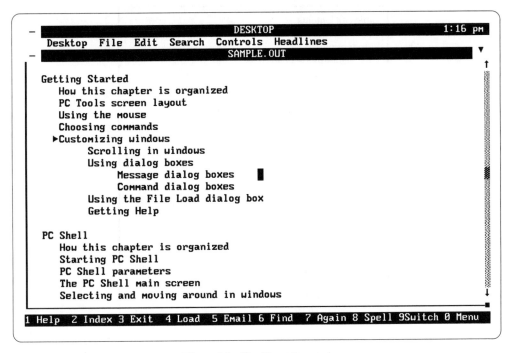

```
 ─                            DESKTOP                        1:16 PM
     Desktop  File  Edit  Search  Controls  Headlines              ▼
 ─                           SAMPLE.OUT
                                                                   ↑
     Getting Started
        How this chapter is organized
        PC Tools screen layout
        Using the mouse
        Choosing commands
       ►Customizing windows
             Scrolling in windows
             Using dialog boxes
                  Message dialog boxes        ▌
                  Command dialog boxes
             Using the File Load dialog box
             Getting Help

     PC Shell
        How this chapter is organized
        Starting PC Shell
        PC Shell parameters
        The PC Shell main screen
        Selecting and moving around in windows                     ↓

  1 Help   2 Index 3 Exit   4 Load  5 Email 6 Find   7 Again 8 Spell 9Switch 0 Menu
```

Figure 8.9. Headlines demoted

Notice also that you demoted more than the one headline you previously promoted. This shows the different effects of promoting and demoting. When you promote a headline, only the current headline is affected. When you demote a headline, you also demote all the levels beneath it.

To promote the five lower-level headlines that were inadvertently demoted, place your cursor on each one in turn and:

Press: [Alt]-[H]-[P]

CREATING AN OUTLINE

Once you've become familiar with the concept of headlines, you should experiment with the various commands to reinforce your understanding. In this section you will recreate the example provided in the SAMPLE.OUT file. Thus, if you don't already have a copy of the file, this recreation will help you learn to use the Outlines module.

Headlines for the SAMPLE.OUT file are displayed in Figure 8.10.

```
Table of Contents

Introduction
        Installing to a hard disk
        PC Setup

Getting Started
        How this chapter is organized
        PC Tools screen layout
        Using the mouse
        Choosing commands
        Customizing windows
                Changing window colors
                Switching the active window
                Moving a window
                Resizing a window
                Closing a window
        Scrolling in windows
        Using dialog boxes
                Message dialog boxes
                Command dialog boxes
        Using the File Load dialog box
        Getting Help

PC Shell
        How this chapter is organized
        Starting PC Shell
        PC Shell parameters
        The PC Shell main menu screen
        Selecting and moving around n windows
                Two list display
                One list display
        Help
```

Figure 8.10. The text for SAMPLE.OUT

The text for SAMPLE.OUT contains thirty-two individual headlines arranged in three levels under eight headings. The four additional lines of text that appear at the top of the file are not part of the outline.

To create this outline, begin at the Desktop main menu:

Press: [O]

Type: SAMPLE

Press: [Enter] twice

Expand the screen to full size, if it's not already that way:

Press: [Alt]-[Spacebar]

Press: [X]

Then:

Type: Table of Contents

Press: [Enter]

Type: Introduction

Press: [Enter]

Press: [Tab]

Type: Installing to a hard disk

Press: [Enter]

Press:[Tab]

Type: PC Setup

Press: [Enter] twice

This moves the cursor down two lines and places it flush against the left margin.

Type: Getting Started

Press: [Enter]

Press: [Tab]

Type: How this chapter is organized

Press: [Enter]

Press: [Tab]

Type: PC Setup

Press: [Enter] twice

This moves the cursor down two lines and sets it flush against the left margin. You can now continue with the rest of the headlines (or text lines) shown in Figure 8.10. To indent the line "Changing window colors" to the third level, which is the deepest you need to go in this outline, simply press [Tab] twice before entering it.

When you're finished entering all the text, and the structure is identical to Figure 8.10, save the file:

    Press: [Alt]-[F]-[S]

    Press: [Enter] three times

After creating this outline, experiment on your own by collapsing, expanding, promoting, and demoting headlines.

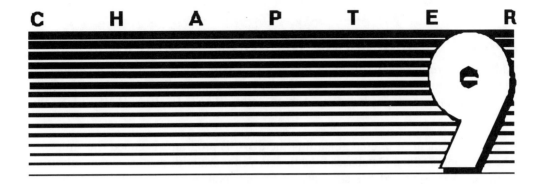

C H A P T E R

9

THE DATABASES MODULE

A database is nothing more than a collection of information that you want to keep together. Encyclopedias, cookbooks, and telephone directories are examples of databases you've used before.

Your own personal address book also is an example of a database. It includes special information that's of particular interest to you. Perhaps you keep track not only of the home and work telephone numbers of your friends and family, but also of their birthdays. This is a database of personally important information.

The microcomputer has finally made computer power available to you for creating a database to maintain personal information. PC Tools utilities provide quick and easy ways for creating, viewing, and editing this information.

dBASE PROGRAMS AND THE DATABASES MODULE

Although there are many different types of database programs for microcomputers, the dBASE implementation has become the most popular. This includes the family of dBASE programs produced by Ashton-Tate: dBASE II, dBASE III PLUS, and dBASE IV.

The main element of interest regarding the dBASE programs is called file structure. The PC Tools Deluxe Databases module lets you work with databases that subscribe to the dBASE standard file structure or format. Not only is the dBASE family of products immensely popular, but also, other database programs subscribe to it. These include FoxBase, Works, Clipper, and dBXL. You can also import and export dBASE data directly while working in Paradox.

While this covers a lot of programs, you should realize that the Databases module in PC Tools doesn't offer you the full functionality of the dBASE programs. There are several important limitations:

- The Databases module is a flat-file database program; it is not relational.

- All activities are run from menu commands. This isn't a limitation if you're a new or infrequent user, but it does limit how far you can go with the program.

- You're limited to 10,000 records in a single database, 128 fields in a record, and 4,000 characters in each field. This is a lot of information capacity for most individual users, but it can fall short for some businesses.

- You can't use memo fields; nor can you use catalogs, filters, reports, or any of the other more technical features available in dBASE programs.

- You can't run dBASE programs, but you can use the Notepads Editor to write dBASE source code. Source code must be compiled in a separate program and will run only in full-fledged dBASE-type programs.

- You can't create your own indexes. The PC Tools program creates a record file for each database that determines how record fields will appear on your screen.

- Once you've created a database structure, your ability to modify it is limited. You can add and delete records, edit field entries, and change field names. But you can't add or delete fields. You'll have to do this sort of work in a dBASE-type program.

This might sound like you're not getting very much in the Databases module, but that's not the case. You can probably accomplish 85% of your routine data work using the PC Tools Databases module. It has several distinct advantages over any dBASE program. The PC Tools program lets you:

- Pop up the Databases module over whatever else you're working with, work with the data, and then pop the module back down to continue your previous task. This alone offers a considerable advantage.
- Create database files more easily and quickly.
- Pop the program up and down more quickly, even when you are running in a standard mode.
- Design your screen display of information more easily.
- Print notes and letters, including information merged from a database, more conveniently.

While these aren't significant advantages for a professional database programmer, they're advantageous enough to make even the many stalwart dBASE programmers prefer to use the PC Tools Databases module for some of their routine chores.

There are ten ways that the Databases module lets you work with data files that subscribe to the dBASE standard. You can:

- Create new database files.
- View and edit records in existing database files (except for memo fields) in the browse and edit modes.
- Delete records and pack database files.
- Select and hide records for special handling.
- Print database record information according to customized formats.
- Change existing database field names.
- Transfer selected records from one database to another.
- Sort data files on a variety of fields.
- Search selected records for text.
- Autodial phone numbers in database records using the Telecommunications module. The dBASE programs cannot do this unless you use a separate communications program that pops up over the dBASE screen.

The rest of this chapter will help you to learn about databases by working with real files.

OPENING THE DATABASES MODULE

You can open the Databases screen the same two ways you can open the PC Tool's other module screens—by viewing an existing file or by creating a new one first and then viewing it. First, you will view an existing file.

With the Desktop main menu showing:

> **Press:** [D]

This opens the Databases dialog box, as shown in Figure 9.1.

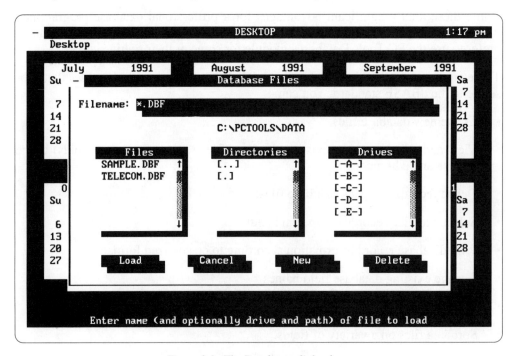

Figure 9.1. The Databases dialog box

If you're still logged onto the default PC Tools directory, three database file names should be displayed in the Databases dialog box: DSKERR.DBF is a database of disk error messages the PC Tools program uses to tell you when you've done something wrong. SAMPLE.DBF is a sample database you can use for practice. TELE-COM.DBF is a database you can use for telecommunications.

DBF, which stands for database file, is the default dBASE database filename extension. The Databases module looks for and displays all files ending with this extension in the selected directory. As with all DOS filenames, you can add any extension to any filename; however, the Databases module will only load files that subscribe to the dBASE file format.

To see the contents of SAMPLE.DBF:

Press: [Enter] twice

This moves the cursor to the filename at the top of the list and selects the file for viewing.

You can also open the file this way:

Type: SAMPLE

Press: [Enter]

Remember, you don't need to type the default file extension appropriate for the module you're using (in this case .DBF) as long as it hasn't been changed.

The Browse Screen

The Browse screen lets you browse through a group of records in a database file and edit the information. Field information is lined up in vertical columns. When SAMPLE.DBF file is loaded, expand it to full-screen size:

Press: [Alt]-[Spacebar]

Press: [X]

The three records in SAMPLE.DBF should appear in browse form, as shown in Figure 9.2.

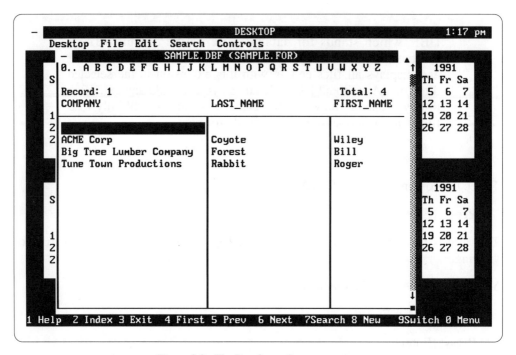

Figure 9.2. The Databases Browse screen

If your screen doesn't look like Figure 9.2:

> **Press**: [Alt]-[F]-[B]

In this screen, a single record occupies one horizontal line. A field occupies a single column. Several fields can usually be displayed on a screen, but this may vary, depending on field sizes. In larger databases you can display other fields by moving right or left, but for SAMPLE.DBF this is not necessary.

In Figure 9.2, there are three records displayed in three fields on the screen: *Company, Last_Name,* and *First_Name.* The first field contains the names of companies, the second and third fields contain the name of someone in each company.

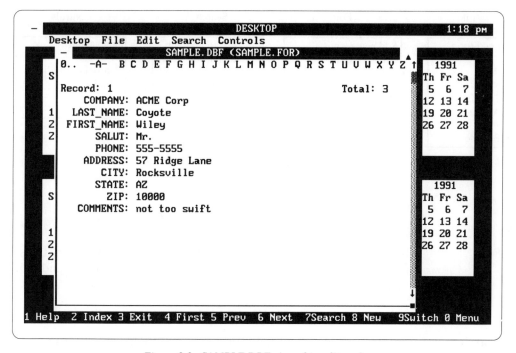

Figure 9.3. *SAMPLE.DBF viewed in edit mode*

The top line of the Browse screen shows the five pull-down menus. The menu map specific to the Databases module is shown in Figure 9.4.

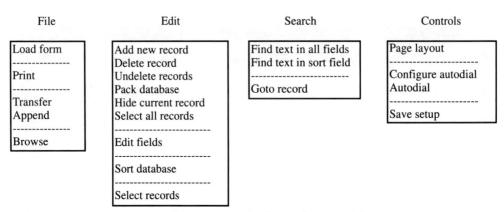

Figure 9.4. Menu map for the Databases module

File   Lets you load different form files, print database information, transfer and append new records, and switch between browse and edit modes.

Edit   Lets you work with records and fields, as well as sort the database.

Search   Searches for text in all fields or just the sort field, and can also go to a specific record number.

Controls   Lets you set default page layout dimensions for printing, configure and use the Autodial feature, and save the current configuration.

The current time is also displayed on the right side of the menu bar. The next line down shows that this is a Databases file, and the third line shows the path and the filename, the record number, and the total number of records in the database file. A vertical scroll bar is on the right side of the screen. These features are identical in both the browse and edit screens.

> Although it's possible to change characters in a highlighted field in the Browse screen, don't change this database. If you do make a change inadvertently, either change the characters back to their original values or press [Esc]. Either of these actions restores the characters that were originally read into the screen.

The ten function keys displayed on the bottom line of the screen have the following assignments attached:

[F1] Help   Opens the general Help screen.

[F2] Index   Opens the Help index.

[F3] Exit   Quits the Databases module and returns to the Desktop menu or to the previous screen you were viewing.

[F4] First   Toggles the cursor between the first and last records in the current database.

[F5] Prev   Moves the cursor to the next lowest record number until the first record is reached.

[F6] Switch   Moves the cursor to the next highest record number, until the last record in the database is reached.

[F7] Search   Opens the Search Sort Field dialog box, which lets you designate a specific record that contains the text you specify in a sorted field. You can find more information in Chapter 10 under the headings "Organizing Records" and "Searching for Records."

[F8] New   Inserts a blank record at the top of the database, where you can enter new record information in the appropriate fields. After information is entered, the insertion point is determined by how you've sorted the database.

[F9] Swap   Switches between active windows.

[F10] Menu   Activates the top menu bar. It has the same effect as pressing [Alt].

When working with a database file, you'll often perform the procedures assigned to the function keys. You might want to experiment with some of these keys now to test their effects. Because altering SAMPLE.DBF in any way will corrupt the file, do not make any changes to it. Make sure you don't add a new record. If you accidentally insert a blank record, leave it empty (do not enter data) and delete it this way:

Highlight: the blank record

Press: [Alt]-[E]-[D]

Moving Around the Databases

All the keys you can use to move around the Browse screen are shown in Table 9.1.

Moving Among Records	
Move right one field	[Tab]
Move left one field	[Shift]-[Tab]
Move down one field	[⇓]
Move down one record	[F6]
Scroll down one line	[Ctrl]-[PgDn]
Move down one screen	[PgDn]
Move to the last record	[Ctrl]-[End]
Move up one field	[⇑]
Move up one record	[F5]
Scroll up one field	[Ctrl]-[PgUp]
Move up one screen	[PgUp]
Move to first record	[Ctrl]-[Home]
Go to a specific record #	[Alt]-[S]-[G]-#
Toggle between 1st/last record	[F4]
Moving Within a Screen	
Move to beginning of window	[Home] twice
Move to end of window	[End] twice
Moving Within a Record	
Move right on field	[Enter]-[Tab]
Move left one field	[Shift]-[Tab]
Moving Within a Field	
Move right on character	[⇒]
Move right one word	[Ctrl]-[⇒]
Move to end of field	[End] once
Move left one character	[⇐]
Move left one word	[Ctrl]-[⇐]
Move to beginning of field	[Home] once

Table 9.1. Keys for moving around the Browse screen

Besides the menu commands that let you go to a particular record, you can move the cursor to the last record in the database by pressing [Ctrl]-[End]. You can move the cursor back to the first record by pressing [Ctrl]-[Home]. If you're at the beginning of the database, you can go to the end by pressing [F4]. Pressing [F4] a second time takes you back to the first record.

Since records are the heart of a database file, you can move from one record to the next in several other ways. For instance, you can move to a record whose sort field begins with a certain letter by pressing that letter key on your keyboard. Let's highlight the record for "Tune Town Productions":

Press: [T]

Notice that the highlight bar jumps to that record. In a database file with only a few records, moving around like this doesn't seem very impressive. But when your database file grows to several hundred records or more, you'll find this feature handy. Note, however, that you cannot use this feature when Modify Data is switched on. You'll see what this means in a moment.

Another way to select a record is to use a menu command. For example, to go to record number 50:

Press: [Alt]-[S]-[G]

Type: 50

Press: [Enter] twice

In this example, it's only coincidental that record numbers and ID_NUMBER numbers are identical; in other files, they may differ. The current record number only shows at the top of the Browse screen after the path and filename; for example: RECORD 3 OF 3.

Using the Browse screen, you can also add, edit, and delete records, select and hide records, and re-sort the entire database. Since we cannot make any changes to SAMPLE.DBF, let's begin to tackle real work by creating a database file of our own.

First, go to the top record:

Press: [F4]

Next, switch to the Edit screen:

Press: [Alt]-[F]-[B]

The Edit Screen

The Edit screen, as shown in Figure 9.3, displays information for a single record, or at least all the information that can fit into a single screen. It's called the Edit Mode screen because you can use it to edit and insert information into a record.

The top three lines are similar to the top three lines on the Browse screen. The menu bar and the function key assignments are identical. The fourth line contains a horizontal scroll bar, and the next line down displays the Line and Column indicators; the name of the current form appears on the right side, in this case SAMPLE.FOR. The fifth line down is the tab line.

These changes make the Databases Edit screen seem more like the Notepads Editor screen. In fact, it is a version of the Notepads Editor screen.

At the top of the screen you see the path and filename you're working with, C:\PCTOOLS\DATA\SAMPLE.DBF, along with the currently displayed record number and total number of records in the file. You can move the cursor around this screen much like the way you move it around the Notepads Editor screen. Additional movement controls are shown in Table 9.2.

Moving Within a Record	
Move right one character	[⇒]
Move right one word	[Ctrl]-[⇒]
Move to end of current line	[End]
Move to end of record	[End] twice
Move left one character	[⇐]
Move left one word	[Ctrl]-[⇐]
Move to start of current line	[Home]
Move to start of record	[Home] twice
Move to start of field date	[Tab]
Moving Among Records	
Move to next record number	[F6]
Move to previous record number	[F5]
Move to last/first record	[F4]

Table 9.2. Cursor movement keys for the Edit screen

You can't move sequentially between database records by pressing [PgDn] or [PgUp]. The only difference between moving around in the Notepads Editor and the Databases Edit screen is that pressing [Tab] in the Databases Edit screen doesn't move the cursor to the next tab stop. Tab stops have no effect in the Databases Edit screen, even though there's a tab line. You can't edit the tab line the way you can in the Notepads Editor screen, nor can you turn it off.

Pressing [Tab] in the Databases Edit screen only moves you to the next word or character after a space.

The best way to understand the fundamental structure of all databases is to create and work with one.

> Because overtype mode is on by default after you load a file into the Databases module, do not immediately begin typing in data. The program presumes that you want to edit data when you enter a database file. If you start pressing keys immediately, you might type over some data in the file. Instead, switch to the insert mode, by pressing [Ins].

CREATING A DATABASES FILE

A database file in its simplest terms consists of individual fields that are repeated for every record. In this section, you will learn about the elements of a database file by creating one yourself.

When you create a database file, you give it a name and then design its structure. You design the structure by deciding what types of fields you want to use and how large you want to make each field type.

Fields are the basic building blocks of a database. Each field is designed to hold individual pieces of information, and the type and size of field you use depend upon the information you want to enter. Once you've created a field structure, you should save it to disk. During the save operation. the PC Tools program will add the extension .DBF to the name you've given the file.

When PC Tools saves the .DBF file, it creates two other files automatically. These help the Databases module to present data correctly on screen. Each file is given the same name as the database file. One file is assigned the extension .REC, which serves as the record file. This is an index file that determines how fields are organized and records displayed on screen.

> In the Databases module, you must use the default extension .DBF. In other modules, you can change the extension.

The second file is assigned the extension .FOR and serves as the default form file. This controls the way data from a database file appears on your screen and is printed out. The default form file serves as the basic template for displaying and printing data until you design and load another form.

If you delete the .REC and .FOR files that match a .DBF file, PC Tools will create new default files. If you ever change the name of a database file, you'll have to change the names of the matching .FOR and .REC files as well.

Let's create a list of people who owe us money. We'll call the database ABLE.DBF and save it to disk. The PC Tools program will then create two additional files, ABLE.REC and ABLE.FOR.

To create your first file, start at the Desktop main menu:

> **Press:** [D]
>
> **Type:** ABLE
>
> **Press:** [Enter] twice

The extension .DBF is added automatically by the program.

Although you can use any filename you want, keep in mind that the Databases dialog box lists filenames in alphabetical order. Therefore, you'll find it handy to use a filename that appears at or near the top of the list. Then all you have to do is press [Enter] twice when the Databases dialog box appears, and you'll move directly into your most frequently used database file. (Not much can come before ABLE.DBF, except perhaps AABLE.DBF.)

Entering Fields

To build a database correctly, you must know beforehand what fields you want to use. For the current project, the minimum information you probably want is the name of the person who owes you money, and the home and work phone numbers. You might also include mailing addresses. This information requires five fields: name, home phone number, home address, work phone, and work address—one field to hold each piece of information.

Actually, you will need more than five fields. Two people may have the same first name, so you have to distinguish between them. This means you'll need two fields for names: first name and last name. Also, you may even need another field for a second work address, such as a post office box.

After typing the filename correctly:

> **Press:** [Enter]

This moves you directly into the Field Editor dialog box, which looks like Figure 9.5.

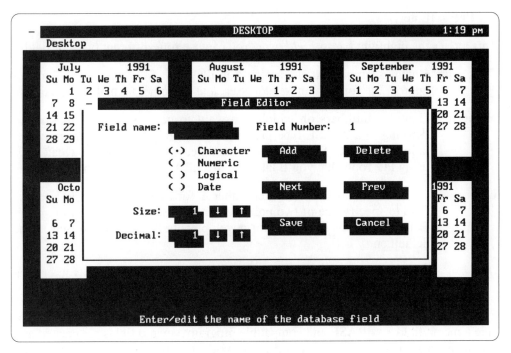

Figure 9.5. Field Editor dialog box

Use this box to define each type of field you want to create. You can move forward through the various selections by pressing [Tab]; move backward by pressing [Shift]-[Tab].

You'll find the cursor blinking in the field after *Field name*. This is where you type the name of the field you want to use. Create the first field to hold a first name. To title this field:

Type: FIRSTNAME

You could as well have typed *Namefirst* or *First_Name* instead. (You must use the underline character to separate field-name information, because dBASE field names cannot contain a dash character.). Use whatever suits you, as long as you stay within the dBASE field-name allowances. You can use all letters and numbers on your keyboard, but you're limited to eleven characters. You can't use dashes or spaces, and you can't begin a field name with a number.

When the field name is as you want it:

Press: [Enter]

This moves the highlight bar to *Field type*. You can use four different types of fields:

Character Contains simple text characters. You'll use this field type most often; it's appropriate for all names, addresses, and any other textual information.

Numeric Contains numbers on which you want to perform calculations when working in a dBASE-type program. Although you can't perform calculations in the PC Tools Databases module, you might want to create files using PC Tools that you'll later use in a dBASE or compatible program.

Logic Contains one logical character, either **T** for true or **F** for false. Use this field to specify one of two possible conditions, such as gender (T=male, F=female), or as an update for developments (T=sent, F=not sent). The default entry is F.

Date Contains date information in an eight-place field. This lets you enter a date using the month/day/year format, as in 12/25/90.

Experienced dBASE users will recognize that the Databases module does not provide a memo field. In dBASE and compatible programs, memo fields are created and stored in separate files, which require more work than the Databases module can perform. However, you can enter up to seventy characters in a Character field, which should be enough for most routine text entries.

Be careful when loading a database file created in a dBASE or compatible program into the PC Tools Databases module. Because of the PC Tools field size limitations, character fields containing more than seventy characters will be truncated—the excess will not be displayed in the Databases screen.

As long as you don't make any changes to the database file, such as saving it or modifying its structure, you can view truncated information in the Databases module screen and then exit the file. The original data will remain intact. If you change or save a database file that contains fields with more characters than can be handled by the PC Tools Databases module, you might lose the excess data.

Since you'll use the Character field most often, it is highlighted by default.

Press: [Enter]

This moves you to the Size field in the Field Editor box, where you declare the maximum number of characters you want to enter into the FIRSTNAME field. Since most first names won't go beyond fifteen characters:

Type: 15

Press: [Enter]

This moves you to the Decimal field. Use this field only when you've selected the numeric field type.

Press: [Enter]

This highlights the Add box. Accepting this box adds the field you've just created into the new database file.

Press: [Enter]

This moves you back to the top of a fresh Field Editor dialog box. The only thing different is that it shows you're creating *Field Number 2*. You can see this more clearly by moving back to the previous field.

Press: [Shift]-[Tab] three times

This should highlight the Prev box.

Press: [Enter]

This moves you back to your first field. Notice that it is *Field Number 1*. To move back to *Field Number 2*:

Press: [Tab] six times

This should highlight the Next box.

Press: [Enter]

This moves you on to the next field, which is Number 2.

The six box commands are:

Add   Adds the field displayed in the Field Editor box to the current database file.

Del   Deletes the field displayed in the Field Editor box from the current database file.

Next   Displays information for the next field in the current database file.

Prev   Displays information for the previous field in the current database file.

Save   Saves all field information for the current database file, completes the building process, and moves you into the Databases display screen showing the current file structure.

Cancel   Cancels building the current database and returns you to the Desktop main menu or to the module you were working in previously.

Finish building the first database structure. When the Field Editor box for Record Number 2 is showing:

Type: LASTNAME

Press: [Enter] twice

Type: 15

Press: [Enter] three times

Type: ADDRESS

Press: [Enter] twice

Type: 35

Addresses usually require more field space than names.

Press: [Enter] three times

Type: CITY

Press: [Enter] twice

Type: 20

Of course, there are city names with more than twenty characters, but you probably won't encounter them that often, and can always abbreviate.

Press: [Enter] three times

Type: STATE

Press: [Enter] twice

Type: 2

Press: [Enter] three times

Type: ZIP

Press: [Enter] twice

You might think that the zip-code field should be numeric because it contains numbers, but numeric fields are only for numbers that will be used for calculations, such as prices and quantities. Since zip codes are not used in calculations—even in full-fledged database programs—use the Character field.

Type: 10

Press: [Enter] three times

Type: PHONE

Press: [Enter] twice

Type: 15

This gives you enough room to enter a phone number and area code, as well as an out-of-building code if you wish. If you intend to call people with extensions in their offices, add a few more digits for the extension number and defining characters; for example, add three more characters for x73, or six more for ext.73.

Press: [Enter] three times

Now create another field type.

Type: MONEY

Press: [Enter] once

When *Field type: Character* is highlighted:

Press: [⇓]

This should highlight *Numeric.*

Press: [Enter] once

Type: 4

Press: [Enter]

Type: 2

This allocates four characters to the left of the decimal point and two characters after the decimal point in the *Money* field, which facilitates entering dollar amounts up to $9,999.99.

Press: [Enter] twice

Type: MAILED

Press: [Enter] once

Press: [⇓]

This should highlight *Logical*.

Press: [Enter] four times

When you create a logical field, you can enter only a True or False reply.

Type: DATE

Press: [Enter]

Press: [⇓]

This should highlight *Date*.

Press: [Enter]

Press: [Enter] four times

When you create a date field, there's also no need to specify the number of characters or decimal points because the program automatically creates the mm/dd/yy format.

Press: [Tab] eight times

This creates the seven fields and saves the structure you've just built. The new structure can be displayed on your screen. To see what this structure looks like, switch to the edit mode:

Press: [Alt]-[F]-[B]

Your screen should look like Figure 9.6.

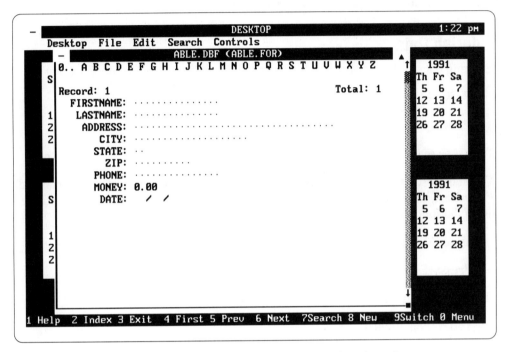

Figure 9.6. The structure for ABLE.DBF displayed in edit mode

This is the template you'll use for every record in ABLE.DBF. You can see the ten fields just created; their names are on the left, and the format of the field is on the right. For each character field, the format shows dots, which indicate the maximum number of characters you can insert in that field. Creating this template yourself gives you a clearer idea of its structure than using a sample database created by someone else.

The three noncharacter fields—*Money, Mailed,* and *Date*—show no dots; instead, they display a form of their own:

- For numeric fields, such as money, the number 0 shows in the first digit position.
- For logic fields, such as *Mailed,* the default character, F (for false), shows in the first position.
- For date fields, such as *Date,* the slashes in mm/dd/yy show, although no month, day, or year numerals appear.

Of course, your personal mail list database may not have the *Money, Mailed,* and *Date* fields. They were included here only as examples of noncharacter field types.

Now use the structure you created to enter data.

Entering Data

Entering data in the Databases Editor screen is easy. First, turn on Modify Data:

> **Press:** [Alt]-[F]

> **Press:** [M]

Then type in the information and press [Enter] to move to the next field. Try it now.

You should see the cursor blinking in the first character position after the first field, *Firstname.* Enter name and address information for your friends and acquaintances using the following example.

> **Type:** Milan

> **Press:** [Enter]

Notice how your cursor pops down to the next line.

> **Type:** Moncilovich

> **Press:** [Enter]

> **Type:** 2 Holly Lane

> **Press:** [Enter]

> **Type:** Beaverton

> **Press:** [Enter]

> **Type:** OR

> **Press:** [Enter]

> **Type:** 97000

> **Press:** [Enter]

> **Type:** 1-503-555-0000

> **Press:** [Enter]

Your screen should look like Figure 9.7.

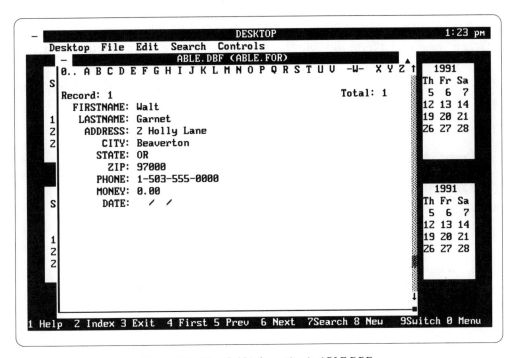

```
 -                            DESKTOP                           1:23 pm
   Desktop  File   Edit   Search   Controls
      -                  ABLE.DBF (ABLE.FOR)                    ▲     1991
      0.. A B C D E F G H I J K L M N O P Q R S T U U  -U-  X Y Z ↑    Th Fr Sa
   S                                                                   5  6  7
      Record: 1                                      Total: 1         12 13 14
        FIRSTNAME: Walt                                               19 20 21
   1     LASTNAME: Garnet                                             26 27 28
   2      ADDRESS: 2 Holly Lane
   2         CITY: Beaverton
            STATE: OR
              ZIP: 97000
            PHONE: 1-503-555-0000
            MONEY: 0.00                                                    1991
   S         DATE:   /  /                                             Th Fr Sa
                                                                       5  6  7
   1                                                                  12 13 14
   2                                                                  19 20 21
   2                                                                  26 27 28
                                                                      ↓
 1 Help   2 Index 3 Exit   4 First 5 Prev  6 Next  7Search 8 New    9Switch 0 Menu
```

Figure 9.7. First field information in ABLE.DBF

You've now inserted the preliminary information for a single record, which contains a name, home address, and phone number.

On your own, enter several more records to get the feel of logging in data. In the rest of this chapter and in the next chapter, you will work with the multirecord database file that you just created.

WORKING WITH FORM FILES

Form files display selected database information in your Edit screen (when the Browse screen is switched off). They also print information to paper or disk. As its name implies, a form file is one that contains the format in which the database information will appear.

The best way to understand form files is find out how they are created and then examine various examples. A default form file can be created under three situations:

- When you first create a database.
- When you first view a database created by another program.
- When you create a form file yourself, designing a format you prefer to use for your own customized needs.

The first two examples, respectively, are the default form files .FOR and .REC that are created automatically by the Databases module.

Take a look at the structure of the default file ABLE.FOR.

> **Press:** [Alt]-[D]-[N]
>
> **Type:** ABLE.FOR
>
> **Press:** [Enter]

> This series of commands works as long as the Notepads and Databases modules are both logged on to the same directory. Otherwise, you'll have to specify the Databases directory when you look for a form file.

When ABLE.FOR appears on your screen, it will look like Figure 9.8.

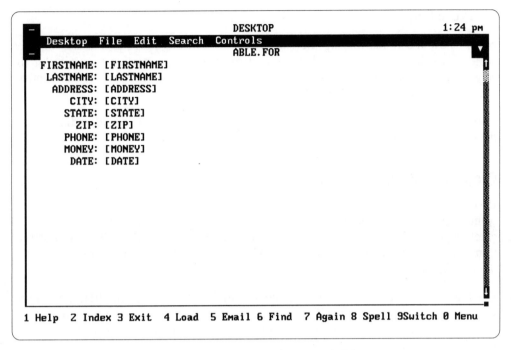

Figure 9.8. ABLE.FOR displayed in the Notepads Editor screen

Notice that each field has been placed on a line of its own, flush against the left margin, and that the name of every field is duplicated on the same line. The first instance is the title of the field. The second instance (in brackets) displays the contents of the matching field name in the selected record of the database you're using. The two names will always be identical.

Remember that this format is similar to what appears when you view the contents of ABLE.DBF in the Databases module screen. You can check this out by opening the matching database file and switching back and forth between it and the form file.

Press: [Alt]-[D]-[D]

Type: ABLE

Press: [Enter]

Make sure you're looking at a record in the Edit Mode screen, which means that information for just one record appears on your screen. Now switch back to the matching form file:

Press: [F9]

Notice how the fields line up the same way in both the Databases screen and the Notepads Editor screen. Switch back and forth until you realize how similar the screens look. This shows you the effect of a form file. The ABLE.FOR file controls the way information in ABLE.DBF appears in the edit view.

You can see this better when you create a different form file and redisplay the database information, which is what you'll do next.

Creating a New Form File for Viewing

If you want to view field information in a different format than the default, or if you want to print it in a custom format (either on paper or on a disk file), you need to create a new form file that corresponds to your appearance specifications. In this section, you'll use form files to view data. Using form files to print data is covered in the next chapter.

Use the Notepads Editor screen to create a form file. Just type in the field names you want to view or print and specify exactly where you want to view or print them. The form file you create will display only the names and phone numbers of the people you listed in ABLE.DBF.

Before creating a form file, you need to know the exact structure of the database file you're working with. You can either write down the structure of the database you're using or open two Notepads screens: one containing the default form file, which displays all the fields, and the other containing your customized form file.

    Press: [Esc]

Now return to ABLE.DBF in the Databases Editor screen. Pop open the Notepads Editor screen over the Databases Edit Mode screen.

To create the new form file:

    Press: [Alt]-[D]-[N]

    Type: NAMENUM.FOR

    Press: [Enter] twice

> Be sure to include the extension .FOR. If you don't, you'll create a text file with the default extension .TXT.
>
> You can create and use a form file with an extension other than .FOR, but you'll have to type the extension each time you want to load the form file.

Consider a shorter name if you use this form often, because you'll have to call it up each time you want to use it. When the second Notepads Editor screen appears, the filename NAMENUM.FOR should appear in the upper-right corner. Next, resize the Notepads Editor screen to let you view the Databases screen underneath:

Press: [Alt]-[W]-[R]

Press: [⇒] approximately 30 times

Press: [⇐] approximately eight times

To fix this new shape:

Press: [Enter]

Now move the smaller current window to the lower-right corner of the screen.

Press: [Alt]-[W]-[M]

Press: [⇒] approximately thirty times

Press: [⇓] approximately five times

Fix this new location:

Press: [Enter]

Your screen should now look like Figure 9.9.

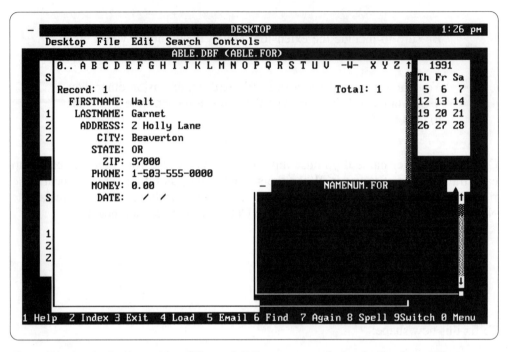

```
 -                          DESKTOP                         1:26 PM
   Desktop  File  Edit  Search  Controls
                      ABLE.DBF (ABLE.FOR)
    0.. A B C D E F G H I J K L M N O P Q R S T U V  -W-  X Y Z ↑   1991
  S                                                             Th Fr Sa
    Record: 1                                  Total: 1          5  6  7
      FIRSTNAME: Walt                                           12 13 14
  1    LASTNAME: Garnet                                         19 20 21
  2     ADDRESS: 2 Holly Lane                                   26 27 28
  2        CITY: Beaverton
           STATE: OR
             ZIP: 97000
           PHONE: 1-503-555-0000
           MONEY: 0.00            -              NAMENUM.FOR
  S          DATE:   /  /                                                ↑


  1
  2
  2


 1 Help  2 Index 3 Exit  4 Load  5 Email 6 Find  7 Again 8 Spell 9Switch 0 Menu
```

Figure 9.9. A resized and repositioned Notepads Editor screen overlaying the Databases Editor screen

Position the cursor in Line 1 Column 1 and type the first field you want to view:

    Type: NAME: [FIRSTNAME] [LASTNAME]

The line might wrap due to the small window size. Don't worry about that.

    Press: [Enter]

This is identical to the first line in the default ABLE.FOR. It's not necessary to use the field name for the first of the two field names, but you will for this example.

The second field name of the pair has to match a valid field name in the database you're using. It can be uppercase or lowercase characters, or a mixture of the two, but it has to match the field name, letter for letter, of the data you want to view.

Now prepare to insert the second field, PHONE:

    Type: PHONE: [PHONE]

Your screen should now look like Figure 9.10.

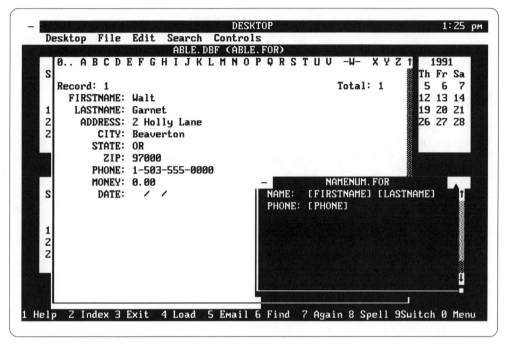

Figure 9.10. The new form NAMENUM.FOR

If the form file is as you want it, save it:

Press: [F5]

Press: [Enter] twice

You can save forms in either PC Tools or ASCII format.

You can change the form if necessary. The first field name in the pair is what appears on screen. You can type anything you want to designate the field. Some users prefer to use uppercase and lowercase letters (for example, *Name*). For this, you could either:

Type: Name: [NAME]

Or:

Type: Person: [NAME]

This would display *Person* on the screen in place of *Name*.

Now that you've created a form file, you can put it to use. First return to the Databases Editor window:

>**Press:** [Esc]

Using a Form File

Whenever you view a database record in the Edit screen, the information will be displayed in a form file that contains the same name as the database file. In most cases, this will be the default form file. To use a form file other than the default, you must load it from the Databases Edit screen.

To load NAMENUM.FOR, first switch back to the Databases module displaying ABLE.DBF.

>**Press:** [F9]

To load the new form:

>**Press:** [Alt]-[F]-[L]

This opens the Form dialog box.

>**Type:** NAMENUM

As long as you're using the current default extension, you only need to type the form filename.

>**Press:** [Enter]

Whenever you use a new form or record file (for example, if you've deleted the previous record file), the Databases Editor screen will appear in its original default mode. The size and colors you've picked before, even if you saved the configuration, won't have an effect.

In a moment, your Databases Editor screen should change to reflect the new form, as shown in Figure 9.11.

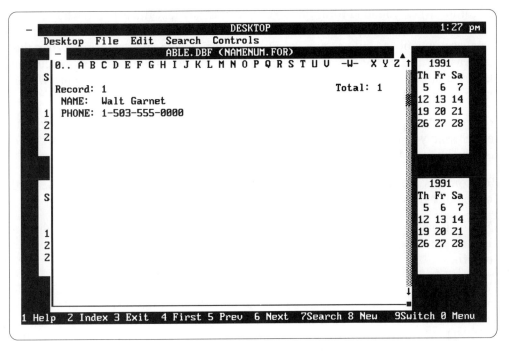

```
  -                              DESKTOP                      1:27 PM
      Desktop  File  Edit  Search  Controls
        -                ABLE.DBF  (NAMENUM.FOR)                  ▲
      |0.. A B C D E F G H I J K L M N O P Q R S T U U  -W-  X Y Z ↑    1991
    S                                                               Th Fr Sa
      Record: 1                                        Total: 1       5  6  7
       NAME:   Walt Garnet                                          12 13 14
    1  PHONE: 1-503-555-0000                                        19 20 21
    2                                                               26 27 28
    2

                                                                       1991
    S                                                               Th Fr Sa
                                                                     5  6  7
                                                                    12 13 14
    1                                                               19 20 21
    2                                                               26 27 28
    2
                                                                          ↓
 1 Help   2 Index 3 Exit   4 First 5 Prev   6 Next   7Search 8 New    9Switch 0 Menu
```

Figure 9.11. ABLE.DBF displayed in NAMENUM.FOR form

Notice how the label NAMENUM.FOR appears in the upper-right corner of your screen; this lets you keep track of which form you're using. Using the custom form NAMENUM, you can move through records in the database and view only the names and phone numbers in your address book.

As long as the form you've just created remains the form in use, you can switch back to the Notepads Editor screen to make changes to the form, save the changes, and then switch back to the Databases Editor screen to view the new effects. This is a great way to build more complex forms and to make sure the information is displayed the way you want it.

To return your display to the default form:

Press: [Alt]-[F]-[L]

Type: ABLE

Press: [Enter]

Be careful when you load form files. You can load any text file as a form file. A text file doesn't have to end with the extension .FOR to appear in the Edit screen of the Databases module as long as you specify the full filename and extension. When this happens, the text of the file appears, but none of the field information in the current database appears. The text file would have to contain a valid field name within brackets for the field data to appear.

You'll use this type of file in the next chapter when you learn how to merge-print letters. Should you inadvertently load a text file, simply repeat the form file process and use a valid form filename.

To avoid this problem, use the default form file extension .FOR for all form files and for no other files.

Once you gain experience working with form files and find that you want to view a certain form more often than the default form, consider switching the name of the form files.

When the Databases module loads a database, it looks for a file ending with .FOR that has the same name as the database and then displays the database information according to that form. Therefore, if you want to view your address book in NAMENUM form more often than the default ABLE form, change the name of the file NAMENUM.FOR to ABLE.FOR and the file ABLE.FOR to NAMENUM.FOR.

If it doesn't find the file, it automatically creates a new one, inserting all the fields in the database. When you view for the first time a database whose structure has been changed, you should delete the current default form file for the database and let PC Tools build a new one for you.

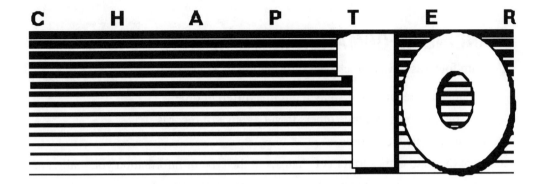

WORKING WITH DATABASES

A good database remains in flux; its information is continuously changing. The value of existing information also changes, with some things becoming more important and others less so. New things appear and old things disappear. All this requires that you keep updating your database or it will soon be outmoded.

CHANGING INFORMATION IN A DATABASE

There are four basic ways to change information in a database:

- Reorganize the records to display them in a different order.
- Select some records and hide others to get a range of records.
- Add, edit, and delete records.
- Change the field names to reflect changes in the type of information you maintain.

For example, if you want to write letters to everyone in ABLE.DBF, you would want to sort the database by name to verify that everyone's listed. If you want to write letters to only those people in California, you would select all records with a California address. You can also add and delete records or edit the record contents, for instance, as your friends move or you gain new friends. Finally, if you want to add the names of people living abroad, you can change the name of the Zip field to *mailcode,* since foreign countries don't use the zip-code system.

These are just a few of the many reasons why you would want to make changes to a database. In this chapter, you'll learn how to make these changes. You'll also discover the various ways can you print database information, so you can maintain paper copies of your database files. This chapter will also describe ways you can automatically dial phone numbers from a database record.

MODIFYING DATABASE RECORDS

Most of your time changing a database will be spent adding new records and editing or deleting existing records.

Editing Records

You can edit information in records just by typing over the original information. You can also delete the old information first by pressing [Del] or [Backspace], but typing over and deleting unneeded information is the best method. Whenever you enter a browse or edit Databases screen, the overtype mode is the default condition. It's a good idea, therefore, to press [Ins] each time you enter a Databases screen so you don't accidentally type over information you want to keep.

> As long as you don't press [Enter], information you type into a field will not be saved. If you accidentally type information you don't want to keep, press [Esc] to exit the Databases screen, then load the file a second time.

If you make changes to a database often, you should create a backup version of the database file to protect against inadvertent changes or to refer back to the original data.

Adding New Records

Once you create a database, you'll be surprised at how fast it grows. Inserting new data is so easy using computers, you'll soon find yourself logging in information you didn't expect to save when you first created the database.

You can add new records to a database in three ways:

- Add them one at a time.
- Transfer them in a block from another database.
- Attach one database to another.

Adding Records One-by-One

To add a new record, you need to first view the database using either the browse or the Edit screen. The Edit screen is more appropriate, since it shows all the fields for a single record when you use the form file created by the program.

To add a record to the current database, use either the *Add New Record* command on the Edit pull-down menu, or the [F8] function key. The easiest way is to:

    Press: [F8]

This opens the blank record screen you saw earlier, in Figure 9.6. This is the screen you used to enter the first records in ABLE.DBF. When adding a record to a database that already has one or more records, you work in the first record screen, but the total count of existing records will show at the top. If you're working in the Browse screen, an empty record slot will appear at the top of the file.

Once you've created a new blank record, turn on Modify Data.

    Press: [Alt]-[F]-[M]

In either screen, just type the record information. Figure 10.1 shows ABLE.DBF containing four records that were added in this way.

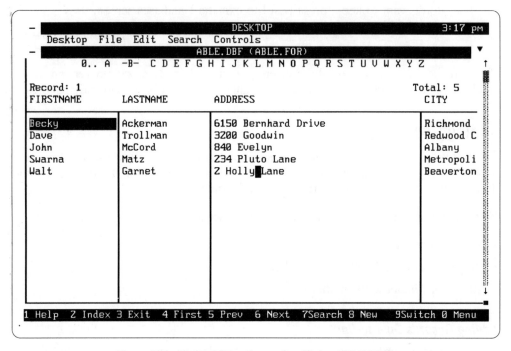

Figure 10.1. Four additional records added to ABLE.DBF

You'll use these records to demonstrate other ways of adding records to a database. For these demonstrations, you'll be adding records of your own. The only requirements for using the examples in this chapter are that you retain the same first and last names in the records shown in Figure 10.1 and you place only two of these records in California (using CA in the State field). You can then enter as many of your own records as you want, up to the PC Tools Deluxe limit of 10,000.

Appending Databases

You can add records to a database by appending another database to it. This procedure requires that you have two databases: the active one that receives the appended records, and the source that supplies the records.

> If you only have one database at this point—say, ABLE.DBF—you can create a new database from scratch or by making a copy of the existing database. To make a copy, use PC Shell, and give the database a different name, for example, BAKER.DBF.

To transfer the contents of BAKER.DBF into ABLE.DBF, make sure you're in the Browse screen of the active database, ABLE.DBF, so you can view the results of appending. Although you can append a database using either the Browse screen or the Edit screen, you can see the results immediately when you're viewing the Browse screen.

Begin the appending process:

Press: [Alt]-[F]-[A]

This opens a version of the Databases dialog box called *Append*.

Type: BAKER

Press: [Enter]

In a moment, the records in BAKER.DBF (which is a copy of ABLE.DBF) will appear in ABLE.DBF, as shown in Figure 10.2. The BAKER.DBF database remains a separate file on your disk.

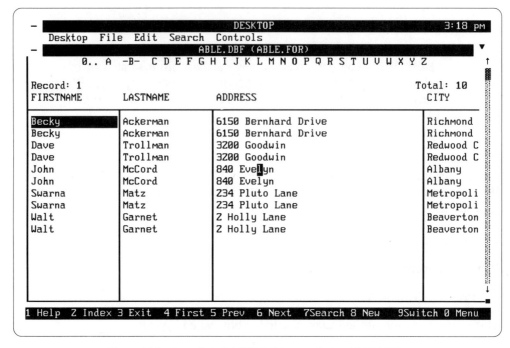

Figure 10.2. Records in BAKER.DBF appended to ABLE.DBF

The records you just appended from BAKER.DBF were added sequentially to the end of ABLE.DBF, but this isn't apparent from the screen display because of the default sort order. The first field you create in a database is designated the primary field. PC Tools automatically sorts the database according to information in this field. Since the first field you created is *firstname*, all the records in ABLE.DBF are organized alphabetically according to the first name of each person in a record. When you appended BAKER.DBF to ABLE.DBF, all the appended records were re-sorted automatically by first name.

> Everything works smoothly when you append records from a database with an identical field structure. But when you append records from a database with different fields, only matching fields will be transferred. Fields that don't exist in the active database (the one receiving the records) will be ignored. You'll be prompted for default entries for fields that don't exist in the appended records but do exist in the active database.

If you want to add some, but not all, of the records from another database, you should use the transfer process, which is described next.

Transferring Selected Records

You can selectively append records from one database to another, which is called transferring records. To do this:

1. Open the source database.

2. Select the records you want to transfer in the source database.

3. Execute the *Transfer* command by specifying the destination database.

4. View the destination database to make sure the records were transferred to it correctly.

Transfer two records from BAKER.DBF, the source, to ABLE.DBF, the destination. First open (load) the source database, BAKER.DBF.

Press: [Alt]-[D]-[D]

Type: BAKER

Press: [Enter]

Now, select the records you want to transfer. For this example, transfer the four records that have addresses in California.

Press: [Alt]-[E]-[R]

This opens the Select Records box.

Type: STATE

Press: [Enter]

Type: CA

Press: [Enter]

Now press either [Tab] or [Enter] as many times as it takes to move the highlight bar to the Select box (about fifteen key presses). Don't press [S] to execute the *Select* command or else you'll insert the letter *s* in a field name or data field.)

You should now be viewing two records on your screen, as shown in Figure 10.3.

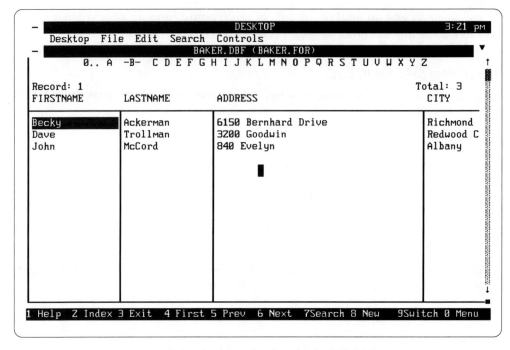

Figure 10.3. Three records selected in BAKER.DBF

These are the records you're going to transfer to ABLE.DBF.

Next, begin the transfer process:

Press: [Alt]-[F]-[T]

This opens a version of the Databases dialog box called *Transfer,* in which you specify ABLE.DBF as the destination database.

Type: ABLE

Press: [Enter]

That's all there is to it. If you want to double-check the success of the transfer, load ABLE.DBF into a Databases screen. If everything went according to plan, your screen should look like Figure 10.4.

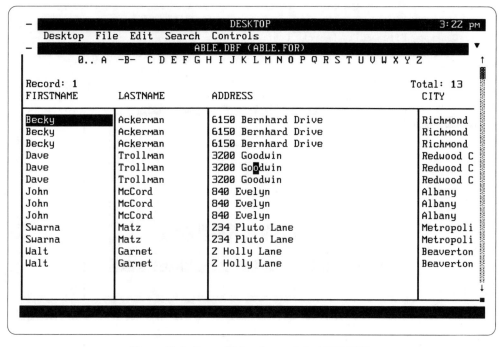

Figure 10.4. Two additional records in ABLE.DBF

If ABLE.DBF was previously loaded into a Databases Editor screen, it doesn't contain the new transferred records. In this case, you'll have to reload the file before you can view the updated information

Deleting Records

Deleting records is a two-step process designed to let you recover any records you've accidentally deleted. The first step marks the record for deletion; the second deletes the record.

For example, suppose you wish to remove the record for Milan from the database. First, view the record in the Edit screen, or highlight it in the Browse screen.

Press: [Alt]-[E]-[D]

The record will disappear from your screen, and the next record will appear in its place. You can only delete records one-by-one. At this point, you can continue deleting other records if you wish. If you delete all but one record from a database, and try to delete the last record, you'll get the security prompt shown in Figure 10.5.

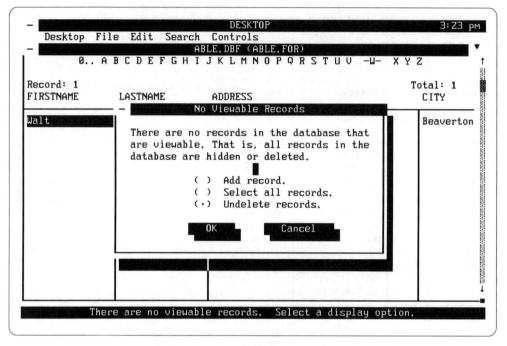

Figure 10.5. The No Viewable Records box

This gives you several options for continuing your work in the current database. After all, if you delete the last record, the database will no longer exist.

You should be aware that the record for Milan you just deleted is not yet gone from the database. Deleting a record only marks it for deletion and hides it from view. The record won't actually be removed until you pack the database.

Undeleting Records

To protect against accidentally marking a record for deletion and losing a valuable record, PC Tools requires that you confirm a record marked for deletion. Confirmation to delete or a decision to retain a record is made when you initiate the packing operation. If you've marked a record but haven't yet started to pack the database, you can recover the marked record:

Press: [Alt]-[E]-[U]

All the records marked for deletion will pop back into view. Although you delete records one-by-one, you undelete all at once any records marked for deletion.

Packing the Database

Once you've decided that you indeed want to delete all the records you've marked, you should pack the database. Packing is a dBASE term that describes the process of removing the marked records and storing the remaining records so that no empty space remains in the database. Obviously, when you remove records, you make the database smaller.

To pack a database containing records marked for deletion:

Press: [Alt]-[E]-[P]

The program will display a security prompt warning you that it's about to pack the database. If you change your mind and decide you don't want to delete certain marked records, you should back out of the pack now.

Press: [C]

This lets you undelete all marked records and begin the deletion process again. If you want to continue the packing process:

Press: [O]

It might take a few moments for the program to complete the packing, depending upon how many records you've marked.

Hiding Records

Hiding a record prevents it from being viewed on screen. This is the best way to protect the record from being changed. You can't mark a hidden record for deletion, nor can you edit information in a record you can't see.

To hide a record, first view it in the Edit screen or highlight it in the Browse screen. Then:

Press: [Alt]-[E]-[H]

When you hide a record, the next record appears in its place. Hiding a record doesn't remove it from the database; the record is only hidden from view until you reveal it again.

To bring the hidden record back to your display:

Press: [Alt]-[E]-[L]

Selecting all records reveals all hidden records at once; you can't reveal them selectively. Because it's possible to hide records and then forget about them, you might want to periodically select all records in the current database just as a reminder.

ORGANIZING RECORDS

You can organize records in a database two ways: by selecting them within a database or by reorganizing the entire database in a special sorted order. Before you learn how to use these two procedures, you should know a little background about how PC Tools remembers the order you specified for displaying records.

About .REC Files

When you first worked with form files in Chapter 9, you learned that the Databases module creates two additional files automatically when you create a database. These are the form file (.FOR extension) and the record file (.REC extension).The record file controls the way records are organized within the matching database. You can't create custom record files the way you can create custom form files. Only one record file can apply to a database; the Databases module creates the record file automatically by scanning the database when you create or change it, and then stores the field entries for the sorted field.

> When a .REC file becomes corrupted or PC Tools can't create a new version of it for a modified database, the message ERROR: BAD .REC FILE, DELETE AND RELOAD DATA BASE will appear. If this happens, follow the displayed instructions. If you continue to have trouble loading a database file, refer to "Backing Up Your Data," later in this chapter.

When you create a database, the order in which you enter the records is considered the sorted order. The first field is the one used for sorting until you select another. Each time you open a database to view or identify its contents, the Databases module reads the matching .REC file and organizes the records according to the file's contents. When you re-sort a database according to another field, the information is saved to a corresponding record file in the new sorted order.

In ABLE.DBF, since the database has not yet been sorted, the order of record listing is by NAME, which is the first field. Take a closer look at this record file. First, use

PC Shell to make a backup copy of ABLE.REC. Name the backup copy ABLEREC.TXT. Next, read ABLEREC.TXT into the Notepads Editor screen:

Press: [Alt]-[D]-[N]

Type: ABLEREC.TXT

Press: [Enter] twice

If the program asks how you want to display the contents of the file, press [A] for ASCII and move into the file. When the contents are displayed on your screen, turn off the highlighting by unmarking the block.

Press: [Alt]-[E]-[U]

You might have to do this twice to remove all the highlighting. (Because there are so many control codes in a .REC file, highlighting is sometimes unpredictable.)

Make sure the Wordwrap and Control character display commands on the Control pull-down menu are turned on (have a mark next to them). Your screen should now resemble Figure 10.6.

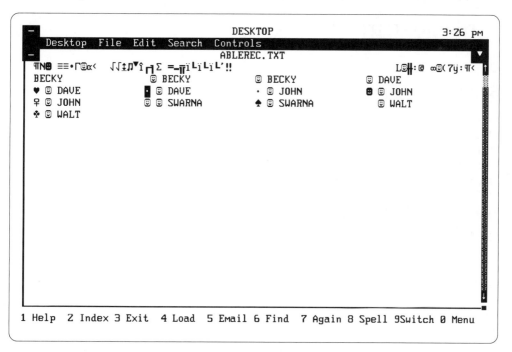

Figure 10.6. Contents of ABLEREC.TXT in the Notepads Editor screen

Most of the file contents might be gibberish to you, but you can make some sense out of the obvious entries.

The characters in the upper-left corner of the screen are crucial to DOS but do not affect this operation. Instead, look at the first name AILING. This is the Firstname field entry for the first sorted record of ABLE.DBF. The second name in ABLEREC.TXT corresponds to the second record in ABLE.DBF. Identical field entries, like these records, are identified by control characters that appear after the name. These characters—the light and dark happy faces, the bullet, the box, and the heart sign, and the others—are the control codes that begin the ASCII character set. That's how records with identical sort-field information are organized.

> Record files are unique to the PC Tools Databases module. No such files exist for any dBASE program. Record files serve as shortcuts for the PC Tools program, so the program gives you quick control over dBASE database files.

For now, close the Notepads screen without saving the file:

Press: [Alt]-[F]-[X]

Selecting Records

The selecting-records technique for organizing database records lets you gather together records that have similar characteristics. You select a group of records by specifying a field value. For example, in ABLE.DBF you can select everyone who lives in California by selecting records that share the value CA in the State field. Once you've selected a group, you can view the group and print it if you want to.

To select these records, display ABLE.DBF on your screen:

Press: [Alt]-[E]-[R]

This opens the Select Records box, as shown in Figure 10.7.

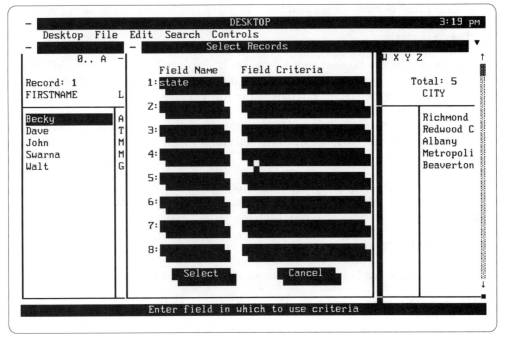

Figure 10.7. The Select Records box

When this box appears, you'll find the cursor in the first field of the Field Name box. The two columns, Field Name and Field Criteria, let you specify the record-selection factors.

To select all records in ABLE.DBF that pertain to people living in California:

Type: STATE

Press: [Enter]

Type: CA

Press: [Enter]

Field names and criteria are case-insensitive, so you can use either upper- or lower-case for these entries. You have to make sure, however, that the field names and criteria are spelled correctly. If you type ST for the field name or CALIF for the field criteria, no records will be selected because the State field name requires five letters and the field criteria allows only two letters.

Now press [Tab] as many times as it takes to move your cursor to the Select box.

> **Press:** [Enter]

The selection process begins, and a message is displayed on the screen. When the entire database has been scanned for all State field entries, the records that match will be displayed. This is most obvious in the Browse screen.

Once a group of records is selected, you can view, edit, and print it. The selecting-records technique limits most of your activities in the database to the selected records.

You can specify up to eight field names in the Select Records box. You can also use the DOS wildcards when specifying ranges and values in the search criteria.

DOS Wildcards

The question mark symbol replaces a single character. For example:

1001?   Selects the numbers 10010, 10011,..., 10019.

?100   Selects the numbers 0100, 2100,..., 9100.

ABLE?   Selects ABLE plus all five Character field entries that begin with ABLE, such as ABLED, ABLEE, and ABLET.

?ABLE   Selects all five Character field entries ending in ABLE, including ABLE, plus such names as CABLE, SABLE, TABLE, 1ABLE, and 2ABLE.

Two periods form a wildcard that has two uses. The first is similar to the use of the asterisk in DOS. For example:

*100..   Selects field entries between 10000 and 10099. Also selects field entries having any characters that appear before the number 100; for example: A100. B100, AB100, or AB9100.

100*   Selects field entries beginning with 100, including 1000, 1001, 100NAMES, and so on.

*ABLE   Selects entries such as TABLE, SABLE, STABLE, and DURABLE.

ABLE*   Selects field entries that begin with ABLE, including ABLE, ABLED, ABLEET, and ABLE10.

The second use specifies a range of first characters. For example:

1 .. 5   Selects field entries that start with the number 1, 2, 3, 4, or 5. You can narrow this down further by specifying something like 35 .. 37, which selects entries beginning with 35, 36, or 37.

A .. C   Selects field entries that start with the letters A, B, or C. You can narrow this down further by specifying AD .. AF, which selects entries beginning with AD, AE, and AF.

To deselect the group of records and view all records in the database:

Press: [Alt]-[E]-[L]

Specifying criteria that no records can match creates an interesting condition for a database—no records show on the screen. When you select this group of records to view, you're really selecting *not* to view the rest of the records. In other words, you're *hiding* the records that were not selected. Thus, if no records match your selection criteria, you hide all records.

To protect against this development, the Databases module asks whether or not you want to hide the last record in the database. Viewing at least one record reminds you that the database contains data and is not empty.

Sorting a Database

Sorting a database means organizing and displaying all the records according to criteria that you specify. PC Tools will organize a database on one field only. For example, suppose you want to sort the records in ABLE.DBF according to the alphabetical order of entries in the Lastname field:

Press: [Alt]-[E]-[S]

This opens the Sort Field Select box, shown in Figure 10.8.

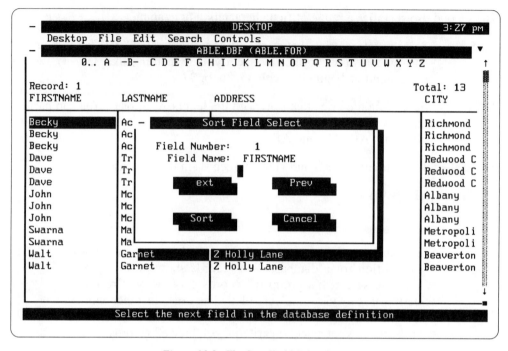

Figure 10.8. The Sort Field Select box

When this box appears, it displays the name and number of a field. If this is not the field through which you want to sort, press [N] (or highlight Next) and move to the next field, until you find the field through which you want to sort. Move backward by pressing [P] (or selecting Prev).

Once you display the correct field name, press [S] (or select Sort, then press [Enter]) to begin the sort. When the sort process ends, records are displayed on screen in the new order. This is most obvious when you're working in the Browse screen.

For this example, sort ABLE.DBF on the Lastname field. To perform this sort:

>**Press:** [Alt]-[E]-[S]

Move to the field through which you want to sort, Lastname, by pressing [N] or [P]:

>**Press:** [S]

In a moment, the contents of ABLE.DBF will return to the screen, displaying records in the newly sorted order, as shown in Figure 10.9.

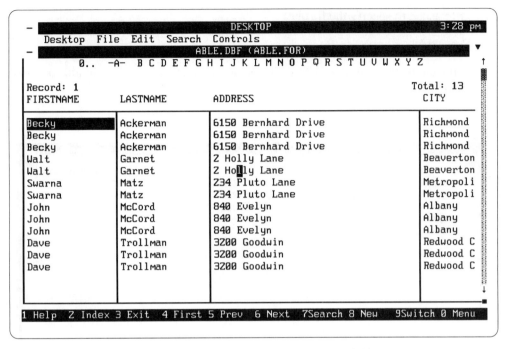

Figure 10.9. ABLE.DBF sorted on Lastname field

> The sort order is always ascending. When you specify a sort field that contains alphabetic characters, the sort will be in alphabetical order. When you specify a field that contains numbers, the sort will start with the lowest number and proceed to the highest.

Notice that the last names are listed in alphabetical order.

Earlier in this chapter you learned about .REC files, which are unique to the PC Tools Databases module. They keep a record of the current organization for the matching database. Now that you've re-sorted ABLE.DBF, look at what happened to the ABLE.REC file. First, copy ABLE.REC to ABLEREC.TXT using PC Shell. When you return to the Desktop Manager, presuming you're still viewing the newly sorted contents of ABLE.DBF:

Press: [Alt]-[D]-[N]

Type: ABLEREC.TXT

If you're asked to specify the format:

> **Press:** [A]

When the contents for ABLEREC.TXT appear on your screen, they should look like Figure 10.10.

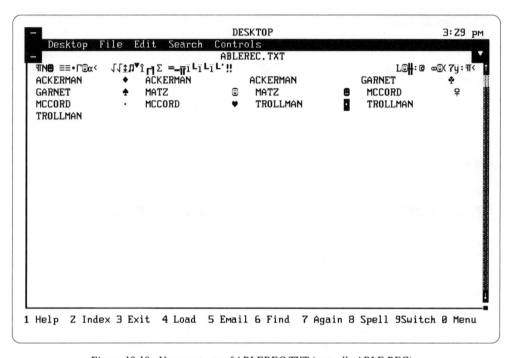

Figure 10.10. New contents of ABLEREC.TXT (actually ABLE.REC)

You can see how the last names have been arranged in the record file matching the database you just sorted. (It is immaterial that each field entry is repeated three times.) This is how PC Tools remembers how to display individual records. When you sort on a field that contains the same data for two or more records, entries in the .REC file will be organized by an internal code, which consists of specific ASCII characters placed before each field to determine its order among other identical fields.

SEARCHING FOR RECORDS

In the Databases module, you can search for specific records three ways. To see your choices:

> **Press:** [Alt]-[S]

This opens the Search pull-down menu and shows that you can search for text in all fields, search for text in the sort field only, or move to a specific record. Moving to a specific record, explained in Chapter 9, is not the same as searching.

The two top search methods both help you to find records when you don't know the record number, but do know something about the data in the record. The more specific method, searching for data in the sort fields, is quicker, but it narrows your search options. The more general method, searching for data in all fields, is slower, but it lets you use anything you can remember about a record.

To remove the Search menu from your screen:

> **Press:** [Esc]

Searching Through the Primary Field

You'll use the more specific method, searching through the sort field, more frequently, because you usually will want to remember the primary field data in a record. In this example, assume that the Name field of ABLE.DBF is the sorted field. (Re-sort ABLE.DBF if you have to.) To find the record of someone you know, all you need to do is search for the name. Because searching is a common procedure in database management, it has been assigned to the function key [F7]. To begin a search on the primary or sort field:

> **Press:** [F7]

This opens the Search Sort Field box, shown in Figure 10.11.

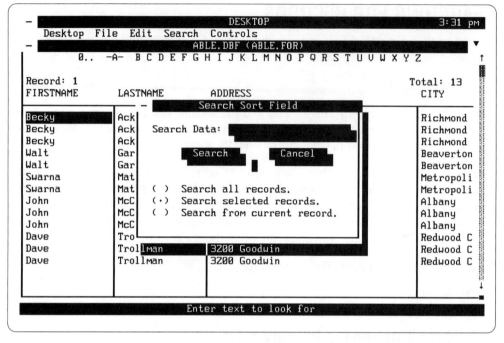

Figure 10.11. The Search Sort Field box

You can also open this box using menu commands:

Press: [Alt]-[S]-[T]

You'll find the cursor blinking in the empty field after *Search Data* heading. This is where you type the data you want to search for. It doesn't have to be all of the data in the field; it can be only a few consecutive characters. For instance, if you want to search for the name Milan Moncilovich, you could type the whole name, just Milan, or just Monc, and probably come up with the same record. Searching is not case-specific; both uppercase and lowercase characters are searched for. For example:

Type: mil

Naturally, the fewer characters you specify, the broader the search, which means that sometimes you'll locate a record that matches the data, but isn't the record you're looking for. The more specific you can make the search data, the more quickly you'll move to the right record.

Once you've specified the string to search for, you're given three record-search options:

1. Searching through all records.

2. Searching through the currently selected records.

3. Searching from the current record to the end of the database.

The default setting is *Search Selected Records,* which searches through the selected group, if you have one, or all the records if you haven't selected any. For example:

>   **Press:** [Enter] twice

This selects the method and begins the search. When the first record that contains "mil" in the Name field is found, the record will be displayed on your screen in Edit mode or highlighted in browse mode. Then the Search Sort Field box will reappear. This lets you move quickly to the next occurrence if you want to.

At this point, look at the first record found. It's for Milan Moncilovich. Since this is not the record you want, just press [Enter] twice to move on. Pressing [Enter] twice switched the default search method to *Search from Current Record.* This prevents you from locating the same record over and over again. The characters you typed remain in the Search Data field. Eventually, you'll get to the record for Milan Moncilovich. Of course, if you had specified this name completely at the beginning, you would have gone directly to the record.

Searching Through All Fields

You can also search for a record by scanning for specific data throughout all fields. To do this:

>   **Press:** [Alt]-[S]-[F]

This opens the Search All Fields box, which is identical to the previous box except for the name. Type the data you want to look for, pick one of the three methods for searching, and begin the search.

CHANGING THE DATABASE STRUCTURE

As you use a database, you'll find you want to change its structure to accommodate more information or save current information in different ways. You can't change the structure very much using PC Tools. The most you can do is change the name of existing field names. You can't insert new field names or delete existing field names, nor can you change the field length.

If you work with dBASE databases a lot, you should keep handy a full-fledged version of dBASE, or a compatible program, to do the things you can't do in the PC Tools Databases module.

Changing Field Names

Changing field names is perhaps the trickiest thing you can do in the Databases module, since you're making a fundamental change to the database structure.

> When you change a field name, it will appear in the database without any data. This means that all the data in the field before the name-change will be lost. To prevent data loss, create a backup file of the original database file before you change any field names in it. You can use dBASE or another full-featured compatible database program to swap data from the old field in the backup file into the new field.

Start by viewing the contents of the database. Next, use the *Edit Fields* command on the Edit pull-down menu:

Press: [Alt]-[E]-[E]

This opens the Field Editor box, which looks like Figure 10.12.

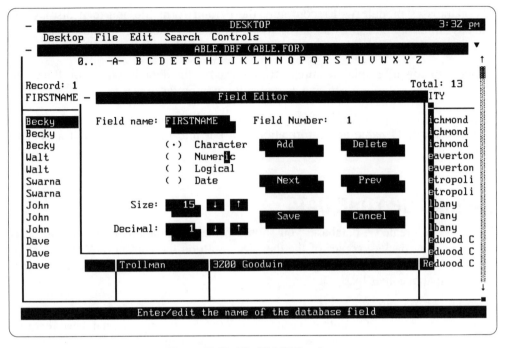

Figure 10.12. The Field Editor box

You might recognize this box. It's the same one you used in Chapter 9 to create fields for ABLE.DBF. The first field name will be displayed along with the information you declared for the field. To change a field, first display its name in the Field Editor box. If you don't want to change the first field, move to the field whose name you want to change and type in the new field name. Then accept and save this name.

For example, to change the Name field in ABLE.DBF to *Person*:

Press: [Alt]-[E]-[E]

Move to the Name field.

Type: PERSON

Press: [Enter]

Press: [A]

Press: [Enter]

Press: [S]

The Databases module will reconfigure the default form file and then display the database information using the new field name. You'll notice that the new field name contains no data. All the data for the field you changed has disappeared.

Notice also how all display features have returned to the default setup. You'll have to reconfigure the colors, screen size, and position you prefer to use.

Once you've changed a field name, you'll have to change any matching form files or else the new field name and information you put into this field will not appear in them.

BACKING UP YOUR DATA

Once you've created a database, you should protect the data as best you can. This means making backup copies of the database, both on the current disk and on floppies, tape, or some other storage medium that allows you to access the database if your original becomes lost.

Database files in dBASE easily become corrupted. Another complication can arise from the practice of PC Tools using its own .REC file to organize database records. You can tell a file is corrupted when you can't load it into the PC Tools Databases module. A corrupted file doesn't mean the data is lost. It only means something has happened to the file that renders it unreadable by your database management program—in this case PC Tools Databases module.

If PC Tools tells you the .DBF is corrupted or the .REC file is damaged, delete the matching .REC file and try to load the database program a second time. PC Tools will attempt to build a new matching record file, and in many cases this is all that's necessary to read the database file correctly.

If that isn't successful, and you work with databases regularly, try to correct the problem by loading the corrupted database file into a full-fledged dBASE-type database management program. This won't construct a .REC file—only PC Tools can do that. But it might straighten out small problems in the database file.

If that doesn't work, you should copy the corrupted database file to a new and separate file. To make a copy, use either the *Copy* command assigned to [F5] in PC Shell or the *Copy File* command on the Files pull-down menu. For example, if you can't load ABLE.DBF into the PC Tools Databases module, copy that file to something like ABLE1.DBF. (Remember to use the .DBF extension.) Now try to read the copy into the Databases module.

In most cases, one of these three tricks should solve the problem. If the problem persists, and you use dBASE files often, you should obtain a dBASE salvage program, which works with more precision on dBASE database files.

If all else fails, you can load the faulty database file into a text editor, strip out all the control codes, delimit the data, and reread the data back into a database file. I won't expand on these instructions; if they don't make sense to you, you shouldn't try the procedure. Whole volumes have been written about salvaging dBASE data.

One of the best ways to back up your data is printing it to a paper or disk file. While it might be tedious to type the data back into a database file, it's a better alternative than losing the data completely.

PRINTING DATABASE INFORMATION

Database information can be printed to two media: through your printer to paper, or to a disk file. The disk file contains text characters arranged in the printed format you want to use, plus the most common printing control characters, such as line feed and carriage return.

To print database information:

1. Design the form file you want to use.

2. Adjust the Page Layout menu settings for the form.

3. Select the way you want to print record information.

4. Select the device you want to print with.

Printing database information is straightforward. You must decide whether to print a default list of all record data or a format of your choice. For a complete list, print from the Browse screen. For a custom format using a form file you've designed, print from the Edit screen.

The format of printed information remains the same whether you print to paper or to disk. You should know a few more details about printing to disk files, however, should you want to use them.

Printing Database Information to a Disk File

There are three reasons to print to a disk file first:

1. To send the file via e-mail or on disk to someone else with a computer.

2. To view the printed file and change the format before printing.

3. To print the file through a printer not supported by PC Tools, such as a PostScript printer. You must use a word-processing program that supports the printer you want to use.

When you print to a disk file, the filename PC Tools uses depends upon whether you start printing the file while viewing the information in the Browse mode or in the Edit mode. If you're viewing the database information in Browse mode, PC Tools uses the same name for the file as the database file you're viewing. The program always adds the extension .PRT. For example, if you're viewing ABLE.DBF in Browse mode and print the file to disk, you'll end up with a disk file called ABLE.PRT.

If you're viewing the database information in Edit mode, PC Tools names the disk file after the form file you're currently using and adds the extension .PRT. For example, if you're viewing ABLE.DBF using NAMENUM.FOR and print to a disk file, the disk filename will be NAMENUM.PRT.

For the rest of this section printing refers to printing through your printer.

Printing a Complete List

The best way to maintain a printed record of all the information in a database is to print the database in tabular format, which is identical to the Browse screen.

To print a list, begin by viewing the database you want to print in Browse mode:

    Press: [Alt]-[F]-[P]

This opens the Print box, which lets you select where you want to print the information. Once you've made the selection:

    Select: PRINT

This begins the printing process. You'll notice a bar appear near the top of your screen telling you that printing is in progress. It disappears when printing is finished. Should you wish to stop the printing before it is completed, press [Esc]. It might take a moment or two before the printing stops, since printers usually contain a buffer that will empty on its own.

Figure 10.13 shows the result of printing ABLE.DBF using the Browse mode screen.

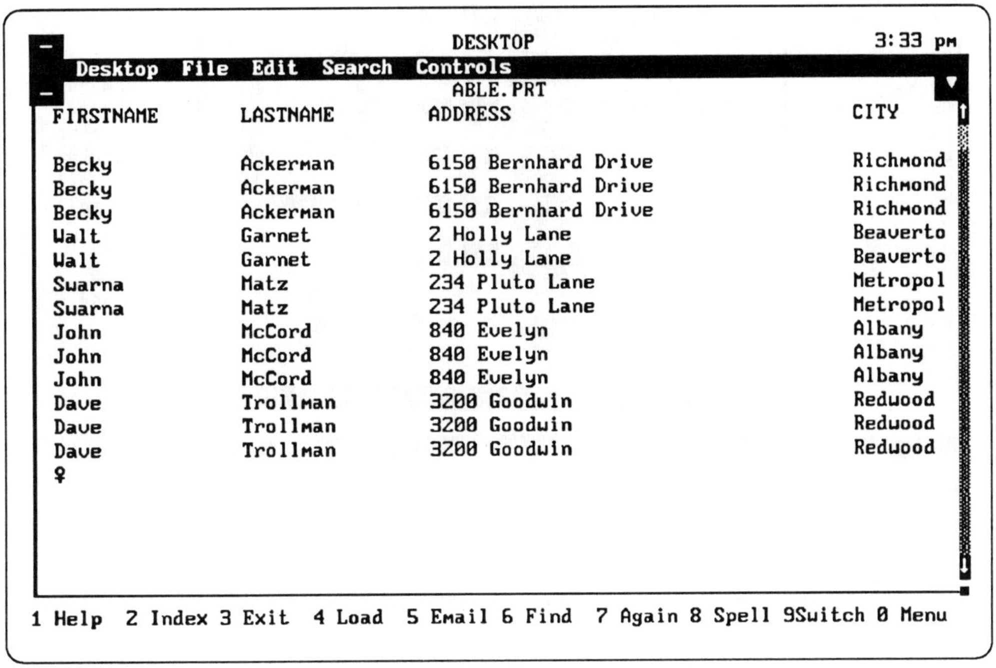

```
┌─────────────────────────────────────────────────────────────────────────────┐
│ ─                          DESKTOP                              3:33 pm       │
│ ▌ Desktop  File  Edit  Search  Controls                                       │
│ ─                           ABLE.PRT                                       ▼  │
│  FIRSTNAME          LASTNAME       ADDRESS                       CITY       ▐ │
│                                                                            ▓ │
│  Becky              Ackerman       6150 Bernhard Drive          Richmond   ▓ │
│  Becky              Ackerman       6150 Bernhard Drive          Richmond   ▓ │
│  Becky              Ackerman       6150 Bernhard Drive          Richmond   ▓ │
│  Walt               Garnet         2 Holly Lane                 Beaverto   ▓ │
│  Walt               Garnet         2 Holly Lane                 Beaverto   ▓ │
│  Swarna             Matz           234 Pluto Lane               Metropol   ▓ │
│  Swarna             Matz           234 Pluto Lane               Metropol   ▓ │
│  John               McCord         840 Evelyn                   Albany     ▓ │
│  John               McCord         840 Evelyn                   Albany     ▓ │
│  John               McCord         840 Evelyn                   Albany     ▓ │
│  Dave               Trollman       3200 Goodwin                 Redwood    ▓ │
│  Dave               Trollman       3200 Goodwin                 Redwood    ▓ │
│  Dave               Trollman       3200 Goodwin                 Redwood    ▓ │
│  ♀                                                                            │
│                                                                               │
│                                                                            ▐ │
│                                                                            ■ │
│ 1 Help  2 Index 3 Exit  4 Load  5 Email 6 Find  7 Again 8 Spell 9Switch 0 Menu│
└─────────────────────────────────────────────────────────────────────────────┘
```

Figure 10.13. Records in ABLE.DBF printed in Browse mode

When you print in Browse mode, only information in the fields that show on screen will be printed. You might want to remember this when you design a database and create individual fields of finite length. You should shorten the field length if you want to show more information on the Browse screen.

To adjust the way field information is printed, you should adjust settings in the Page Layout box, shown in Figure 10.14:

Press: [Alt]-[C]-[P]

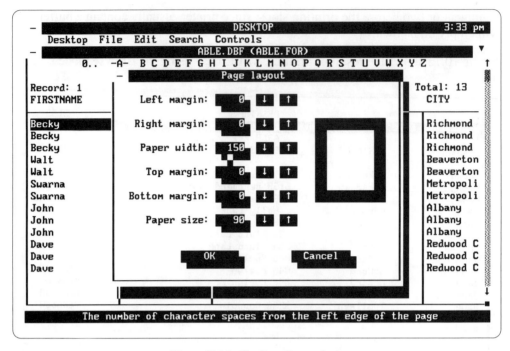

Figure 10.14. The Page Layout box

The menu is identical to the page layout settings for the Notepads and Outlines Editor screens. It lets you set the four margins, paper size, line spacing, and the first page to print. You'll need to adjust the right and left margins to control how much information is printed on a single line. You can't control how much information is printed for each field.

Each time you change these settings, save the new configuration:

   Press: [Alt]-[C]-[S]

The settings remain current until the next time you change and save them.

Designing a Form File for Printing

To customize the positions where individual field information appears when printed, you should use the Edit screen, design a form file for the format you want to use, then readjust the page layout settings to accommodate the form file.

You can use the same form file for both viewing and printing database information. Viewing form information on screen is probably the best way to see how the printed results will look.

For the next example, you'll create a form file that prints the names and addresses of people in ABLE.FOR in label form. To do this, open the Notepads Editor screen:

Press: [Alt]-[D]-[N]

Type: LABELS.FOR

Press: [Enter] twice

Type the field names according to the format of a label. With your cursor in Line 1, Column 1:

Type: [FIRSTNAME] [LASTNAME]

Press: [Enter]

Notice that you don't have to use a preliminary label such as NAME: or Person>. If you had, the field names would also be printed on your labels.

Type: [ADDRESS]

Press: [Enter]

Type: [CITY], [STATE] [ZIP]

This places the city and state names (separated by a comma) and zip code on the same line. Your screen should now look like Figure 10.15.

Switch back to the Databases Editor screen for ABLE.DBF and load this new form file, then look at the results in Edit mode. Your screen should look like Figure 10.16.

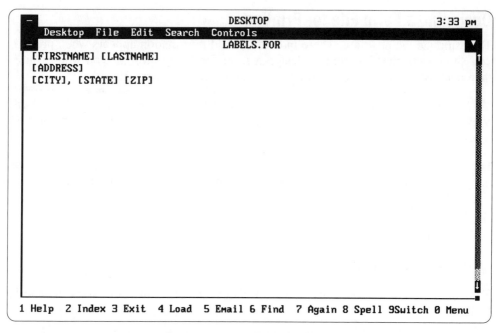

Figure 10.15. Form file for LABELS.FOR on screen

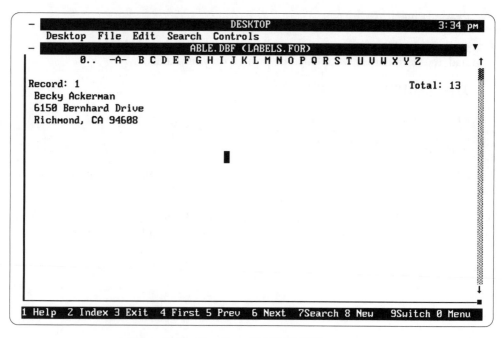

Figure 10.16. The effect of LABELS.FOR on screen

Adjusting Page Layout

When you print a database file, its form file will be controlled by settings in the current page layout configuration. To view the configuration:

Press: [Alt]-[C]-[P]

Suppose you're using a long strip of labels measuring one inch high and three inches wide. With these dimensions, you can fit up to six lines of text on each column, and each column can hold about thirty characters. The exact number of characters depends upon your pitch setting.

> To print labels using a laser printer that doesn't accept strip labels or to print master labels that you can duplicate in a copy machine using multicolumn label paper, you should first print the labels to a disk file then read the disk file into a text editor that supports the printing of columns.

To make sure you don't print on the left edge of the label (unless the left edge of the label paper is inserted to the left of Column 0 on the printer), set the left margin to 5.

To prevent unwanted text wraparound, set the right margin to 40. A setting of 40 is longer than the width of the labels you're using. You can also adjust the right margin to the longest line length you'll use, even if that means losing some characters off the right side of the label.

Set the top margin to 0, the bottom margin to 6, and the paper size to 66. This forces a page break after every sixth line. You should view each label as a single page.

Selecting Record Information

Now that you've set the form and page layout, prepare to print the labels. Make sure you're viewing the information in ABLE.DBF using the form LABELS.FOR.

Press: [Alt]-[F]-[P]

This opens the Print Selection box, which looks like Figure 10.17.

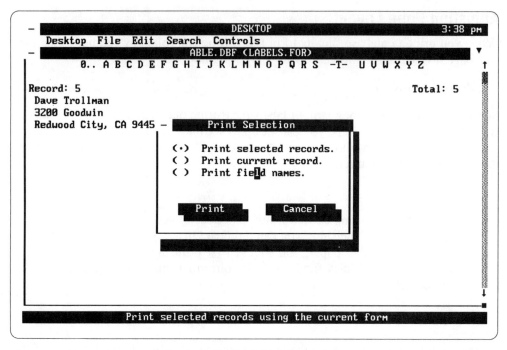

Figure 10.17. The Print Selection box

You're given three options for printing record information:

Print selected records   Prints all selected records in the current database according to the current form file and page layout configurations. If you haven't selected a group, this option will print all records.

Print current record   Prints only the currently displayed record according to the current form file.

Print field names   Prints a record of all the field names in the current database.

For your labels, select the first option. This moves you to the Print box. Select the device you want to use and the number of copies you want to print, then select PRINT.

The contents of each label will be printed on screen as they are printed to paper. When all your labels are printed, they'll look like Figure 10.18.

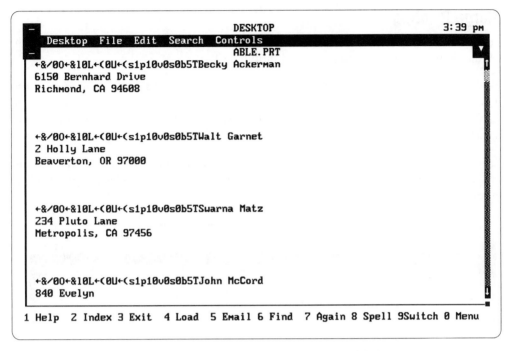

Figure 10.18. Records in ABLE.DBF printed as labels

The codes that appear in front of each name are formatting codes specific to my printer, a Hewlett-Packard LaserJet.

You'll have to remove the page numbers using an editor. Printing lists and labels is straightforward, but the way you adjust your page layout and customize the form file is a little more complex. Experiment with these settings and see what happens when you change them.

> If you print database information to a disk file, remember that the name of the file is taken from the form file, not the database. If you printed the example shown in Figure 10.18 to disk, you'd end up with a disk file LABELS.PRT.

Merge Printing

You can also use form files to insert record information into merge letters, which contain identical text but are addressed individually.

You've already created form files to change the way record information appears on your screen and is printed to labels. Creating a form file for merge letters is almost as easy. All you do is create a form file that contains the text you want to print, then insert field names where you want individual record information to appear.

For example, suppose you wanted to send a copy of this book to your friends listed in ABLE.DBF. You could use the form file shown in Figure 10.19 for just such a purpose.

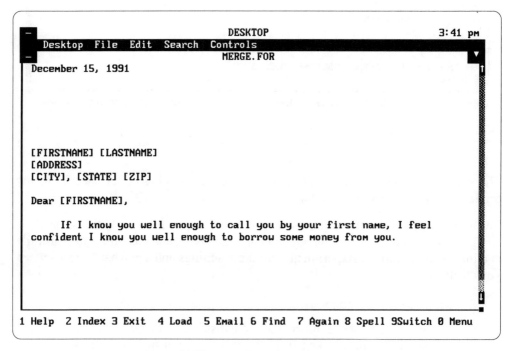

Figure 10.19. Merge letter form file on screen

The text of the file appears just like the text in a letter. However, field names (enclosed in brackets) appear at the places you want individual names to be printed. As usual, double check your page layout settings and make sure they are set to normal page printing: left margin in Column 10, right margin in Column 65, top and bottom margins on Line 6, page length of 66 lines, and so on.

In this case, you might not want to send letters to your friends on your list who are engineers. To do this, you either need to insert a field that displays you friends' occupation of those on your list, or you can hide the records of your engineer friends.

To print the merge letters, return to the Databases screen currently displaying ABLE.DBF. Load the form file MERGE.FOR (the name should appear in the upper-right corner of your Databases Editor screen).

> **Press:** [Alt]-[F]-[P]

> **Press:** [Enter] twice

When the Print box appears, select the device, then begin the printing.

Printing a List of Field Names

Printing a list of field names is an excellent way to keep a record of the structure of a database.

To print a list of all field names in a database, begin by viewing the database in Edit mode. It makes no difference which form file you're using. All field names in the current database will be printed, regardless of which form you're viewing.

> **Press:** [Alt]-[F]-[P]

> **Select:** Print field names

Next, select the device, then PRINT. You'll see the list appear on your screen briefly. When you print the field names in ABLE.DBF, the results on the screen should look like Figure 10.20.

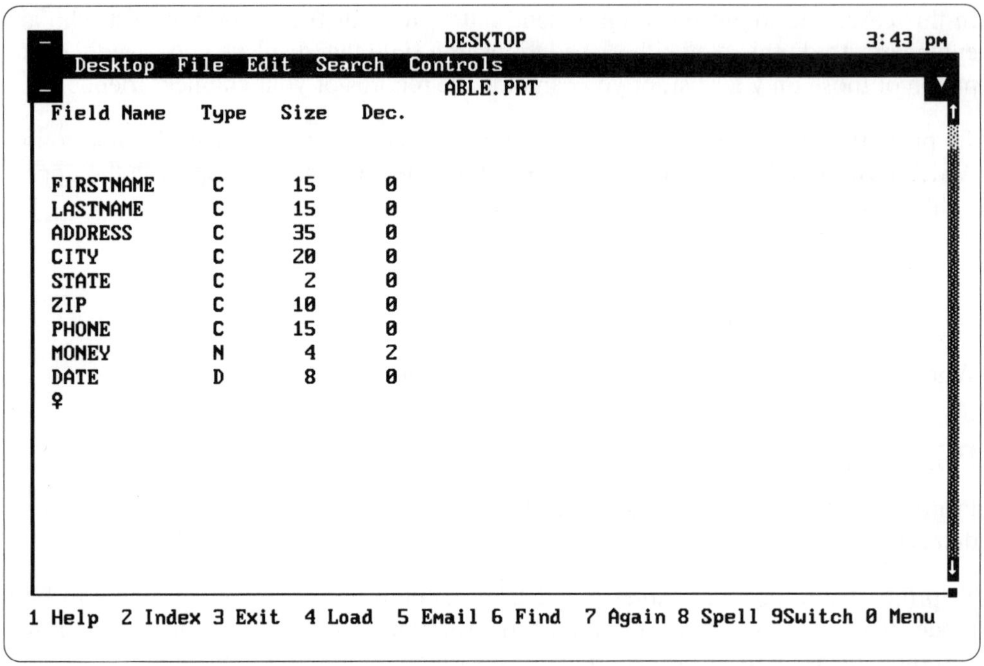

```
                                    DESKTOP                          3:43 PM
        Desktop  File  Edit  Search  Controls
                                    ABLE.PRT                                 ▼
      Field Name    Type   Size   Dec.                                       ↑


      FIRSTNAME      C      15      0
      LASTNAME       C      15      0
      ADDRESS        C      35      0
      CITY           C      20      0
      STATE          C       2      0
      ZIP            C      10      0
      PHONE          C      15      0
      MONEY          N       4      2
      DATE           D       8      0
      ♀


                                                                             ↓

    1 Help  2 Index 3 Exit  4 Load  5 Email 6 Find  7 Again 8 Spell 9Switch 0 Menu
```

Figure 10.20. Field names in ABLE.DBF printed to disk

Printing a list of field names is the one exception to the rule that a form file controls the fields that appear in a printed layout. When you print a list of field names, all the field names for the database will appear, not just those that appear in the current form file.

USING AUTODIAL

You can use the Autodial feature in the Databases module to make a voice phone call. This feature dials a phone number that appears in a record field. There are two ways you can execute Autodial in the Databases module:

- Use Screen Autodial by pressing the hotkeys [Ctrl]-[O].
- Use Autodial configured for the Databases module by pressing [Alt]-[C]-[A]. You should configure the program for your hardware first. Autodial in the Databases module automatically dials the first valid phone number it runs across in the current record.

You can use a database supplied by PC Tools called TELECOMM.DBF to record and use various phone numbers that you might want to send messages to via e-mail. This database applies only to your work in the Telecommunications module. You'll use the information you learned in this and the previous chapter for your work with TELECOMM.DBF. However, a description of how you actually use TELECOMM.DBF is discussed in chapters 11 through 13, which describe the Telecommunications module.

The first valid phone number is a crucial phrase in the Databases Autodial method. It means that Autodial will begin to dial the first number with three or more digits in the series of fields for the displayed record. This lets you dial people on another extension in your company phone system. If an address field comes before the phone field and the address begins with three or more numbers (like some of the addresses in ABLE.DBF), then Autodial will try to dial the address number. There is no way to change this procedure.

When you execute Autodial, it scans the series of fields as they exist in the database, which is not necessarily the order that shows on your screen. Suppose you're using a form other than the default form, and you've designed it so the phone field comes before any other field that contains numbers. In this case, executing Autodial will dial the phone number, because Autodial works off the actual structure of the database, not what's displayed on your screen.

When viewing a database, you can also use the standard form of Autodial by pressing [Ctrl]-[O], unless you've changed these hotkeys. The version specific to the Databases module allows you to quickly call a number in a specific field.

Before you can use the version of Autodial specific to the Databases module, you must configure certain hardware settings.

Configuring Autodial

To configure Autodial in the Databases module:

Press: [Alt]-[C]-[C]

This opens the Configure Autodialer box, which looks like Figure 10.21.

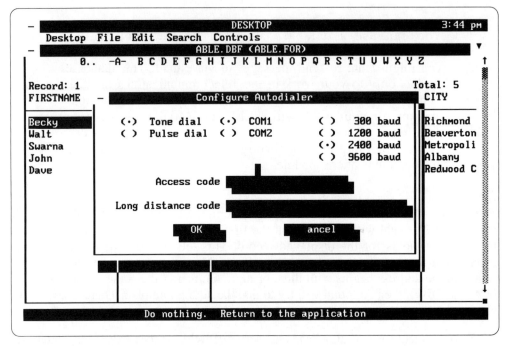

Figure 10.21. The Configure Autodialer box

You'll find the Cancel box highlighted. Press [Tab] to highlight the settings you need to change. Once you've entered the settings you want to use:

Select: OK

Making a Call

To make a call using Autodial in the Databases module, highlight the record you want to call and:

Press: [Alt]-[C]-[A]

This begins Autodial. When the first valid number for the current record is found, your screen will look like Figure 10.22.

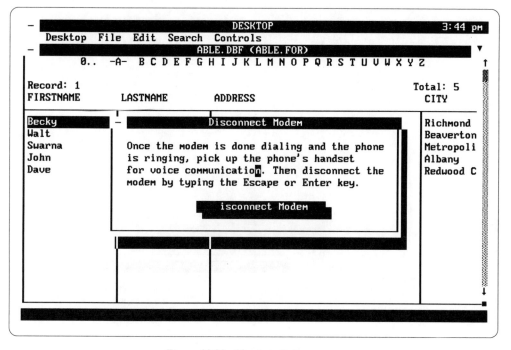

Figure 10.22. The Autodial message

You can cancel the call by pressing [Enter], which disconnects the modem. Otherwise, the call will proceed.

You can always use the programwide Autodial by pressing [Ctrl]-[O] and selecting appropriate commands.

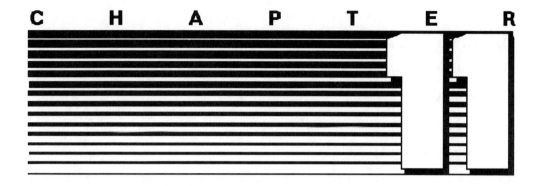

C H A P T E R

11

WORKING WITH THE APPOINTMENT SCHEDULER

The Appointment Scheduler was designed to let people manage their time efficiently. You can use it just to check the current date, to log-in important appointments, to set alarms for your working day, to remind you to check your mail or pick up your children from school, and so forth.

You can also make the Appointment Scheduler start other programs or macros at pre-set times to perform complex functions automatically, such as downloading your e-mail or routinely compressing files on your hard disk.

OPENING THE APPOINTMENT SCHEDULER

To open the Appointment Scheduler from the main menu:

Press: [A]

To open the Appointment Scheduler from another module:

Press: [Alt]-[D]-[A]

This opens a dialog box that filters for files ending in the extension .TM. You can remember this as *time manager.* To create an appointment file called A.TM:

Press: [A]

Press: [Enter] twice

One file should be large enough to accommodate most of your appointments. A file with the name A.TM will appear at the top of the Appointment Scheduler dialog box every time you enter this module. When the Appointment Scheduler screen for a new file appears, it looks like Figure 11.1.

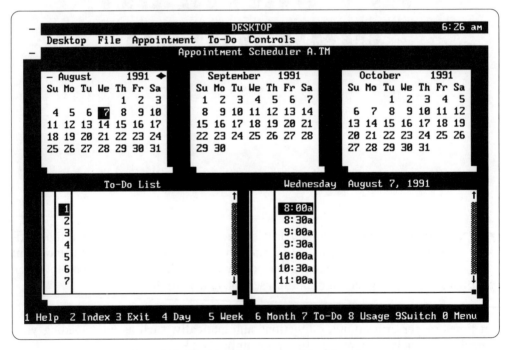

Figure 11.1. The blank Appointment Scheduler screen

From now on, to enter A.TM from the Desktop menu, all you have to do is press [A] and then [Enter]. You'll notice the screen is divided into three sections:

1. A calendar in the upper half of the screen

2. An hourly schedule on the lower right

3. A To-Do list in the lower left

You can move forward through the calendar, the daily schedule, and the To-Do list by pressing [Tab]. You can move backward by pressing [Shift]-[Tab]. You can tell that a section is active by its highlighted title. Notice that each section has its own scroll bars (in the calendar these are arrows) that let you use a mouse to move around the section you're working with.

Pull-Down Menus

The top line on your screen shows four pull-down menus specific to the Appointment Scheduler:

File   Duplicates the commands in the Notepads and Outlines File pull-down menus, letting you load and save schedules, customize Autosave, print schedules, and exit without saving.

Appointment   Gives you eight commands for working with appointments in the daily scheduler. Five of these commands are duplicated on function keys active in this screen.

To-Do   Gives you three commands for working with items on your To-Do list. One of these commands is duplicated on a function key.

Controls   Gives you four customizing commands; three work in the daily schedule, and the fourth toggles the wide display on and off.

The menu map specific for the Appointment Scheduler is shown in Figure 11.2.

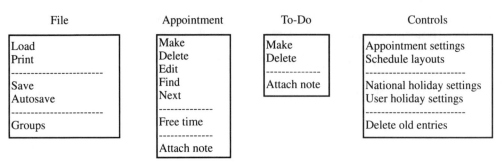

File	Appointment	To-Do	Controls
Load	Make	Make	Appointment settings
Print	Delete	Delete	Schedule layouts
----------------------	Edit	--------------	-------------------------
Save	Find	Attach note	National holiday settings
Autosave	Next		User holiday settings
----------------------	--------------		-------------------------
Groups	Free time		Delete old entries

	Attach note		

Figure 11.2. Pull-down menus in the Appointment Scheduler

You can set the amount of time Autosave will save in the schedule:

Press: [Alt]-[F]-[A]

This opens the Autosave window, as shown in Figure 11.3.

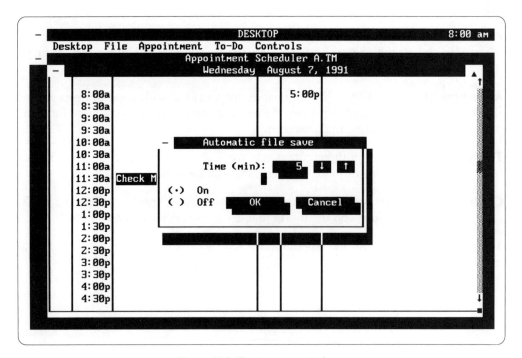

Figure 11.3. The Autosave window.

Active Function Keys

You can find all ten function keys defined at the bottom of your screen:

[F1] Help   Opens the general Help screen.

[F2] Index   Opens the Help index.

[F3] Exit   Exits the Scheduler screen and returns you to your previous work.

[F4] Day   Toggles the daily schedule on and off.

[F5] Week   Toggles the weekly schedule on and off (see Figure 11.4).

[F6] Month   Toggles the monthly schedule on and off.

[F7] To Do   Toggles the To Do list on and off.

[F8] Usage   Shows your current schedule usage (see Figure 11.5).

[F9] Switch   Switches to the next active module.

[F10] Menu   Activates the top menu bar.

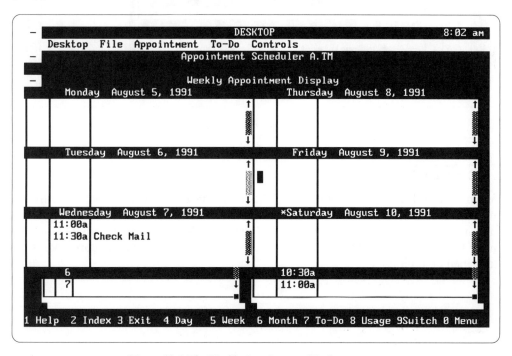

Figure 11.4. The Weekly Appointment Display screen.

These commands will work only after you've inserted appointments in a schedule.

When you press [F8], your screen displays the Time Usage Graph, which shows weekly appointments in graph form, so you can see if there is any free time or conflicts. It is shown in Figure 11.5.

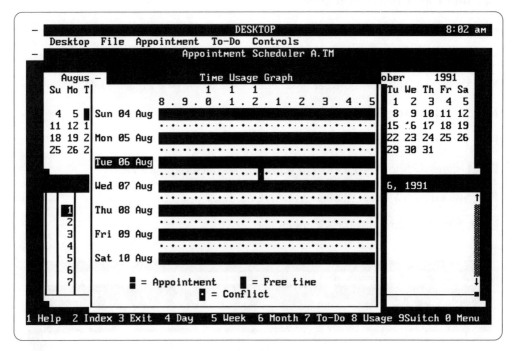

Figure 11.5. The Time Usage graph

THE CALENDAR

When you call up the Appointment Scheduler, the calendar displays the current month and highlights the current day. To make the calendar active, press [Tab] until the name of the month and year are highlighted in the upper-right corner. You can move to other days, months, and even years in the calendar using the cursor keys as described in Table 11.1.

Action	Press	Action	Press
Ahead one day	[⇒]	Back one day	[⇐]
Ahead one week	[⇓]	Back one week	[⇑]
Ahead one month	[PgDn]	Back one month	[PgUp]
Ahead one year	[Ctrl]-[PgDn]	Back one year	[Ctrl]-[PgUp]
Current date [Home]			

Table 11.1. How to change dates in the calendar

As you use these keys to change calendar dates, notice that the date and month change at the top of the calendar. Notice also that the date for the daily schedule changes to match the highlighted calendar date. When you move from one week to the next, the same day of the week will remain highlighted. When you move from one month or year to the next, the same date will remain highlighted. Return to the current date before you begin experimenting with appointments:

Press: [Home]

WORKING IN THE DAILY SCHEDULER

The Daily Scheduler is on the right side of the Appointment Schedule window. It is the core of the Appointment Scheduler.

Once you've selected a date to work with, switch to the daily schedule:

Press: [Tab] eight times

Once the daily schedule appears, expand it to full-screen size:

Press: [Alt]-[Spacebar]

Press: [X]

When maximized, the daily schedule shows the range of times, on the half-hour, between 8:30 and 5:00.

Making an Appointment

The easiest way to make an appointment is to highlight the appointment time slot and press [Enter]. For example, suppose you want to check your mail at 11:30 every morning:

Highlight: 11:30a

Press: [Enter]

This opens the Make Appointment window, which looks Figure 11.6.

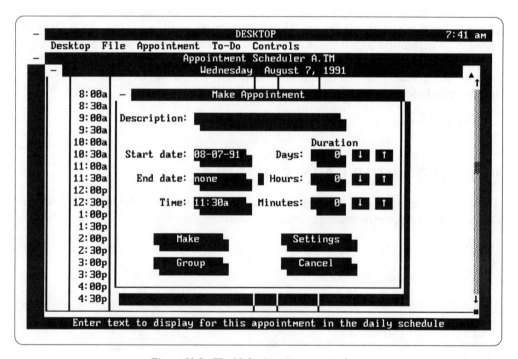

Figure 11.3. The Make Appointment window

You can also open this menu using the *Make Appointment* command on the Appointment menu by pressing [Alt]-[A]-[M].

The selected date and time are displayed at the top of the window. You can find your cursor in the Note field. This is where the text that shows in the Daily Scheduler time slot is typed. For this example:

Type: Check Mail

Press: [Enter] eight times

This moves you through the eight options on this screen and selects the *OK* command. You can also press [Tab] to move through the options on this screen. Once the command *Make* is highlighted:

Press: [Enter]

This inserts the new appointment in your schedule, as shown in Figure 11.7.

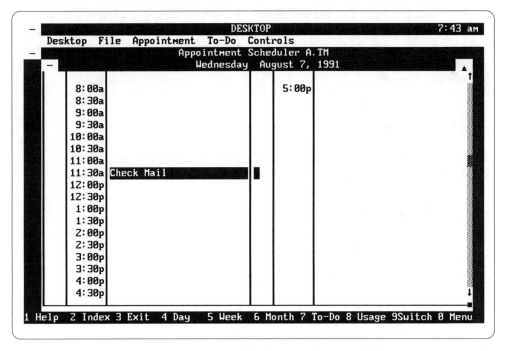

–	DESKTOP	7:43 am

Desktop   File   Appointment   To-Do   Controls

–   Appointment Scheduler A. TM
      –   Wednesday   August 7, 1991

```
 8:00a                              5:00p
 8:30a
 9:00a
 9:30a
10:00a
10:30a
11:00a
11:30a Check Mail                    ▌
12:00p
12:30p
 1:00p
 1:30p
 2:00p
 2:30p
 3:00p
 3:30p
 4:00p
 4:30p
```

1 Help   2 Index 3 Exit   4 Day   5 Week   6 Month 7 To-Do 8 Usage 9Switch 0 Menu

Figure 11.7. Your new appointment inserted

Alarms

Alarms alert you to pending appointments as well as to other activities you've logged into your schedule. A simple alarm displays the appointment message on your screen at the starting time of the appointment. You can set an alarm to give you advance warnings of five or ten minutes.

The musical note denotes that an alarm has been set.

When the appointment time arrives, the message *check mail* appears on your screen along with two options: Snooze and OK. Pressing [Enter] accepts OK and removes the message from your screen for good. Selecting Snooze also removes the message from your screen, but it will return in five minutes, much like a snooze alarm on a clock. The message will keep reappearing every five minutes until you select OK.

Now let's take a closer look at the important commands in the Make Appointment window.

The times are self-explanatory. This is where you set the starting and stopping times for your appointments. The starting time is important when you want to schedule the alarm to appear on your screen. The stopping time is important when you want to make sure you've blocked out enough time for the appointment, and don't want any conflicts. The two important commands in the Make Appointment window are *Settings* and *Group*.

Special Settings

When you insert an appointment, you can attach special settings to it. First, open the Special Appointment Settings window, then the Make Appointment window:

> **Press:** [Alt]-[A]

> **Press:** [Enter]

When the Make Appointment window appears:

> **Press:** [Alt]-[S]

Your screen should change to look like Figure 11.8.

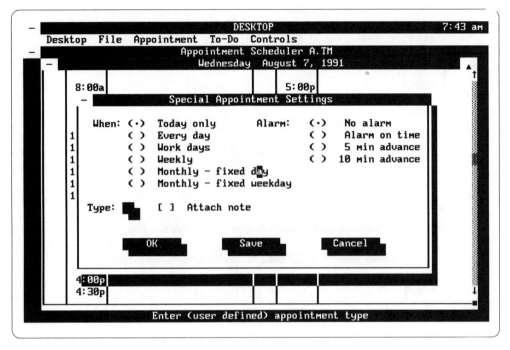

Figure 11.8. The Special Appointment Settings box

These settings let you determine how often the appointment will serve, whether an alarm should be attached, how much advance warning you'll get with the alarm, and the type of appointment (personal, business, social, and so on).

Once you've selected the settings you want to use, close the Special Appointment Settings box and the Make Appointment screen by pressing [Esc] twice.

Using Groups

The concept of groups applies to personal computers that are linked on a network and want to share the same appointments as a group. Before you can use the *Group* command in the Make Appointment box, you must establish a group. Use the *Group* command on the File pull-down menu to do this.

> **Press:** [Alt]-[F]-[G]

This opens the Subscribe to a Group window, as shown in Figure 11.9.

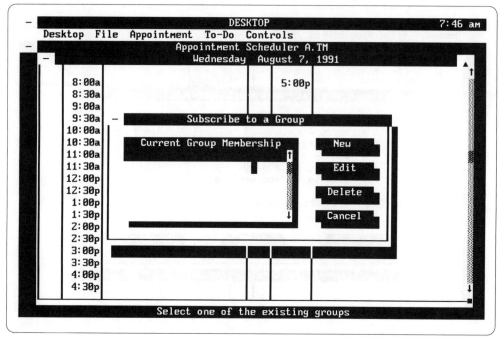

Figure 11.9. The Current Group Membership window

To insert the name of a group:

Press: [Alt]-[N]

This executes the *New* command to open the Group Membership window, as shown in Figure 11.10.

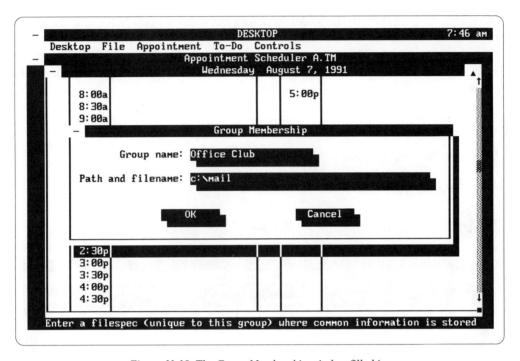

Figure 11.10. The Group Membership window filled in

To insert the group name "Office Club," for instance,

> **Type:** Office Club

> **Press:** [Enter]

This inserts the group name characters and moves your cursor to the second field, Path and Filename. For an appointment to be shared on a network, you must declare the network directory

> **Type:** C:\MAIL

> **Press:** [Enter] twice

This inserts the network directory, accepts it, and closes the Group Membership window.

Now when you go back to the Make Appointment window, you can access the group *Office Club* to share an appointment.

First, highlight the appointment you want to share, then open the Make Appointment window:

       Press: [Alt]-[A]-{M]

Next open the Select Group window:

       Press: [Alt]-[G]

The Select Group window is shown in Figure 11.11.

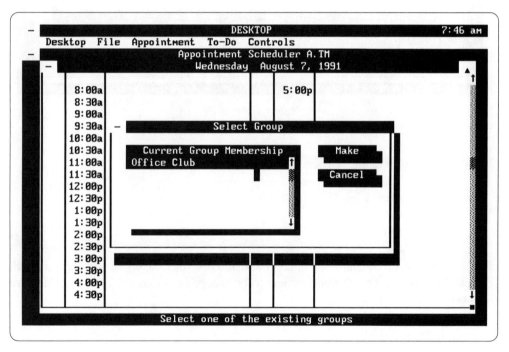

Figure 11.11. The Select Group window

Highlight the group you want to use and press [Enter]. Since there is only one group in the window:

       Press: [Enter]

The Select Group window disappears and a duplicate time slot appears for the appointment time. This means it is being shared.

You don't share all appointments on a schedule when you insert a group appointment, only the one selected to be shared.

Attaching a Note

You can attach a note to an appointment if you need additional information. For example, this could be a list of people attending a meeting and what their role will be, the minutes of the meeting, or an agenda. When the appointment time arrives, the Notepads Editor screen appears and displays the text of the note.

You can create a note for an appointment by using the *Attach Note* command on the Appointment or To-Do pull-down menus, or by toggling on the option in the Make Appointment screen.

All of these move you directly to the Notepads dialog box. The program will create the first part of the note for you by automatically inserting the date and time. The filename will be the same as in the Appointment Schedule you're using. Next, the program assigns a three-digit number as the extension. The first note for the current appointment schedule will be given the extension .001, the second note .002, and so on, up to 999 notes for each appointment schedule. (At least, that's the way it's supposed to work, though I've had notes begin with extension numbers higher than .001.)

When PC Tools has inserted the complete filename, you'll move into the Notepads Editor screen. PC Tools then inserts the date and time information of the appointment at the beginning of the note. The note for the check-mail appointment is shown in Figure 11.12.

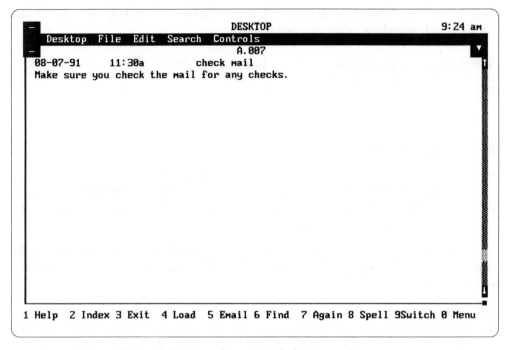

Figure 11.12. A sample note attached to an appointment

After saving the note files, you'll automatically return to the Appointment Schedule screen, not Desktop. Notice that the letter N has been inserted to the left of the appointment time slot. This means a note has been attached to the appointment.

The second way you can create a note is to attach it to an already existing appointment. The easiest way to do this is to highlight the appointment in the Daily Schedule and press [F6]. You can also press [Enter] and select Alter Note or use the menu commands [Alt]-[A]-[A]. This executes the *Attach Note* command on the pull-down menu. This begins the process whereby the program creates the note file and leaves you in the Notepads Editor screen.

Finding Appointment Information

There are two ways to find an appointment in a schedule: the *Find* and *Next* commands on the Appointment pull-down menu.

To find a specific appointment:

> **Press:** [Alt]-[A]-[F]

This opens the Find Appointment box, as shown in Figure 11.13.

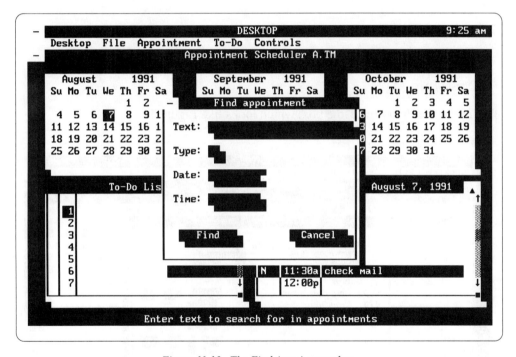

Figure 11.13. The Find Appointment box

The Find Appointment box lets you find an appointment by specifying some information about the appointment. You can search for text in the name of the appointment, for the type of appointment (P or B), for the suspected date of the appointment, or for the suspected time of the appointment.

This box lets you insert part or all of the text you're looking for, as well as the type, date, and time of the appointment. Once you enter information into this box and press [Enter], the program looks for the first entry that matches the information you've entered.

The more specific you are when entering information, the better your chances of finding the appointment you want. The less specific you are, the more appointments you'll have to review before finding the right one. If the first appointment you find is not the one you're looking for:

Press: [Alt]-[A]-[N]

This executes the *Next* command on the Appointment pull-down menu, and resumes the search according to the information you've inserted most recently into the Find Appointment box.

Searching for Free Time

You can find out what free time you have in a day by searching for free time.

Press: [Alt]-[A]-[F]

This opens the Find Free Time box, which looks like Figure 11.14.

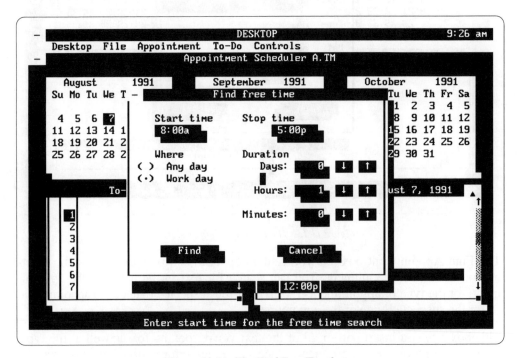

Figure 11.14. The Find Free Time box

You can specify the range of start and stop times as well as days of the week that you want to use to narrow your search. You can also specify the amount of free time you want to search for using fields for days, hours, and minutes.

Move through each selection, set the parameters you want to use, then select *Find*. This takes you to the first empty time slot for the current day. You can continue searching for free time until you find a slot you want to use. You'll find all your appointments, free time, and any conflicts marked on these time lines.

Printing a Schedule

To print a copy of the current appointment schedule to your printer or a disk file:

Press: [Alt]-[F]-[P]

This opens the Print box, which looks like Figure 11.15.

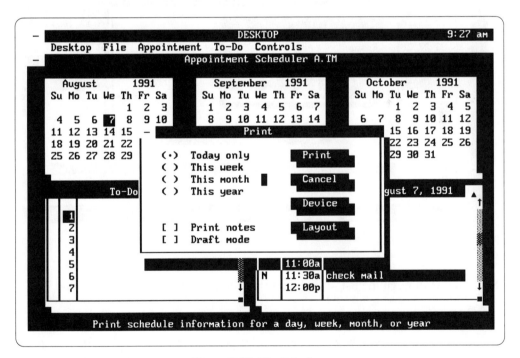

Figure 11.15. The Print box

You can print out the day's schedule, or the schedule for any of the other standard ranges of time, such as week, month, and year. You can also opt to print notes along with your schedule, and determine whether to print in draft (light) mode or nondraft (standard) mode.

To select the device to print through:

Press: [Alt]-[D]

This opens the Select Printer box, as shown in Figure 11.16.

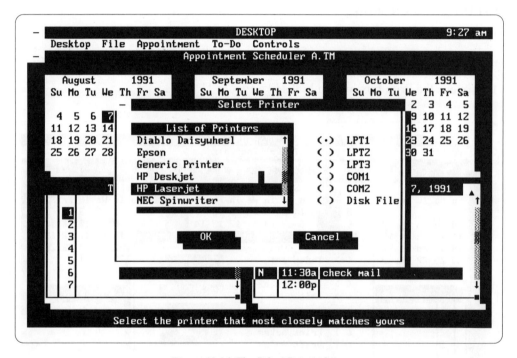

Figure 11.16. The Select Printer box

Scroll down through the list to find the printer you want to use. Once you find it:

Press: [Enter]

Next, select the port you want to use. In most cases, this will be *LPT1* for your printer and *Disk File* when you want to print to a disk. The question of which port to use is determined by your computer configuration.

Once you've selected the printer and port you want to use, return to the Print box by highlighting *OK* and:

Press: [Enter]

Now, view the layout controls:

Press: [Alt]-[L]

This opens the Schedule Printout Options, as shown in Figure 11.17.

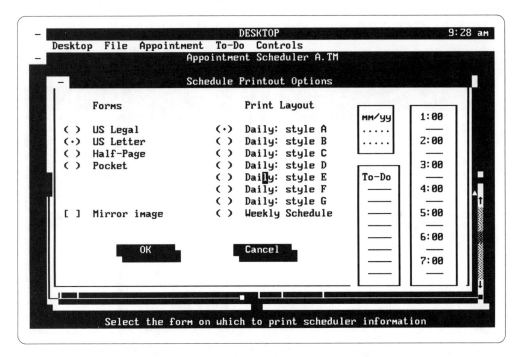

Figure 11.17. The Schedule Printout Options box

This screen lets you select one of four forms to use, one of eight layouts, and whether you want a mirror image printed.

You can view the arrangement of each layout on the right side of the Print Layout screen. Just highlight the name of the layout you're interested in—for example, *Daily: Style D*—and the layout of that style will appear on the right side.

A mirror image exchanges information on the right side of the printout with information on the left.

USING THE TO-DO LIST

The third feature on the full version of the Appointment Schedule screen is the To-Do list. This displays a list of reminders. You can display this list when you first load the Desktop Manager using the /RA switch.

Inserting Items

To insert an item in the To-Do list, first make the list active by pressing [Tab] until *To-Do List* is highlighted. If you're inserting the first item, press [Enter]. This opens the New To-Do Entry box, which looks like Figure 11.18.

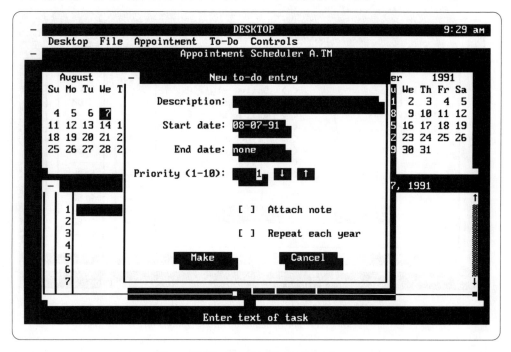

Figure 11.18. The New To-Do Entry box

You'll find the cursor in the Note field. The current date appears as the *Start Date,* A priority of 1 will be assigned automatically, since this is the first item you've inserted into the list. When you have entered more than one item into the list you can display them according to priority.

You can attach a note to any item on the list, just as you can attach a note to any appointment. When you attach a note to an item on the To-Do list, the letter *N* will precede the item on the list.

You can also repeat an item each year; for example, to remind you of birthdays and anniversaries.

For this example, create several items to do:

Type: Call Henry Holt

Press: [Enter]

Press: [Tab] five times

This skips over the fields that are not to be changed and moves you to *Make*.

Press: [Enter]

The box will disappear, and your screen should look something like Figure 11.19.

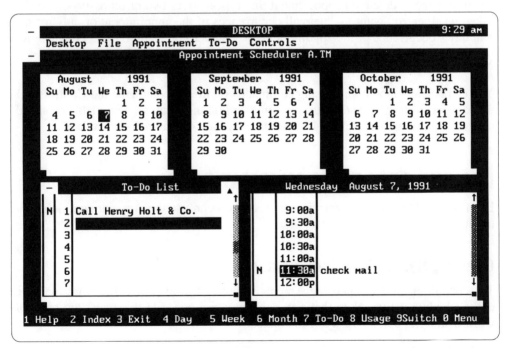

Figure 11.19. First item in To-Do list

Editing and Deleting Items

To edit or delete an item on the list, highlight the item:

   Press: [Enter]

To complete the editing, press one of following four keys:

Delete   Deletes the item from the list.

Edit   Opens the New To-Do Entry box, displaying settings for the high-
                  lighted item. This lets you change any part of the item. If you attach
                  a note and later edit the item and toggle off *Attach Note*, the note file
                  will remain on disk and should be deleted.

Alter Note   Alters the text in a note attached to a To-Do item.

Cancel   Cancels any changes you want to make to an item.

When you try to delete an appointment that repeats over two or more days, you'll be
asked whether you want to delete all occurrences of the appointment or only the current day's occurrence of the appointment, or whether you want to cancel the deletion.

You can also edit appointments using the Appointment pull-down menu.

You can delete appointments using commands on the Appointment and Controls pull-
down menus. The *Delete Old Entries* command on the Controls menu lets you specify
a date; the program will delete all appointments that were set before that date.

LOADING PROGRAMS AUTOMATICALLY

Even if you don't budget your time closely, you can use the Appointment Scheduler
to run specific programs at preset times.

Opening Notepads Automatically

To schedule a time to open the Notepads screen and display a file, first make the
daily schedule active. Note that you can't create a new file this way, you can only
work with a file that's already been created.

Highlight the time you want the Notepads Editor to open, and press a bar symbol (|),
then enter the name of the file you want to appear in the Editor screen. On most keyboards, you can insert the bar symbol by pressing [Shift]-[\].

Next, specify the path of the file if it's not in the default path as shown in the Notepads dialog box.

For example, to open the file DOWOP.TXT in the PCTOOLS directory at 10 A.M., begin in the daily schedule:

Highlight: 10:00a

Type: | DOWOP.TXT (the space between the bar and text is optional).

Press: [Enter]

This opens the Make Appointment box. Here you can set other parameters such as a five-minute warning that Notepads is about to appear.

Once you set the time a program is to appear, it will appear in the daily schedule like any other appointment, but it will be indicated with a bar symbol.

If you want to display a warning message that the Notepads Editor screen is about to appear, place the message before the bar:

Type: Here comes DOWOP | DOWOP.TXT

When the warning time arrives, you'll see the message: `Here comes DOWOP`

Loading an Outside Application

You can load an outside application the same way you opened the Notepads Editor screen. If you want to spend an hour a day putting data into a database, you can schedule the time of day when the Appointment Scheduler will load your database management program and the specific file you want to work with.

To load dBASE at 2 P.M. every day, open the Appointment Scheduler and move to the daily schedule.

Highlight: 2:00p

Type: load data! | <cmd>1:00 dbase

You should recognize most of the commands in this example. The message text comes first, then the bar, then the name of the file that loads the program you want to use. The program filename must end with the extension .BAT, .COM, or .EXE. The file must be in your path, or you must specify its path as part of the filename.

The syntax of this appointment also borrows from the PC Tools macro language. The new command, *<cmd>1:00,* gives PC Tools one minute to bail out and call the dBASE filename from DOS. You need this much time at the very minimum, or the command will not work.

When 2:00 P.M. rolls around every day, the Appointment Scheduler passes the filename to DOS and loads the program, if you've specified a valid filename. If you don't specify a filename to load, the program will automatically default to the Notepads Editor screen and load the program in that module.

You're given room for only twenty-four characters of text in an appointment slot, which isn't very much. If you don't have enough room to type in all the information—the warning message, the filename, the current path—you can write the text in a batch file in your root directory and then run the batch file as the program to run in your appointment.

Using a Batch File to Run Programs

A batch file is a simple text file containing DOS commands. You can run a batch program as well as .COM and .EXE programs in Appointments. This is a great help when you want to run a program that's not on your path, or a program that can parse the DOS command line for switches or a specific filename.

You can use the Notepads Editor to create the batch file; just make sure you don't insert any control characters and that you save the file in ASCII mode. For example, suppose you want to load the dBASE program at 2:00 P.M. every day and enter data in the database file MYDATA.DBF. Assume your dBASE program file is called DBASE.COM and that it's not on your path, but in a first-level directory called C:\DBASE. The database file MYDATA.DBF is in the path C:\DBASE\DATA. To open the program and the file, you insert this line into a simple ASCII text file:

Type: | <cmd>1:00 C:\DBASE\DBASE C:\DBASE\DATA MYDATA.DBF

The macro command *<cmd>1:00>* delays the call for one minute, as required by the PC Tools program. The first group of commands tells the Appointment Scheduler to search the DBASE directory off the root for the executable file DBASE. The second group of commands is interpreted solely by the dBASE program, which searches for a file MYDATA.DBF in the path DBASE\DATA off the root directory.

You can precede this appointment with a message by placing the message text before the bar.

USING MACROS WITH THE APPOINTMENT SCHEDULER

When used in conjunction with macros, the Appointment Scheduler can also be used as a timer to do other things you want done on your computer at specific times.

This is such a useful technique, PC Tools provides a sample macro you'll probably want to use often if you have an MCI Mail box. The sample macro is the last example in SAMPLE.PRO. It looks like this:

```
Read MCI mail:
<begdef><ctrlf9><desk>T<enter><cmd>d20:0<enter><esc><esc><enddef>
```

There are eleven commands in this macro. Lets go through them one-by-one.

<begdef>	Begins the string of commands.
<ctrlf9>	Attaches this macro to the keys [Ctrl]-[F9], so that when you press them together, the macro executes.
<desk>	Opens the Desktop Manager if it's been installed in resident mode.
T	Opens the Telecommunications module on the Desktop menu (same as pressing T).
<enter>	Selects the first entry in PHONE.TEL and begins the phone call (same as pressing [Enter]).
<cmd>d20:0	Pauses all activity from your computer for 20 seconds. This lets the script MCI.SCR run long enough to log your computer on to MCI Mail and check your mailbox. If it finds any mail, it downloads the messages and saves them to disk regardless of how long it takes. Each command must play out before the next one is called. Once you start downloading mail, you don't have to worry about inserting any more delays.
<enter>	Inserts a carriage return.
<esc>	This appears twice and is designed to unload the Desktop Manager from your screen if you aren't using background communications. The first time it returns you to the Desktop menu. The second time it unloads the Desktop Manager from your screen.
<enddef>	Ends the string of commands.

This macro is helpful when running your communications in background. It loads the Desktop Manager, opens the Telecommunications screen, makes a call to MCI Mail using the MCI.SCR, reads your mailbox and downloads the messages, saves them to disk, then exits MCI Mail, Telecommunications, and the Desktop Manager—all in the background.

Once you've activated this macro, all you need to do is press [Ctrl]-[F9] to download your MCI Mail box, while you continue working in other things.

Read Chapter 15 describing the Macro Editor for more information about how you can view, edit, activate, and deactivate this and other macros.

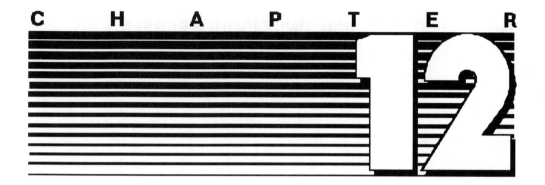

CHAPTER

12

THE TELECOMMUNICATIONS MODULE

T he information for working in the Telecommunications module has been divided into three chapters. This chapter describes basic aspects of computer communications and basic features of the Telecommunications module. Chapter 13 provides working examples about the Telecommunications module. Chapter 14 describes telecommunications using the PC Tools script programming language.

Telecommunications is the ability to communicate electronically over wire and broadcast transmissions. With telecommunications you can communicate with a computer halfway around the world or one on the desk next to yours. To do this you need a communications software program, a modem, and an active telephone line.

The Telecommunications module is a communications program. It facilitates your telecommunications ability by keeping track of all the activities going on during a call.

THE TELECOMMUNICATIONS MODULE SCREEN

To open the Telecommunications menu from the Desktop menu:

Press: [Enter]

Press: [T]

If you're working in another module:

Press: [Alt]-[D]-[T]

Either of these will open the Telecommunications menu, which gives you four choices:

Modem Telecommunications	Lets you send and receive messages directly with a modem.
Electronic Mail	Lets you check electronic mail activity.
Send a Fax	Lets you send and receive faxes using a fax board that subscribes to the Intel standard.
Check the Fax Log	Displays entries in your fax log directory.

MODEM TELECOMMUNICATIONS

To open Modem Telecommunications:

Press: [Enter]

This moves you directly into the default phonebook called PHONE.TEL.

> If someone else has already created another phonebook with the .TEL extension, you'll see the Telecommunications dialog box first, which lets you select which phonebook file you want to work with. This dialog box filters for files ending with .TEL.

When the Telecommunications screen appears for the first time, it resembles Figure 12.1.

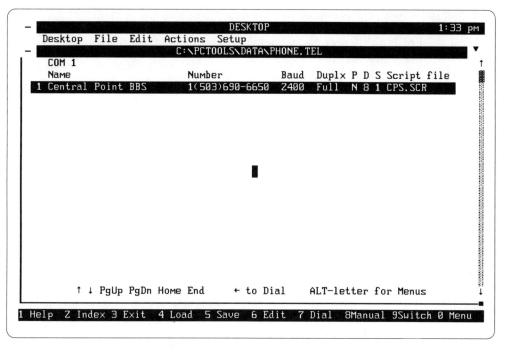

Figure 12.1. The default phonebook PHONE.TEL

The label COM1 on the top-left side shows you're connected to the COM1 serial port. PHONE.TEL on the right side shows the phonebook you're viewing.

When you view this screen for the first time, four default phonebook entries will appear: MCI Mail, EasyLink (CompuServe's mail program), CompuServe, and the Central Point Software bulletin board.

The bottom line of the screen tells you how you select phonebook entries, how to make a call, and how to access menus.

The light bar highlights the entry to be selected for a call. To move down or up one entry at a time, press the arrow keys. When you add several entries you can move around the phonebook with [PgUp], [PgDn], [End], and [Home]. You can also type the number displayed to the left of the entry you want to use.

To make a call, highlight the entry to be called and press [Enter].

As in other Desktop modules, to activate the top menu bar, you press [Alt] or [F10].

The four pull-down menus unique to the Telecommunications module are:

File   Loads a different phonebook and saves the current phonebook if you've made any changes.

Edit   Creates, edits, and deletes entries in the phonebook you're viewing.

Actions   Dials a phone number either automatically or manually, and hangs up a finished phone connection.

Setup   Sets up your modem configuration and toggles the size of your On-Line screen after you've established a connection with another computer.

Figure 12.2 shows a menu map of the Telecommunications pull-down menu.

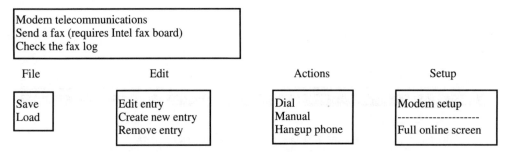

Figure 12.2. Menu map for the Telecommunications module

All ten function keys have assignments in the Telecommunications screen:

[F1] Help   Opens the general Help screen.

[F2] Index   Opens the Help index.

[F3] Exit   Exits the Telecommunications screen, returning you to your previous work.

[F4] Load   Opens the Telecommunications dialog box and lets you load another phonebook.

[F5] Save   Saves the current phonebook to the disk file of the same name or a different name.

[F6] Edit   Opens the Edit Phone Directory window, and lets you create a new entry or edit an existing entry.

[F7] Dial   Automatically dials the highlighted entry number.

304

[F8] Manual   Opens the On-Line screen, which lets you communicate with another computer connected to yours via a hard-wire link (minimum three-wire cable containing a null modem).

[F9] Switch   Switches you between active windows.

[F10] Menu   Activates the top menu bar.

Function keys F4 through F8 contain unique communications commands, explained in detail in the next chapter.

SETTING UP YOUR MODEM

You should have no trouble making modem settings, as the program does most of the work for you.

    Press: [Alt]-[S]-[M]

This opens the Modem Setup window, which for my modem looks like Figure 12.3.

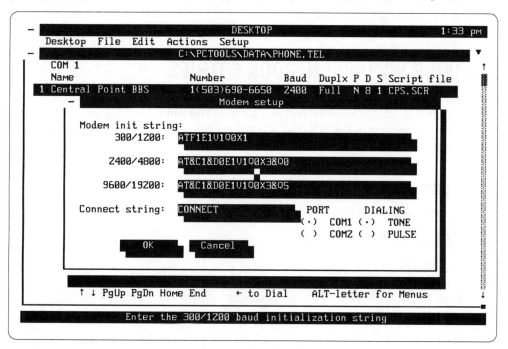

Figure 12.3. The Modem Setup window

This screen lets you tell PC Tools the speed of your modem, so that it will assign the proper modem-initialization string. To set the speed of your modem, highlight the proper baud-rate category and press [Enter]. You can move forward through fields by pressing [Tab], and backward by pressing [Shift]-[Tab].

Once you've selected an entry, to accept it:

> **Press:** [Tab]

> **Press:** [Enter]

If you're not using a Hayes-compatible modem, highlight the Connect field and type the string of characters specific to your modem. You should be able to find this string of characters printed in the modem's documentation. If you can't, call the modem manufacturer customer support number. Once you've typed the string:

> **Highlight:** OK

> **Press:** [Enter]

Once you enter a string, the Modem Setup window will close, and you'll be returned to the Telecommunications window.

WORKING WITH PHONEBOOK ENTRIES

A phonebook entry *must* contain the number you want to call and the communications parameters you've selected for the number. You can add additional information later, such as whose number it is and other ways you might want to contact the person or company. You can create new entries, change or edit them, and delete them.

Editing an Entry

Edit the first entry in PHONE.TEL, as shown in Figure 12.1. To begin the edit:

> **Highlight:** MCI Mail

> **Press:** [F6]

This opens the Edit Phone Directory window, as shown in Figure 12.4.

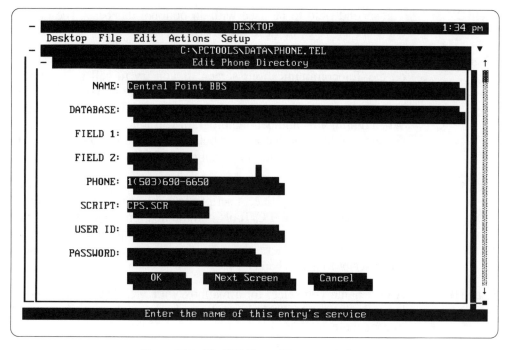

Figure 12.4. The Edit Phone Directory window

There are two groups of settings in this window. The top group lets you insert characters and define the entry. The bottom group contains eleven communications parameters that control the way communications are sent and received by your computer. Some of these are crucial, such as the modem and port settings; others have a less dramatic effect, such as end-of-line and parity settings. The default settings for the four default entries are recommended, although you might have to adjust the modem and communication port settings.

Defining an Entry

The eight fields in this screen let you define an entry:

Name   The name of the person or company. You can enter up to 54 characters here. The name will be displayed on the Telecommunications screen.

Database   The database you want to use to provide numbers for your call.

Field 1   The first field to be used with an optional database. The default entry is MCI_ID, a field in TELECOM.DBF.

Field 2	The second field to be used with an optional database. The default entry is *Fax_Telex* in the TELECOM.DBF.
Phone	The phone number. This is the only required entry, and it also shows on the Telecommunications screen. If you try to call an entry that doesn't have a phone number, PC Tools will prompt you to enter the number manually. You can enter up to twenty-five characters here. When dialing this number, the program will ignore any spaces, dashes, and parentheses that appear between numbers. For example, 1-555-528-1040 will do the same thing as 15555281040.
Script	The script file assigned to this entry. This shows on the far right of each phonebook entry line. A script file is a text file containing commands specific to the PC Tools communication program that automate many of the routine tasks of communicating. You can enter up to twelve characters here, the limit of a filename. You'll learn more about script files in Chapter 14.
User ID	A user name you select for a mailbox with MCI Mail. You need to log in both your MCI Mail user ID and password whenever you try to connect to MCI Mail.
Password	A password assigned to your MCI Mail account. When you type in your password, the characters will not appear.

Communications Parameters

There are eleven communications parameters that control the way data is sent and received by your computer. To view and change these parameters, you must open up the second Edit Phone Directory screen while viewing the first one. To do this:

Press: [Alt]-[N]

Or press [Tab] to highlight the command *Next Screen,* then press [Enter].

The second Edit Phone Directory screen is shown in Figure 12.5.

Figure 12.5. The second Edit Phone Directory screen

Baud Rate   The speed rate of data transmission: one baud equals one bit per second. A 1200 baud rate means that 1,200 bits per second can be transmitted.

Parity   Sets the parity bit, used to verify correct communications. The most popular setting is *Even*. It is displayed on the Telecommunications screen under *P.*

Terminal   You can use one of four terminal displays:

1. TTY (for TeleTYpe), the original and simplest screen, displays characters and numbers only.

2. ANSI (American National Standard Institute) displays the full range of ASCII characters.

3. VT100 emulates the Digital Equipment Corp. (DEC) VT100 terminal

4. VT52 emulates the DEC VT52 terminal.

Flow Control   Also called *handshaking,* the receiving computer determines when it can receive data and how much data it wants. If you switch XON/XOFF on, the computer receiving data controls the flow of data by sending an XON signal when it wants to receive data, and an XOFF signal when it wants a computer to stop sending data. In this way, the receiving computer digests information without becoming overloaded. *On* is the most popular setting.

EOL Receive   *Receive* is an *End-of-Line parameter.* It determines how line feed (LF) and carriage-return (CR) characters are received by your computer. How you set it depends on the computer you're communicating with. In most cases, you should set Receive to *None.*

EOL Send   *Send* is also an *End-of-Line parameter.* It determines how line-feed and carriage-return characters are sent by your computer. If you intend to send messages created in the Notepads Editor through MCI Mail, you should set Send to *Strip LF.* This strips line feed characters from your messages. If you do not select *Strip LF,* single-spaced messages will be sent double-spaced.

Data-Bits   Sets a byte to hold either seven or eight bits of data. If you're using any sort of parity, one bit is reserved for checking parity, so you should switch data bits to seven. If you're not using any parity, then switch to eight data bits. When you're using seven data bits, you can only transmit and receive the lower 128 characters of the ASCII character set. The number of data-bits is displayed on the Telecommunications screen under *D.*

Stop-Bits   Determines the end-of-character bit. Most computers use 1, but some use 2.

Duplex   Controls the transmission of data. Full-duplex instructs the computer you're connected with to send back all the characters you send it; half-duplex does not send back the characters. If you see two characters on your screen for every one character you type, you should switch to half-duplex. If you don't see any characters on your screen when you type a character, you should switch to full-duplex.

When you communicate with an e-mail service like MCI Mail, or a bulletin board service such as CompuServe and Central Point Software BBS, the ideal PDS settings are E71 for even parity, seven data bits, and one stop bit. When you communicate with another computer over a hardware connection using a null modem, the ideal PDS setting is probably N81 for no parity, eight data bits, and one stop bit.

Most of your communications with specific entries won't change until you buy new equipment.

Changing an Entry

To learn how to change a phonebook entry, let's customize the entry for MCI Mail. If you're a subscriber to MCI, you should use your own local MCI phone number. If you're not an MCI subscriber, experiment by calling the Central Point BBS or a local BBS number.

If the Edit Phone Directory box is not showing:

> **Press:** [F6]
>
> **Type:** MCI Mail
>
> **Press:** [Enter]
>
> **Type:** 1-800-234-6245 (or a local bulletin board number instead).
>
> **Press:** [Enter] seven times

This moves you over the various Character field entries and onto the first parameter, Terminal. For most of your purposes on a personal computer, the two most common types of terminals, ANSI and TTY, will serve. I prefer ANSI.

To accept ANSI:

> **Press:** [⇓]
>
> **Press:** [Enter]

This moves you to the second parameter, Receive:

> **Select:** NONE
>
> **Press:** [Enter]
>
> **Select:** STRIP LF

For Port, you should probably accept COM1, but this depends on your computer setup.

For Duplex, accept Full.

For Dialing, select Tone or Pulse, depending on your phone system.

For Baud, pick the rate that suits your modem.

For Parity, pick Even.

For Data-bits, pick 7.

For Stop-bits, pick 1.

Set Flow Control to XON.

When you've picked the last setting, highlight *Accept:*

> **Press:** [Enter]

To accept all the changes you've made, insert them in the current phonebook, and close the Edit Phone Directory box:

> **Press:** [Enter]

If you want to go back and change any of the settings, you can open the box, press [Tab] to go to the setting you want to change, make the change, and then press [A] to select Accept. Don't press [A] unless you're on a communications parameter setting, otherwise you'll enter the letter *a* in one of the character fields. If you exit the screen by pressing [Esc] or [C] for Cancel without selecting ACCEPT, none of your changes will be accepted.

As soon as the Edit Phone Directory box closes, the new entry should be first one on the Telecommunications screen. Its PDS settings should be E71.

Making a Call

To make a call, turn on your modem, highlight the entry you want to call, and press [Enter] or [F7]. For example, to call your new entry, highlight entry 1:

> **Press:** [1]

> **Press:** [Enter]

The bottom line of the Telecommunications screen should change to read: `Dialing - Press ESC to Cancel`

If your call goes through, the On-Line screen will appear, showing that you have connected with another computer. You can identify this screen when different pull-down menu titles appear on the top line and different commands appear on the bottom two lines of your screen. The middle section will be blank.

Disconnect from the BBS you have signed onto to save subscription and telephone service charges:

Press: [F8]

The message `Disconnecting` will appear at the bottom of the screen for a few seconds, and then you'll return to the Telecommunications screen.

THE ON-LINE SCREEN

The best way to study the On-Line screen is to view it using manual calling. This will allow you to view all the features on the On-Line screen without connecting to another computer, saving you long-distance and subscription charges.

To move onto the On-Line screen, shown in Figure 12.6:

Press: [F8]

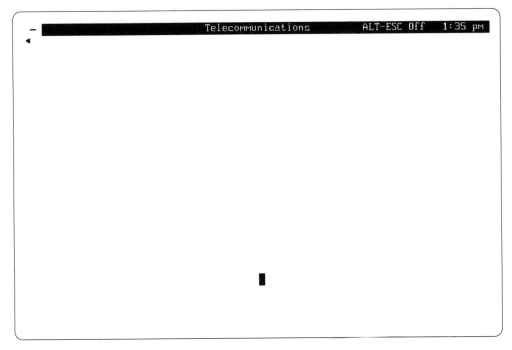

Figure 12.6. The On-Line screen

Regardless of which type of terminal you've set as a parameter, the On-Line screen will always look the same when it first appears.

The top menu bar gives you three unique pull-down menus:

Actions   Hangs up the phone and ends a file transfer.

Receive   Allows you to select ASCII or XMODEM protocols to receive files (you can also press [F6] or [F7], respectively). Use ASCII for simple text files and XMODEM for binary or program files.

Send   Allows you to select either ASCII or XMODEM protocols to send files (for which you can also press [F4] and [F5], respectively).

Notice that only the overtype mode is functional in this screen and that [Del] does not delete characters. To delete characters, place your cursor before the character you want to delete and press [End].

The current time is displayed on the right end of the top line. Just to the left of the time display is the `ALT-ESC Off` label, which indicates that special control of the [Esc] key is turned off. This means when you press [Esc], it will exit the On-Line screen:

Press: [Esc]

You'll return to the Telecommunications screen. However, when you press [Esc] to exit the On-Line screen, you're still logged onto the On-Line screen. You can switch to another phonebook, work in another Desktop module, or switch to PC Shell, but technically the On-Line screen is still your primary screen.

To return to the On-Line screen from the Telecommunications screen:

Press: [Enter]

You can see how you're still tied to the On-Line screen by exiting the Desktop Manager and then returning to it:

Press: [Esc] three times

This should return you to your DOS prompt:

Press: [Ctrl]-[Spacebar]

Press: [T]

This should return you directly to the On-Line screen, bypassing the Telecommunications screen.

You can change the effect of the [Esc] key so that it inserts an *escape character* instead of exiting from the On-Line screen. This can be of value when you communicate with another computer directly and want to send an escape character to the other computer. To make this change, start by viewing the On-Line screen:

Press: [Alt]-[Esc]

Notice that the label on the right end of the top line turns on the ALT-ESC setting. It also removes your access to help. To find out how this change affects the program:

Press: [Esc]

The On-Line screen didn't close. You did insert an escape character, however, even though you can't see it. If you were connected to another computer, you would have sent that character to the other computer.

This works for all keys, not only [Esc]. When ALT-ESC is on, you're operating in what can be called *raw mode*. When you press a key or keys, the scan code assigned by IBM to that key is inserted on your screen and sent to the other computer.

To see what has happened to help:

Press: [F1]

This inserts the letter P. Normally, pressing [F1] opens the Help screen, but when you're operating in raw mode all keys have been assigned scan codes.

When the ALT-ESC is on, the new key assignment to exit the On-Line screen is [Shift]-[Esc], as shown on the second-to-bottom line.

The bottom two lines contain status messages and function-key assignments. There are six items on the second-to-bottom line:

Connected   Shows you're connected to another computer.

Send   Controls the way you send files; applies to the two function-key assignments in this group, [F4] and [F5].

Receive   Controls the way you receive files; applies to the two function-key assignments in this group, [F6] and [F7].

1200 E71　　　　Shows current settings: baud of 1200, even parity, 7 data bits, and 1 stop bit.

FDX　　　　Shows duplex setting: full.

ANSI　　　　Shows type of terminal: ANSI.

All ten function keys have assignments in the On-Line window:

[F1] Help　　　　Opens the general Help screen.

[F2] Index　　　　Opens the Help index.

[F3] Exit　　　　Exits the On-Line screen and returns you to the Telecommunications screen. You will still be logged onto the On-Line screen, until you hang up by pressing [F8].

[F4] ASCII　　　　Opens the Send ASCII dialog box, which lets you select the file you want to send according to the ASCII protocol. This should be reserved for simple text messages only.

[F5] XMODEM　　　　Opens the Send XMODEM dialog box, which lets you select the file you want to send according to the XMODEM protocol. This should be reserved for binary files, or text files containing special control codes.

[F6] ASCII　　　　Opens the Save File to Disk box, where you specify the name of the file you're about to receive. This receives the file according to the ASCII protocol, which is designed for simple ASCII text files. You don't have to be as careful receiving text files as you do receiving binary files. If stray characters are also received, you'll probably notice them immediately. You can later go back into the file you've saved and clean up these characters.

[F7] XMODEM　　　　Opens the Save File to Disk box, where you specify the name of the file you're about to receive. This receives the file according to the XMODEM protocol, which is designed for binary files and heavily formatted text files. Since files received according to the XMODEM protocol must be received precisely, a second box, which shows the progress of the transmission and error checking, appears after you've specified the filename to save.

[F8] Hangup　　　　Hangs up your connection and returns you to the Telecommunications screen. This is the only way to log off of the On-Line screen.

[F9] Switch   Switches you between active windows.

[F10] Menu   Activates the top menu bar.

Once you become familiar with communicating in PC Tools, you can do most of your work with the function keys [F4] through [F7].

Disconnecting

To disconnect from the On-Line screen and return to the Telecommunications screen:

> **Press:** [F8]

Unless you press [F8] every time you want to disconnect from the On-Line screen in either the manual or automatic modes or every time you call up the Telecommunications module, the On-Line screen will appear.

CREATING OTHER PHONEBOOKS

You can create, edit, and delete new phonebooks because they exist as separate disk files. The Telecommunications screen will always display the contents of the phonebook that you were viewing when you last exited the Telecommunications module.

Creating a New phonebook

To create a new phonebook called MY.TEL, view the Telecommunications screen and:

> **Press:** [F4]

When the Communication dialog box opens:

> **Type:** MY

> **Press:** [Enter] twice

This designates the phone-book filename and tells the program to create it as a new file. The .TEL extension is added automatically. If you specify another extension, you must use it each time you want to open that phonebook.

You cannot open more than one phonebook at a time. A new phonebook will replace the old phonebook in the Telecommunications screen.

When MY.TEL first appears on your screen, it will contain no entries, as shown in Figure 12.7.

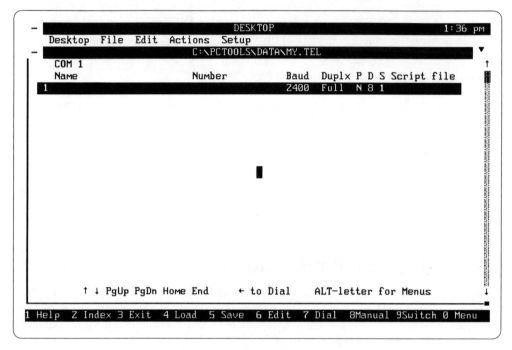

Figure 12.7. A new phonebook without entries

Notice how the necessary communication parameters from the previous phonebook are automatically inserted into the first entry fields. You can now insert new entries and edit them as you did for PHONE.TEL.

If you want to make a call right away:

Press: [Enter]

This opens a box that lets you enter the number you want to call, shown in Figure 12.8.

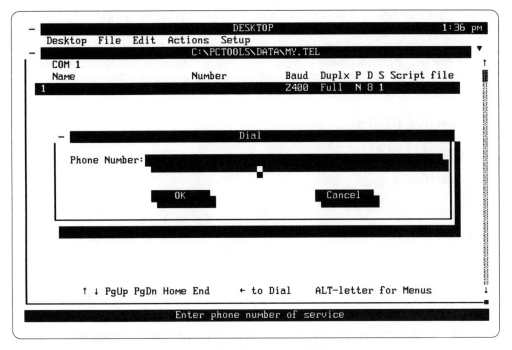

Figure 12.8. The Phone Number Entry box

To dial the number, type it into the Phone Number Entry box and select *Accept*. The number will not be inserted in the current phonebook. You need to insert a new entry or edit an existing entry to record a number.

Deleting a Phonebook

If you want to delete the phonebook MY.TEL, you can use PC Shell and delete the phonebook as a file. You can also open the Communications dialog box, highlight MY.TEL, tab over to DELETE, and press [Enter].

USING TELECOM.DBF

Earlier in this chapter, you edited the first entry in PHONE.TEL either the Edit Phone Directory box to make the changes. You may have noticed the three character fields at the top of this screen: Database, Field 1, and Field 2. These three fields are filled with information from a database program called TELECOM.DBF, supplied with PC Tools Deluxe.

You can use this database to make calls to other phone numbers, especially fax numbers, using the menu-driven interface that appears as part of the MCI.SCR and CIS.SCR files. You can also design your own script files that make calls to this database or to another database of your own design. The best way to understand how to do this is to see how TELECOM.DBF coordinates with the Telecommunications screen. Use the Databases module to open TELECOM.DBF:

Press: [Alt]-[D]-[D]

Type: TELECOM

Press: [Enter]

Now expand the window to full-screen size:

Press: [Alt]-[Spacebar]

Press: [X]

When TELECOM.DBF appears, your screen should look like Figure 12.9.

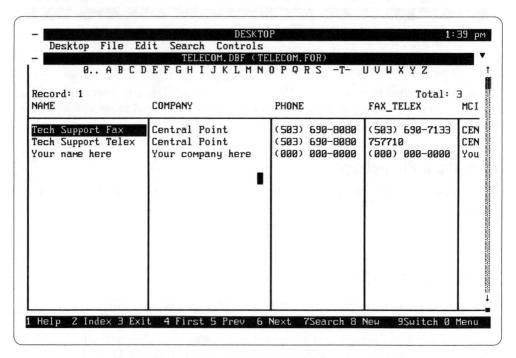

Figure 12.9. Contents of TELECOM.DBF in browse mode

Highlight the entry for Tech Support Fax and switch to edit mode:

Press: [Alt]-[F]-[B]

Your screen should now look like Figure 12.10.

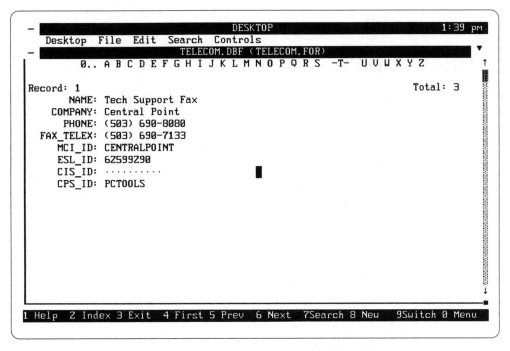

Figure 12.10. Tech Support Fax record in edit mode

The database contains eight fields: one for the name of the department, another for the name of the company, two for voice and fax phone numbers, and four more fields for the three most popular electronic connection services and the Central Point Software bulletin board. Only the CPS_ID field is empty, to be filled in after you log onto the Central Point bulletin board, described in Chapter 13.

To learn how to use this information in phone-book entries, refer back to Figure 12.5, the entry for MCI Mail that you edited. In this figure, the database file contains the path and filename C:\PCTOOLS\TELECOM.DBF, which designates the TELE-COM.DBF as an alternate source for numbers. The Field 1 field is filled with MCI_ID, and the Field 2 field is filled with Fax_Telex. When you call MCI Mail using the MCI.SCR script file, you're given a menu of selections for things to do while logged on to MCI Mail. One of these is to send a message to another MCI

Mail box. When you pick this selection, MCI asks who you want to send the message to, and automatically opens TELECOM.DBF. You can now highlight the entry you want to use in TELECOM.DBF. The MCI.SCR script file then prepares the message for the MCI Mail account number located in the MCI_ID field.

Another selection on the MCI Mail menu is to send an electronic fax message. When you choose this selection, TELECOM.DBF again appears. You pick the record entry you want, the number in the Fax_Telex field is called, and your fax is sent.

ELECTRONIC MAIL

Electronic mail—or e-mail—is a relatively new way of communicating. It's like an electronic post office, except that different companies operate nationwide or international e-mail networks to which computer-users can subscribe. Using e-mail, you can send and receive messages electronically; instead of receiving "paper mail," you can read messages on your computer screen and then save them to disk if you want to.

The second selection on the Desktop Telecommunications menu lets you work with electronic mail. To open this module when the Desktop menu is showing, first open the Telecommunications menu:

Press: [T]

Next, open the Electronic Mail window:

Press: [E]

The Electronic Mail module Inbox screen looks like Figure 12.11. The Outbox and the Sent screens in the Electronic Mail module are very similar to the Inbox screen.

In fact, the same pull-down menus appear in all three screens:

View   Lets you view the contents of your inbox, outbox, and sent box.

Actions   Lets you read your mail and create messages.

Setup   Lets you declare a mail service and set schedules for automatically reading and sending e-mail.

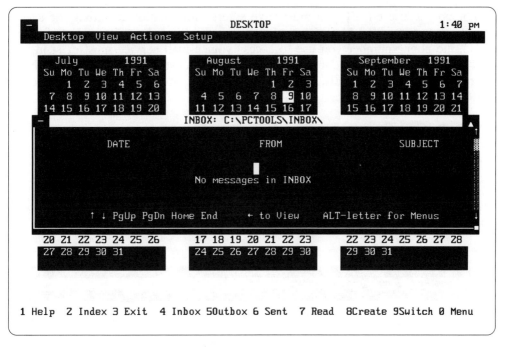

Figure 12.11. The Electronic Mail Inbox window

When the E-mail window is open, you can use these function-key commands:

[F1] Help   Opens context-sensitive help for electronic mail.

[F2] Index   Opens the Help index for electronic mail.

[F3] Exit   Closes the window and returns you to the Desktop main menu.

[F4] Inbox   Checks your inbox for messages you have received.

[F5] Outbox   Checks your outbox for messages you want to send.

[F6] Sent   Checks the sent box for messages you've sent.

[F7] Read   Reads the selected file.

[F8] Create   Lets you create a message to send over your e-mail service.

[F9] Switch   Switches between active Desktop windows.

[F10] Menu   Activates the top menu bar.

To be able to use e-mail, you must have entered information regarding the service you want to use—MCI Mail, CompuServe, EasyLink, or any of a number of others. Also, the phone number you use to access your e-mail service must exist in your PHONE.TEL. For example, to use MCI Mail, you must insert your local MCI Mail number into PHONE.TEL. The Electronic Mail module uses information in PHONE.TEL to place the calls.

To set up a carrier:

> **Press:** [Alt]-[S]

> **Press:** [Enter]

This selects the *Mail Service* command, and opens the Electronic Mail Service, as shown in Figure 12.12.

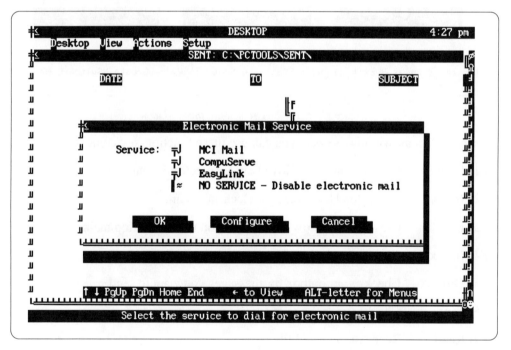

Figure 12.12. The Create Electronic Mail Service window

This screen lets you select one of the e-mail services, or disable the service. Once you've selected a service, open the Configure screen, shown in Figure 12.13.

> **Press:** [Alt]-[C]

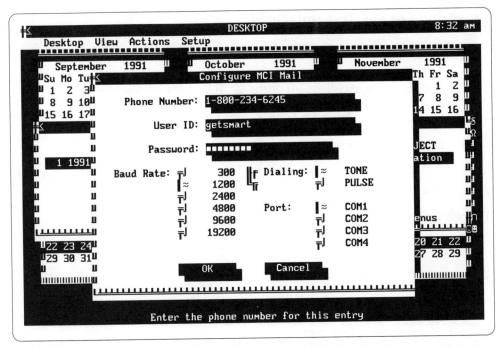

Figure 12.13. The Configure MCI Mail screen

The screens for all the services look alike; the name of the service you're using will appear at the top, where you insert the User ID number and password. Your password will appear as you type it, but will later be camouflaged. You also set your baud rate, type of phone (tone or pulse), and communications port.

FAX TRANSMISSIONS

The Telecommunications module is used to send and receive fax transmissions, if you've installed an acceptable fax board. The two types of boards that can be used with PC Tools are Intel's Connection CoProcessor board and the board from SpectraFax. A fax board from another manufacturer, it might work; if the board is incompatible, you'll receive a Non-CCP status message when you try to send a fax.

Before you can send or receive transmissions over a fax board, you need to install the board in your computer, make the necessary connection to your phone line, and install the software that runs the fax board. How you install the equipment depends upon the type of computer and board you're using. Refer to the instructions that came with your equipment.

Preparing For Fax Transmissions

When you select Telecommunications on the Desktop main menu, you're given three choices:

1. *Modem telecommunications* opens the Telecommunications window.

2. *Send a fax (requires a fax board)* opens the Send Fax Directory screen.

3. *Check the fax log* opens the Fax Directory screen.

Before you can send a fax, you need to configure your Fax Directory the same way you configured your phonebook for standard e-mail communications.

To open the Fax Directory window from the Desktop main menu:

Press: [Alt]-[T]-[S]

Your screen will change to look like Figure 12.14.

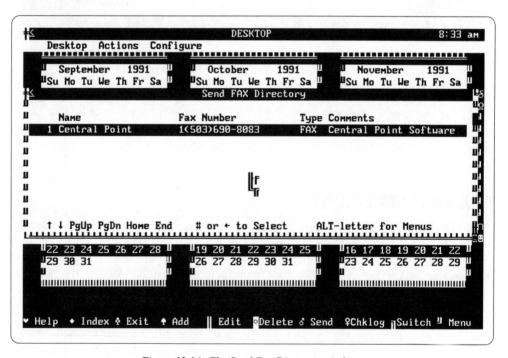

Figure 12.14. The Send Fax Directory window

If you receive an error message that no fax driver has been installed in your fax directory, you can still enter the Fax Directory screen by pressing [Enter].

The ten assignments to the function keys are:

[F1] Help Opens context-sensitive help for fax transmissions.

[F2] Index Opens the Help index for fax transmissions.

[F3] Exit Closes the Fax Directory window and returns you to your previous work.

[F4] Add Adds an entry to the Fax Directory window.

[F5] Edit Edits the highlighted entry.

[F6] Delete Deletes the highlighted entry.

[F7] Send Makes a call and sends a fax message to the number highlighted in the Fax Directory box.

[F8] Chklog Opens the Fax Log so you can check the status of fax messages you've sent and received.

[F9] Switch Switches between active windows.

[F10] Menu Activates the top menu bar. Same as pressing [Alt].

You're given two pull-down menus, shown in Figure 12.15, to use while working with fax transmissions:

Actions Lets you add, edit, and delete entries in your Fax Directory, send messages, and check your fax log.

Configure Lets you enter or set the following parameters:

    Fax Drive Selects the drive that contains the fax messages you want to send.

    Page Length Selects the page length for a fax message. If it's only a short message and the receiver has a fax machine that prints out paper messages, you can save them paper by setting a short page length.

Cover Page	Toggles the cover page on or off. If the receiver is picking up your message at a fax bureau, toggling this to *No* saves the receiver some money. If the receiver works in a large company, toggling this to YES makes sure the message gets routed correctly.
Time Format	Toggles between 12- (A.M./P.M.) and 24-hour formats.
Sent From	This can be your name or your company name.

When the Fax Directory window appears for the first time, the Central Point Software fax number is inserted by default. You can use this number to experiment with, or you can insert another valid fax phone number.

Actions

Add a new entry	F4
Edit the current entry	F5
Delete the current entry	F6
Send files to the selected entry	F7
Check Fax log	F8

Configure

Fax drive	
Page Length	11
Cover Page:	YES
Time Format:	24 hr
Sent from	

Figure 12.15. Menu map of the Send a Fax screen

Working With Fax Number Entries

With the function keys you can add ([F4]), edit ([F5]), and delete ([F6]) entries in the Fax Directory.

To insert a new fax number:

Press: [F4]

This opens the Fax Details window, which looks like Figure 12.16.

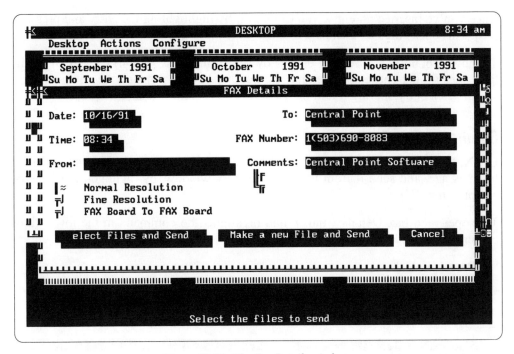

Figure 12.16. The Fax Details window

You'll find your cursor in the To field. This where you insert the name of the person or company you'll send faxes to. You insert the fax phone number in the Fax Number field. The Comments field lets you designate the kind of faxes you send this person or company, and is only for your own reference. You're given three ways to send fax messages:

Normal Resolution

Selected by default, this is the standard method for sending text files that contain no graphics.

Fine Resolution

Use this setting for files containing graphic features that should be transmitted in unusually clear detail. Transmission is considerably slower than Normal Resolution, which means that sending a fine-resolution fax long-distance will result in higher telephone connection charges.

Fax Board to Fax Board

This lets you send binary files from one fax board to another. Use this setting only when you want to send program files that need to run on a computer.

Once you've inserted an entry, you can edit it by highlighting the entry and pressing [F5]. This opens the Fax Details window for the highlighted entry.

To move around Fax Directory entries by screenful, press [PgDn] or [PgUp]; highlight specific fax entries by pressing the number keys that match the entry number. To delete an entry, highlight it in the Fax Directory window and press [F6].

Sending a Fax Transmission

Use Notepads, Outlines, or a more sophisticated word processing program to create a fax message, and send it from the Fax Directory window, by highlighting the entry and pressing [F7].

This opens the Fax Details window and highlights the command in the lower-right corner of the window, *Select Files and Send.*

Press: [Enter]

This opens the Files To Select box, shown in Figure 12.17.

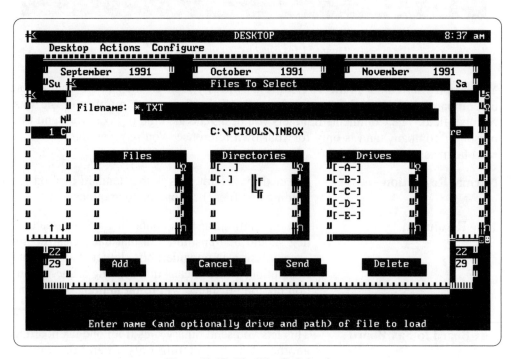

Figure 12.17. The Files To Select box

Either type the filename of the message you want to send, or highlight it in the file-name list. Then:

Press: [Enter]

The Fax Log

When you send a message, you're immediately switched to the Fax Log screen, shown in Figure 12.18, which monitors the progress of your call and the success of transmission.

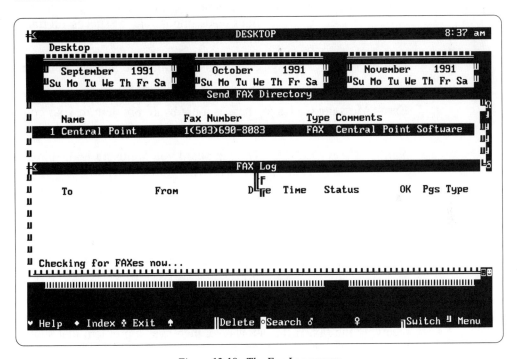

Figure 12.18. The Fax Log screen

You can enter this window either directly from the Telecommunications submenu by selecting *Check Fax Log,* or from the Fax Directory window by pressing [F8]. This lets you view previous fax activities.

The Fax Log window displays eight columns of information about each message you've sent:

To   The person or company receiving the message.

From   The name of the person or company who sent the message.

Date   The date the message was sent or received.

Time   The time the message was sent or received.

Status   The current status of the message. You can receive eight specific messages, or one of several error-message codes:

Aborted   You've canceled the fax message you were going to send.

Bad Phone, Drop	A transmission problem in the telephone lines made impossible the successful transmission of the fax you were sending.
Dialing	PC Tools is dialing the number you want to send a fax message to.
Error Message Codes	There is a hardware problem in your computer or telephone equipment.
Non CCP	The fax board you are using is incompatible with the standard required for PC Tools fax transmissions.
Receiving	Your fax board is presently receiving a fax message.
Sending	Your fax board is sending a fax message.
Sent	The message has been sent successfully.

OK   If this shows *Yes,* there were no problems encountered in sending or receiving the fax. If this shows *No,* there was a problem that should be defined by the status field.

Pgs   The number of pages in the fax according to the page length you've specified and whether a cover page was included.

Type   The type of fax message sent or received. If it was a normal fax message, this will show *Fax* if it was a binary file, this will show *File.*

You can use seven function keys in the Fax Log window:

[F1] Help   Opens context-sensitive help.

[F2] Index   Opens the Help index.

[F3] Exit   Closes the Fax Log window and returns you to the Fax Directory window.

[F5] Delete   Deletes a fax entry in the fax log.

[F6] Search   Searches for a specific item in the fax log by name.

[F9] Switch   Switches you between active windows in the Desktop Manager.

[F10] Menu   Activates the top menu bar.

The two pull-down menus in the Fax Log window share the names of the pull-down menus in the Fax Directory screen, but they execute different commands:

Actions   Deletes or searches for a log entry.

Configures   Changes fax drives or changes the *Auto Update* setting.

The two menus are shown in Figure 12.19.

Actions		Configure
Delete the selected entry	F5	Fax drive
Search	F6	Auto update

Figure 12.19. Menu map for the Check Fax Log window

All entries in the fax log are made automatically by the PC Tools program. You can delete entries by highlighting them and pressing [F5]. You can search for entries that don't appear in the window by pressing [PgDn] or [PgUp], or by pressing [F6] and specifying some parameters of the file you're looking for.

Auto Update

The fax transmission section of Telecommunications contains a feature called *Auto-Update,* which updates the fax log periodically, since you can receive fax transmissions at any time of the day or night, even while you're working in the Fax Directory or Fax Log window. It also lets you send faxes at prearranged times using the Appointment Scheduler. The default time setting for Auto Update is sixty seconds. You'll receive a message when updating occurs.

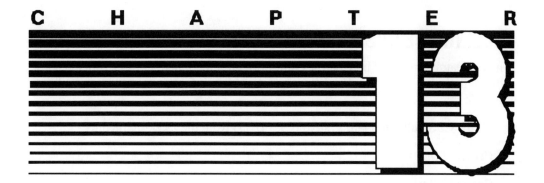

USING
TELECOMMUNICATIONS

T his chapter shows you how to log onto the Central Point Software bulletin board, how to use MCI Mail and CompuServe, and how to work e-mail. You will learn how to use the Telecommunications module to send and receive messages and download binary files.

CALLING THE CPS HELP BULLETIN BOARD

A novel feature provided by Central Point Software, the makers of PC Tools Deluxe, is the bulletin board system that allows you to obtain information and upgraded program files.

To call the CPS bulletin board system (CPS BBS) from the Desktop menu:

Press: [T]-[M]

Press: [Enter]

If you're working in any other Desktop module:

Press: [Alt]-[D]-[T]-[M]

Press: [Enter]

The default Telecommunications screen provides an entry for the Central Point Software bulletin board in slot 4. The script file CPS.SCR is attached to this entry, but I recommend that you deactivate it for your first call. This is because you must register with the bulletin board and select two log-on names; once you've declared the log-on names you want to use, you can enter them in CPS.SCR. Then the script file can do all the log-on work for you.

Deactivating the Script File

To deactivate this script file, first highlight the Central Point Software entry:

Press: [4]

Highlight the Script field:

Press: [F6]

Press: [Enter] twice

Your cursor should appear after the last letter of the CPS.SCR. To delete the script filename:

Press: [Backspace] seven times

Now, to enter the communications parameters, which begin at TERMINAL:

Press: [Tab] until you enter the communications parameters

To accept the change and return to the Telecommunications window:

Press: [A]

If no filename shows for the Script field for entry 4, you have deactivated the Central Point Software script file. The script file is still on disk; it just won't be activated when you make a call using the CPS BBS entry.

Making the Call

During your first call to the CPS BBS, you need to establish a unique user name and password so that you can enter the bulletin board directly and CPS can keep track of you. First, connect with the Central Point Software BBS. Make sure entry 4 is highlighted:

Press: [4]

Now, make the call:

Press: [Enter]

You can also make the call by pressing [F7], or the menu command [Alt]-[A]-[D].

As soon as you press [Enter], the following message appears on the bottom line of your screen:

```
Dialing - Press ESC to Cancel
```

If the audio controls of your modem are on, you'll hear the number being dialed, the sound of a connection, and then a hissing noise. This is the sound of the other computer replying that it's ready to connect to yours. This signal automatically opens your On-Line screen. Wait a few moments to see if the two computers can get to communicating by themselves. If they do not, press [Enter] to speed up making the connection.

When connection is made, CPS BBS will ask:

```
Can you display ANSI graphics?
If you are not sure select "N".
Would you like ANSI? (Y/N)
```

You'll find your cursor just after the (Y/N) question. If your monitor can display ANSI graphics, you can answer yes, but it's not too important. If you answer yes, you get to see a few colors and flashing text. If you select no, you'll just see plain text:

Press: [N]

Press: [Enter]

This begins a series of questions scrolling through several screenfuls of text. Your screen should look like Figure 13.1.

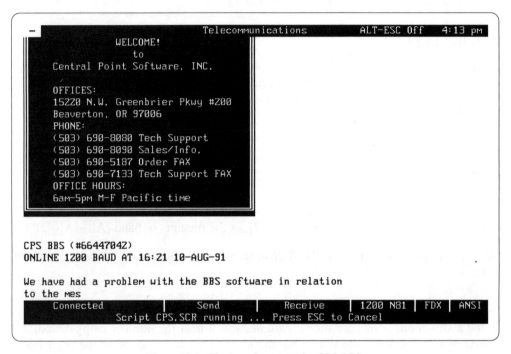

Figure 13.1. The Log-On screen for CPS BBS

The first screen is a welcome message. The message will stop scrolling when it asks whether you're a new subscriber. You'll find your cursor after the colon. At this point, you might want to start recording the text.

Recording Text

You can record text characters that appear on your screen by saving the dialog to a simple text file. To do this:

Press: [F6]

This opens the Save File to Disk box. This lets you declare the filename to hold the dialog, and looks like Figure 13.2.

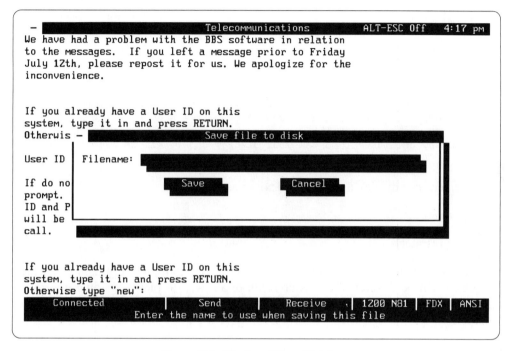

Figure 13.2. The Save File to Disk box

To begin the recording:

Type: RECORD.TXT

Press: [Enter] twice

Notice the message that appears at the bottom of your screen:

```
record.txt 0 lines received, ESC end.
```

This will record all text characters that appear on your screen during your dialogue with CPS BBS. As the dialogue progresses, the line count will increase. This is how you *download,* or *receive,* a simple text file.

Continuing the Dialog

To continue with your first communication with CPS BBS:

> **Type:** NEW

> **Press:** [Enter]

The message will continue:

```
Welcome. Before you can use the system we need to get some information.
After we get this information, you will have free access to the system. So
that we can format output for you properly, how wide is your screen? That
is, how many columns across can your display show, left to right?
```

Most screens can display a width of 80 columns.

> **Type:** 80

> **Press:** [Enter]

CPS BBS starts asking information about you. I've highlighted my answers, which of course will be different from yours. You're allowed to pick your own user name and password, but if you pick a name that's already in use, you'll be asked to select another.

> Central Point Software is always updating the bulletin board, so the text and menu choices displayed in this book might change.

```
Good!  Your answer has been used to control the "word-wrap" feature, as you
can see.  Now if you'll tell us a little about yourself, we'll get underway.
Please enter your first and last name:
Charles Ackerman

Now enter your company name, or just press RETURN if none:
getsmart

Enter the first line of your address (your street address or P. O. Box):
810 Contra Costa Drive

Enter the second line of your address (city, state, and ZIP code):
El Cerrito, CA 94530
Now enter the telephone number where you can be reached during the day:
415-555-0000
```

We would also like to know what kind of system you are using, so that we can serve you better. Do you have...

    1. An IBM PC or compatible
    2. An Apple Macintosh
    3. An Apple other than Macintosh
    4. A Commodore Amiga
    5. An Atari, any model
    6. A Radio Shack unit, any model
    7. A CP/M system of any sort
    0. None of the above

Select a number from 0 to 7: **1**

Now you need to choose a "User-ID" for yourself. Your User-ID will be your "code name" on this system. You will use it to identify yourself to the system when you log on and other users will know you by this name. Your User-ID must be 3 to 9 letters long. There are no digits, spaces or punctuation allowed. The system will automatically capitalize the first letter of your User-ID and set all of the other letters to lower-case.

Enter the User-ID you want to use to identify yourself: **chas**

Sorry someone else is already using "Chas". Try a different one...

Enter the User-ID you want to use to identify yourself: **Click**

Here is a simulated message, showing how your User-ID will appear to other users:

    From Click: This BBS is very helpful.

Are you satisfied with your choice of User-ID (Yes/No) ? **y**

Ok Click, that will be your User-ID from now on. Now you'll also need to select a password so you can keep other people from using your name without your permission. Make it short and memorable, but not obvious. The security of your account depends on nobody else knowing what your password is.

Enter the password you plan to use: **clack**

The following account has been created:

    User-ID.... Click
    Password... clack

WRITE THIS INFORMATION DOWN if you haven't already. There will be nothing anyone can do for you if you forget either one of these. We don't give out people's passwords by mail or over the phone, even if they "sound" totally honest.

```
KEEP YOUR PASSWORD TO YOURSELF.

Press RETURN when you have written down your User-ID and password...

Welcome.
To: CPS BBS

    1 ... Central Point Software Inc.
    2 ... Technical Information
    3 ... Sales Information
    4 ... Download files
    5 ... BBS Information
    6 ... Leave a message
    7 ... Read your messages
    X ... EXIT the system

Select an option, X to EXIT or ? for help: 7
```

This brings you to the Central Point Software bulletin board main menu. You can explore this bulletin board at your leisure.

When you're finished exploring the board, return to the main menu:

> **Press and hold:** [X]

Hold down [X] until the main menu reappears. When you press [X] at the main menu, the CPS BBS will tell you:

```
You are about to terminate this telephone connection!

Are you sure (Y/N, or R to re-logon)?
```

Before logging off, turn off the recording of this dialog:

> **Press:** [Esc]

The function key assignments for the On-Line screen should return to your screen. You've saved the dialog to a text file called RECORD.TXT.

You can view the contents of RECORD.TXT in the Notepads Editor screen. You can then delete the parts you don't want to keep, or delete the entire file if it has no value to you.

Now log off the CPS BBS:

> **Type:** Y

Press: [Enter]

```
OK, thanks for calling CPS BBS.
Hope to see you back again real soon!!

Have a nice day...

MJQ~
NO CARRIER
```

The NO CARRIER sign shows you're no longer connected to the other computer. It will appear whenever you exit the other computer's program. To disconnect:

Press: [F8]

You'll see the message Disconnecting at the bottom of your screen. When the disconnect is complete, the On-Line screen will close and you'll return to the Telecommunications screen.

Once you've declared a user name and password, you can log onto the bulletin board quickly with subsequent calls. You can also insert your user name and password into the script file CPS.SCR, and have that file log you on automatically. This is described in the next chapter.

Now log back onto the CPS BBS to send a message and receive a file.

When the Telecommunications screen is showing, highlight the entry for CPS:

Press: [4]

Press: [Enter]

When CPS BBS asks you about screen type:

Press: Y

Press: [Enter]

Enter your user name and password when CPS BBS asks you for them. This moves you directly to the main menu.

Sending a Message

You can send a message two ways: interactively, if the other computer provides an editor, and by *uploading* (or *sending*) a text file you created earlier. If the message is short, no more than a couple of lines, you can use the other computer's editor. If the message is longer than one or two lines, you should create it first and then upload it onto the other computer.

Creating and uploading a message involves the following steps:

1. Compose a message using a text editor of your own, such as the Notepads screen.

2. Save the file to disk.

3. Send the file when the other computer is prepared to receive it.

Uploading is the preferred method of placing messages on other computers, because you don't waste time connected to the other computer while composing the message. Your long-distance charges are minimized, although they will climb quickly if you don't pay attention to them. Using your own editor also allows you time to compose and edit more detailed messages without feeling rushed.

However, if you want to type in an extremely short message, it might be more efficient to type the message directly onto the other computer using the other computer's interactive editor, because it involves fewer steps.

To send a message in this way, first connect with the CPS BBS main menu and select the option that lets you leave messages:

Press: [6]

This selects the *Leave a Message* option, which opens with the following information:

```
CPS BBS
MESSAGE

Currently, the turnaround time for Tech Support questions is approximately
4 days. Please select option "I" (Important Information) before leaving
messages. Your cooperation is appreciated, thank you.
Technical Support

    1 ... Tech Support - PC Tools V6
    2 ... Tech Support - PC Tools V5
    3 ... Tech Support - PC Tools V4
```

```
 4 ... Tech Support - Option Board
 5 ... Tech Support - Copy II PC
 6 ... Tech Support - Copy II Mac
 7 ... Tech Support - Copy II Plus
 8 ... Tech Support - Copy II 64/128
 9 ... Tech Support - PC Tools Mac
10 ... Product Suggestions
 S ... General Sales Questions
 I ... Important Information
```

```
Select an option, X to EXIT or ? for help:
```

For this example:

> **Press:** [1]

This logs you onto help for the current version of the PC Tools Deluxe program.

You'll now be asked a series of questions, which you answer depending upon the type of message you want to send. As before, my answers appear in boldface.

```
The message you send can be up to 1920 characters long.  When done, type OK
on a line by itself.  (Or, type /S to save and proceed, without editing).
```

Just testing.
OK

```
EDITOR OPTIONS:

  S)ave message      R)e-type a line
  A)ppend message    D)elete line
  L)ist message      I)nsert line(s)
  C)hange text       N)ew message
  H)elp              T)opic change
```

```
Select an option from the above list: s

Do you wish to "attach" a file to this message (Y/N)? n

Do you want a "return receipt" when this message is read (Y/N)? n

<<< CONFIRMED: MESSAGE #29840 WRITTEN TO DISK >>>

Do you want to send a copy of this message to anyone (Y/N)? n

The following E-Mail services are available:

  R => Read message(s)
  W => Write a message
```

```
M => Modify a message
E => Erase a message
X => Exit from E-Mail
```

Select a letter from the above list, or ? for more info:

Uploading a Message

Suppose you have created a text file called QUESTION.TXT, which contains technical questions you'd like the CPS BBS tech support group to answer. Upload this file,
with the preceding E-Mail menu still showing:

Press: [W]

When the screen asks you to write the message:

Press: [F4]

This opens the Send ASCII box. This is the dialog box for sending ASCII text files
and looks like Figure 13.3.

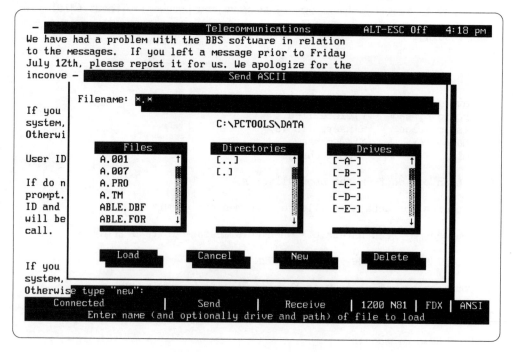

Figure 13.3. The Send ASCII box

This box behaves the same way as the other dialog boxes, but there is no filter for the filenames. Filenames in the selected directory will appear in alphabetical order.

Type: QUESTION.TXT

Press: [Enter]

This begins the sending of the file. Notice how the bottom line shows the filename and path, and how many lines of the file have been sent. Once the message has been sent:

Type: OK

Press: [Enter]

That's all there is to it.

Downloading a Binary File

Downloading a file means receiving it from the other computer. You've already downloaded a simple text file when you recorded the dialog of registering on CPS BBS to RECORD.TXT. In this section, you'll download a *binary file,* a file that's written in *machine code.* Machine code is a series of 1s and 0s that signify values that your computer uses to perform software operations.

Binary files are more complex than simple ASCII text files and require special handling to make sure that transmission is correct. You can usually tell when ASCII characters get mixed up in transmission. The transposition of an occasional 1 with a 0 is undetectable, and it will cause lots of trouble.

Download one of the binary files in the CPS BBS user library. To get to this section, begin at the CPS BBS main menu:

Press: [4]

Press: [Enter]

This moves you through the following text:

```
CPS

CENTRAL POINT SOFTWARE FILES
These files are intended ONLY as upgrades for registered owners of CPS
products. They are not to be considered freeware or shareware and should
not be uploaded to other Bulletin Board Systems. Thank you.
```

```
1 ... PC Tools V5.5 files
2 ... Option Board files
3 ... PC Tools V1.1 Macintosh files
4 ... Copy II Plus In-House Parms
U ... User files
```

```
Select an option, X to EXIT or ? for help:
```

To look at the user files:

Type: U

Press: [Enter]

```
CPS BBS
USERS
```

```
The files in this area are provided for your convenience and in some cases
were not written or tested by Central Point Software.
```

```
F ... List of files
D ... Download files
U ... Upload files
```

```
Select an option, X to EXIT or ? for help:
```

Look at the list:

Press: F

Press: [Enter]

> This list changes from time to time, so you if you're an active PC
> Tools user, you should probably check this list occasionally to see if
> there are any new files that can help your work.

For this example, download the file called TELSORT.EXE, a useful utility that sorts
entries in alphabetical order in a PC Tools phone book.

To prepare for downloading the file:

Press: [D]

Press: [Enter]

The bulletin board asks you which file you want to download:

```
File name(s), keyword, date (MM/DD/YY), or days ago (-DD):
```

> **Type:** TELSORT.EXE

> **Press:** [Enter]

The bulletin board will first display some facts about the file you want to download. For TELSORT.EXE, the information looks like this:

```
TELSORT.EXE    Sort PC Tools (5.5) dialing directories
Date:  09/02/89    From:  Abrava        Downloads:  751
Time:  21:14:44    Size:  39680 bytes   Download time:  8 minutes

Keywords:  directory  sort  telephone  utility

TELSORT sorts PC Tools version 5.5 dialing directories.  To run the program,
type TELSORT [filename].  [Filename] must include its extension.  TELSORT
will default to PHONE.TEL if no filename is specified.  The program will
create a backup directory before proceeding.  Sorting is alphabetical.

    A -> Download using ASCII text protocol < only on ASCII files >
    C -> Download using XMODEM-CRC
    M -> Download using XMODEM <If using CrossTalk "tm">
    Y -> Download using YMODEM
    Z -> Download using ZMODEM

Please select an option or X to EXIT.
```

Copy this screen to the Clipboard so you can remember the details about TELSORT.EXE:

> **Press:** [Ctrl]-[Del]

Move your cursor to the upper-left corner of the screen.

> **Press:** [Enter]

Now move your cursor to the lower-right corner of the screen to highlight the text that describes the file TELSORT.EXE.

> **Press:** [Enter]

This records the screen text to the Clipboard. After you finish with the download, paste the Clipboard text into a Notepads text file and save it to disk.

Note that the estimated time to download the file is eight minutes. Since TEL-

SORT.EXE is a binary file, use an error-checking mode while downloading it:

Press: [C]

Press: [Enter]

You're given the message:

```
Ready to begin XMODEM CRC download (CTRL-X to cancel) . . .
```

To prepare PC Tools to receive a binary file:

Press: [F7]

This opens a box that displays the progress of downloading (see Figure 13.4).

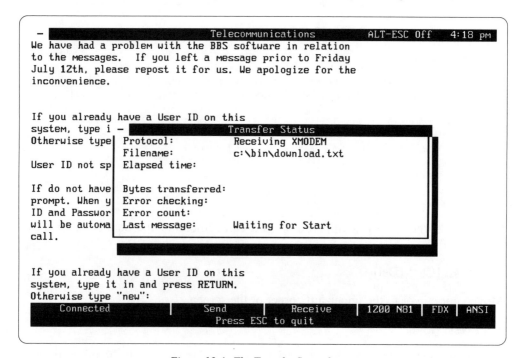

Figure 13.4. The Transfer Status box

The appearance of this box will trigger the beginning of the download. Numbers will appear in the fields after *Elapsed time, Bytes transferred,* and *Last message* as the downloading progresses. You'll hear a beep when the file has been completely download, and you'll seethe message:

```
Transfer Complete - Press any Key to Continue.
```

You will return to the CPS BBS main menu. Exit the bulletin board.

Once you've downloaded a binary file and exited the bulletin board, you should check to ensure that it works. To run the program, first make sure TELSORT.EXE is in your PCTOOLS directory.

> **Type:** TELSORT

> **Press:** [Enter]

You'll see the following text displayed on screen:

```
ORT - Sort PHONE.TEL dialing directory
Version 1.0 - Victor Abrahamsen / Silicon‾ Memory Systems

SYNTAX: TELSORT [filename.ext], where [filename.ext] corresponds to a PC
Tools
            Deluxe dialing directory's DOS filename.   Default directory:
PHONE.TEL

PHONE.TEL entries: 12

Sorting...

   Writing...

      Complete!

Entries sorted: new PHONE.TEL created; original file is now PHONE.OLD
```

If you look at the contents of PHONE.TEL, or whatever phone book you specified, you'll see that the entries have been reorganized alphabetically.

USING MCI MAIL

MCI Mail is an electronic subscription service. One of the services is the exchange of messages among MCI Mail subscribers and subscribers to other e-mail services. MCI Mail charges for each message you send, depending upon the size of the message. However, you are not charged for the time you are connected to the MCI Mail computer.

To send or receive messages using MCI Mail, you must have joined the service and been given a mail box, a user name, a password, and an MCI Mail account number.

Basic and Advanced services are available. MCI Mail lets you choose your own user name. Most people take the first letter of their first name and add the first seven characters of their last name. If I used this technique my user name would be *cackerma*. Once you have these things, you can look up the local MCI Mail telephone number and log it into your Telecommunications phone book as described in Chapter 12.

> Since I use MCI Mail a lot, I've made my local MCI Mail number as the first entry in PHONE.TEL. This way, when the Telecommunications screen appears, all I have to do is press [Enter] to make the call.

The details for logging on, logging off, and using MCI Mail are explained in the information package you receive when you subscribe to the service. The package includes a description of all MCI Mail services and the commands to access them. A sample log-on screen is shown in Figure 13.5.

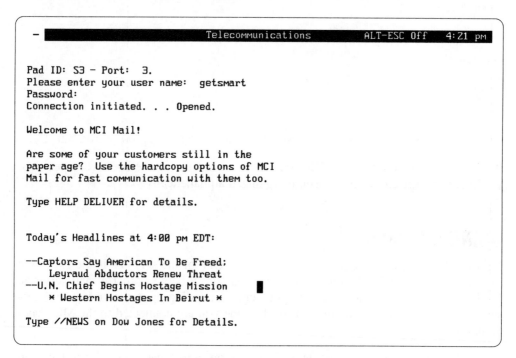

Figure 13.5. The log-on screen for MCI Mail

Sending Notepads Disk Files

When using MCI Mail with PC Tools, watch out for one problem. Sending a text file through MCI Mail that has been printed to disk in the Notepads Editor sometimes results in receiving a long string of repeated questions from MCI Mail. When you print a Notepads text file to disk, the program often adds a string of hard-carriage returns after the slash mark. The hard-carriage returns saved to the disk file keep giving the wrong answer to the *Send?* command from MCI Mail.

Figure 13.6 shows what these hard-carriage-return symbols look like when you turn control character display on.

You should view the disk file before you send it and delete the hard-carriage-return symbols. This will save you the trouble of watching the same question repeat itself over and over on your screen.

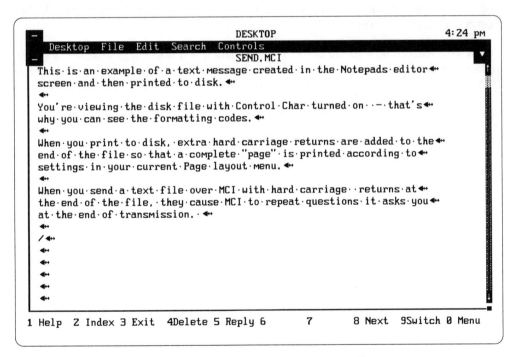

Figure 13.6. Hard-carriage returns in a text file

USING COMPUSERVE

CompuServe is a subscriber electronic database service that connects you to a larger variety of informational bulletin boards. It also provides a mail-exchange service called EasyLink. This service is similar to MCI Mail, but the crucial difference is that you're charged for each minute you're connected to CompuServe. This means that the rapid downloading and uploading of data is more important than when working with MCI Mail.

As with MCI Mail, you have to be a paid subscriber before you can use their services. When you subscribe, you will receive a user name and password, which you can use to log on to the CompuServe main menu.

USING E-MAIL

In the last chapter, you were introduced to the E-mail module of Telecommunications. In this chapter you'll learn how to use it.

You've also learned how to log onto MCI Mail and CompuServe. Sometimes it's convenient to do this yourself. Other times, it's more convenient to log onto your favorite e-mail service automatically. You can use the E-mail module to do this.

First, open e-mail from the Desktop main menu:

Press: [T]

Press: [E]

Your Electronic Mail Inbox screen will appear next, as shown in Figure 13.7.

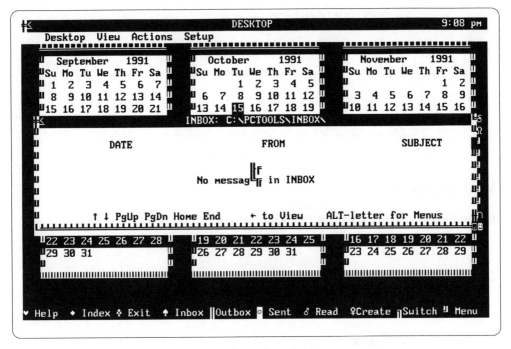

Figure 13.7. The Electronic Mail Inbox screen.

Next, declare your mail service.

Press: [Alt]-[S]

Press: [Enter]

This opens the screen, as shown in Figure 12.13.

We'll use MCI Mail as your example. Make sure the radio button next to MCI Mail is on, then press [Enter] twice. Now, configure MCI Mail:

Press: [Alt]-[C]

Follow these steps to configure:

1. Type the local phone number you use to access MCI Mail, then press [Enter].

2. Type your User ID (this is the code MCI Mail usually lets you select), then press [Enter].

3. Type your password (MCI Mail gives you this), then press [Enter].

4. Select your baud rate, then press [Tab].

5. Select your type of dialing, then press [Tab}.

6. Finally, select the port you use for modem communications, then press [Tab].

7. If all the settings are as you want them, press [Enter] to accept OK. Otherwise, press [Ctrl]-[Tab] to go back through the selections, find the one you want to change, change it, then move back to OK by pressing [Tab].

Making a Call

To make a call and log on to MCI Mail:

Press: [F7]

The E-mail module will automatically switch over to Modem Communications, and dial your MCI Mail number. Using the MCI.SCR, it will read your MCI Mail inbox, download any messages, log off of MCI Mail, then return to the e-mail screen.

Checking Your Boxes

You should periodically check your mailboxes to find out the status of your messages.

To check your inbox:

Press: [F4]

To check the contents of your outbox:

Press: [F5]

To check the contents of the mail you've sent:

Press: [F6]

When you've received a message, read it by highlighting the filename in the Inbox window, and pressing [Alt]-[A].

This opens the Action pull-down menu.

Press: [Enter]

This executes the first command on the menu, *View Highlighted Message*. Figure 13.8 shows a message viewed on screen.

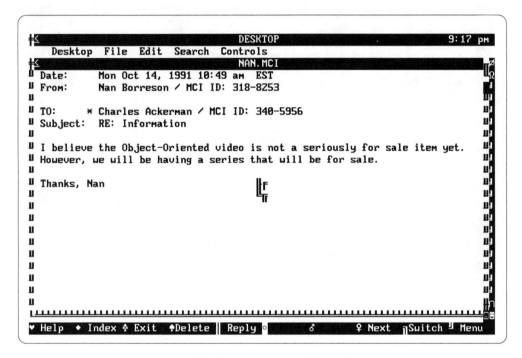

Figure 13.8. Viewing contents of file in inbox

Scheduling Mail

You can set time schedules for the E-mail module to check your e-mail service and send and receive automatically. For this technique to work successfully, you need to load Desktop in resident mode, so that its control is always available. If you want to do other things while Desktop handles your mail automatically, you'll have to install backtalk communications.

To set a schedule to send or upload messages automatically:

   Press: [Alt]-[S]-[S]

This opens the Send Mail Schedule box, as shown in Figure 13.9.

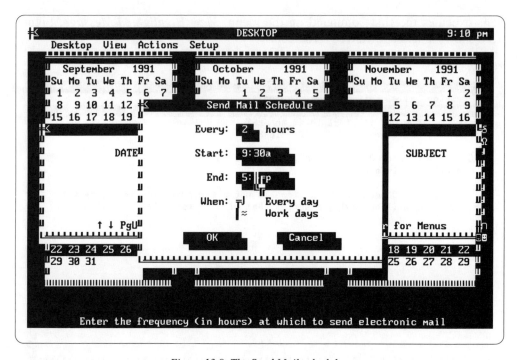

Figure 13.9. The Send Mail schedule

Using this box, you can set the number of hours that should elapse between each log-on, and the times of day you want the process to start and stop.

You use the Receive Mail box, shown in Figure 13.10, to set the schedule for receiving mail.

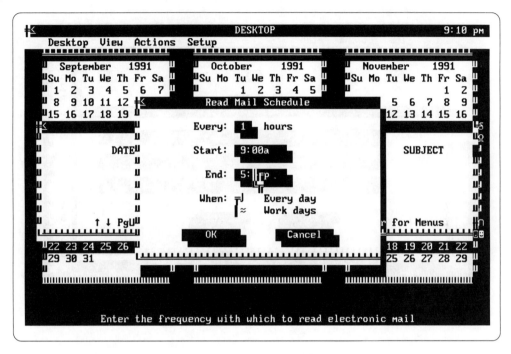

Figure 13.10. The Receive Mail box

To use the send and receive mail boxes correctly, you should configure the directories that will hold the mail.

Press: [Alt]-[S]-[M]

This opens the Electronic Mail Directories box, as shown in Figure 13.11.

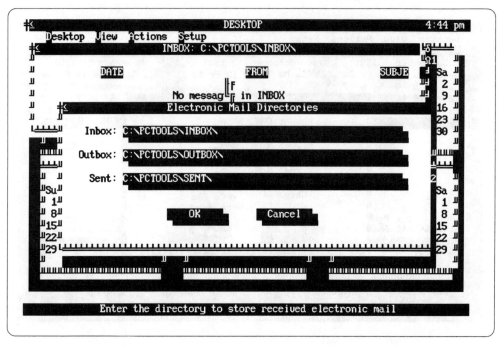

Figure 13.11. The Electronic Mail Directories box

The default settings are the directories created by the PC Tools Install program: C:\PCTOOLS\INBOX for the inbox, C:\PCTOOLS\OUTBOX for the outbox, and C:PCTOOLS\SENT for the sent box. You can change these settings to any other drive or directory accessible by PC Tools Desktop.

USING A DIRECT TELEPHONE LINK

You can also use the Telecommunications module to send and receive messages with another computer to which you're connected through a modem, with no electronic service to act as the intermediary. Just dial manually and type an initialization string and phone number in the On-Line screen, then press [Enter] to process these numbers. You're using PC Tools Telecommunications, but the other computer can use either PC Tools or any of a variety of communications programs.

Begin in the Telecommunications screen. Highlight an entry that contains the communications parameters you want to use:

Press: [F8]

You can also use the menu commands [Alt]-[A]-[M].

Now, type the proper initialization code. If you're using a Hayes or Hayes-compatible modem, the string will most likely be ATDT.

> Refer back to the Modem Setup window, Figure 12.3. All three modem initialization strings begin with the letters AT, which wake up the modem. *D* stands for *Dial*, which is what you'll do next. *T* stands for *tone*, the more common dialing method. If you're using a pulse-type phone, you should use the string *ATDP*. If you're not using a Hayes-compatible modem, you should contact the modem manufacturer for the correct string.

Once you've entered the correct modem initialization string, type the phone number for the computer you want to reach. You can press [Backspace] to delete incorrect characters, but that's about the limit of your editing controls in this screen. When the numbers are correct, press [Enter] to send them through your modem.

When the connection is complete, send a message:

Type: HI!

Press: [Enter]

Arrange beforehand with the operator of the other computer to wait for your message, then reply with one of his or her own. Only one person can type at a time. When you press [Enter], the cursor moves back to the beginning of the current line. Characters from the other computer will replace those you've typed. Work out a shorthand message that indicates when each of you is finished typing.

When your message goes through and you get the reply you're looking for, the connection is secure. You can now send and receive ASCII and binary messages.

To send an ASCII text message, press [F4], type the name of the message you want to send, and press [Enter] twice. The other computer must be set up to receive.

To receive an ASCII message, press [F6], type the name of the disk file to which you want to save the message, and press [Enter] twice. As long as the operator on the other computer has entered the correct commands for sending the text file, everything should work smoothly. You'll see the text scroll by on your screen. When the message is finished, press [Esc].

To send a binary file, press [F5], type the name of the file, and press [Enter] twice. You can view the progress of the file being sent and of error checking. The other computer must be set up to receive the message.

To receive a binary file, press [F7], type the name of the disk file you want to save, and press [Enter] twice. If the operator on the other computer has correctly started to send the file, you should receive it on your computer.

Obviously, communicating with a direct telephone link requires close teamwork with the operator of the other computer. You have to synchronize your activities so that one is sending and the other is receiving. If you don't coordinate your efforts, communication won't be successful. It might not make sense to communicate this way, if you need to transfer only one or two disk files. But if you want to transfer many files, for example an entire hard disk's worth, a direct telephone link is the best way to do it.

USING A HARDWIRE CONNECTION

You can also communicate directly with another computer through a hardwire connection. This is a cable that contains at least three wires passing through a null modem. In most cases, a hardwire connection begins to fail if it's over fifty feet in length.

The procedure is almost identical to communicating with a direct telephone link. Once you've established the hardwire connection, you should turn on both computers and load suitable communication programs. Select an entry that uses communications parameters identical to the parameters used by the other computer.

   Press: [F8]

This moves you into the On-Line screen. You don't need to type an initialization string or a phone number. You should already be connected via the hardwire. Type a message to make sure you're connected correctly to the other computer. The characters should appear on your screen and on the other computer's screen. When you press [Enter], the cursor will move back to the beginning of the line, but it will not move down a line. You should not try to type something when the operator of the other computer is typing. Use shorthand messages to indicate that you have completed your message.

You can now send and receive messages with the other computer using the instructions explained in the preceding section, "Using a Direct Telephone Link."

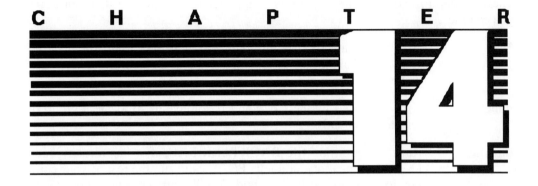

USING SCRIPT FILES

A script file is a program that controls the behavior of your computer when it communicates with another computer. Script files can automate many of the procedures performed in telecommunications. Even if you've never done any programming before, you'll find the PC Tools script easy to work with.

The first step to understanding PC Tools script files is learning the nineteen terms you can use.

*	A symbol that precedes all comments you may want to put into a script file. This means the characters that follow won't be processed by the program.
:label	A marker used by the *GoTo* and *If* commands to locate a group of related commands.
Backtalk	Runs the program file BACKTALK.EXE, if it has already been loaded into memory, and tells PC Tools to run the rest of your communications in the background. You'll find out more about background communications at the end of this chapter.
Database	Runs the database declared in the phonebook entry you used for the call, and works with variables V1 and V2 to send the entries for two fields in the database. The default database entry is TELECOM.DBF, and the two default fields are MCI_ID and FAX_TELEX.
Download	Receives a file from the other computer, as long as the receiving protocol has been specified.
Echo	Toggles on and off the screen display of characters. This is useful when you try to debug sections of a new script.
GoTo	Tells the program to go to a group of commands associated with a specific label. (See **:label**).
HangUp	Breaks the connection between your computer and the telephone link, or discontinues a file transfer if one is in progress.
If	A conditional command, this tells PC Tools to go to a group of commands associated with a specific label depending upon whether a condition is true or not.
Input	Lets you store up to eighty characters ending in a carriage return or line-feed character in three different variables, V1, V2, and V3.
Pause	Pauses the execution of the script for the specified number of seconds. If no number is given, the pause lasts for one second.
Print	Prints characters on your screen, including the characters defined for variables you might include.

Receive   Accepts a string of up to eighty characters ending with a carriage return or line-feed character sent from the other computer, and stores them in one or more of the three variables V1, V2, and V3.

Send   Sends a string of up to eighty characters ending with a carriage return or line-feed character to the other computer. You can store up to three different strings in the variables V1, V2, and V3.

TrOff   Turns off the effect of the *TrOn* command. Stands for *trace off*.

TrOn   Displays, at the bottom of your screen, the characters for each line of commands in a script file that's running on your computer. After a line is displayed, the program pauses and waits for you to press [Spacebar] to execute the next line of commands. Pressing [Esc] cancels the script. Stands for *trace on*.

Upload   Sends a file from one computer to another, as long as the sending protocol has been specified.

V1/V2/V3   Variables that hold character strings for sending and receiving optional character strings.

WaitFor   Preceding a string of characters, this tells the program to halt all action until the specified string is received from the other computer.

Some of these commands work with the variables V1, V2, and V3. Working with variables is probably the most complicated part of writing script files, so first let's cover the basics.

Script terms are not case-sensitive; you can use either uppercase or lowercase letters for them. The PC Tools script glossary, or list of command words, is a lean set. This prevents you from designing complex script files, but makes it easier to learn the language.

The best way to learn how to use these commands is to take a look at how they've been used in the several sample script files provided as part of the PC Tools programs.

THE DEFAULT SCRIPT FILES

You get four script files already prepared for your use as part of the PC Tools program.

CPS.SCR   Logs you onto the Central Point Software bulletin board.

CIS.SCR   Logs you onto your account with the CompuServe bulletin board.

ESL.SCR   Logs you onto your account with EasyLink mail.

MCI.SCR   Logs you onto your account with MCI Mail and opens a menu for your use.

In the previous two chapters on telecommunications you familiarized yourself with the module and logged on manually. In this chapter, we'll automate some of the work.

Script files are all simple ASCII text files. This means you can create, view, and edit them in the Notepads Editor screen. You might even want to print them out so you can study them in closer detail. There's no better way to learn about script files than by studying someone else's files and figuring out how they work.

The CPS.SCR File

The first script file we'll look at is CPS.SCR, which automatically logs you onto the Central Point Software bulletin board. If you're still viewing the Telecommunications screen:

>   **Press:** [Alt]-[D]-[N]

>   **Type:** CPS.SCR

>   **Press:** [Enter]

You can also select the Notepads module from the main menu. When your Notepads window is zoomed to full-screen size, it should look like Figure 14.1.

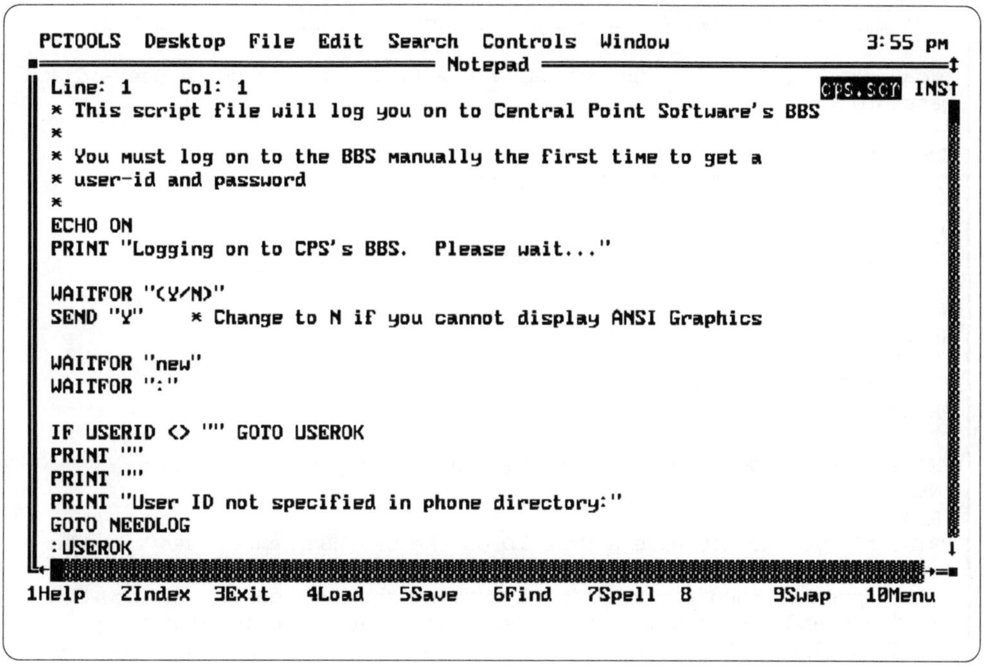

```
 PCTOOLS  Desktop  File  Edit  Search  Controls  Window          3:55 pm
 ════════════════════════════════ Notepad ════════════════════════════╪
 Line: 1     Col: 1                                          CPS.SCR INS↑
 * This script file will log you on to Central Point Software's BBS
 *
 * You must log on to the BBS manually the first time to get a
 * user-id and password
 *
 ECHO ON
 PRINT "Logging on to CPS's BBS.  Please wait..."

 WAITFOR "(Y/N)"
 SEND "Y"     * Change to N if you cannot display ANSI Graphics

 WAITFOR "new"
 WAITFOR ":"

 IF USERID <> "" GOTO USEROK
 PRINT ""
 PRINT ""
 PRINT "User ID not specified in phone directory:"
 GOTO NEEDLOG
 :USEROK
 1Help   2Index  3Exit  4Load  5Save  6Find  7Spell  8    9Swap  10Menu
```

Figure 14.1. The top of CPS.SCR in the Notepads Editor

You'll have to press [PgDn] three times to view all of the commands. The full contents of CPS.SCR are shown in Table 14.1.

```
* This script file will log you on to Central Point Software's BBS
*
*You must log on to the BBS manually the first time to get a user-id and
password
*
ECHO ON
PRINT "Logging on to CPS's BBS. Please wait..."

WAITFOR"(Y/N)"
SEND 'Y'     *Change to N if you cannot display ANSI Graphics

WAITFOR "new"
WAITFOR ":"

IF USERID ,. '' GOTO USEROK
PRINT ''
PRINT''
PRINT "User ID not specified in phone directory:"
:NEEDLOG
PRINT ""
PRINT "If you do not have a User ID on the CPS BBS, enter 'new' at the
next"
PRINT "prompt. When you are finished using the BBS, enter your new User"
PRINT "ID and Password into your Telecommunications phone directory. You"
PRINT "will be automatically logged on to the system the next time you"
PRINT "call."
SEND""
GOTO BYE
:PASSOK

SEND USERID
WAITFOR "Password"
SEND PASSWORD
:BYE
```

Table 14.1. The complete listing of CPS.SCR

There are eight commands in this file: *, *:label, Echo, GoTo, If, Print, Send* and *WaitFor*. Let's take a look at them individually. (You won't find *:label* as such—you'll find various names, such as :USEROK and :NEEDLOG, after the colon.)

The five asterisks at the top of CPS.SCR designate those lines as comments, which define the file but have no effect upon its execution. You can find a sixth asterisk further down the file, before the line *Change to N if*. The asterisk turns off any effect the words after it might have as commands. As soon as a carriage return or line feed appears, the effects of the asterisk disappear.

The second command is *Echo On*, which will display all the characters received during a *WaitFor* command.

The third command is *Print*. This prints the text that follows the command in quotation marks, in this case beginning with "Logging on to CPS's . . .".

The fourth command is our first *WaitFor* command. It waits for the text specified between quotation marks, in this case (Y/N). These appear when the CPS bulletin board asks if you want to view characters on your screen in ANSI form.

The fifth command is another *Send* command. It automatically sends the text in quotation marks that follows it, in this case *Y* for yes. The comment after this command tells you to change the character to N if you don't want to view characters in ANSI form.

The sixth and seventh commands are both *WaitFor* commands. The first waits for the word *new*, which asks if you are a new user. The second waits for the colon that follows *new*. You have to specify the colon after *new*, or else PC Tools will proceed with the script file when it runs across the colon between hours and minutes a few lines below the opening logo screen.

The eighth command begins a new command construction. It begins with the conditional *If* and ends by going to the USEROK label (:USEROK). The line looks like this:

```
IF USERID <> " " GOTO USEROK
```

This calls on the entry in the User ID field of the phonebook entry you're using. Refer back to Figure 12.3, where you'll find User ID as the fourth field from the top. You can enter your CPS BBS user name here, and CPS.SCR will call on it when it needs to.

If you use a valid CPS BBS user name, you'll go to the group of commands under :USEROK. If you're not using a valid name, or you haven't specified one, you'll see the message:

```
User ID not specified in phone directory.
```

This moves you to the label :NEEDLOG, which walks you through the commands for logging on to the CPS BBS for the first time.

The most important construction in CPS.BBS is the use of labels. The command *If* creates a condition that moves you to a specific group of commands. Otherwise, PC Tools proceeds through the script in linear fashion, starting at the top, unless a *GoTo* command sends it back to an earlier label, from which the progression continues. Obviously, using labels in a logical fashion is crucial to the success of any script you write and use.

Using CPS.SCR

To use CPS.SCR, return to the Telecommunications screen and call the CPS bulletin board a second time. If you popped up the Notepads Editor screen into Telecommunications:

   Press: [Esc]

If you started out in the Notepads Editor screen:

   Press: [Alt]-[D]-[T]

Otherwise, enter the Telecommunications screen from the Desktop main menu. When the Telecommunications screen appears:

   Press: [4]

   Press: [Enter]

The bottom line of your screen shows you which script is active. To cancel a script, press [Esc].

> Pressing [Esc] while a script is running cancels the script. In most cases, you'll revert to manual control of the computer with which you are communicating. In rare instances, all communication will stop and you will have to hang up and start again.

This time the revised script file should walk you through all the commands of logging on. When the script is finished executing, you should find yourself at the Central Point Software main menu. This script will repeat itself automatically each time you make a call using an entry that has CPS.SCR in the *Script File* column of the Telecommunications screen.

The MCI.SCR Script

The script file MCI.SCR lets you log onto MCI Mail and presents you with a menu. Before you use MCI.SCR, make sure your phonebook entry for MCI Mail contains your MCI user name and password in the appropriate fields. Open the phonebook you use to call MCI Mail in your Telecommunications screen, then highlight the MCI Mail entry and press [F6]. This opens the window that lets you edit entries.

There should be two fields in this window: USER ID and PASSWORD. After inserting your user ID and password, close the window and make a call to MCI Mail. When you connect, your screen should look like Figure 14.2.

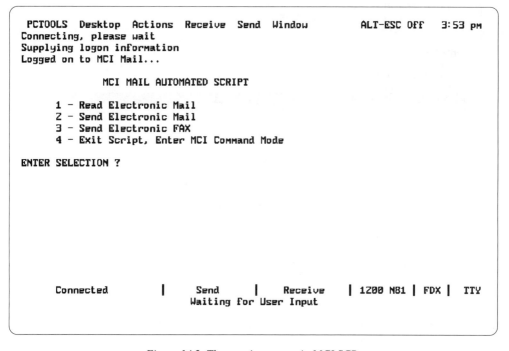

```
 PCTOOLS  Desktop  Actions  Receive  Send  Window        ALT-ESC Off   3:53 pm
Connecting, please wait
Supplying logon information
Logged on to MCI Mail...

            MCI MAIL AUTOMATED SCRIPT

   1 - Read Electronic Mail
   2 - Send Electronic Mail
   3 - Send Electronic FAX
   4 - Exit Script, Enter MCI Command Mode

ENTER SELECTION ?




   Connected          |     Send    |    Receive   | 1200 N81 | FDX |  TTY
                            Waiting for User Input
```

Figure 14.2. The opening screen in MCI.SCR

MCI.SCR contains fifteen commands. You've seen eight of them in CPS.SCR; seven are new: *Backtalk, Database, Download, HangUp, Receive, Upload,* and *V1.* To view this file, load it into the Notepads Editor screen. When it is loaded, your screen should look like Figure 14.3.

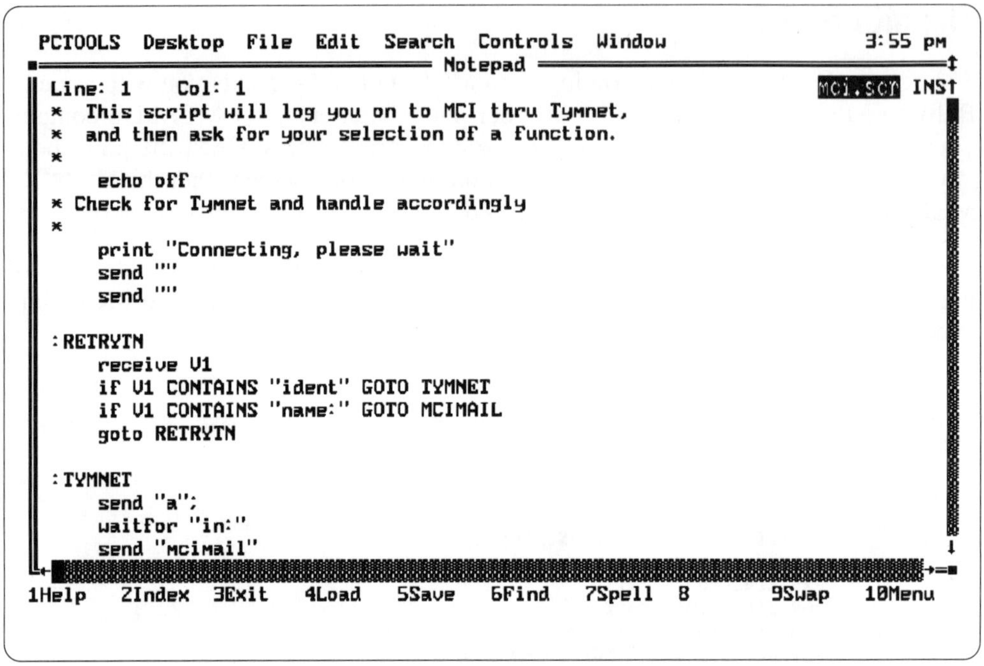

```
 PCTOOLS  Desktop  File  Edit  Search  Controls  Window          3:55 PM
 ━━━━━━━━━━━━━━━━━━━━━━━━━━━━━━ Notepad ━━━━━━━━━━━━━━━━━━━━━━━━━━━━━━━━┷
 Line: 1     Col: 1                                          MCI.SCR  INS↑
 *  This script will log you on to MCI thru Tymnet,
 *  and then ask for your selection of a function.
 *
     echo off
 * Check for Tymnet and handle accordingly
 *
     print "Connecting, please wait"
     send ""
     send ""

 : RETRYTN
     receive V1
     if V1 CONTAINS "ident" GOTO TYMNET
     if V1 CONTAINS "name:" GOTO MCIMAIL
     goto RETRYTN

 : TYMNET
     send "a";
     waitfor "in:"
     send "mcimail"                                                      ↓
 ↳━━━━━━━━━━━━━━━━━━━━━━━━━━━━━━━━━━━━━━━━━━━━━━━━━━━━━━━━━━━━━━━━━━━━━◆═■
 1Help   2Index  3Exit   4Load   5Save   6Find   7Spell  8       9Swap   10Menu
```

Figure 14.3. The top of MCI.SCR in the Notepads Editor screen

The first several lines are introductory comments. The first command, *Echo Off*, reduces the amount of text echoed back to your screen. It's nice to see this text when you first start out, but after awhile you won't pay attention to it. However, if you want to follow the progress of MCI.SCR more closely, turn echo on.

After the *Echo Off* command, there's one *Print* and two *Send* commands. These tell you PC Tools is logging on.

PC Tools then reads linearly to the :RETRYTN label. This group of commands uses the variable V1, which reads the reply from your screen and figures out what to do.

Variables

A variable in PC Tools script language is a series of text characters that can vary from one time to the next. You can store up to three variables in PC Tools' memory, and can change these variables when you want to. Variables are the crucial elements of a dialogue with another computer.

The command *Receive V1* takes you the next text line that appears on your screen (sent by your connection), stores it in memory, and then compares the contents of this line to certain *If* conditions. For our example, PC Tools takes the line and first searches for *ident*. This is part of a larger message unique to the Tymnet service. If PC Tools finds these characters, it goes to the Tymnet group of commands under the label :TYMNET. If those characters aren't found, PC Tools checks for *name*. This is a unique part of the MCI Mail connection message. If it finds these characters, PC Tools goes to the label :MCIMAIL.

If for some reason neither group of characters is found, the next command, *GoTo Retrytn*, returns you to the top of the current group and walks you through the commands all over again.

If you don't use Tymnet to connect to MCI Mail, delete the commands down to and, including the label :MCIMAIL. Though these would just be ignored by the PC Tools programs, it's better not to include more lines of code than you actually need.

You can also use variables to read your own information. The commands under the label :*Retryas* begins by showing a menu. To select one of the four operations, press the key that matches your selection. This number is put into the variable V1, which is then checked against the list of conditions that follow. PC Tools will route itself to the label, or group of commands, that apply to the desired activity.

Back to MCI.SCR

The program can automatically pick up mail for you to read. The command BACK-TALK calls on the program BACKTALK.EXE, which must have been loaded prior to your running this script. If it has, you'll exit the On-Line screen and do other things on your computer, since all activity takes place in the background. You can find out more about background communications at the end of this chapter.

The following commands download any awaiting mail to the file TODAYS.MCI:

```
print "Capturing mail to 'TODAYS.MCI'"
send "PRINT INBOX"
DOWNLOAD ASCII "todays.mci"
```

When all the mail has been downloaded, the program tells you it is finished and proceeds to the :EXIT label, which exits MCI Mail and hangs up for you.

Further down the file, you can find the following commands:

```
database V1
if V1 <> "" goto SMAILOK
print "Enter MCI User Name to send Mail to:"
input V1]
```

This opens the database whose name is in the current phone entry.

You should be able to decipher the meanings of most of the remaining commands and groups of commands with these few lessons.

The *Pause* command lets you pause execution of the script for a certain number of seconds, which you enter after the command; for instance, *Pause 1* means wait one second, and *Pause 10* means wait ten seconds.

TrOff and *TrOn* are used to trace problems you might experience when writing script files of your own. They trace the progress of PC Tools through the script file by displaying each line as it is called on the bottom of your screen. The execution is paused until you press [Spacebar], giving you time to check each line. You can insert *TrOff On* and *TrOff Off* commands through a file to check those parts and skip over other sections you know work well.

Input and *Upload* are used, respectively, to store characters from your keyboard and to send a file to another computer. You'll seldom perform either of these activities on an automated basis.

CREATING A NEW SCRIPT FILE

You can create all sorts of script files. The contents depend only upon what you want to do when you communicate with another computer.

We're going to create two script files in this section. The first will log you onto CPS BBS, see if you have any messages waiting, download them if you do, send a message you've already created, and then log you off. The second script file will be a refinement of the first: It will send a file only if you downloaded a message from the bulletin board.

Logging Onto CPS BBS and Leaving a Message

The first script you will create will log you onto the Central Point Software bulletin board, leave questions you would like answered, receive any messages waiting for you (presumably, replies to previous questions), and then log off. We'll assume that you've already created the message you want to send in a subdirectory called MAIL, and given it the name QUESTION.TXT. The file will be referred to as C:\MAIL\QUESTION.TXT. You can give the file any name you want and put it in any path, as long as you insert the name and path in the script file that sends it.

First, create the script file CPSMAIL.SCR that sends the file. At the Desktop menu:

> **Press:** [N]
>
> **Type:** C:\PCTOOLS\CPSMAIL.SCR
>
> **Press:** [Enter] twice

When the empty Notepads Editor screen appears:

> **Type:** * Script file to send messages to CPS BBS
>
> **Press:** Enter]

The entire file should look like Table 14.2.

```
* Script file to send messages to CPS BBS
ECHO ON
WAITFOR "(Y/N)"
SEND "Y"
WAITFOR "new"
WAITFOR ":"
SEND "place your user name here"
WAITFOR "Password"
SEND "place your password here"
WAITFOR "help:"
SEND "6"
WAITFOR "help:"
SEND "1"
WAITFOR "editing)."
PRINT "Path and name of file to send"
INPUT V3
UPLOAD ASCII V3
SEND "/S"
WAITFOR "(Y/N)?"
SEND "N"
WAITFOR "(Y/N)?"
SEND "N"
WAITFOR "(Y/N)?"
SEND "N"
WAITFOR "info:"
SEND "X"
WAITFOR ">>"
SEND "X"
WAITFOR "help:"
SEND "X"
WAITFOR "re-logon)?"
SEND "Y"
HANGUP
```

Table 14.2. The Script file to send messages to CPS BBS

The first few commands are abbreviated from CPS.SCR so you can log on correctly. Entering your user name and password directly from entries in the script file saves a few milliseconds. It's not as elegant, but you can see how they work. You could make this file considerably shorter by removing all the commands after saving your file with SEND /S and replacing them with HANGUP.

You might need to edit some of the commands in CPSMAIL.SCR if Central Point changes their bulletin board.

Checking for Errors

Check for errors in a new or revised script file in two ways. First proofread, then make a call using the script file. It helps to have the command *Echo On* at the top of a file you're using for the first time, so you can see all messages displayed on screen.

The PC Tools Telecommunications program has a learning component built into it. When the program runs across a command that doesn't make sense, it will display the command on screen and show it as an error. You can skip over the command and continue with your call by pressing [Enter], or you can hang up by pressing [F8]. You can then return to the Notepads Editor screen, make the necessary change, and try the call again. This can be tedious, but it is foolproof.

Try using your script CPSMAIL.SCR now. Return to your Telecommunications screen. If you're working in the Notepads Editor screen, switch active windows. Otherwise, open the Notepads Editor screen:

> **Press:** [Alt]-[D]-[T]

Now, create a second entry for CPS BBS, as shown in Figure 14.4.

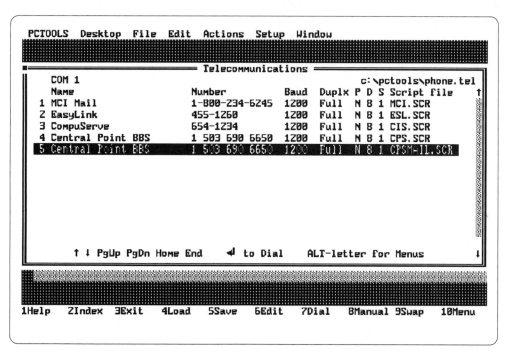

Figure 14.4. A new CPS BBS entry

Type in the CPSMAIL.SCR filename in the third field from the top of the Edit window. Once all parameters are set, accept this entry and make your first call.

If you run across a problem and the program displays an error message, write it down, press [F8] to disconnect, and return to the Notepads Editor screen (press [F9]) to make the necessary adjustments. You'll probably run into problems when you start creating script files on your own.

Revising

You might want to revise CPSMAIL.SCR. Of course, you can use several different script files for accessing CPS BBS, and create separate phone entries for each one.

For example, let's make sending mail conditional upon receiving mail, since if Central Point Software Tech Support hasn't yet answered your last question, there's no point in overloading them with more questions.

To do this, you would place a few more commands and two new routines into CPS-MAIL.SCR, so it would look like Table 14.3.

```
* Script file to send messages to CPS BBS
ECHO ON
WAITFOR "(Y/N)"
SEND "Y"
WAITFOR "new"
WAITFOR ":"
SEND "place your user name here"
WAITFOR "Password"
SEND "place your password here"
WAITFOR "help:"
SEND "7"
RECEIVE V1
IF V1 CONTAINS "Sorry" GOTO BYE
IF V1 CONTAINS " one ?" GOTO PROCEED
:PROCEED
SEND "6"
WAITFOR "help:"
SEND "1"
WAITFOR "editing)."
PRINT "Path and name of file to send"
INPUT V3
UPLOAD ASCII V3
SEND "/S"
WAITFOR "(Y/N)?"
SEND "N"
WAITFOR "(Y/N)?"
SEND "N"
WAITFOR "(Y/N)?"
SEND "N"
WAITFOR "info:"
SEND "X"
WAITFOR ">>"
SEND "X"
WAITFOR "help:"
SEND "X"
WAITFOR "re-logon)?"
SEND "Y"
:BYE
    HANGUP
```

Table 14.3. The revised script file to send messages to CPS BBS

This file first checks for any waiting mail. If there is no mail waiting, you end the call by proceeding to the :BYE label. If there is some mail, the script file proceeds to send your new message using the V3 variable.

We could insert more commands that download your waiting mail, but I didn't want to make this example too complex.

BACKGROUND COMMUNICATIONS

The can communicate in the background if all you want to do is send and receive files. Communicating in the background lets you do other things with your computer while the screen goes through commands. Communications takes place in the background in DOS the same way the PC Tools programs can go resident. A TSR program manages your communications out of sight.

To communicate in the background, you must load the background communications driver file BACKTALK.EXE, which simply enables background communications without changing the way the PC Tools Telecommunications program behaves.

You must also automate communications using a script file that logs you onto the communication service you want to use and passes to the service commands that describe what you want to do while communicating.

You can also use the Appointment Scheduler to set the times when you want certain calls to be made. This would fully automate your communications; all you would have to do is create the files you want to send (using the same names you've logged into the script file), and read the mail you get after it's been saved to disk. This is the handiest way to use background communications if you're a frequent user of e-mail services. This way you can download your mail automatically without bothering about it and the read your mail when it's convenient. You can even have your computer tell you when it is downloading messages, so you can decide whether you want to read them right away or wait for a more convenient time.

All this requires that you know how to write script files in the Notepads Editor screen and create appointments that call Telecommunications in the Appointment Schedule. You might want to review chapters in this book that describe those features if you haven't done so already.

Loading BACKTALK.EXE

The documentation says you have to load BACKTALK.EXE as a command in your AUTOEXEC.BAT file, but that's not strictly true. You can load BACKTALK.EXE any time you want to perform background communications, and remove it from memory when you no longer need it by running KILL.EXE. The BACKTALK.EXE program is a separate TSR program that can be loaded and unloaded on its own.

To enable background communications, begin at the DOS prompt:

Type: BACKTALK

Press: [Enter]

In a moment, you should see the line *Background communications installed for COM1*. The serial port COM1 is the default port, which you can change using a switch with the *Backtalk* command. For instance, to install background communications for COM3:

Type: BACKTALK\3

Press: [Enter]

You must use a serial port for communications, but you can install background communications for serial ports COM1 through COM4.

Communicating in the Background

You'll communicate automatically in the background once you install BACK-TALK.EXE and make a call using a script file that uses the *Backtalk* command. As soon as Backtalk is called, you'll exit the On-Line screen and return to the Desktop main menu. A blinking *B* will appear in the upper right corner of your screen to remind you that background communication is taking place.

This *B* will appear in all your DOS and applications screens. If the mark stays longer than you think it should, you can kill background communications by removing BACKTALK.EXE from memory. Just return to your DOS prompt:

Type: KILL

Press: [Enter]

When you plan to send or receive files while communicating in the background, you need to enter the names of the files you want to send beforehand in the script file. You also need to declare which filename or series of filenames will record the files you plan to receive. Since all communication goes on in the background, once you start the call, the program proceeds on its own until it is finished, or until it encounters a problem.

You mark files to send or receive by inserting their names in the script file you're using. If you're not sure how many files you're going to receive, you can copy them all to the same file and then break them out later.

You can run into all sorts of problems when communicating. This happens more frequently when you communicate in the background because you aren't monitoring the program's success or failure. Good background communications require that you write perfect script files.

Using the XMODEM Protocol

The XMODEM protocol is used to double check the transfer of all files you send and receive. Whenever you use this protocol while communicating in the background, the PC Tools program will automatically create a file called TRANSFER.LOG, which logs in critical messages relating to each file transferred using XMODEM by the PC Tools program.

Critical messages can consist of all sorts of information. If you want to save this information, you should change the name of TRANSFER.LOG to another unique filename. Since TRANSFER.LOG is created automatically each time you work in background communications, the new version will always overwrite the old, unless you change the name of the old to another filename.

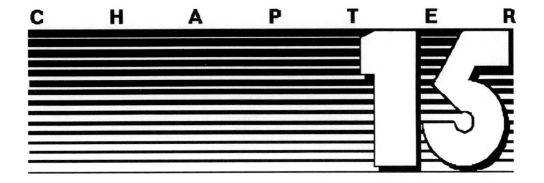

WORKING WITH MACROS

A *macro* is sequence of commands that can be replayed whenever you want to execute those commands. Five sample macro files have been provided as part of the PC Tools program. Four of these help you to print special formatting in your Notepads text files. The details of these macro printer files are described at the end of Chapter 6. The fifth sample macro file provided is called SAMPLE.PRO. This file provides a collection of macros that automate some of the commands frequently performed in PC Tools Deluxe.

OPENING THE MACROS EDITOR

To open the Macros Editor dialog box when the Desktop menu is showing:

Press: [M]

To open the box from any other Desktop module:

Press: [Alt]-[D]-[M]

When the Macros dialog box appears:

Type: SAMPLE

Press: [Enter]

The following sequence works only if PCTOOLS is in your default directory and SAMPLE.PRO has been installed. If not, you'll have to switch directories. Make sure your Macros Editor screen has been expanded to full size. If it hasn't been:

Press: [Alt]-[W]-[Z]

Your screen should now look like Figure 15.1.

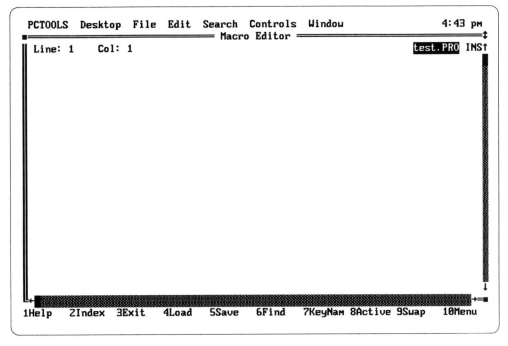

```
PCTOOLS  Desktop  File  Edit  Search  Controls  Window              4:43 PM
════════════════════════════════════ Macro Editor ═══════════════════════════
  Line: 1      Col: 1                                          test.PRO INS↑


                                                                             █
                                                                             █
                                                                             █
                                                                             █
                                                                             █
                                                                             █
                                                                             █
                                                                             █
                                                                             █
                                                                             █
                                                                             █
                                                                             █
                                                                             █
                                                                             ↓
  ◄                                                                         →▪
 1Help   2Index   3Exit   4Load   5Save   6Find   7KeyNam 8Active 9Swap   10Menu
```

Figure 15.1. The expanded Macros Editor screen

This screen is similar in appearance to the Notepads Editor screen. The only differences are in the menus and function-key assignments:

- The File pull-down menu has a new command, *Macro Activation*, in place of the commands *Print* and *Edit Without Saving*. If you want to print a macro file, you must load it into the Notepads Editor screen and print it there.

- The Edit pull-down menu doesn't have the three spell-checking commands. If you want to spell-check a macro file, do so in the Notepads Editor screen.

- The Controls pull-down menu retains only one command from its Notepads equivalent: *Save Setup*. Three new commands are specific to macro work: *Erase All Macros, Playback Delay,* and *Learn Mode*.

Figure 15.2 shows the pull-down menus for the Macros Editor.

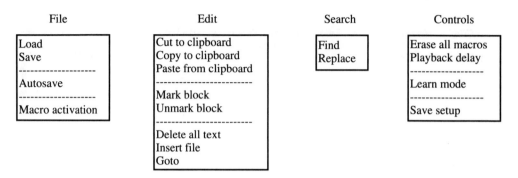

Figure 15.2. Pull-down menus in the Macros Editor screen

You can find six function-key assignments at the bottom of the Macros Editor screen.

[F1] Help   Opens the general Help screen.

[F2] Index   Opens the Help index.

[F3] Exit   Closes the current Macros Editor screen and returns you to the Desktop menu, or whatever you were working in before opening the Macros Editor.

[F4] Load   Opens the dialog box that lets you select or specify another macro file to work with.

[F5] Save   Saves the current macro file to disk.

[F6] Find   Opens the Find and Replace box.

[F7] Keyname   Lets you enter a key name directly into the macro file you're building.

[F8] Active   Lets you save the current macro file so it can perform in one of four possible ways.

[F9] Switch   Switches you between active windows.

[F10] Menu   Activates the top menu bar.

Only the functions of [F7] and [F8] differ from the Notepads. In the Notepads Editor screen, pressing [F7] begins spell-checking, and [F8] is not assigned.

WORKING WITH SAMPLE.PRO

Activate some examples in SAMPLE.PRO to figure out how the PC Tools macro command language works. To scroll through all the contents of this file:

Press: [PgDn] five times

Don't pay much attention to the individual commands. If you don't have a copy of the file, duplicate the commands, which are listed below.

[Ctrl]-[F8] Loads the SAMPLE.DBF database file, asks for the client you want to find, then dials the phone number for that entry:

```
<begdef><ctrlf8><desk>DSAMPLE.DBF<enter><alts>
T<vfld>..<vfld><alts><altc><altc><alta><cmd>d15
<enter><enddef>
```

[Ctrl]-[N] Creates or loads a daily notepad file:

```
<begdef><ctrln><desk>N<date>.TXT<enter><enter>
<enddef>
```

[Ctrl]-[F9] Reads your MCI Mail:

```
<begdef><ctrlf9><desk>TM1<enter.1<enter><esc>x
<enddef>
```

[Ctrl]-[R] Demonstrates a fixed-length fill-in-the-blanks. This prints *DIR* on your DOS command line, then waits for you to type the drive letter:

```
<begdef><ctrlr>DIR <ffld>#<ffld>:<enter>
<enddef>
```

[Ctrl]-[F] Demonstrates how you use a variable fill-in-the-blanks. This prints *DIR* on your DOS command line, then waits for you to enter a filename:

```
<begdef><ctrlf>DIR <vfld>..<vfld><enter>
<enddef>
```

[Ctrl]-[F5] Runs the PC Tools Compress program:

```
<begdef><ctrlf5>cd\PCTOOLS<enter.Compress C:
/CF<enter><enddef>
```

[Ctrl]-[F6]   Pops up Desktop Manager, loads the file SAMPLE.TXT, then finds the entry for ACME in the SAMPLE.DBF database file:

```
<begdef><ctrlf6><desk>NSAMPLE.TXT<enter><desk>
DSAMPLE.DBF<enter><alts>TACME<alts><altc>
<enddef>
```

[Ctrl]-[F7]   Pops up Desktop Manager and asks which Notepads file you want to load, then asks which customer you want to find in the SAMPLE.DBF database:

```
<begdef><ctrlf7><desk>N<vfld>..<vfld><enter>
<desk>DSAMPLE.DBF<enter><alts>T<vfld>..<vfld>
<alts><altc><enddef>
```

[Ctrl]-[F1]   Loads Desktop Manager:

```
<begdef><ctrlf1><desk><enddef>
```

[Ctrl]-[F2]   Loads Desktop Manager, then opens the Algebraic Calculator:

```
<begdef><ctrlf2><desk><CA<enddef>
```

[Ctrl]-[F3]   Runs the PC Backup program:

```
<begdef><ctrlf3>cd\PCTOOLS<enter>PCBACKUP>
<enter><enddef>
```

[Shift]-[F3]   Demonstrates how you use linked macros:

```
<begdef><shiftf1>This is a test of one
macro<enddef>
<begdef><shiftf2>calling two others<enddef>
<begdef><shiftf3><shiftf1><shiftf2><enddef>
```

[Ctrl]-[D]   Demonstrates how you use the date and time stamps in a macro:

```
<begdef><ctrld><date>, <time><enddef>
```

[Ctrl]-[F4]   Demonstrates how you use a delay in a macro:

```
<begdef><ctrlf4>wait 4 seconds...<cmd>d4<enter>
Done<enddef>
```

These commands might not make much sense to you now, but you'll learn how they work by activating the file and experimenting with various commands. First, move back to the top of SAMPLE.PRO:

Press: [Ctrl]-[Home]

The first paragraph tells you that the macro file assigns macro commands to sixteen key combinations.

[Ctrl]-[F1] Opens the Desktop main menu.

[Ctrl]-[F2] Opens the Algebraic calculator.

[Ctrl]-[F3] Loads the PC Backup program when run at the DOS prompt.

[Ctrl]-[F4] Displays the string: `wait 4 seconds...`, waits four seconds, then inserts a hard-carriage return and displays `Done`. This key combination not only specifies a time delay, but also demonstrates how the text character is used in a text editor.

[Ctrl]-[F5] Loads the PC Compress programs when run at your DOS prompt. You might want to view this play-out in an Editor screen.

[Ctrl]-[F6] Loads the SAMPLE.TXT file in the Notepads Editor screen, overlays it with the Databases Editor screen, loads SAMPLE.DBF, and goes to the ACME company record. This is a display of menu commands, popping open one module, and then going to another.

[Ctrl]-[F7] Opens the Notepads dialog box.

[Ctrl]-[F8] Loads the SAMPLE.DBF in the Databases Editor screen and opens the Search Sort Field box, letting you type the text necessary to specify which record you want to go to.

[Ctrl]-[F9] Opens your Telecommunications screen, calls MCI, reads your mail, and then hangs up. This is a handy way to download your MCI mail.

[Ctrl]-[D] Automatically types the current date and time at your cursor position (D stands for Date).

[Ctrl]-[F] Runs the DOS command DIR and lets you fill in the filename you want to list. Start at your DOS prompt and press [Ctrl]-[F]. After DIR appears, type the name of a file you want to list. This is a demonstration of a *variable fill-in-the-blanks,* a variable you supply.

[Ctrl]-[N]	Creates a Notepads file using the current date for a filename; for example, 12-18-89.TXT (N stands for Notepads).
[Ctrl]-[R]	Runs the DOS command DIR and lets you type the drive you want to check. Start at your DOS prompt. Press [Ctrl]-[R] and after DIR appears, type the drive you want to check. This is a demonstration of a *fixed-length fill-in-the-blanks*.
[Shift]-[F1]	Prints the string: `This is a test of one macro.` Make sure you're working in an editor or word processor when you activate this command.
[Shift]-[F2]	Prints the string: `calling two others.` Make sure you're working in an editor or word processor when you activate this command.
[Shift]-[F3]	Prints the string: `This is a test of one macro calling two others.` Calls the commands assigned to [Shift]-[F1] and the commands assigned to [Shift]-[F2]. Make sure you're working in an editor or word processor when you activate this command.

The best way to learn the commands assigned to these macros is to activate this macro file and run one or two of them to see their effects. Then go back to analyze the command structure and see how they seized control of the program.

Activating SAMPLE.PRO

You must be viewing the SAMPLE.PRO file to activate it. While SAMPLE.PRO is showing in the Macros Editor screen:

> **Press:** [F8]

This opens the Macros Active box. The four options in this window broaden the discussion of macro performance.

Not Active	Deactivates a macro file that's been made active, essentially turning off all the commands. Once *Not Active* is initiated, you will have to reactivate the macro file using one of the three following options.
Active When In Desktop	Allows the macro to operate only while you're working within PC Tools, either in standard or resident mode.

Active When Not In Desktop   Allows the macro to operate only when you're working outside of PC Tools—in, for example, DOS, WordPerfect, or dBASE—when PC Tools has been installed in resident mode.

Active Everywhere   The macro will work everywhere, both inside and outside of PC Tools, as long as the program has been installed in resident mode.

For example, to highlight *Active Everywhere:*

> **Press:** [⇓] three times

> **Press:** [Enter] twice

Now all commands in SAMPLE.PRO have been made part of the Desktop program.

To see how some of the macro commands behave, bail out of Desktop:

> **Press:** [Ctrl]-[Spacebar]

You will return to the DOS prompt or to the application you were working in.

Running Some Examples

To test the first key combination:

> **Press:** [Ctrl]-[F1]

This should bring the Desktop menu on screen. You can now access any of the commands on this menu. While pressing [Ctrl]-[F1] is not much different from pressing [Ctrl]-[Spacebar], it does show you how a macro works.

To get rid of the Desktop menu:

> **Press:** [Esc]

Now try another key combination reassigned by SAMPLE.PRO.

> **Press:** [Ctrl]-[F2]

This opens the Algebraic calculator. This macro does save you a step; you do not have to go through the Desktop menu and the Utilities menu.

Press: [Esc] twice

You can try a few more combinations, referring to the sixteen macro commands earlier in this section.

Deactivating SAMPLE.PRO

You might find that these new key assignments conflict with commands you want to use in other programs. For example, I use Sprint for much of my word processing, and I save these files by pressing [Ctrl]-[F2]. After I activate SAMPLE.PRO, the PC Tools macro command assigned to those two keys override my Sprint command. Since I use the Algebraic calculator less than I do Sprint, I want to deactivate that command. Unfortunately, to remove the macro [Ctrl]-[F2], I have to deactivate the entire SAMPLE.PRO macro file.

To deactivate SAMPLE.PRO, return to the Macros Editor with the file contents for SAMPLE.PRO showing on your screen:

Press: [F8]

Highlight: Not active

Press: [Enter] twice

You can verify that a macro has been deactivated by trying any of the keys it reassigns:

Press: [Ctrl]-[F2]

If nothing happens, you have successfully deactivated SAMPLE.PRO.

ALL ABOUT MACROS

Before you can really understand the various macro commands assigned to examples in SAMPLE.PRO, you should learn the features basic to all macro files. Then you'll learn how to use these features to build your own simple macro files.

Macro File Anatomy

Building macros so they perform successfully requires that you follow certain rules. This is similar to other forms of computer programming. The only difference is that building macros is much less difficult than working with computer languages.

A macro command must contain the following four elements in the order shown for it to work:

```
<begdef><key assignment><commands><enddef>
```

Take a closer look at each of these elements:

\<begdef\>   BEGins the DEFinition of the macro command.

\<key assignment\> Identifies the key combinations you want to assign to the macro command.

\<commands\>   Identifies one or more acceptable macro commands strung together that will be acted on in sequence.

\<enddef\>   ENDs the DEFinition of the macro command.

Only the two elements \<key assignment\> and \<commands\> change from one macro to the next. The first determines how you execute a macro. The second determines what the macro does. The \<begdef\> and \<enddef\> elements must always appear at the beginning and the end, respectively, of each macro command.

Before going further, I should clear up the terms *macro, macro command,* and *macro file.*

- A macro is a series of commands.
- A macro command is a single command from the list of valid macro command names in PC Tools.
- A macro file contains at least three valid macro commands and a key assignment. It is usually saved to disk with the .PRO extension, but you can use another extension if you want to specify it each time you view, deactivate, and reactive the file.

To understand these terms better, create a simple macro that puts your name into a text file. Open a new file in the Macros Editor. Beginning at the Desktop menu:

Press: [M]

Type: NAME

Press: [Enter] twice

This opens the macro file NAME.PRO. When the blank Macros Editor screen appears:

Type: \<begdef\>

Press: [Enter] twice

Type: <enddef>

Press: [⇑]

This inserts the mandatory beginning and ending macro commands and a blank line between them where your cursor will appear, as shown in Figure 15.3.

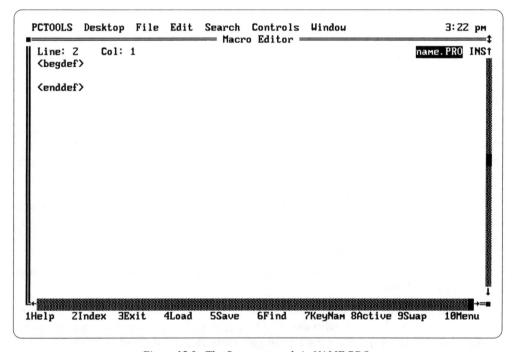

```
 PCTOOLS  Desktop  File  Edit  Search  Controls  Window              3:22 PM
 ═══════════════════════════════════ Macro Editor ═══════════════════════════╪
 ║ Line: 2     Col: 1                                            name.PRO INS↑
 ║ <begdef>
 ║
 ║ <enddef>
 ║
 ║
 ║
 ║
 ║
 ║
 ║
 ║
 ║
 ║
 ║
 ║
 ║
 ║
 ║
 ║←                                                                        →▪
 1Help   2Index  3Exit   4Load   5Save   6Find   7KeyNam 8Active 9Swap  10Menu
```

Figure 15.3. The first commands in NAME.PRO

You don't need to insert both beginning and ending macro commands when you start out. I do it out of habit.

> You can also use shortcuts for entering the required beginning and ending macro commands. Pressing [Alt]-[+] will insert <begdef> and pressing [Alt]-[-] will insert <enddef>. These keys aren't helpful unless you're working in learn mode, described later in this chapter. I find it easier just to type the commands.

Next, assign keys to activate the macro. To assign [Ctrl]-[X] to the macro:

Type: <ctrlx>

You have to make sure you aren't reassigning a key combination you used for something else. You should avoid using [Alt] key combinations, since pressing [Alt] is a common way for activating the top menu bar.

To insert your name in the cursor position:

Type: Your name

Each time you press [Ctrl]-[X] your name will appear at the cursor.

That's all there is to it. Four lines of commands should appear on your screen and look like this:

```
<begdef>
<ctrlx>
Your name
<enddef>
```

I prefer to arrange commands or command sequences in a vertical row, like the four lines above, but it's also correct to place all the commands on a single line:

```
<begdef><ctrlx>Your name<enddef>
```

However, when you start creating a larger macro file, like the example at the end of this chapter, you'll find placing parts of the file on different lines will help you to make sense of the commands.

These commands are not case-sensitive, except when you type the text you want the macro command to insert, such as your name.

Saving and Activating Macro Files

After building a macro file, you need to save it to a disk file, and then activate it. It is not absolutely necessary that you save the file, but it is strongly recommended. You can activate a file that appears on screen and hasn't yet been saved to disk; it will still work, but you will not have a record of it if you want to go back and deactivate it or check it for errors. If you don't save the file before activating it, you might lose the file.

To save the file NAME.PRO:

> **Press:** [F5]

This opens the Save File to Disk box, which is identical in appearance and behavior to the same-named box in the Notepads Editor.

To save the file to the name you've given it, and accept all the default options in the box:

> **Press:** [Enter] twice

If you want to use menus to save a file:

> **Press:** [Alt]-[F]-[S]

The file is now saved, but it is not part of the program. You must now activate it. To open the Macros Active box:

> **Press:** [F8]

> **Highlight:** Active when in PCTOOLS Desktop

> **Press:** [Enter] twice

You can also activate a macro file using menus by pressing [Alt]-[F]-[M].

To test this macro in the file you're working in:

> **Press:** [Ctrl]-[X]

Your name will appear at your cursor position. Now, any time you want to type your name, just press [Ctrl]-[X]. Your name will appear each time, until you deactivate the macro NAME.PRO.

Erasing All Macros

To erase all the macros you have previously activated:

> **Press:** [Alt]-[C]-[E]

WORKING WITH MACRO COMMANDS

There are eight commands you can use to build a macro file:

\<begdef>   Marks the beginning of a string of macro commands that form a single complete macro. This command must come before all others.

\<cmd>d#   Sets a time delay specified by #, or the amount of delay. You use the format hh:mm:ss:t to specify hours, minutes, seconds, and tenths of a second. A slot with no number specified defaults to seconds. Use \<cmd>d5 to set a delay of five seconds. To set a five-hour delay, use \<cmd>d5:0:0. To set a five-minute delay, use \<cmd>d5:0. And to set a half-second delay (or 5/10ths of a second), use \<cmd>d.5. You can specify a delay as short as 1/10th of a second (\<cmd>d.1) or as long as 256 hours (\<cmd>d256:0:0).

\<date>   Inserts the current date at your cursor position, using the mm/dd/yy format.

\<desk>   Opens the Desktop main menu when it is loaded in resident mode. A macro cannot call the currently assigned hotkey combination to pop open this menu.

\<enddef>   Marks the end of a string of macro commands that form a single complete macro. This command must come after all others.

\<ffld>#   Inserts variable information of a known length at the time you run the macro. For example, if you want to check the directory entries of one of several disks, design the macro so that it runs the DOS command DIR, then type the disk drive letter you want to check. The disk drive can vary from one run of the macro to the next, but the drive letter will always be only one character long. This command is often called a *fixed-length fill-in-the-blanks* variable.

\<time>   Inserts the current time at your cursor position, using the *hh:mm* format.

\<vfld>   Inserts variable information of varying length at the time you run the macro. For example, if you want to check a specific range of entries on a disk, design the macro so it runs the DOS command DIR, then type the entry information, or as much of it as you want to, including DOS wildcards. This command is often called a *variable-length fill-in-the-blanks variable*.

The next several examples will help you learn how to use these commands.

Inserting Time and Date Stamps

You can insert time and date stamps into your files using the <time> and <date> commands. For example, create a macro file called TIMEDATE.PRO. When the empty Macros Editor screen for this file appears, insert these commands:

```
<begdef><ctrlt><time><enddef>
<begdef><ctrld><date><enddef>
<begdef><ctrlb><date><time><enddef>
```

The first line creates a command that inserts the current time when you press [Ctrl]-[T]. The second command inserts the current date when you press [Ctrl]-[D]. The third command inserts both date and time when you press [Ctrl]-[B]. The mnemonic key assignments are T for time, D for date, and B for both.

Activate the macro file:

Press: [F8]

Press: [Enter] twice

You're ready to try them out. If for some reason they don't work correctly, deactivate the file so you free up the three key assignments.

USING THE LEARN MODE

The learn mode is designed to let you build macros by entering commands from the keyboard. These are saved to memory and then recorded to a file that you can subsequently view and edit.

Use the learn mode to build a macro that takes you on a brief tour of the Desktop Manager.

Switch learn mode on:

Press: [Alt]-[C]-[L]

Make sure the check-mark appears next to the *Learn Mode* command. Now exit the Macros Editor screen and return to your DOS screen:

Press: [Esc] twice

Don't hotkey out of the Desktop Manager. Since you're going to take a tour of the Desktop Manager program, you want the Desktop main menu to appear as the first feature. If you hotkey out of the Macros Editor screen and then call the Desktop Manager program, you'll move right back into the Macros Editor screen.

If you were building a macro in an underlying application where you didn't need to access the Desktop main menu, you could hotkey out of the Desktop Manager by pressing [Ctrl]-[Spacebar].

When you see your cursor blinking at the DOS prompt:

Press: [Alt]-[+] (Use the [+/=] key on the top row of your typewriter keyboard)

Pressing these two keys begins a macro in learn mode. It's the only way you can insert the <begdef> command in the memory buffer of PC Tools. Notice that your cursor changes to a block shape (unless that's the way you see your cursor normally). The change in cursor shape shows that you're working in learn mode.

Now, walk through the following brief tour of the Desktop Manager. Remember that every keystroke you perform will be stored in memory. Don't worry if you make a mistake, just make your corrections and continue with the tour. Later you can edit your keystrokes.

First, you must declare the keys you want to assign to this macro:

Press: [Ctrl]-[T]

Now, begin the tour.

Press: [Ctrl]-[Spacebar]

This should open the Desktop main menu.

Press: [N]

Type: TEST

Press: [Enter] twice

Type: This is the Notepads screen

Press: [Alt]-[D]

This should open the Desktop menu in the Notepads Editor screen.

> **Press:** [O]
>
> **Type:** TEST
>
> **Press:** [Enter] twice
>
> **Type:** This is the Outlines screen
>
> **Press:** [Alt]-[D]

This should open the Desktop menu in the Outlines Editor screen.

> **Press:** [D]
>
> **Type:** TEST
>
> **Press:** [Enter] twice
>
> **Type:** Hi!
>
> **Press:** [Esc] four times

This should return you to your DOS prompt. If it doesn't, keep pressing [Esc]. Now, check the files you've created.

> **Type:** CD PCTOOLS
>
> **Press:** [Enter]
>
> **Type:** DIR TEST*.*
>
> **Press:** [Enter]

As long as all the files that show in the filtered list are file names you created during the tour, delete them.

> **Type:** DEL TEST*.*
>
> **Press:** [Enter]

Now sign off:

> **Type:** That's all, folks!

Now stop the learn mode:

Press: [Alt]-[-] (use the hyphen/underline key)

This should change your cursor back to its original shape.

In some cases, your cursor might take a third shape. Exiting and entering a few applications should change it back to the shape you're familiar with.

Now, re-enter the Macros Editor screen and toggle off the learn mode:

Press: [Alt]-[C]-[L]

The keystrokes you've just placed into memory remain in a file called LEARN.PRO. Take a look at them:

Press: [Alt]-[F]-[L]

Type: LEARN

Press: [Enter]

When the file appears on screen, it looks like Figure 15.4.

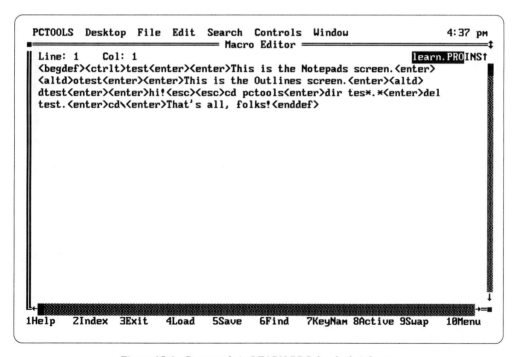

Figure 15.4. Commands in LEARN.PRO for the brief tour

You can now edit these commands. One change you'll have to make is to insert the command <desk> between <ctrlt> and *test*. When you popped open the Desktop main menu to start the tour, you pressed [Ctrl]-[Spacebar], but the hotkeys do not operate in a macro. You need to use the command <desk> to pop open the Desktop main menu (although you can use [Esc] to exit the Desktop Manager).

Once you start editing LEARN.PRO, you should change its filename, so you can keep a permanent file of the macro commands. Use PC Shell and change the name to TOUR.PRO. Once you've done this, view TOUR.PRO in the Macros Editor, edit it further, and activate it. The changes I made to TOUR.PRO are shown in Figure 15.5.

Figure 15.5. A modified TOUR.PRO

The substantial changes are to insert delays of a half-second each between opening the Desktop main menu and selecting the three modules: Notepads, Outlines, and Databases, using the command <cmd>d.5.

Save this macro by pressing [F5] and selecting the ASCII format. Next, deactivate all macros:

Press: [Alt]-[C]-[E]

Press: [Enter]

It's a good idea to clear out all macros while you're building one in learn mode.

Now make TOUR.PRO active everywhere.

Once you've gotten TOUR.PRO to work, you should probably deactivate it and then delete it. I don't recommend assigning the keys [Ctrl]-[T] to any macro, because they are used in many word processing programs for deleting the word following your cursor.

THINGS TO WATCH OUT FOR

There are several constraints you should watch out for when using macros, but they apply at different times to different operations.

- For a macro to call up the Desktop Manager using the <desk> command, the program must be running in resident mode.
- The Desktop manager must be loaded in resident mode to use the learn mode.
- You can call up PC Shell in either standard or resident mode, but you can't call any of the commands in the shell. Once you enter PC Shell, you're on your own.
- You can call other utility programs that serve as part of PC Tools Deluxe.
- If you find you can't get a macro to work correctly, try to deactivate it, erase the file, and start all over. You might have to erase all macros to start clean (press [Alt]-[C]-[E]).

LOADING PRINTER MACRO FILES

Printer macro files were introduced in Chapter 6. They are used to enhance the look of printed text files.

Once you've activated the macro file specific for the printer you want to employ, you can use these commands in your Notepads, Outlines, and Databases form files to print your files with special formatting effects.

To load any one of the printer macro files, begin by viewing it in the Macros Editor screen, then:

Press: [F8]

Select: Active when in PC Tools Desktop

Press: [Enter] twice

You can try to design printer macros for other types of printers, but you'll need the printer documentation. Most printers call special escape codes that you'll need to insert as part of the commands you want to use.

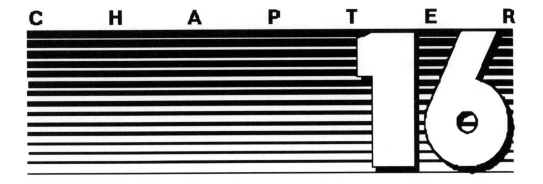

CHAPTER 16

WORKING WITH CALCULATORS

I n this chapter you will learn how to work with the four calculators provided in the Calculator module: Algebraic, Financial, Programmer's, and Scientific. This chapter is not designed to teach you how to make all the calculations possible within each calculator; entire books have been written about each type. What you will learn are the various commands you can use in each calculator, as well as the basic steps for making all calculations within each calculator.

OPENING THE CALCULATOR MODULE

To open the Calculator module from the main menu:

    Press: [C]

To open it from any other Desktop module:

    Press: [Alt]-[D]-[C]

This opens a menu that gives you a choice of four calculators:

Algebraic Calculator	Performs routine mathematical and algebraic calculations.
Financial Calculator	Performs advanced financial calculations emulating a Hewlett-Packard HP-12C hand-held calculator.
Programmer's (Hex) Calculator	Converts numbers between hex, octal, binary, decimal, and ASCII equivalents, among other programming calculations. This calculator emulates the HP-16C.
Scientific Calculator	Lets you perform advanced scientific calculations simulating a Hewlett-Packard HP-11C.

> If you intend to use one of these calculators intensively, I recommend that you supplement your reading with a book describing the equivalent Hewlett-Packard hand-held calculator.

You can use the same basic procedures in each of the calculators, although there are also crucial differences between them.

THE ALGEBRAIC CALCULATOR

The Algebraic calculator lets you perform most common algebraic calculations, including addition, division, subtraction, percentage, multiplication, and changing signs. Since the Algebraic calculator is frequently used, PC Tools designers have provided a handy macro that opens it from any place in your computer, if the Desktop Manager is loaded.

Recall that in Chapter 15, you learned that the macro that comes as part of SAMPLE.PRO looks like this: `<begdef><ctrlf2><desk>CA<enddef>`.

Once you activate this macro, you'll move into the Algebraic calculator each time you press [Ctrl]-[F2].

To open the Algebraic calculator, shown in Figure 6.1, when the Calculators menu is showing:

Press: [A]

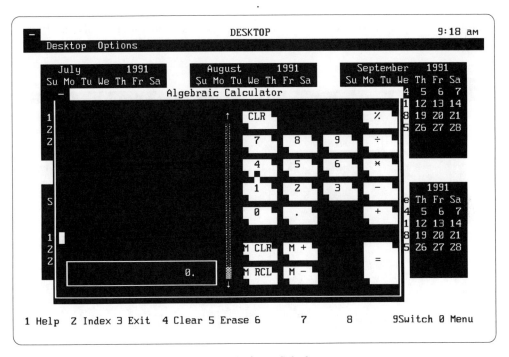

Figure 16.1. The Algebraic Calculator screen

This is a fairly simple display. The number keys are on the right, and the display register is on the left, with a window above it that simulates a tape. As you enter numbers and perform calculations on them, your results will appear in the register and the tape window. Each new calculation result replaces the previous number in the display register. New calculations in the tape scroll upward as you add more numbers. You can edit the tape and move to numbers that have scrolled off the top.

The right half of the Calculator screen is intended for use with a mouse. If you're using a mouse, you just point to the key you want to use and press a button.

To enter numbers without a mouse, type the numbers with the numeric keypad, usually on the right side of the keyboard.

I recommend that you leave the right side of the Algebraic calculator showing, because the key display can remind you of many commands. But if you wish, you can toggle the right side on and off with the wide display, which is on by default. To switch it off:

Press: [Alt]-[O]-[W]

When wide display is off, your Algebraic Calculator screen should look like Figure 16.2.

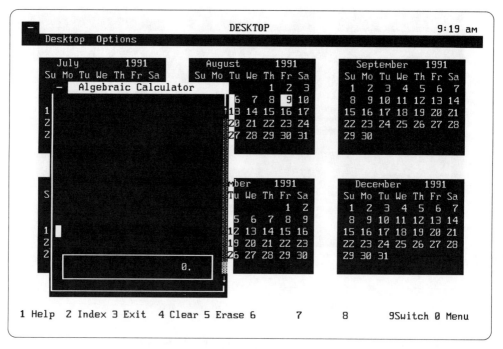

Figure 16.2. The Algebraic calculator with wide display off

After toggling the wide display back on, try a simple calculation. First, make sure [Num Lock] is on:

Press: [Num Lock]

To multiply 2 x 4:

Press: [2]

Press: [*] (As an alternative to pressing * for multiplication, you can press [X])

Press: [4]

Press: [=]

The result, 8, should appear in the display register. Your tape should now look like Figure 16.3

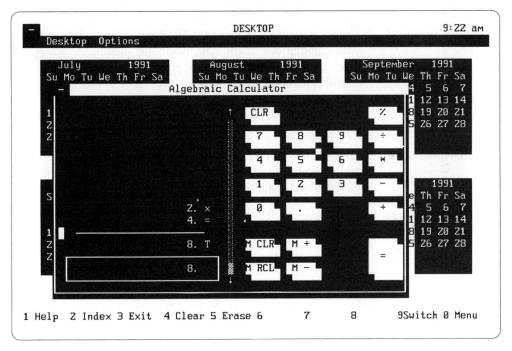

Figure 16.3. The Algebraic calculator tape display

The exact keys you press depend upon what type of keyboard you're using. If you have a separate keypad, then you should use those keys. Most keypads also have a separate asterisk key; however, you can press [Shift]-[8] to get the same effect.

If 8 does not appear on your display, clear it by pressing [F4] or [C]. This will insert a zero in the tape followed by C, to show that all calculations up to that point have been cleared.

To clear the tape:

Press: [F5]

Now, look at the menus. The Desktop and Window menus are the same ones you get in the other modules. There's only one new menu—Options ([Alt]-[O]), which contains five commands:

Clear Display   Clears the current display. Same as pressing [F4] or [C].

Erase Tape   Clears the tape on screen. Same as pressing [F5].

Copy to Clipboard   Copies the current tape to the Clipboard. This lets you move your calculations to another document, such as the Notepads screen, or to an outside application, such as a document in WordPerfect or Lotus 1-2-3.

Print Tape   Opens the Print window, which lets you select the print device.

Wide Display   Toggles the calculator display between wide (Figure 16.1) and narrow (Figure 16.2). You need only the wide display if you're using a mouse.

You need only a few menu commands, because working with the Algebraic calculator is simple and straightforward. Table 16.1 shows the commands you can use.

Function	Keyboard	Mouse
Add	[+]	[+]
Subtract	[-]	[-]
Multiply	[*] or [X]	[*]
Divide	[/]	[/]
Equal	[=] or [Enter]	[=]
Total	[=] or [Enter]	[=]
Clear	[C]	[CLR]
Percentage	[%]	[%]
Memory		
Add	[M]-[+]	[M]-[+]
Subtract	[M]-[-]	[M]-[-]
Recall	[M]-[R]	[MR]
Erase	[M]-[C]	[MC]
Edit Tape ([Num Lock] off)		
Up one line	[⇑]	move up
Up one window	[PgUp]	
Down one line	[⇓]	
Down one window	[PgDn]	
Decimal places set	[D] + decimal places	
Toggle comma on and off	[,]	[,]

Table 16.1. List of commands in the Algebraic calculator

To display a number to five decimal places:

Press: [D]-[5]

To turn off decimal display:

Press: [D]-[0]

The bottom line of your screen shows seven function-key assignments:

[F1] Help Opens the definition of the Algebraic calculator, from which you can move into the Help index.

[F2] Index Opens the Help index list.

[F3] Exit Closes the Algebraic calculator and returns you to the Desktop menu or to whatever you had been working in.

[F4] Clear Clears the display register.

[F5] Erase Erases all contents on the current tape.

[F9] Switch   Switches you to other active windows.

[F10] Menu   Activates the top menu bar.

Using the Tape

You can work with the tape in several ways.

You can change the figures displayed in the tape and then run a new calculation on the figures. The tape can only show twelve lines of numbers, but it can hold up to a thousand lines. After that, the oldest calculation is erased to make room for the new. However, you can save the tape to a file periodically by copying the contents of the tape to the Clipboard, where you can paste it into a file in the Notepads Editor screen or into an outside application. First, however, make sure the wide display is toggled back on. If it isn't:

> **Press:** [Alt]-[O]-[W]

Editing the Tape

The basic procedure for editing the tape is to highlight the number you want to change, make the change, and then perform the calculation again by pressing [End]. The scroll bar down the center of the wide version of the calculator shows the relative position on the current tape.

In the previous calculation, you multiplied 2 x 4 and got 8. Edit the calculation to multiply 2 x 8.

Turn off Num Lock :

> **Press:** [Num Lock]

> **Press:** [⇑] once

Even though the 4 is two lines up from the display, you only need to press [⇑] once. You can only edit figures you've entered into the tape, so you skip over the first number, 8, which is the product of the first calculation.

When the number 4 appears on the display register:

> **Press:** [8]

Now recalculate the new numbers:

Press: [End]

The result is 16. Your screen should look like Figure 16.4.

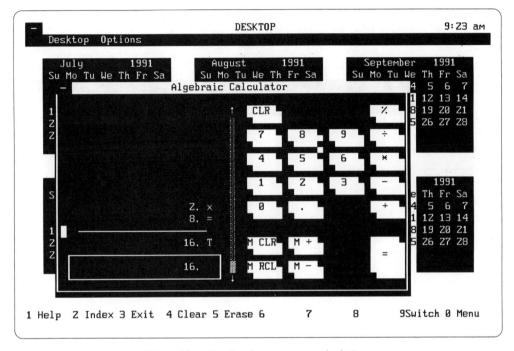

Figure 16.4. Results of running a recalculation

Whenever you recalculate numbers, you cannot press [=] to make the recalculation, you must press [End].

Copying the Tape to the Clipboard

Often you'll want to use one of the calculators to make a quick check on some figures and then return to your work in another application. You can use the calculator, copy the result to the Clipboard, and then paste it from the Clipboard to whatever application you're working with.

For example, copy the calculation you just performed, 2 x 8. (Your screen should look like Figure 16.4.)

Press: [Alt]-[O]-[O]

This copies the current contents of the tape to a disk file called CALC.TMP, and also to the Clipboard. To verify that this worked:

Press: [Alt]-[D]-[B]

Your display screen should look like Figure 16.5.

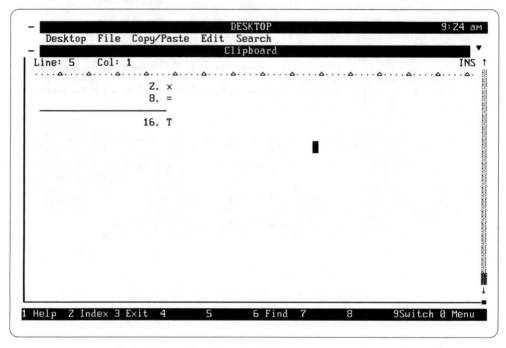

Figure 16.5. Copying the calculator tape into the Clipboard

To paste the contents of the clipboard into another application, refer to Chapter 7.

Printing the Tape

You can print the current contents of the Algebraic calculator tape to your printer or to a disk file. You must print the entire contents of the tape, but if you print it to a disk file first, you can edit the file using the Notepads Editor, and then save and print only the part you want.

To print a calculator tape:

> **Press:** [Alt]-[O]-[P]

This opens the Print box, which lets you determine the receiving device for the file. When you print to disk, the tape contents are saved to a file called CALC.PRT. If you save your tape contents periodically (so you don't encounter the thousand-line limit), you'll have to change the name of this file after you print it. You can use the PC Shell File menu command, *Rename*. For example, you could rename the files CALC1.PRT, CALC2.PRT, and so on.

Using Memory

In the Algebraic calculator, you can store one number into memory. The three other calculators can store up to twenty numbers. Storing a number is convenient when you are using it repeatedly, for example, when you are multiplying a series of numbers by a constant.

Putting a Number into Memory

To place the number 2 into memory:

> **Press:** [2]

> **Press:** [M]-[+]

When you place a number into memory, the letter *M* will show on the left side of the tape, just above the display register.

To recall the contents of memory:

> **Press:** [M]-[R]

This stands for *memory recall*. It places the number in the display register to be used for calculations.

Changing a Number in Memory

You can change a number in memory by increasing or decreasing its value. To increase the value, type the value you want to increase it by, and press [M]-[+]. For example, to increase the number in current memory by 6, or from 2 to 8:

> **Press:** [6]-[M]-[+]

You can now check the results by pressing [M]-[R]. Be sure to press [F4] to clear the register so you don't use this new number inadvertently.

To decrease the number in memory, press [M]-[-]. For example, to decrease the number in current memory by 3, or from 8 to 5:

> **Press:** [3]-[M]-[-]

Check the results by pressing [M]-[R], then [F4].

Clearing Memory

Clearing memory is simple:

> **Press:** [M]-[C].

You can verify that your memory is cleared when the letter *M* disappears from the lower-left corner of the tape. The current value in memory will be dumped into the display register and on tape. To clear the register:

> **Press:** [F4]

THE FINANCIAL CALCULATOR

Use the Financial calculator to perform calculations for:

- Simple and compound interest rates, including annual percentage rates.
- Financial five-key problems involved with loans, including calculations for interest, remaining principal and balance, and periodic payments.
- Mortgage calculations, including discounted rates, prepaid charges, wraparounds, variable rates, and amortization schedules.
- Discounted cash-flow analysis, including net present value, internal rate of return, and yield and rate conversions.
- Computing depreciation and appreciation.
- Statistical analyses such as finding mean averages, and linear projections.

To enter the Financial calculator, when the Calculator menu is showing:

> **Press:** [F]

This opens a calculator that fills your entire screen and looks like Figure 16.6.

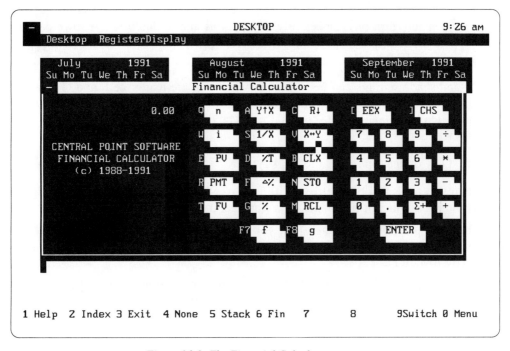

Figure 16.6. The Financial Calculator screen

You can't toggle the wide display on and off in this or any of the other more sophisticated calculators in PC Tools, because the key display is crucial to operating these calculators.

Like the lack of a wide-display toggle, many of the rules that apply to the Financial calculator also apply to the Programmer's and Scientific calculators, described later in this chapter.

The F and G Function Keys

Most of the keys in the Financial calculator have several functions displayed in and above each key. Each key is identified by the letter to its left.

For example, the top five keys are assigned to the letters Q, W, E, R, and T. These keys have three functions each. You execute the one in the middle of the key when you press the letter key by itself. You execute the function above the key when you press [F7] and then the key. And you execute the lower function when you press [F8] and then the letter key.

If you look in the lower-left corner of the calculator keypad, you'll see the [F7] and [F8] keys. These turn on, respectively, *F functions* and *G functions*. A lowercase *F* will appear in the display register after you press [F7], and a lowercase *G* will appear after you press [F8].

Color and shade settings can be important when you are using the F and G function assignments. On color screens, the [F7] key shows up as a red F and the [F8] key as a blue G. On black-and-white screens, they'll be different shades. The functions they control will correspond.

The first key on the top row is the [Q] key:

- When you press [Q] by itself, you'll insert *n*, which is a specific register designed to hold the number of payments for a financial transaction (signified by *n*).
- When you press [F7] and then [Q], you'll insert the F function assigned to the Q key, which calculates the amortization of using payment and interest figures (signified by AMORT).
- When you press [F8] and then [Q], you'll insert the G function assigned to the Q key, which multiplies the number by 12. This is usually used to calculate the yearly total from the monthly rate.

The complete range of functions assigned to the keys displayed in the Financial Calculator screen are as follows.

[Q]   Number of periods (n). F function: Amortization (AMORT); G function: 12 times (12x).

[W]   Interest rate (i). F function: Interest rate (INT); G function: Into 12 (12÷).

[E]   Present value (PV). F function: Net present value (NPV); G function: Initial cash flow group (CFo).

[R]   Payment (PMT). F function: Rounding values (RND); G function: Next cash flow group (CFj).

[T]   Future value (FV). F function: Internal rate of return (IRR); G function: Number of periods for cash flow (Nj).

[A]   Exponential power Y^X. F function: Bond price (PRICE); G function: Square root ($\sqrt{x}$).

[S]   Reciprocal power or inverse (1/X). F function: Bond yield to maturity (YTM); G function: Exponent (EXP).

[D]   Percent of total (%T). F function: Straight-line depreciation (SL); G function: Natural log of displayed number (LN).

[F]   Percentage difference (Δ%). F function: Sum-of-the-year's-digits depreciation (SOYD); G function: Digits after decimal point into display (FRC).

[G]   Percent (%). F function: Declining balance depreciation (DB); G function: Digits before decimal point into display (INT).

[X]   Change sign (CHS). F function: Clear (Σ); G function: Date (DAT).

[[ ]   Exponent (EEX). G function: Change (ΔDY).

[Enter] Enter key. G function: Recalls last number displayed into X (LST).

[0]   Insert 0. F function: No decimal places; G function: Calculates mean average (x).

[1]   Insert 1. F function: One decimal place; G function: Calculates correlation coefficient (x, r).

[2]   Insert 2. F function: Two decimal places; G function: Calculates linear projection (y, r).

[3]   Insert 3. F function: Three decimal places; G function: Calculates factorial (n!).

[4]   Insert 4. F function: Four decimal places; G function: Day/month/year format in display (DMY).

[5]   Insert 5. F function: Five decimal places; G function: Month/day/year format in display (MDY).

[6]   Insert 6. F function: Six decimal places; G function: Statistical weighted mean (xw).

[7]   Insert 7. F function: Seven decimal places; G function: Beginning payment period calculation (BEG).

[8]   Insert 8. F function: Eight decimal places; G function: Ending payment period calculation (END).

[9]   Insert 9. F function: Nine decimal places; G function: None.

[,]   Toggles comma on and off.

[&]   Calculating statistics (Σ+). G function: Reverse statistical calculation (Σ-).

[+]   Addition (+).

[-]   Subtraction (-).

[/]   Division ($\div$).

[*]   Multiplication (x).

Some keys have been gathered into related groups. The top five keys, QWERT, perform your most basic financial calculations. The A and S keys work with bond calculations (although you'll use other keys in the process). The D, F, and G keys work with depreciation, and X, C, V, and B clear various registers.

The Financial calculator provides a menu of its own, Register Display, which contains three choices:

Stack Register   Lets you perform standard math—subtraction, multiplication, and division—and stack the intermediate results. You can display this series of registers by pressing [F5] or [Alt]-[R]-[S].

Financial Register   Lets you perform financial calculations by storing four values and calculating a fifth value from them. You can display this series of registers by pressing [F6] or [Alt]-[R]-[F].

Data Register   Stores twenty numbers to be recalled later. You can display this series of registers by pressing [F8] or [Alt]-[R]-[D].

Error Messages

The Financial, Programmer, and Scientific calculators provide error messages when you make a mistake. For example, the error messages that can appear in the Financial calculator are:

Error   Incorrect key sequence.

Error 0   An impossible calculation.

Error 1   Too many values in registers.

Error 2   Incorrect statistical calculation.

These error messages do not illuminate problems as clearly as a new user would like.

An incorrect key sequence can show up as an impossible or incorrect calculation, depending upon what keys you pressed. If you move quickly, the error message can disappear before you have a chance to read it. Pressing any key after an error message removes the message.

When you get an error message, even if you pass over it, check the contents of your registers. It's possible that values were entered accidentally, even though the display register has returned to 0.00. You might want to clear all registers as a matter of habit whenever an error message appears.

Press: [F7]-[B]

Working With Registers

You worked with a single register in the Algebraic calculator. The Financial calculator, along with the Programmer's and Scientific calculators, contain more memory registers. You can see the contents of these registers in all three calculators using the Register Display pull-down menu:

Press: [Alt]-[R]

This opens a menu with three choices of registers: stack register, financial register, and data register. Only the Financial calculator contains the financial register. The stack and data registers are available in all three.

The Stack Register

The stack registers are designed to hold numbers for standard arithmetic calculations: addition, subtraction, multiplication, and division. To see the stack register display:

Press: [F4]

Your screen should resemble Figure 16.7.

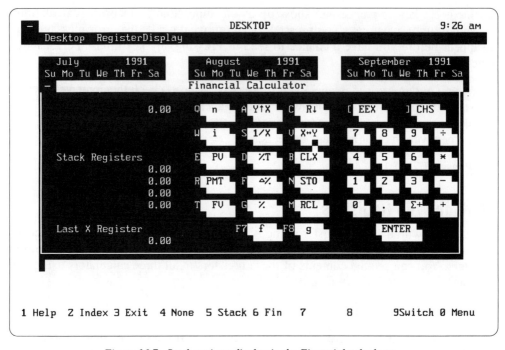

Figure 16.7. Stack register display in the Financial calculator

The five stack registers show the position of five values that have been stored in a stack. The T register stands for the top value on the stack. The Z, Y, and X registers refer to values that have been added since, with X, the most recent value, at the bottom of the stack. The number in the display register is automatically inserted in the X register.

As you add numbers from the bottom, the numbers above are pushed toward the top The numbers pushed upward come down as values are removed from the bottom of the stack. LSTX means the last value that appeared in the X register before the most recent calculation. This lets you refer back one step to a previous value.

To close the stack register display:

    Press: [Alt]-[R]-[N]

To multiply 3 x 3, make sure [Num Lock] is turned on:

    Type: 3

Press: [Enter]

Type: 3

Type: *

The answer, 9, should show in the display register.

Notice that when you performed similar math in the Algebraic calculator, you didn't have to press [Enter]. That's because the Algebraic calculator is designed specifically for standard math. The Financial calculator is designed for more sophisticated calculations, but you can also perform more simple calculations as long as you press [Enter] first.

The figures you used to calculate the simple multiplication have been loaded into the stack registers. To see them:

Press: [F4]

Your stack register display should look like Figure 16.8.

REGISTER	
T	0.00
Z	0.00
Y	0.00
X	9.00
LSTX	3.00

Figure 16.8. The Stack register

The calculated value of 9 has been placed in the X register, where it can be used in other calculations.

The LSTX register shows 3, because that value was inserted in the X register when you first typed 3 and pressed [Enter].

Try a more complex calculation. Close the stack register display:

Press: [Esc]

Find the square root of 16:

Type: 16

Press: [F8]-[A]

The answer, 4, appears immediately in the display register. The key that calculates square root is the G function of [A]. Now take a look at how this value has been added to the stack:

Press: [F4]

Your screen should look like Figure 16.9.

```
REGISTER
     T                    0.00
     Z                    0.00
     Y                    9.00
     X                    4.00

  LSTX                   16.00
```

Figure 16.9. The Stack register contents

The result of your most recent calculation, 4, appears in the X register. This bumped up the previous calculated value of 9 to the Y register. The number 16 shows in the LSTX register because this was the most recent value to appear in the X register.

Now switch the values in the X and Y registers. Notice that the V key has been given this assignment (X↔Y):

Press: [V]

The display register changes to 9.00, which is the value that appeared before 4.00 in the Y register. Double-check the stack registers:

Press: [F4]

They should look like Figure 16.10.

```
REGISTER
     T                    0.00
     Z                    0.00
     Y                    4.00
     X                    9.00

  LSTX                   16.00
```

Figure 16.10. The Stack register display

The values in the X and Y registers have changed places, and the previous value inserted in the display register, 16, now appears in LSTX.

Clearing Registers

You can clear stored values in registers several ways. The established way is to use the F function for the [B] key. This is marked REG, and will clear all registers:

>   **Press:** [F7]-[B]

Now check the stack registers:

>   **Press:** [F4]

They should be empty, showing 0.

You can selectively clear only the X register by just pressing [B] by itself. This is marked CLX, which stands for *CLearing the X register*.

You can also clear all values from all registers in any calculator by pressing [Esc] and then re-entering the calculator.

The Financial Registers

The financial registers are used for specific financial calculations. To see this register display:

>   **Press:** [Alt]-[R]-[F]

These five registers have specific properties:

n   The number of payments covered by a financial transaction. You enter the number of time periods in the display register using the [Q] key, which transfers the value to this register. When the program calculates the number of payments, it stores it here for future calculations.

i   The interest applying to a financial transaction. You enter the interest rate in the display register using the [W] key, which transfers the value to this register. When the program calculates the interest rate, it stores it here for future calculations.

PV   The present value of a financial transaction. You enter the present value in the display register using the [E] key. When the program calculates the present value, it stores it here for future calculations.

PMT The payment amount for a single periodic payment. You enter the payment amount in the display register using the [R] key, which transfers the value to this register. When the program calculates the payment, it stores it here for future calculations.

FV The future value of a financial transaction. You enter the future value in the display register using the [T] key, which stores the value to this register. When the program calculates the present value, it stores it here for future calculations.

You store numbers in these five registers to process them according to various financial calculations. For example, suppose you want to take out a one-year loan for $5,000 at 16.75% interest:

Type: 5000

Press: [E]

This inserts the present value. Type in the interest rate:

Type: 16.75

Press: [W]

Make sure you've entered these numbers correctly:

Press: [F6]

To recall any of these stored financial values to the display register, you need to use the STO key, [N]. For example, to recall the interest rate in the previous example:

Press: [N]-[W]

The value in the i register will appear in the display register.

To perform a financial calculation, you must place sufficient values into the financial registers and then calculate them. For example, suppose you want to calculate the payment amount for a loan when you know the present value, interest (18%), payment periods (5 years, or 60 months), and present value ($5,000).

First, clear all registers:

Press: [B]

Now enter the four values you know:

Press: [F8]-[8]

This makes sure payments are at month's end.

Type: 60

Press: [Q]

Type: 18

Press: [F8]-[W]

Type: 5000

Press: [T]

Press: [R]

The answer is -$126.97, or a periodic payment of $126.97. To view the Financial registers:

Press: [F5]

The Data Registers

The data registers store up to twenty figures. The [N] key (called STO) stores numbers in the data registers; the [M] key (called RCL) recalls the stored numbers.

To see the registers:

Press: [F6]

The first column of ten data registers are marked R0 through R9, and the second column is marked R.0 to R.9. To insert and recall numbers from these twenty registers, you only need to refer to the number 0, 1, ..., 9 or .0, .1, ..., .9.

To enter a value into any one of these registers, type the value, press [N] (the STO key), and then the number of the register into which you want to insert the value. To recall a stored number, press [M] (the RCL key) and then the number of the register containing the number you want to recall.

For example, to insert 16 into R0:

Type: 16

> **Press:** [N]
>
> **Type:** 0

To view the results so far:

> **Press:** [F6]

To store 100 in R1, first close the register display:

> **Press:** [Esc]
>
> **Type:** 100
>
> **Press:** [N]
>
> **Type:** 1

Now, to recall the number in the R0 register:

> **Press:** [M]-[0]

The number 16 should appear in the display register. To calculate the square root of this number:

> **Press:** [F8]-[A]

You can continue to store and recall numbers in the twenty registers this way, and then perform calculations using the various keys.

THE PROGRAMMER'S CALCULATOR

The Programmer's calculator can perform all sorts of complicated programming calculations. It is modeled after the HP-16C, but in the PC Tools version you cannot use any of the programming capabilities provided in the HP-16C.

To open the Programmer's Calculator screen (shown in Figure 16.11) from the Calculators menu:

> **Press:** [P]

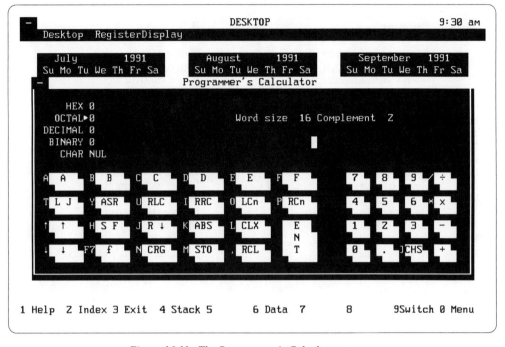

Figure 16.11. The Programmer's Calculator screen

The Register Display menu is identical to its counterpart in the Scientific calculator; however, the bottom-line function-key bar differs, showing only three assignments:

[Esc] Cancel   Cancels the current calculation.

[F4] Stack Registers   Displays the stack registers.

[F6] Data Registers   Displays the data registers.

The five standard function keys for all four calculators continue to work: [F1] Help, [F2] Index, [F3] Quit, [F9] Swap, and [F10] Menu. You can find all key assignments in Table 16.2.

Key	Performs	[F7]
[A]	Insert A in hex register	Shift left (SL)
[B]	Insert B in hex register	Shift right (SR)
[C]	Insert C in hex register	Rotate left (RL)
[D]	Insert D in hex register	Rotate right (RR)
[E]	Insert E in hex register	Rotate left # (RLn)
[F]	Insert F in hex register	Rotate right # (RRn)
[T]	Left justify (LJ)	Number of bits (#B)
[Y]	Arithmetic shift right (ASR)	Double remainder (DBR)
[U]	Rotate left carry through (RLC)	Double divide (DBR)
[I]	Rotate right carry through (RRC)	Double multiply (DBX)
[O]	Rotate left carry though # of bits (LCn)	Square root (sym[214]x)
[P]	Rotate right carry through # of bits (RCn)	Reciprocal (l/X)
[⇑]	Up one register	Restore start-up date (RST)
[H]	Set flag (SF)	Clar flag (CF)
[J]	Roll down (R⇓)	Roll up (R⇑)
[K]	Absolute value (ABS)	Exchange X and Y registers (X↔Y)
[L]	Clear X (CLX)	Backspace (BSP)
[⇓]	Down one register	
[F7]	Activate F key (F7)	
[N]	Clear register (CRG)	Clear prefix (CPX)
[M]	Store number (STO)	Word size (WSZ)
[,]	Recall number (RCL)	Precision (PRC)
[Enter]		Last X register (LST)
[0]	Insert 0 all registers	
[1]	Insert 1 all registers	1's complement mode (1s)
[2]	Insert 2 all registers	2's complement mode (2s)
[3]	Insert 3 all registers	3's complement mode (3s)
[4]	Insert 4 all registers	Set bit (SB)
[5]	Insert 5 all registers	Clear bit (CB)
[6]	Insert 6 all registers	Leading zeros (ZER)
[7]	Insert 7 all registers	Mask left (MKL)
[8]	Insert 8 all registers	Mask right (MKR)
[9]	Insert 9 all registers	Remainder after division (RMD)
[.]	Insert decimal	
[ ]]	Change sign (CHS)	
[÷]	Division	Logical or (OR)
[*]	Multiplication (x)	Logical and (AND)
[-]	Subtraction	Logical operation (NOT)
[+]	Addition	Logical sum (OR)

Table 16.2. Key commands in the Programmer's calculator

Notice that only F functions are available in this calculator. Also, you can press [F7] and [/] for the exclusive OR (XOR).

The Display Register

The display register in the Programmer's calculator is a bit more complicated than its equivalent in the other calculators. This is because there are several ways to view number values for programming purposes, and different ways you can display the results of various computations.

Eight features appear on the default display register of the Programmer's calculator:

Hex

The hexadecimal equivalent of a number. The hex system, as it's called, is a number system with base 16. This is the most popular system to use for programming because it requires the fewest digits to express a value. The first ten digits are the same as the decimal system: 0, 1, 2, 3, ..., 9. The remaining six digits are A, B, C D, E, and F. For example, decimal 16 is equal to hex F.

Octal

This system has a base of 8, but is not used much any more.

Decimal

Base 10. The most commonly used notational system, it became popular because most humans have ten fingers.

Binary

Base 2. There are only two digits in this system: 0 and 1. This is the most basic system, and reflects the fundamental pairing positive and negative.

Char

The ASCII character equivalent, if any, to the number in question.

Word size

The size of a programming word or data bit, which can be from 1 to 64 bits long. The default is 16 bits.

Complement

One of three possible complements: 1, 2, or unsigned mode (which shows as U). Complement 2 is the default.

System flag

One of four possible flags: C for carry over (the default), Z for leading zero control, G for greater-than-range, and P for pending.

The first five items listed above are simply different notational systems that express the same value. The arrow that appears after one of these on your screen shows which system is active, or into which you can put a value. You can move the arrow by pressing [⇑] or [⇓].

Notational Conversion

The easiest thing you can do in the Programmer's calculator is convert number values between the four commonly used programming notational systems: hex, octal, decimal, and binary. You can see these names on the left side of the display register.

Because this is called the Programmer's calculator, and programmers use the hexadecimal system most often, this calculator is also called the hex calculator.

> If you aren't familiar with these notational systems, this isn't the calculator for you. You need a fundamental grounding in hex and binary notational systems to program correctly, and if you can't program there's little practical use in working with this calculator.
>
> You can, however, use this calculator to get a start on understanding the relationships among the notational systems. By placing a number in the decimal display, which is the notational system we use every day, you can see how its value changes in the other notational displays.

The best way to start out is to enter a decimal number you're familiar with, and view its equivalent in the other notational systems.

Highlight: DECIMAL

This moves the red arrow next to *Decimal*. Now:

Type: 1

Your display should now look like this:

```
HEX   1
OCTAL   1              Word Size   16
Complement   2
DECIMAL   1
BINARY   1
CHAR   SOH
```

The first four fields all display the same value, since they all begin with 1. To continue the lesson:

Press: [0]

Now things begin to get interesting. Your display should look like this:

```
HEX    A
OCTAL  12              Word size 16
Complement 2
DECIMAL  10
BINARY  1010
CHAR     LF
```

You can continue adding to the current decimal number to see how the others change. Or you can check entirely new numbers by clearing the display and entering a new number, using the decimal system or one of the other systems.

Clearing the Display

You can clear all five notational fields in the display register in three ways:

1. Press [L]. This executes the CLX function, which clears the five notational fields and prepares for a new entry in the current field.

2. Press [⇑] or [⇓] to switch to another notational system, then press [0]. This clears all five notational fields and lets you enter a new number to convert.

3. Press [F7]-[L]. This lets you remove digits one-by-one by backspacing. This erases only the rightmost value in all five fields.

The numbers you are working with and converting are always being added to the stack register. Press [F4] to see the contents of the stack register and [F6] to see the contents of the data registers. To clear the display, stack, and data registers all at the same time:

Press: [F7]-[⇑]

This executes the restore function (RST) and removes everything.

Displaying ASCII Characters

If you want to view specific ASCII characters assigned to keys on your keyboard:

Highlight: CHAR

Type: A

As long as you don't press [Shift] with this key, you should get decimal 97.0. Now try another key, such as *b*. Notice how the characters are arranged in sequence; that

433

is, the letter *a* is decimal 97, *b* is decimal 98, and so on. The uppercase equivalents are in a different series.

There are 17 keys that don't bring up an ASCII character: [F1], [F2], [F3], [F4], [F5], [F9], [Alt], [Caps Lock], [Shift], [Ctrl], [PrintScrn], [Scroll Lock], [Num Lock], [Pause], the [5] key on the keypad, and the [⇑] and [⇓] keys. These last two highlight other notational names in the register.

Before moving on to the registers, you might want to double-check the results of the Programmer's calculator with another feature in the Desktop Manager, the ASCII table. To overlay the Programmer's calculator with the ASCII table:

   Press: [Alt]-[D]-[U]-[A]

This should open the ASCII table from the Utilities menu. If you position the ASCII Table window correctly, you can get your screen to look like Figure 16.12.

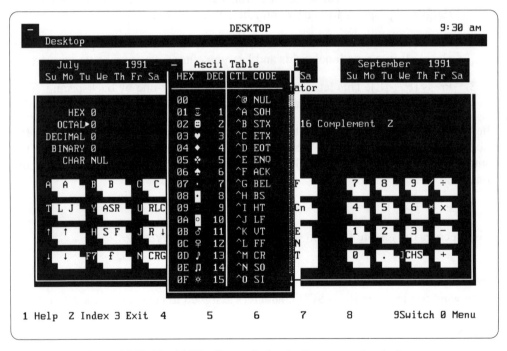

Figure 16.12. The ASCII table overlaying the Programmer's calculator

If you read down the first column in the ASCII Table window and come to character 0A (which is the hex number), you can read across the line and see the ASCII character that matches this value, the decimal value 10. You also see the control code assigned to this character, and the ASCII notation. Three of these values appear in the Programmer's calculator display: the hex and decimal values and the ASCII notation.

About Word Size

A *programming word* is a group of bits stored in a computer's memory. The size of the programming word you want to use can be crucial for many programming commands.

The size of the word you can use depends upon the capacity of your computer's memory. The phrases *16-bit computer* and *32-bit computer* define the maximum decimal word size the computer can handle. Word size can range from 1 to 64 decimal bits. The default word size is 16 decimal bits. The size of the current word setting also controls how many digits can appear in the display.

To change the size of the current word, enter the bit size of the number you want to use and press [F7]-[M]. This executes the WSZ, or word size, function. The bit-size number you enter will be controlled by whatever notational system is highlighted. For example, to enter the 32-bit-size word:

Highlight: DEC

Type: 32

Press: [F7]-[M]

> The bit-size numbers—16, 32, and 64—are decimal numbers. If another notational system name is selected when you try to change the word bit-size, you'll end up with a different decimal value. For example, if the Hex field is selected and you type 32 and then press [F7]-[M], you're going to get a word size of decimal 50 bits. The word size always shows up in a decimal value, although you can control the number using any of the four notational system fields. To get a decimal 32-bit word as a hex number, you must enter 20 in the Hex field.

You can set the maximum word size of 64 by just pressing [F7]-[M]. It doesn't matter which notational field is current.

You can return the word size to the default value of 16 by pressing [F7]-[⇑]. This executes the restore function marked RST on the left side of the keyboard.

When you change the word size, you change only future values, not values already stored in the stack or data registers. If you want these values changed as well, you need to re-enter those values using the new word size.

About Complements

Complements refer to methods for adding and subtracting binary number values and displaying the results. The 1's complement refers to binary addition, and 2's complement refers to binary subtraction. Unsigned complement refers to binary numbers without an additional digit designed to serve as a flag denoting positive or negative status (the sign). The 2's complement is the default setting.

To set 1's complement:

> **Press:** [F7]-[1]

You'll see the number 1 appear after the Complement field. To set the unsigned complement:

> **Press:** [F7]-[3]

To return the default:

> **Press:** [F7]-[2]

System Flags

There are four system flags, and each one denotes a special condition concerning the most recent calculation. These can be turned on automatically by some calculations, or you can turn them on yourself for certain types of control.

Z   Denotes *leading zero control*. This determines how many zeros are displayed. This flag is off by default, which means that only the zeros you enter as digits appear in display fields, as long as these zeros separate other digits higher than zero. (You can't enter a string of zeros if the Z flag is off.)

> To toggle this flag on:
>
> > **Press:** [F7]-[6]
>
> This executes the zero function (ZER). You'll notice zeros appearing in three of the four notational fields (four in HEX, six in OCTAL, and 16 in BINARY—leading zeros are always suppressed in DECIMAL). You can toggle

the flag off by repeating the above command, or by setting and clearing flag 3, as described for the following flags.

C   Denotes *carry-over*. This flag appears whenever a math calculation results in a remainder that can't appear on screen, or when you've shifted or rotated bits beyond the limits of the field. When this flag appears, and you want to toggle it off:

> **Press:** [F7]-[H]-[4]

This executes the clear flag (CF) function for flag 4.

G   Denotes *greater-than-the-range*. This flag appears whenever the result of a calculation is too large to appear in the display register under conditions imposed by the current word size and complement setting. To clear this flag after it appears:

> **Press:** [F7]-[H]-[5]

This executes the clear flag (CF) function for flag 5.

P   Denotes *pending*. This flag appears when the calculator presumes it is waiting for more information from you; it is pending more data or commands. To clear this flag:

> **Press:** [F7]-[N]

This executes the clear prefix function (CPX).

Flags are designed to keep you informed of the status of your calculation. When they appear, you should check the information you've just entered, as well as the status of current stack and data registers.

Error Messages

The documentation says there's only one error message in the Programmer's calculator: Illegal digit for this number base.

This is the error you'll probably get most of the time, but you can also get several others, for instance Improper mathematical operation and Improper flag number. These are invariably specific and self-explanatory.

Using Registers and Floating-Point Precision

You can use two sets of registers in the Programmer's calculator: stack and data. These are essentially the same types of registers as their counterparts in the Financial calculator. All current values in both the stack and data registers will be displayed according to the currently selected notational system.

The Stack Registers

Five stack registers (X, Y, Z, T, and LSTX) store values that you can see when you press [F4]. These behave the same way as the stack registers in the Financial calculator:

- The selected number in the display register appears in the X register.
- Subsequent values move previous values up the stack to the Y, Z, and T registers in turn.
- When you make a calculation, the number in the X register moves to the LSTX register, should you want to save it.
- The X↔Y procedure switches values in the X and Y registers.
- The R⇓ rolls the value in a specified register down one register.
- The STO and RCL procedures store and recall numbers in specified registers.

There's one feature unique to the stack register in the Programmer's calculator: The R⇑ procedure rolls the value in a specified register up one register.

The Data Registers

The data registers store values in ten registers, marked R0 through R9, which you can see when you press [F6]. These are identical to the function of the data registers R0-R9 and R.0-R.9 in the Financial calculator, except that you can also roll values up one register using R⇑.

Floating-Point Precision

The term *floating point* refers to a decimal point that moves (or "floats" around), depending on the result of a calculation. For example, look at these two calculations:

4.0 x 4.5 = 18

4.5 x 4.5 = 20.25

The first is actually equal to 18.0, but you probably don't need the 0 after the decimal point. However, if in the second calculation you want to use numbers that share the same format, you'll have to show them as 4.50 x 4.50 = 20.25.

The first example shows floating-point precision, or how many decimal places you want to show, turned on; the second shows it turned off. You can specify floating-point precision by:

• Typing a period where you want it to appear in a number.

• Using the PRC procedures.

To use the PRC procedure, type the number of digits after the decimal you want to use, and then select the PRC procedure. For example, to set a floating-point precision of five decimal places:

> **Type:** 5

> **Press:** [F7]-[,]

Notice that five zeros appear after the decimal point in the Decimal field. Floating point applies to decimal numbers only. If another field is selected when you set floating-point precision, the arrow will move to the Decimal field.

Notice also that the word size increases to the maximum value of 64 bits. The Programmer's calculator can store up to eighteen digits in the maximum word size of 64 bits.

To clear precision, just set the value to 0.

THE SCIENTIFIC CALCULATOR

The Scientific calculator is designed to emulate parts of the HP-11C calculator.

To open the Scientific calculator, on the Calculators menu:

> **Press:** [S]

When the calculator appears, your screen will look like Figure 16.13.

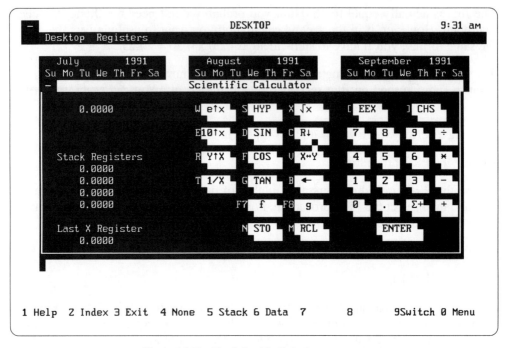

Figure 16.13. The Scientific Calculator screen

This screen looks less complicated than the Financial Calculator screen, but you might find it a bit harder to work with, if you're not familiar with scientific calculations. Many of us work with financial figures in one form or another every day, but there is not commonly a need for scientific calculation.

The only pull-down menu unique to the Scientific calculator is the Register Display menu, which contains two choices: stack registers and data registers. The function-key assignments at the bottom of this screen are identical to those in the Financial calculator, except that [F5] for the Financial register is unavailable.

The key display and assigned functions are considerably different from the Financial calculator key display. The following list shows what each key does.

[W]   Raises e to the power of x. G function: Computes the natural log (LN).

[E]   Raises 10 to the displayed number. G function: Computes the common log of a displayed number.

[R]   Raises # in Y register to power of displayed #. G function: Computes displayed value % of Y register.

[T]   Computes reciprocal of displayed number. G function: Computes % change of Y register.

[S]   Computes hyperbolic sine, cosine, or tangent in display. G function: Computes inverse sine, cosine, or tangent of displayed number.

[D]   Computes sine of displayed number. G function: Computes the arc sine of displayed number.

[F]   Computes cosine of displayed number. G function: Computes the arc cosine of displayed number.

[G]   Computes tangent of displayed number. G function: Computes tangent of displayed number.

[X]   Computes square root of displayed number. G function: Computes square of displayed number.

[C]   Rolls down the stack contents. G function: Rolls up the stack contents.

[V]   Exchanges contents in X and Y registers. F function: Clears all registers; G function: Rounds the mantissa of 10 digit # in X to match Y.

[B]   Deletes numbers from display. F function; Cancels partial instructions; G function: Clears contents of X register to zero.

[F7]   Activates F functions.

[F8]   Activates G functions.

[N]   Stores twenty numbers in registers. F function: Displays digits after the decimal; G function: Displays digits before the decimal.

[M]   Recalls stored numbers.

[ ]]   Changes sign or exponent of 10 in display. F function: Places value of pi in display; G function: Returns absolute value of displayed number.

[[ ]   Prepares to display number in exponent of 10. F function: Converts polar magnitudes in X/Y to rectangular; G function: Converts rectangular magnitudes in X/Y to polar.

[ENT]   Enters X register value into Y. G function: Recalls displayed value before previous function.

[,]   Inserts comma. F function: Computes sample standard deviation; G function: Computes linear/correlation coefficient.

[&]   Collects statistics of X and Y from R0-R5. F function: Computes linear regression Σ+. G function: Subtracts statistics of X and Y from R0-R5.

[0]   Inserts 0. F function: Computes factorial x; G function: Computes mean average of X and Y using Σ+.

[1]   Inserts 1. F function: Computes possible combination sets; G function: Computes possible permutations.

[2]   Inserts 2. F function: Converts hours, minutes, and seconds to decimal; G function: Converst decimal hours, minutes, and seconds to standard.

[3]   Inserts 3. F function: Converts degrees to radians; G function: Converts radians to degrees.

[4]   Inserts 4.

[5]   Inserts 5.

[6]   Inserts 6.

[7]   Inserts 7. F function: Fixes the number of displayed decimals; G function: Changes display to trig functions.

[8]   Inserts 8. F function: Displays scientific notation; G function: Displays radians for trig functions.

[9]   Inserts 9. F function: Displays grads for trig functions; G function: Displays engineering notation.

All of the commands assigned to these keys operate as they do in the other calculators, except that you must follow the *reverse Polish* notation method, and not the *infix* method used by the other calculators.

About Reverse Polish Notation

You can work with various types of calculation systems in the Scientific calculator, such as reverse Polish notation, engineering, and scientific. The default mode is reverse Polish notation. This means that you enter all the numbers for the calculation first, then enter the operators to perform the calculation.

> Reverse Polish notation was devised by Jan Lukasiewicz, a Pole, half a century ago to reorganize numerical calculations so they could be processed by machines.

There are various notational systems you can use when making calculations. For the previous three calculators, you've used a method called *infix* notation. This is where you enter numbers and operators in what appears to the human mind to be a logical sequence. For example, in the Algebraic calculator you multiplied 3 x 3 to get 9. Your actual steps were:

Type: 3

Press: [*]

Type: 3

Press: [=]

You interspersed numbers with operators, which were processed in a logical order. In reverse Polish notation, you would enter the first 3, then the second 3, and then perform multiplication on the two numbers.

Scientific Registers

The Scientific calculator provides you with the same five stack registers and twenty data registers as the Financial calculator.

There are an additional six statistical registers, which you can't view, but the calculator uses them for statistical calculations:

R0	Number of data points collected
R1	Σx, the sum of the x values
R2	Σx^2, the sum of the squares of the x values
R3	Σy, the sum of the y values
R4	Σy^2, the sum of the squares of the y values
R5	Σxy, the sum of the products of the x and y values

You should make sure these registers are clear between each calculation. To clear the statistical registers:

Press: [F7]-[&]

Error Messages

There are three error message in the Scientific calculator:

Error 0   An impossible calculation.

Error 1   No more room in storage registers.

Error 2   An incorrect sequence of statistical calculations.

LOADING A CALCULATOR AUTOMATICALLY

Using program switches, you can load the Desktop Manager and directly display an often-used calculator.

For example, if you're a programmer and you want to use the Programmer's calculator when you load the Desktop Manager:

Type: DESKTOP/CP

If you wanted Desktop to go resident:

Type: DESKTOP/R/CP

To load the Algebraic calculator, use the /CA switch; the Financial calculator, the /CF switch; and the Scientific calculator, the /CS switch.

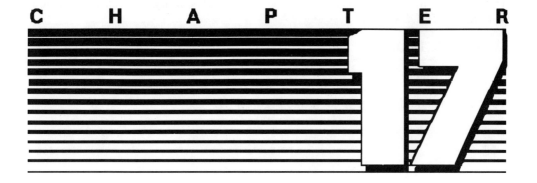

C H A P T E R

17

UTILITY PROGRAMS

I n addition to PC Shell and Desktop Manager, there are other programs in the PC Tools package called *utility* programs, which radically enhance the quality of your work and the security of your files.

This chapter describes the PC Tools utility programs that work under DOS. The next chapter describes the PC Tools utility programs that work under Windows.

All but two of the PC Tools utility programs can be accessed using the PC Tools menu. VDefend (for Virus Defend) and Memory Information are not accessible from the PC Tools menu, and are described at the end of this chapter.

The best way to get an overview of the DOS PC Tools utility programs is to run the program PCTOOLS.EXE.

Type: PCTOOLS

Press: [Enter]

Your screen should change to look like Figure 17.1.

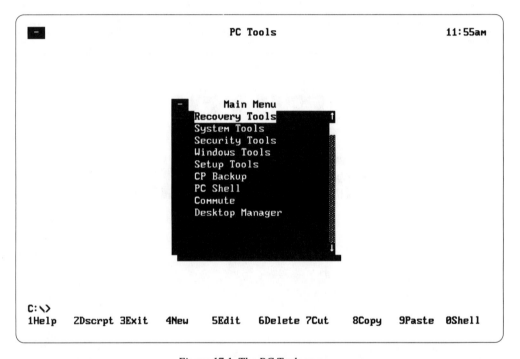

Figure 17.1. The PC Tools screen

This shows the main menu of the PC Tools program. The first five commands on it lead to other menus.

Recovery Tools Opens a menu letting you access DiskFix, File Fix, Undelete, and Unformat.

System Tools Opens a menu letting you access Compress, FileFind, System Information, Directory Maintenance, View, and PC Format.

Security Tools Opens a menu letting you access PC Secure, Data Monitor, and Wipe.

Windows Tools	Opens a menu letting you access CP Backup and Undelete.
Setup Tools	Opens a menu letting you access Install and PC Config.
CP Backup	Lets you access the DOS Backup program.
PC Shell	Opens PC Shell.
Commute	Lets you access the Commute program.
Desktop Manager	Lets you open the Desktop main menu.

All of these programs are accessible from the PC Tools main menu, as well as from your DOS prompt. To load any of these programs from your DOS prompt, just type the filename and press [Enter]. For example, to start the program File Find:

Type: FF

Press: [Enter]

When you highlight a utility program name on the PC Tools menu, you'll see the command sequence for loading the program several lines above the bottom of your screen. For example, when you highlight FileFind on the System Tools menu, you'll see the command line `C:\>C:\PCTOOLS\FF.EXE` at the bottom of your screen. This means you can type FF (as long as your PCTOOLS directory is on your path) and press [Enter] to start the FileFind program.

You can also install any of these programs on your Program List menu in PC Shell. Just make sure to mark them as a PC Tools program.

RECOVERY TOOLS

The *Recovery Tools* command on the PC Tools main menu opens a submenu that contains the names of five programs that help you recover data from your disks.

DiskFix

This program analyzes, diagnoses, and fixes errors and incompatibilities on disks. It is designed to fix problems you may encounter because of errors recorded to crucial parts of your operating disk. These problems aren't always apparent when they occur, so you can also run the DiskFix program to protect against insidious errors that can grow over time. The program is fully menu-driven and very easy to use.

To run DiskFix from the PC Tools menu, open the Recovery Tools menu, highlight *DiskFix*, and press [Enter].

To open DiskFix from your DOS prompt:

Type: DISKFIX

Press: [Enter]

The first thing you'll see is a warning about unloading any disk-caching software other than PC Cache. No software can access the disk while DiskFix does its work. Diskfix automatically unloads PC Cache. To move through this warning:

Press: [Enter]

DiskFix will proceed to check your equipment, then display the Diskfix main menu, as shown in Figure 17.2.

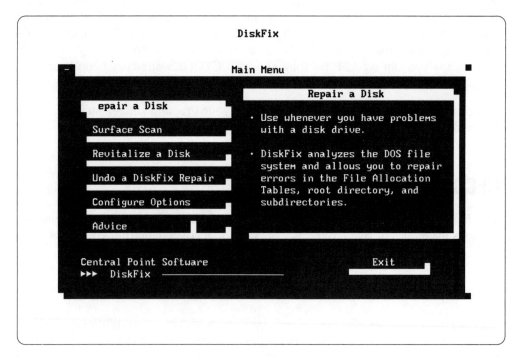

Figure 17.2: The DiskFix main menu

You select one of these six commands to analyze or repair some aspect of one of your disks:

Repair a Disk Runs the major part of the DiskFix program, which analyzes the specified disk for errors in boot sector, FAT integrity, FAT comparison, media description, FAT data analysis, directory structure, and lost clusters. You can print the report to a printer or disk, or you can skip the report and return to the main menu.

Surface Scan Checks the surface of the specified disk for errors.

Revitalize a Disk Revitalizes a floppy disk if it doesn't read or write correctly. Once you select a drive, three tests are run to check the disk-drive performance. *Testing System Integrity* checks partition RAM, system controller, controller RAM, timing system, and archive caching. *Testing Disk Timing Characteristics* tests three aspects of disk read/write activity. *Determining Physical Parameters* checks physical characteristics of the disk.

Undo a DiskFix Repair Undoes a DiskFix repair, as long as an Undo file has been created by DiskFix.

Configure Options Lets you select four options to configure the DiskFix program. See below for more information.

Advice Provides information on various aspects of the DiskFix program.

All of these commands are self-running. All you do is select the drive to check and press [Enter].

Configure Options

This command lets you set four configuration options:

Test Partition Information Test partition information each time a test is run.

Check Boot sector for viruses Checks your boot sector for any viruses before tests are run.

Look for Mirror file	Looks for a mirror file on the disk you specify before running any tests.
Use Custom Error Message	You can create what's called a "custom message" by selecting *Edit Custom Message* command at the bottom of the window. This prevents DiskFix from correcting any errors it finds. Instead, when the program locates an error, it displays the custom message you design. Pressing [Enter] removes the custom message and lets DiskFix proceed to look for the next error. Custom messages you might want to use could be "Contact System Administrator" or "See Your Boss First." DiskFix won't correct any errors until you turn off the *Use Custom Error Message* setting.

Switches When Loading

When loading DiskFix, you can use the following three switches.

/?	Display switches you can use. Same as /H.
/H	Display switches you can use.
/BW	Display black and white attributes on a color monitor.

File Fix

The File Fix program lets you fix three types of commonly used data files for the programs dBASE, Lotus 1-2-3, and Symphony.

To load this program, select the FileFix command on the Recovery Tools menu for the PC Tools program, or at your DOS prompt:

Type: FILEFIX

Press: [Enter]

When the program is loaded, you'll see the screen shown in Figure 17.3.

450

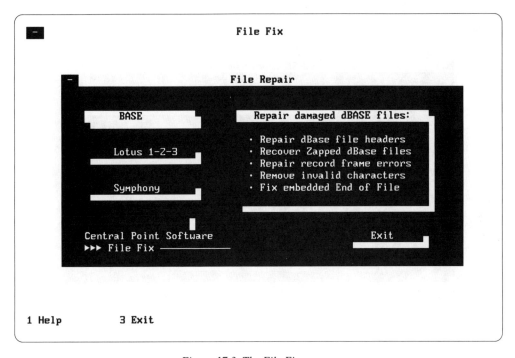

Figure 17.3. The File Fix screen

To use this program:

1. Select the program name whose file type you want to fix, then press [Enter]. This opens a Select File to Fix screen, and lists all the files in the current directory that can be read by the program you've selected. For example, for dBASE, you'll see listed all files ending in .DBF. For Lotus 1-2-3, you'll see all files listed ending with .WK.

2. Highlight the file you want to fix and press [Enter]. This moves you into a series of screens specific to the file type you want to fix. For example, Figure 17.4 shows the dBASE Repair Options screen.

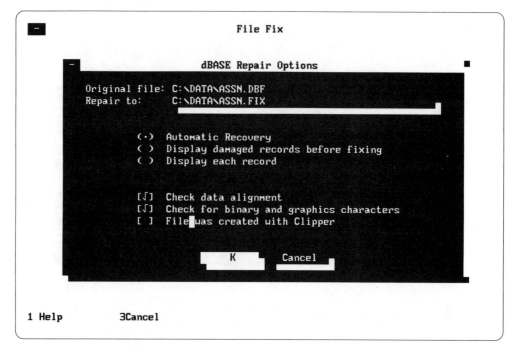

Figure 17.4. The dBASE Repair Options screen

Once you set the conditions you want to repair, press [Enter] to proceed. This opens the File Repair screen, which shows the repairs' progress. Once repairs have been made, you can review the contents of the file by highlighting *Review* at the bottom of the screen, then pressing [Enter].

Undelete

The PC Tools undelete program is particularly easy to use and good at recovering deleted files and directories.You should explore the Undelete program before you have to use it.

Undeleting files is easy to do—most of the time.

If you've already deleted information you want to keep, the first thing to do is DON'T DO ANYTHING ELSE—for a moment. Relax. *Then* begin the undelete process:

You can load the PC Tools Undelete program in three ways:

1. From PC Tools: Open the Recovery menu in PC Tools, highlight *Undelete,* and press [Enter].

2. From your DOS prompt:

    Type: UNDEL

    Press: [Enter]

3. From PC Shell: Press [Alt]-[F], then [U] to select the *Undelete* command on the File pull-down menu.

All three methods load the same program. When the Undelete program is loaded, you'll see the screen shown in Figure 17.5.

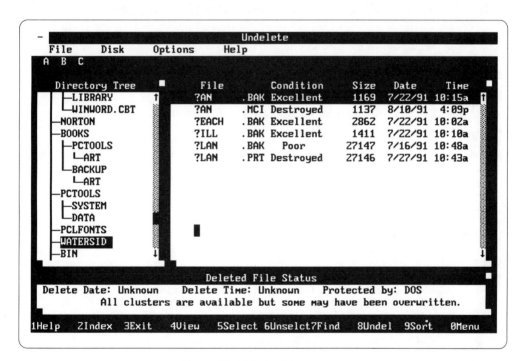

Figure 17.5. The Undelete screen

Figure 17.5 looks like the single-list PC Shell screen. You'll find a tree list in the left panel and a file list in the right. You can move up and down the tree list by highlighting that panel and using your cursor keys. To select a file or files to undelete, press

[Tab] to highlight the right panel, then highlight the file or files you want to recover.

The panel below these two is called *Deleted File Status*. This shows information for the deleted file currently highlighted in the file list panel.

You can use commands on four pull-down menus:

File   Lets you undelete files, find undeleted files, view file contents, and use Advanced Delete.

Disk   Lets you scan for deleted file information in various ways on your data disk.

Options   Lets you sort filenames in various ways; also lets you show existing files and select a Mirror file to use.

Help   Provides help on a variety of topics in the Undelete program.

Figure 17.6 shows a menu map of all commands on these menus.

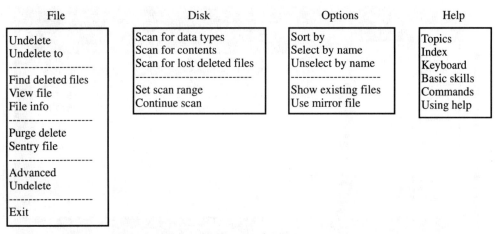

Figure 17.6. Menu map for the Undelete program

All ten function keys have assignments in the Undelete program.

[F1] Help   Opens context-sensitive interactive help.

[F2] Index   Provides a Help index you can use to select a topic for more information.

[F3] Exit   Lets you exit Undelete and return to your previous work.

[F4] View   Lets you view the contents of a deleted file.

[F5] Select   Lets you select more than one file to undelete.

[F6] Unselect Lets you unselect a group of selected files.

[F7] Find   Lets you find a specific file by name.

[F8] Undel   Begins the undelete process for highlighted or selected filenames.

[F9] Sort   Lets you arrange files in the file list panel according to a variety of conditions.

[F10] Menu   Activates the top menu bar so you can use a pull-down menu.

When the Undelete program lists deleted files in the right panel, it will also display its best guess regarding your ability to restore a deleted file:

Perfect   Your chances of recovering this file are perfect. The file has been protected by both the Delete Sentry and Delete Tracker tools.

Excellent Your chances are excellent that Undelete will assemble all sections of data back into the original file. This file was not protected by any other PC Tools program. Some of the data might be overwritten, but you can probably reassemble most it into a good file.

Good   Your chances are good for restoring most or all of the data. The Undelete program might be able to do all of the work. Most likely, you'll have to assemble some of the lost sections yourself.

Poor   Your chances for recovering this file are not good. You might be able to recover some of the data using the Advanced Undelete method.

Destroyed You probably cannot restore the contents of this file, although you might be able to resurrect some or most of the data by moving around the disk and assembling parts of the data.

Existing   This marks a file that has been created using the Advanced Undelete method. You do this for the purpose of assembling data from another deleted file.

Recovered The file was just recovered.

There are two methods you can use to recover a deleted file: automatic and manual. Which method you use depends upon the state of the deleted file. If the file is marked *Good, Excellent,* or *Perfect,* you can probably use the automatic method.

When DOS deletes a file, it removes the first letter only from the filename. This is enough to let DOS ignore the file completely, and presume that all clusters that were filled with data and assigned to the file are now free for another file's data.

If you delete a file, then go on to other work, it's possible that some of the new file data will write over the data in the deleted file. Just how much data is overwritten, and whether or not you can reassemble the deleted file's data, determines your chances for success when undeleting the file.

The Automatic Method

The automatic method for undeleting files simply requires that you insert a new first letter for the deleted filename. As long as the deleted file data has not been overwritten, the Undelete program can reassemble all deleted file clusters automatically.

To undelete a file automatically, highlight the filename, then:

> **Press:** [Alt]-[F]

> **Press:** [Enter]

This selects *Undelete*, the first command on the menu. If the file can be undeleted automatically, you'll be asked to type the first letter of the filename. Type the letter you want to use, then press [Enter] twice. This renames the file, and reallocates the clusters attached to this filename as a valid DOS file.

When you encounter a message that says the file cannot be undeleted automatically, you must use the manual method.

The Manual Method

The manual method for undeleting a file requires that you assemble the data from the deleted file clusters manually. To use the manual method:

1. Highlight the name of the deleted file you want to recover.

2. Press [Alt]-[F] to open the File pull-down menu, select the command *Advanced Undelete*, and press [Enter]. This opens a submenu. The top two commands should be enabled (highlighted), while the bottom two will be disabled (shaded).

3. Press [Enter] to select the command *Manual Undelete,* then press [Enter]. This opens a screen similar to the one shown in Figure 17.6, where you're asked to select the first letter for the filename.

4. Type a first letter and press [Enter] twice. This moves you into the Manual Undelete screen, shown in Figure 17.7. There is a shortcut to opening this screen:

      Press: [Alt]-[F]

      Press: [A]

      Press: [M]

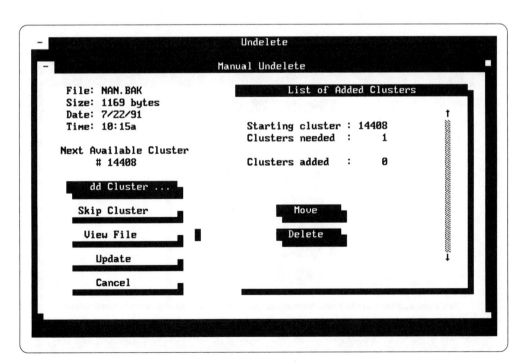

Figure 17.7. The Manual Undelete screen

You'll use the Manual Undelete screen to assemble clusters on your hard disk with data you want to save into the deleted filename. If the deleted file hasn't been severely impaired, you'll start off working in the first cluster on record, listed in the upper-right corner of the screen, under *Next Available Cluster.*

Skip Cluster   Skips the current cluster and moves to the next in sequence.

View File   Lets you view any part of the undeleted file that you've already assembled. You must add at least one cluster to a file to view it.

Update   Returns you to the Undelete File screen, and updates file status.

Cancel   Cancels the manual delete operation.

To begin recovering a file by adding clusters:

> **Highlight:** Add Cluster

> **Press:** [Enter]

This opens the Cluster Options window, as shown in Figure 17.8.

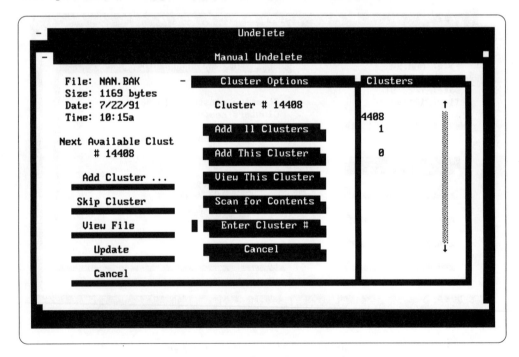

Figure 17.8. The Cluster Options window

The six commands on this screen let you do the actual assembling.

Add All Clusters	Add all clusters originally assigned to the file.
Add this Cluster	Adds the current cluster only.
View this Cluster	Lets you view the contents of the current cluster.
Scan for Contents	Lets you scan the contents of the current cluster.
Enter Cluster #	Lets you specify a cluster by number.
Cancel	Cancels the *Add Cluster* command.

Once you've added the clusters you want to save:

> **Press:** [Esc]

This closes the Cluster Options menu and returns you to the Manual Undelete screen.

> **Highlight:** Update

> **Press:** [Enter]

You should be able to view the filename you've just undeleted in the right panel marked *Recovered*.

To close the Undelete program:

> **Press:** [Esc]

If you were working in PC Shell, you'll return to PC Shell. If you were working in PC Tools, you'll return to that menu. If you were working at your DOS prompt, that's where you'll return.

Unformat

The Unformat program is used when a disk has been formatted accidentally and you want to recover some of the data erased during the formatting.

If you used the PC Tools Mirror program to create one of your recovery files, then the unformatting process is much easier. You can still recover data if you didn't use the Mirror program—it's just less reliable.

To load the Unformat program, select the program name from the PC Tools Recovery Tools menu, or at your DOS prompt:

Type: UNFORMAT

Press: [Enter]

The first step asks you to specify which drive contains the disk you want to unformat. After you specify the drive, the program will validate the drive.

The second step asks whether you created a Mirror file for the disk. If you select *Yes*, the Undelete program will look for the Mirror file you want to use. If you select *No*, you'll be shown any files that remain on the disk you're about to unformat. This gives you a chance to save these files, which otherwise might be destroyed during unformatting.

The final step before unformatting analyzes the drive you want to unformat using the screen shown in Figure 17.9.

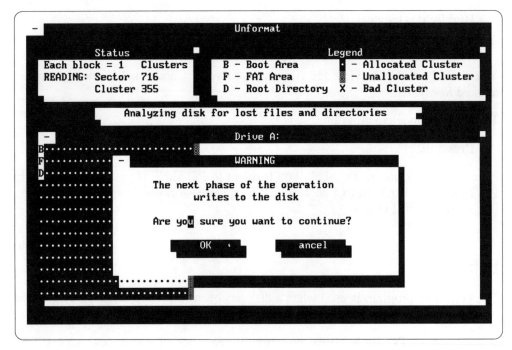

Figure 17.9. The Undelete Analyzing screen

Once the program has analyzed the surface of the disk you want to format, it will unformat the disk and look for files that existed on the disk previous to the formatting.

SYSTEM TOOLS

The System Tools menu provides access to six different utility programs that let you enhance your work with disk files.

Compress

The Compress program optimizes your disk space usage. This program does not compress your files; PC Secure does that. Compress rearranges file segments on the specified disk so they appear in a more logical order for your computer to process.

When you run the Compress program, it:

1. Analyzes the specified disk

2. Defragments files

3. Looks for unmarked errors on the disk and moves file data off these areas

4. Places your directories at the beginning of a disk

5. Sorts all directory contents

The most important procedure is defragmenting your disk file data. File fragmentation occurs when you create and save files to disk, then go back and modify the files several times and add new files. The first time you create and save a file on an empty disk, it is saved in a continuous block. Your computer continues to save other files as long as contiguous blocks of space are available. When it can't save a file's data in one block, your computer searches around for any available space and squeezes data into various locations.

As you continue to add, erase, and modify files, fragmentation gets increasingly worse. The more a file is fragmented, the longer it takes your disk head to find the data and read it into your computer's memory.

The Compress program solves this problem by plowing through the data on a disk cluster by "cluster lifting" all the data sections from a single file off the disk and rerecording them in a continuous block. This not only speeds up your disk-head access time, it reduces that chances that you'll encounter lost chains, which happens when DOS forgets which disk clusters have been erased and which ones contain good data.

You can run Compress from your DOS prompt or from the PC Shell Applications menu, as long as you entered the shell from the DOS prompt.

Loading Compress

To launch Compress from your DOS command line:

Type: COMPRESS

Press: [Enter]

When the Compress screen appears, it looks like Figure 17.10.

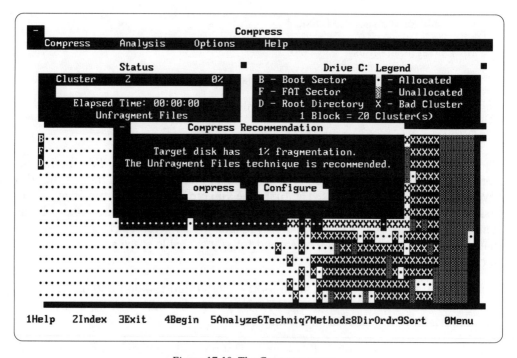

Figure 17.10. The Compress screen

The current disk will be highlighted on the left side of the second line from the top, in this case disk DRV C. The most prominent feature on this screen is the cluster map of file data on the selected disk. The map you view will most likely be different from the map shown in Figure 17.1.

Five features that appear on the map are defined just below the map:

Boot Sector   Contains two DOS files your computer needs to boot up.

FAT Sector   Contains two copies of the file allocation table, or an assignment of the file sections assigned to each cluster.

Root Directory   Contains the information for your root directory, which is the first or topmost directory, which you see when you boot up your computer.

Allocated Cluster   A cluster that's been allocated to a valid file, or a file that hasn't been deleted.

Unallocated Cluster A cluster that's not been allocated to a valid file. An unallocated cluster may very well contain data—it's just data for an erased file or a file lost by DOS.

The allocated cluster at the very end of the disk, in the lower-right corner of the map, is used by MIRRORSAV.FIL. This file is created by the Mirror program and saves information about your boot directory, FAT, and boot record. The Mirror program puts it here because most disk damage occurs at the front end of the disk, especially during an accidental DOS format that is aborted. By placing the file at the end of the disk, the information necessary to rebuild your disk is stored in the least risky position.

You can use four pull-down menus in this screen:

Sort   Lets you select several different ways to sort the files on disk.

Analysis Lets you analyze the disk three ways.

Compress Lets you compress the files on the disk according to a variety of settings, and issue a report on the compress if you want one.

Help   Opens the Help index for Compress.

The Compress pull-down menu map is shown in Figure 17.11.

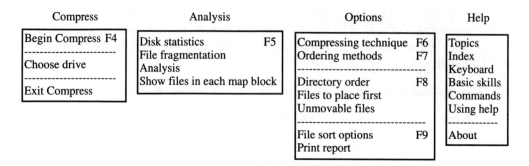

Figure 17.11. Menu map for the Compress program

Commands have been assigned to all ten function keys.

[F1] Help   Opens help for Compress.

[F2] Index   Opens the Help index for Compress.

[F3] Exit   Closes the Compress screen and return to your previous work.

[F4] Begin   Begins the Compress program according to existing settings in the Sort and Compress pull-down menus. Same as pressing [Alt]-[C], then [B].

[F5] Analyze   Performs an analysis of the file organization of the current disk.

[F6] Technique Lets you choose which compression technique you want to use.

[F7] Methods   Lets you select which compression method to use.

[F8] DirOrdr   Lets you choose the order in which directories are arranged.

[F9] Sort   Lets you choose the order in which files in a directory are arranged.

[F10] Menu   Activates top menu bar. Same as pressing [Alt].

Once you've set the sort order and method of analysis, you can start the compression program. When the program has finished, you should reboot your computer.

Switches to Use When Loading

You can use the following switches to modify the behavior of the Compress program upon start-up:

/350   Loads the program so it can be displayed in VGA mode, or 350 horizontal lines.

/BW   Loads the Compress program in black-and-white video mode. This is supposed to give you a better screen display if you're using a color card with a monochrome screen.

/CC   Runs a full compression and clears all unused sectors. CC stands for *Compress and Clear*.

/CF   Runs a full compress only. CF stands for *Compression Full*.

/CU   *Unfragments* your hard disk with a minimum of compression.

drive: The drive letter where you want the Compress program to do its work.

/NM   Stands for *No Mirror*, and prevents the Mirror program from running once Compress has stopped. It is recommended that you run Mirror once you've compressed a disk, so you can update your recovery file.

/OD   Stands for *Order DOS,* and arranges all files, including subdirectories, in normal DOS order.

/OO   Arranges files, placing subdirectories first.

/OP   Arranges files so that program files (those that end with .COM or. EXE) come first.

/OS   Arranges files using the standard or existing order.

/SA   Sorts the filenames in ascending order.

/SD   Sorts the filenames in descending order.

/SE   Sorts filenames by extension characters.

/SF   Sorts filenames by filename.

/SS   Sorts filenames by file size.

/ST   Sorts filenames by time of creation or last save.

These commands fall into several groups marked by the first letter of the switch. The /C group runs various compress options, the /O group controls file order, and the /S group controls sort order.

You can use several of these commands at the same time, as long as you don't use more than one command from each group.

File Find

The File Find program lets you search for specific files and groups of files on your disks. Once files are found, you can view their contents.

To load the program:

Type: FF

Press: [Enter]

In a moment, your screen will change to look like Figure 17.12.

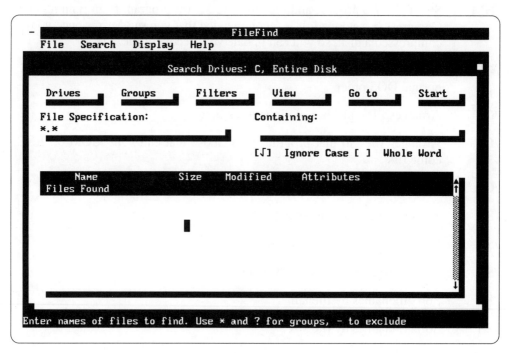

Figure 17.12. The FileFind screen

The top line displays the name of the program and the Control menu button. The second line down contains the names of the four pull-down menus. A menu map of all commands on these menus is shown in Figure 17.13.

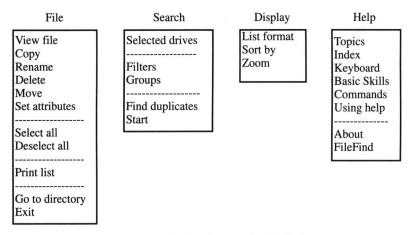

File

| View file |
| Copy |
| Rename |
| Delete |
| Move |
Set attributes
Select all
Deselect all
Print list
Go to directory
Exit

Search

Selected drives
Filters
Groups
Find duplicates
Start

Display

| List format |
| Sort by |
| Zoom |

Help

| Topics |
| Index |
| Keyboard |
| Basic Skills |
| Commands |
Using help
About
FileFind

Figure 17.13. Menu map in FileFind

The rest of the screen is divided into three areas: commands for controlling the search, the filename display screen occupying the largest part, and the ten function key assignments at the bottom of the screen. The commands for controlling the search are:

Drives   Opens the Select Drives/Directory window, where you select which drives you want to backup. You can select the entire directory, the current directory and all directories below it, or just the current directory.

Groups   Opens the Search Groups window, which lets you select certain groups of files to look for, such as all zipped files, or all Windows Write files.

Filters   Opens the Search Filters window, which lets you set filters that control your search.

View   Displays the contents of the currently highlighted file in an appropriate viewer, such as dBASE III and Lotus 1-2-3.

Go to   Moves you directly to the directory containing the current file, and bails out of the FileFind program.

Start   Starts the finding process.

Two fields let you enter information.

File Specification   Lets you specify while files to search through. The DOS wild-cards * and ? can specify groups of filenames, and the hyphen (-) is a wildcard indicating "do not include." For example, if you want to search for all files that begin with *D*, you could use the file specification D*.*. If you want to search for files whose first character is immaterial, you could use ?FILE.TXT. If you want to make sure the program doesn't search through your DOS directory, you could use -DOS.

Containing   Lets you specify a string of characters to search for in the files.

Once you've entered information in both of these categories, press [Enter] to start the search. FileFind will display the files it finds that meet your criteria in the large area in the central portion of the screen.

For example, let's search for all database files on the C drive.

    Type: *.DBF

Notice how previous characters disappear when you enter text.

    Press: [Enter]

This starts the search. File Find counts the files it finds that match your criteria, and displays this count on screen. The program tells you when it has scanned the entire disk (or the range you've specified), and tells you how many records it has found.

You can stop a search at any time by pressing [Esc]. This opens the Pausing Search screen, which asks whether you want to cancel the search.

Say you wanted to find .DBF files that contain the name "Ackerman":

    Press: [Tab]

This should highlight the File Specification field. (If you don't have any .DBF files, type the file extension of the database files you do keep and press [Enter].)

    Press: [Tab]

This highlights the Containing field.

    Type: Ackerman

Press: [Enter]

This begins the search. File Find will probably find fewer matches this time.

System Information

System Information provides accurate information about your computer setup and current usage. You can enter this program three ways:

1. From PC Shell: Press [Alt]-[S]-[S]

2. From the PC Tools menu: Open the Systems Tools menu, highlight System Information, and press [Enter].

3. From your DOS prompt: Type SI, and press [Enter].

This opens the System Information screen, as shown in Figure 17.14.

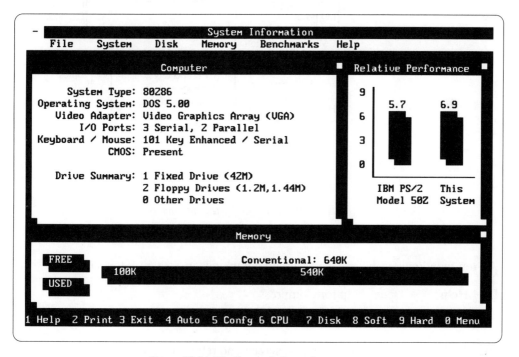

Figure 17.14. The System Information screen

This screen provides six pull-down menus:

File   Lets you view file information.

System   Lets you view system information.

Disk   Lets you view disk information.

Memory   Lets you view various aspects of memory information.

Benchmarks   Lets you run several benchmark tests.

Help   Opens a list of help subjects you can view in greater detail.

Figure 17.15 displays a menu map for all the commands on these menus.

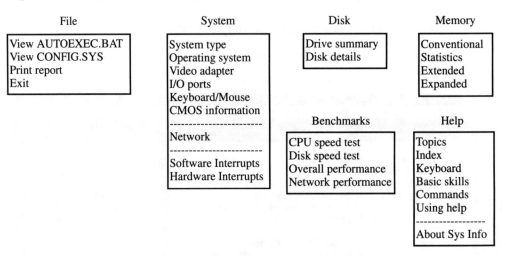

Figure 17.15. Menu map for System Information

All ten function keys have been assigned commands in System Information.

[F1] Help   Opens help for Compress.

[F2] Index   Opens the Help index for Compress.

[F3] Exit   Closes the Compress screen and return to your previous work.

[F4] Auto   Displays the contents of your AUTOEXEC.BAT file.

[F5] Config   Displays the contents of your CONFIG.SYS file.

[F6] CPU   Displays information about the central processing units (CPU) installed in your computer.

[F7] Disk   Displays information about your disk drives.

[F8] Soft   Displays information about your software interrupts.

[F9] Hard   Displays information about your hardware interrupts.

[F10] Menu   Activates the top menu bar.

You can't change any aspect of your system using System Information. This is designed solely to display information about your current setup, configuration and usage.

Directory Maintenance

The Directory Maintenance program lets you move around and maintain the directory structure on your disks. You can use the program on stand-alone disk drives or networked disk drives. You can access the program directly from DOS, or as a command in PC Shell.

You can load Directory Maintenance in three ways:

1. From PC Shell: Press [Alt]-[D], then [M].

2. From the PC Tools menu: Open the System Tools menu, highlight Directory Maintenance and press [Enter].

3. From your DOS prompt:

    Type: DM

    Press: [Enter].

When the Directory Maintenance screen appears, it will look like Figure 17.16.

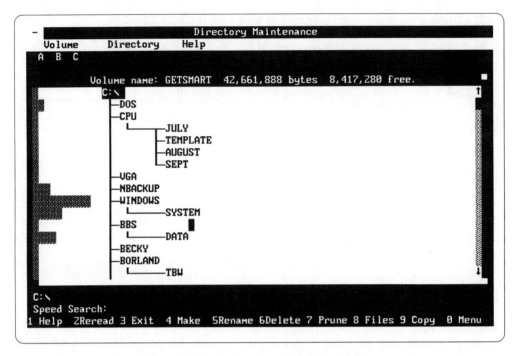

Figure 17.16. The Directory Maintenance screen

The details of your tree structure will look different from those shown in Figure 17.16, which displays the contents of my tree structure.

There are six features to the Directory Maintenance screen. The top line displays the Control menu button, the name of the screen you're working with (Directory Maintenance), and the current time.

The second line from the top shows the names of the three pull-down menus:

Volume   Lets you work with volume and tree information.

Directory Lets you work with directory features, DOS file attributes, and network rights.

Help   Lets you view help information about features in Directory Maintenance.

The third and fourth lines of your screen show disk-drive letters that have been installed in your computer. Most of the rest of the screen displays information about your current disk- drive tree structure.

The third line from the bottom of your screen displays the current directory name.

The second line from the bottom displays the Speed Search field. You'll learn more about speed searching in just a moment.

The bottom line of your screen displays the commands assigned to the ten function keys:

[F1] Help	Displays on-line context-sensitive help for the highlighted feature.
[F2] Reread	Rereads the current directory tree and displays it on screen.
[F3] Exit	Closes the Directory Maintenance program and returns you to your previous work.
[F4] Make	Makes a new directory in the current cursor location. Same as the DOS command *MD*.
[F5] Rename	Lets you rename an existing directory.
[F6] Delete	Lets you delete the current directory, as long as it is empty. You cannot delete a file that contains files or other directories. Same as the DOS command *RD*.
[F7] Prune	Lets you move an existing directory, along with all the files and directories it contains, to a new location. This is also called "prune and graft."
[F8] Files	Lists the filenames in the current directory.
[F9] Print	Prints the current directory tree to your printer.
[F10] Menu	Lets you work with the pull-down menus. You can also press [Alt] to activate the menu.

Using Directory Maintenance

To work with Directory Maintenance, you must understand the features in the middle of the screen. First, the left side of this screen contains the *relative-size graph*. This is a series of colored (or shaded) horizontal bars that provide a graphic display of the size of the directory to the right of the bar. You can change this display to numbers by using the *Tree Data Display* command on the Volume pull-down menu.

The Directory Maintenance screen contains a cursor that can move from one directory name to another. You can move this cursor by pressing the arrow keys ([⇩] or [⇒] moves the cursor down, [⇧] or [⇐] moves the cursor up) or by speed-searching a directory name.

You can work with any of the six commands on the Volume pull-down menu, regardless of where your directory cursor is located:

Rename Volume   Lets you rename the currently highlighted drive.

Reread Tree   Rereads the tree for the current drive.

Change Drive   Lets you change the current drive.

Print Tree   Lets you print the contents of the current tree to your printer or a disk file. The disk file will be named TREELIST.PRN, and will be saved in the same directory that contains the Directory Maintenance program file DM.EXE (most likely your PCTOOLS directory).

Tree Data Display   Lets you control the way tree data is displayed on screen. This command opens the Tree Data Display window, which lets you select one of five ways to display data: bar graph (the default), size, creation date, owner, and rights. The last three are available only if the data pertains to shared files.

Exit   Lets you exit the Directory Maintenance program and return to your previous work. If you entered the program through PC Shell, that's where you will return.

There are nine commands on the Directory menu:

Make Directory   Lets you make a new directory below the currently highlighted directory.

Rename Directory   Lets you rename the currently highlighted directory.

Delete Directory   Lets you delete the currently highlighted directory.

Copy Tree   Copies the contents of the currently highlighted directory, along with the directory name, to another location on the tree.

Prune & Graft   Lets you move the currently highlighted drive, including files and subdirectories, to become a directory in a new location.

Branch Size   Lets you determine the depth of directory level to display.

Modify Attributes   Lets you modify directory attributes.

Show Files   Shows all the filenames in the current directory.

Network Rights   Lets you observe your network rights. This command will be disabled unless you've installed a network driver.

Figure 17.17 shows a menu map for individual commands on all pull-down menus in Directory Maintenance.

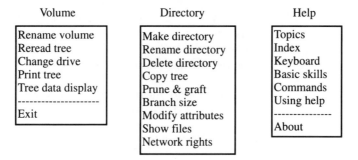

Volume	Directory	Help
Rename volume	Make directory	Topics
Reread tree	Rename directory	Index
Change drive	Delete directory	Keyboard
Print tree	Copy tree	Basic skills
Tree data display	Prune & graft	Commands
------------------	Branch size	Using help
Exit	Modify attributes	---------------
	Show files	About
	Network rights	

Figure 17.17. Directory Maintenance menu map

Speed Searching

You can move around directories in the Directory Maintenance screen by typing the first few letters of the directory you want to go to. When you press a character key, the character will also appear in the Speed Search field, which is located on the second line from the bottom of your screen.

If you want to go to a directory that shares the first two or three letters with another directory—for example, BOOKS and BORLAND—you need to enter enough letters to make the directory name unique. You have to type at least three letters for Directory Maintenance to differentiate between BOOKS and BORLAND.

You can delete a character in the Speed Search field by pressing [⇐].

You can also move around directories by pressing your arrow keys. To move the cursor down the directory tree, use [⇒] or [⇓]. To move it up, use [⇐] or [⇑]

Command Line Options

You can load Directory Maintenance without viewing the Directory Maintenance screen by loading from your DOS prompt and adding one or more of these options:

d:
Lets you specify which drive to read when the program is loaded. Saves loading time.

directory name
Lets you specify the name of a directory you want to be current when Directory Maintenance loads.

DD path
This command means *delete directory*. It deletes the directory you specify in the path. If the directory contains any items, you will be asked whether you want to delete its contents. You must type the correct path to the directory for this command to work.

MD path
This command means *make directory*. It makes the directory you specify in the path.

RV name
Stands for *rename volume*. It renames the volume label of the current drive using the name you specify.

RN oldpath newdir
Renames the directory specified in the "oldpath" to the new directory name specified by "newdir."

PG prunepath graftpath
This stands for *prune directory* It moves the directory specified in "prunepath" and makes it a subdirectory of the directory specified in "graftpath."

MA path HSRA
This stands for *modify attributes*. It changes any of the four attributes you specify (H: hidden, S: system, R: read only, and A: archive) for the directory you specify in path.

/R
Stands for *reread the tree*; this command rereads the directory tree for the current drive and updates the TREELIST file.

The syntax for using these switches is *DM switch*. For example, DM A reads the disk in A drive, and DM /R rereads the directory structure for the current drive. You can also use these command options in groups. For example, DM A: /R rereads the disk in your A drive.

These commands are not case-sensitive.

View

You use the View program to select a file and view its contents on screen. This covers all popular word processing files, database and spreadsheets files, graphic files, and even compiled binary files (as long as you don't mind viewing them in binary or ASCII format).

You can load View from the PC Tools menu or from your DOS prompt:

Type: VIEW

Press: [Enter]

When the View screen appears, it lists the name of the subdirectories and files in the current drive and directory. Figure 17.18 shows the View program displaying the contents of my root directory.

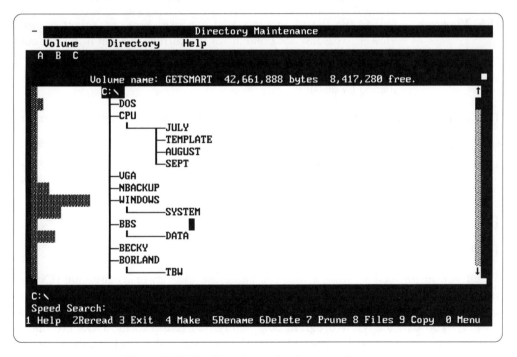

Figure 17.18. The View screen showing a root directory

To display the contents of a directory, highlight its name and press [Enter].

To view the contents of a file, highlight the filename and press [Enter]. View figures out the format of the file and loads the appropriate viewer, named at the top of the screen. All viewers provided have these ten commands assigned to the function keys:

[F1] Help   Displays help information about the View program.

[F2] Info   Displays information about the file you're viewing.

[F3] Exit   Closes the View program and returns you to your previous work.

[F4] Files   Opens the View window and display files and directories in the current drive and directory. You can view another file directly this way.

[F5] GoTo   Lets you go to a specific line and column in the current file.

[F6] Viewer   Opens the list of viewers you can use. You can select another viewer to display the contents of the current file, but if the file contents are not suitable for the viewer (for example, you want to view an ASCII text file in a database viewer), the Binary Viewer will be loaded by default.

[F7] Search   Lets you search for a string of text characters using whole-word or case-insensitive conditions.

[F8] Unzm   Reduces the display size of the viewer to half screen. This changes the designation of F9 to Zoom. Pressing F9 a second time expands the display space to full-screen size

[F9] Prev   Displays the previous screen.

[F10] Next   Displays the next screen.

When you're finished viewing a file, you can close the viewer by pressing [Esc] or [F3]. In both cases, you're given a prompt that asks whether you want to exit or cancel the exit. Unfortunately, when you press [Enter] to exit, you don't just exit the viewer—you exit the View program completely and return to the DOS prompt. If this happens and you want to return to the View screen, just press [F3], then [Enter]. This reinserts the command VIEW you typed previously, then loads the program.

PC Format

The PC Format program is a versatile disk formatter that you might well want to use instead of the DOS command FORMAT. In fact, when you first install the PC Tools programs using PC Tools Install, you're asked whether you want the program to change the name of DOS program FORMAT.COM so you can use the PC Tools FORMAT.COM command instead, which is handier and safer. If you accept this option, all files called FORMAT.COM will be renamed FORMAT!.COM, while the PC Tools program PCFORMAT.COM will be renamed FORMAT.COM. You can load PC Format from the PC Tools menu or from your DOS prompt:

> If you decide not to change the name of the PC Tools program PCFORMAT.COM to FORMAT.COM, type PCFORMAT to run the program, then press [Enter].

Type: FORMAT

Press: [Enter]

When the PC Format program is loaded, the first thing you'll be asked is which disk to format. After selecting a disk and pressing [Enter], you'll move into the PC Format screen, as shown in Figure 17.19.

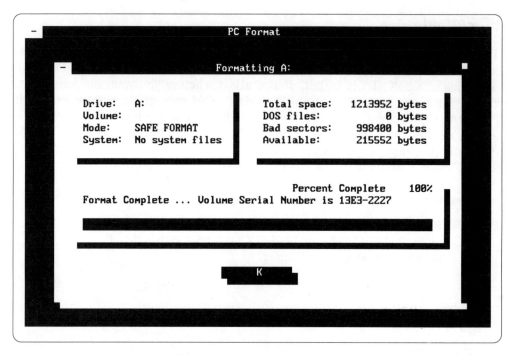

Figure 17.19. The PC Format screen

This screen lets you declare the type of format, and the way certain system and Mirror files will be handled during formatting. Once you've made your selections and pressed [Enter], you'll move into the format progress screen, which tracks and displays the progress of the formatting.

You can also run the PC Format program using command line switches. This means you can bypass the screens and start your formatting, as long as you enter the right commands. There are six formatting parameters and eight disk parameters.

The formatting parameters are:

/V   Prompts you for a new volume or disk label.

/V:label   Lets you specify the new volume or disk label on the DOS command line.

/S   Includes DOS system files to make the formatted disk a bootable disk.

/Q   Quickly erases a previously formatted disk.

/P   Prints all messages to your screen and the LPT1 port.

/TEST   Simulates a format without writing anything to disk.

For example, to run a quick version of PC Format, you would:

Type: FORMAT /Q

Press: [Enter].

The are disk parameters are:

/1   Formats a disk on a single side only.

/4   Formats a 360 Kbyte disk in a 1.2 Mbyte drive.

/8   Formats eight sectors per disk track.

/N:s/T:t   Formats a certain number of tracks, where T can equal 40 or 80, and sectors per track, where S can equal 8, 15, 18, or 36.

/F:ddd   Formats for various diskette sizes, where ddd can equal 160, 180, 320, 360, 720, 1,440, and 2,880.

/R   Reads each track on the diskette, reformats each track, and rewrites the original data.

/F   Works like the /R switch, except it deletes all files.

/DESTROY   Formats and erases all data.

For example, to run a quick format that destroys all data:

Type: FORMAT /Q /DESTROY

Press: [Enter]

SECURITY TOOLS

The Security Tools menu provides access to two PC Tools utility programs that help secure your disk file data.

PC Secure

The PC Secure program lets you encrypt files or directories of files so only you can use them. It also allows you to decrypt encrypted files and directories.

The first time you run the program, you'll be asked to install it using a master key password. This key can decrypt any file when the password assigned to a file has been lost.

You type the password once, then again for verification, then press [Enter]. Once you've declared a password, you won't see this first screen again.

When the PC Secure screen appears, it looks like Figure 17.20.

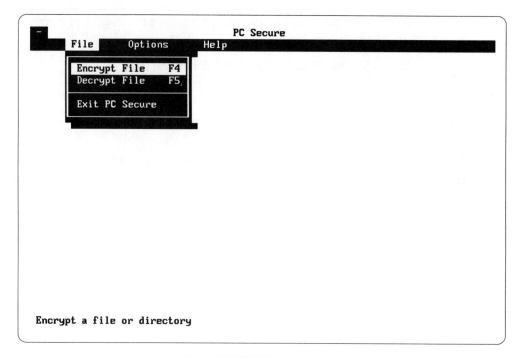

Figure 17.20. PC Secure screen

The PC Secure screen provides three pull-down menus:

File   Lets you begin encrypting or decrypting a file.

Options   Lets you set options for encryption.

Help   Lets you select a topic from a list for more information about the topic.

Figure 17.21 shows a menu map of the commands on these three menus.

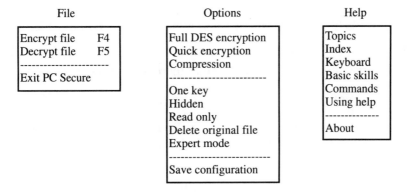

File	Options	Help
Encrypt file F4	Full DES encryption	Topics
Decrypt file F5	Quick encryption	Index
-----------------------	Compression	Keyboard
Exit PC Secure	-----------------------	Basic skills
	One key	Commands
	Hidden	Using help
	Read only	--------------
	Delete original file	About
	Expert mode	

	Save configuration	

Figure 17.21. Menu map for PC Secure

You can press [Esc] to close the File pull-down menu. When you do this, you'll see six function key assignments:

[F1] Help   Displays help information about the View program.

[F2] Info   Displays information about the file you're viewing.

[F3] Exit   Closes the View program and returns you to your previous work.

[F4] Encrypt   Opens the File Selection window, which lets you select the file or directory to encrypt.

[F5] Decrypt   Opens the File Selection window, which lets you select the file or directory to decrypt.

[F10] Menu   Activates the top menu bar.

To encrypt a file:

> **Press:** [F4]

This opens the File Selection window. Select the directory that contains the file you want to encrypt. Then select the filename and press [Enter]. You'll be asked to specify a password. Type one in, then press [Enter].

To decrypt an encrypted file:

> **Press:** [F5]

Now select the file, enter the password you assigned to encrypt the file, and press [Enter].

You can fine-tune your encryption using one or more of the following options:

Full DES Encryption   Lets you use the full data encryption standard algorithm.

Quick Encryption   Lets you use a form of encryption that's quicker than the DES method but not as secure.

Compression   Lets you compress a file while it's being encrypted. This makes the file occupy less space on the disk.

One Key   Lets you use one password for more than one file.

Hidden   Hides the file from display when you run the DOS command DIR.

Read Only   Prevents the file from being deleted.

Delete Original File   Deletes the original file after making an encrypted copy. You cannot recover the deleted original file using Undelete, or any other undelete file program.

Expert Mode   Disables the master password key.

Save Configuration   Saves the options you have selected.

You can tell when an option has been selected because a musical note will appear to the left of the option name.

Data Monitor

The Data Monitor program lets you protect your data and computer system in several ways. To load the program, select the Data Monitor command on the Security Tools menu, or at your DOS prompt:

Type: DM

Press: [Enter]

When the Data Monitor screen appears, it looks like Figure 17.22.

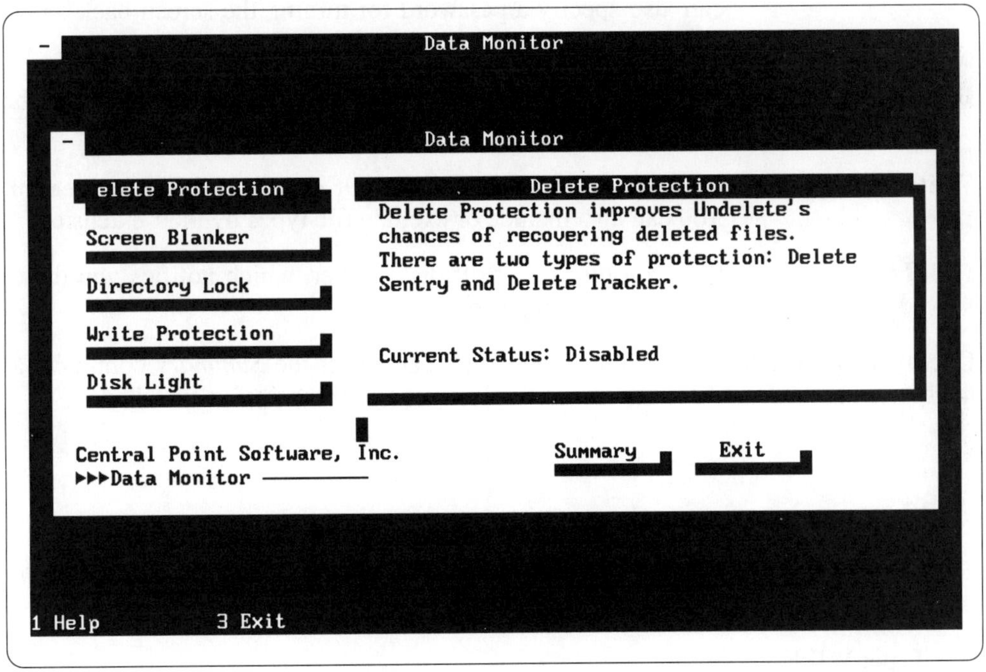

Figure 17.22. The Data Monitor screen

Thc left side of the Data Monitor screen lists the Data Monitor features you can install. The right side defines each option as you highlight it.

Delete Protection   Lets you install Delete Sentry and Delete Tracker, two tools that improve your chances of recovering lost data when you use the Undelete program. Delete Tracker keeps a track of where deleted files are kept. Delete Sentry moves deleted files to a hidden directory. You can install one or both of these tools.

Screen Blanker   Blanks your screen after a period of time that you define. You can also specify a password for turning the screen back on, as well as a set of hot keys.

Directory Lock   Lets you maintain data in an encrypted directory that can be accessed only with a password, if you want.

Write Protection   Lets you protect portions of your disk from being written on. You can also include or exclude file types by their extension.

Disk Light   Lets you turn on or off disk flicker, which notifies you that a disk drive is being used.

Once you've installed any of these tools, you can select the *Summary* command at the bottom of the Data Monitor screen to review the settings you've installed.

Wipe

The Wipe program wipes data clean from your disk. You can load the program from the PC Tools menu, or from your DOS prompt:

Type: WIPE

Press: [Enter]

This brings up the Wipe Main Menu screen, as shown in Figure 17.23.

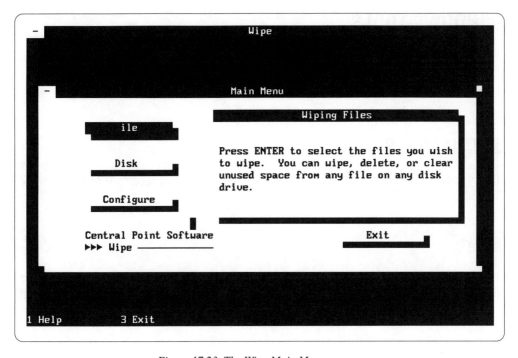

Figure 17.23. The Wipe Main Menu screen

This lets you specify whether you want to wipe a file or disk, or configure the program first.

If you select *File*, the File Options screen opens. This lets you toggle on or off the selections that determine how and when files should be wiped.

If you select *Disk*, you are given the options of wiping the entire disk or just the unused sections of the disk.

If you select *Configure*, you're allowed to select *Fast wipe* or *DOD wipe*, which is more thorough but slower. You can select the overwrite character for *Fast wipe*. You can determine the number of times *DOD wipe* occurs.

You can use the following two function keys while working in View:

[F1] Help   Provides on-line context-sensitive help.

[F3] Exit   Lets you exit the Wipe program and return to your previous work.

WINDOWS TOOLS

The Windows Tools Utility menu provides access to two utility programs that run under Windows: CP Backup and Undelete. You can find the details for running these programs, and other Central Point Windows programs, in the next chapter.

SETUP TOOLS

The Setup menu provides access to two PC Tools utility programs that help you set up and configure the various PC Tools programs.

Install

The Install program, when run from the PC Tools main menu, runs the reduced version of the Install program. Read Appendix A for more information about the Install program.

PC Config

The PC Config program lets you determine the way your terminal screen behaves, as well as how your mouse and keyboard respond. Once you make the selections you want to use, you can save them to a configuration file that PC Tools programs call on for settings.

You can load PC Config from the PC Tools menu, or from your DOS prompt:

> **Type:** PCCONFIG

> **Press:** Enter

This brings up the Configuration Options screen, as which looks like Figure 17.24.

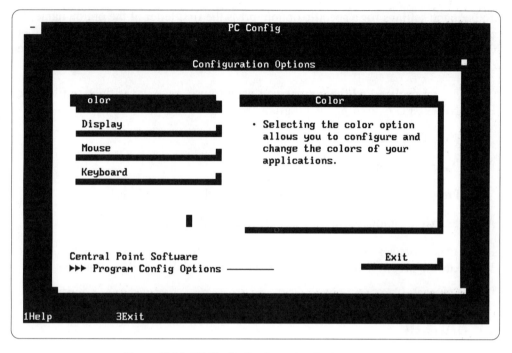

Figure 17.24. PC Config Configuration Options screen

You're given four options to work with:

Color   Lets you select various color options for PC Shell if your terminal can display color.

Display   Lets you select one of four display terminal settings, as well as text or graphics mode. You must have a monitor that matches the setting you select, such as EGA or VGA, or else the PC Tool program you want to use will default to the original settings.

Mouse   Lets you select four conditions for your mouse to work with, such as the speed of mouse response.

Keyboard   Lets you select the rate and delay time for your keyboard response.

To find out how PC Tools describes each option, press [⇓] to highlight the option you're curious about and look at the Exit window to the right of the option list. To find out more about an option, highlight the option and press [F1] for help.

To open the settings for a specific option, press the first letter of the option name; for example, press [M] to set Mouse options. This opens the Mouse Options screen, which lets you switch on or off four different mouse settings, and control the speed of your mouse performance.

Once you've declared all the options you want to use, save the settings to file called PCCONFIG.CFG by exiting the program. You can do this three ways:

1. Press [F3], then [Enter].

2. Press [X], then [Enter].

3. Press [Tab] to highlight the *Exit* command, then press [Enter].

All three exit techniques will save any changes you've made.

If you make changes and then decide you don't want them, press [Esc], then [Enter]. This exits the program and retains the previous PCCONFIG.CFG file on disk.

CP BACKUP

The CP Backup program lets you backup disk files on a hard disk to a floppy disk, a series of floppy disks, or tape drive.

There are two parts to the PC Backup program. The first part backs up data on your hard disk to another storage device, such as floppy disks or tape. PC Backup backs up data on a disk to another disk or tape storage device that you can save for later use if the original disk or files become damaged, or if you lose files on the original disk that you can't undelete.

The PC Backup program uses a unique format that squeezes more data onto the backup storage device than usual. This saves you time and trouble when you backup an entire hard disk to a series of floppy disks, which is the most frequent method for preserving data.

The second part restores this data from the backup media to the original disk. You can backup all or part of your files, and you can restore all or part of your files. You'll use the various menu settings to control these options.

When you run PC Backup, you can use a DOS-compatible backup procedure or an alternative high-speed DMA procedure.

Switches When Loading

You can use the following ten switches when you load the program to change the way it appears or behaves:

/?   Displays a Help screen.

/BW   Loads the Backup program in back-and-white video mode. This is supposed to give you a better screen display if you're using a color card with a monochrome screen.

/DOB   Stands for Deluxe Options Board. This switch turns automatic detection for this board on. PC Tools Deluxe supports the use of this board, which can dramatically reduce the amount of time it takes to format disks and write information to them.

drive: The drive letter that will write the backup files.

/filename Declares the backup sets of files using the extension .SET.

/LCD   Displays the program for LCD screens on laptop computers.

/LE   Stands for *Left Exchange*, which switches command assignments between the left and right button on your mouse.

/NO   Stands for *No Overlap*. This switch overrides simultaneous DMA (direct memory access) to both floppy and hard disks. On older computers, or computers that are not truly compatible, the Backup program might not perform the way it's supposed to. If you experience problems running Backup, you might want to reload the program using the /NO switch.

/PS2   Reconfigures the program on IBM PS/2 computers that fail to control some older models of mouse input devices.

/R   Stands for *Restore*; this loads the program and starts it out in restore mode. This relieves you of waiting while the program reads the disk directory structure and information about the current files. The first thing it asks you to do is insert the first disk of the series you want to restore.

To run PC Backup, select the program name from the PC Tools menu, or from your DOS prompt:

Type: PCBACKUP

Press: [Enter]

The program will read your disk first. If you haven't configured the program for your computer, you'll be walked through two screens to do this. Next, the program tests your hardware equipment.

You should declare the various floppy disk drives you use in this window, which moves you into the second screen. Once you've configured your version of PC Backup, you'll be shown the PC Backup screen, which looks like Figure 17.25.

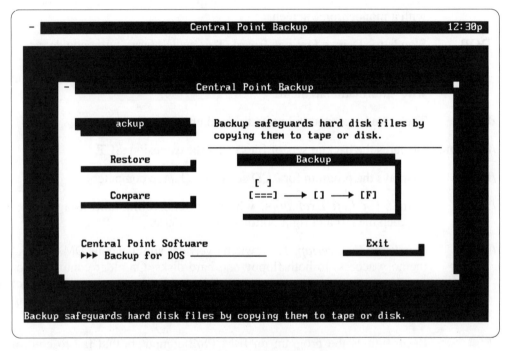

Figure 17.25. The PC Backup screen

This is a modified version of the PC Shell screen, with a tree list on the left and file-names on the right. You can press [Tab] or [Shift]-[Tab] to switch activity between the two windows. Filenames appear in the right window for the directory highlighted in the left window. Once you've configured the program, this is the first screen that appears.

You can find the menu bar at the top with five pull down menus:

Backup   Lets you start the backup procedure, chose the directories you want to backup, and exit the program.

Restore   Lets you configure the restore program, start the restore program, and compare disks.

Options   Lets you load a setup file, save a setup file, and declare many other options that control the way you backup your files.

Configure   Lets you select various options, such as the drive and media you want to use, other special equipment, the backup speed, current user level, and color selection of various features in the program.

Help   Opens the basic Help screen.

The menu map for PC Backup is shown in Figure 17.26.

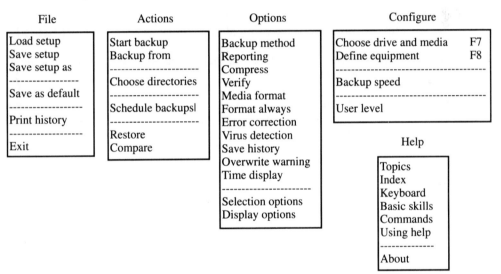

Figure 17.26. Menu map for PC Backup

The two lines below the top menu bar show the drive you're backing up, the drive you're backing up to, the Setup file you're using, if any, and the user level.

The left window shows the top part of your current tree, and the right window shows the files in the current directory.

The second-to-bottom line of your screen shows six pieces of information about the disk you want to backup: the number of directories, total number of files, disk space occupied by these files, the number of disk you'll probably need to backup all the files, and the approximate time it will take to complete the backup operation.

You can use nine function keys as shown at the bottom of the screen.

F1 Help   Opens the context-sensitive Help screen.

F3 Exit   Closes the PC Backup screen and returns you to the DOS command line. Same as pressing [Alt]-[B]-[X].

F4 Select   Opens the Choose Drive & Media window, which lets you declare what type of backup device you're using. Same as pressing [Alt]-[B]-[H].

F5 Backup   Starts the backup procedure. You should select this after you've set the various backup options. Same as pressing [Alt]-[B]-[S].

F6 Restore   Runs the restore program, which restores information from backed-up disks or tape to the original disk. Same as pressing [Alt]-[R]-[S].

F7 Device   Lets you choose the drive and media you want to backup to. Same as pressing [Alt]-[C]-[M].

F8 Setup   Runs the setup program, which walks you through the two screens you used to configure your version of PC Backup. Same as pressing [Alt]-[C]-[C].

F9 Compare   Starts the disk compare program, which compares backed up files on the backup disk to the files on the original disk. Same as pressing [Alt]-[R]-[C].

F10 Menu   Same as pressing [Alt].

To backup files, you should set the various conditions you want to use use to backup or restore your disk files, make sure your backup media is installed and ready, then begin the backup procedure by pressing [F5]

When you want to restore backed-up file information, you should make sure to declare the restore settings you want to use, install the backed-up media in the proper device, then press[F6].

Running a Backup

When you run your first complete backup, you'll be given a screen that asks you to insert the first disk in the series. The progress of PC Backup through your disk will be noted at the bottom of your screen.

The PC Backup program begins at the top of your directory tree on the left and proceeds to backup each file in the right window. The file being backed up will be highlighted. As one disk fills up, the program will prompt you to replace it with the next disk. Be sure to mark disks in order, so you can feed the disks into the restore program in the same order. This is necessary because the backup program is so precise that it will break a file over two disks, and the second disk has to follow the first or else a program file will be unfinished.

When the backing up is complete, the program will write the directory structure to the last disk, and tell you when it is doing this. When the program is finished, it will display a report screen.

Using Setup Files

The PC Backup program is very complex. I usually use it to backup my entire hard disk using default settings, but I often restore a single file or a group of files while ignoring the rest of the backed up data.

You can create and save special setup files that include optional settings for certain situations, such as restoring a single file, or restoring only those files that have been changed since the last time you backed up the files. To do this, declare the options you want to save using the various menus in the PC Backup program, then press [Alt]-[O]-[S]. This opens a screen that lets you type the name you want to give the setup file.

When you want to use the specific setup file, press [Alt]-[O]-[L], type the name of the file, and press [Enter].

Picking a User Level

Once you've taken a look at the PC Backup program, you may prefer to configure it for your level of skill or confidence. As with PC Shell, you can choose Beginner, Intermediate, or Advanced user level. Advanced is the default. The higher the level, the more menu commands you can use.

To select a user level:

> **Press:** [Alt]-[C]-[U]

This opens the Select User Level menu, which lets you pick one of three levels. Press [Tab] to highlight the level you want to use, then press [Enter].

COMMUTE

The Commute program lets you work with two computers at the same time and control the disk files on both computers. This means you can view and transfer files from one computer to another, and run programs on the remote computer using the computer at hand.

There are only two things you have to decide when you want to run Commute. The first is how you'll make the connection between the computers. The second is which computer will control the other.

> **Type:** COMMUTE

> **Press:** [Enter]

The first time you enter the program, you'll be asked to declare a user name. Once you type this name, it will control your entrance into the program.

When the program is fully loaded, you'll see the Commute screen, as shown in Figure 17.27.

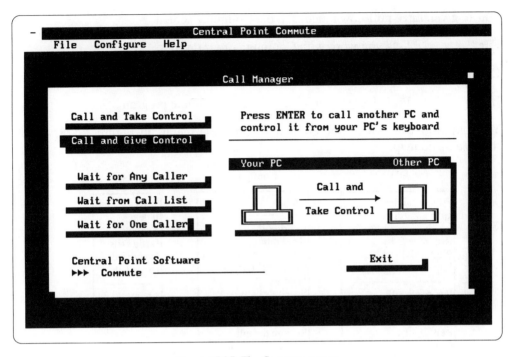

Figure 17.27. The Commute screen

This gives you five situations on the left and a graphic depiction of the relationship between you and the other computer on the right.

Call Manager Window   Lets you work in the Commute screen.

Call and Take Control   Lets you call another computer and take control of that computer.

Call and Give Control   Lets you call another computer and give control of your computer to the other computer.

Wait for Any Caller   Lets you wait for another computer to call your computer.

Wait from Call List   Lets you wait for another computer on your call list to call your computer.

Wait for One Caller   Lets you wait for a specific caller to call your computer.

You're given three pull-down menus in the Commute screen:

File   Lets you work with Commute program files.

Configure   Lets you control the way the Commute program behaves.

Help   Provides help on features in the Commute program.

You can view a list of all the commands on these menus in Figure 17.28, which shows a menu map.

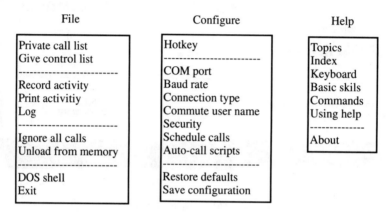

```
        File                       Configure                    Help

 ┌─────────────────────┐   ┌─────────────────────┐   ┌──────────────────┐
 │Private call list    │   │Hotkey               │   │Topics            │
 │Give control list    │   │---------------------│   │Index             │
 │---------------------│   │COM port             │   │Keyboard          │
 │Record activity      │   │Baud rate            │   │Basic skils       │
 │Print activitiy      │   │Connection type      │   │Commands          │
 │Log                  │   │Commute user name    │   │Using help        │
 │---------------------│   │Security             │   │--------------    │
 │Ignore all calls     │   │Schedule calls       │   │About             │
 │Unload from memory   │   │Auto-call scripts    │   └──────────────────┘
 │---------------------│   │---------------------│
 │DOS shell            │   │Restore defaults     │
 │Exit                 │   │Save configuration   │
 └─────────────────────┘   └─────────────────────┘
```

Figure 17.28. Menu map of the Commute program

The File Menu

The File pull-down menu in the Commute program provides the following eight commands.

Private Call List   Lets you use a list of computers you want to call privately.

Give Control List   Lets you use a list of computers you are willing to give control of your computer to.

Record Activity   Lets you keep a record of your commuting activity.

Print Activity Log   Lets you print a copy of your activity log.

Ignore All Calls   Lets you ignore all incoming calls.

Unload from Memory	Unloads the Commute program from your computer's memory.
DOS Shell	Returns you to DOS temporarily. Type EXIT and press [Enter] to return to the Commute program.
Exit	Lets you exit the Commute program and return to your previous work, either your DOS screen or the PC Tools program main menu.

The Configure Menu

The Configure pull-down menu in the Commute program provides the following eleven commands.

Hotkey	Lets you change the hot key setting.
Modem List	Lets you select the modem you want to use.
COM Port	Lets you select the COM port you want to use.
Baud Rate	Lets you select the BAUD rate you want to use.
Connection Type	Lets you select the type of connection you want to make with the other computer.
Commute User Name	Lets you specify your user name.
Security	Lets you select security settings that apply to your computer and the computer you're communicating with.
Schedule Calls	Lets you schedule calls at appointed dates and time.
Auto-Call Scripts	Lets you list calls made automatically with scripts.
Restore Defaults	Lets you restore all default configuration settings.
Save Configuration	Lets you save changes you've made to the configuration.

Working with the Commute program takes some practice. You'll find you'll get better at it, and become familiar with the commands you like to use, when actually working with the program and another computer.

VDEFEND

The VDefend program is also called Virus Defend, and protects your disk system areas from becoming fouled by any replicating viruses. This program is loaded resident into your computer's memory, and keeps constant vigil over any attempts to write to the system areas on your hard disk or to perform a low-level format. You'll be alerted if any attempt is made. You can then take the appropriate steps, either preventing the writing to disk or proceeding with it.

To load Vdefend:

Type: VDEFEND

Press: [Enter]

It takes only a moment for the program to load, after which you'll see your DOS prompt. You'll also see a message on your screen notifying you that the program has been successfully loaded.

You might want to make sure VDefend is always at work when your computer is turned on. In this case, you should probably load VDefend into memory automatically each time you boot using the VDEFEND command in AUTOEXEC.BAT.

If you ever want to unload VDefend from memory, at your DOS prompt:

Type: KILL

Press: [Enter]

MEMORY INFORMATION

This program displays your current memory usage in various ways. You can only run the program from your DOS prompt, but it's a good way to check your memory if you switch between lots of programs, or use programs that tax your computer memory limits.

To run the MI program:

Type: MI

Press: [Enter]

Your screen will change to look something like shown in Figure 17.29.

```
C:\>mi
Memory Info V7
(c)1991 Central Point Software, Inc.

Addr.   Total bytes   Program or device driver
-----   -----------   --------------------------
0255h       33,104    Device=FASTBIOS  Attr=8000h   Name=__FBIOS_
0A6Bh        1,184    Device=HIMEM     Attr=A000h   Name=XMSXXXX0
0AB6h       12,624    Device=MOUSE     Attr=8000h   Name=MS$MOUSE
0DCCh       13,392    Device=SMARTDRV  Attr=C800h   Name=SMARTAAR
1239h        2,624    COMMAND
12F0h       23,392    GRAB      C:\HSG\GRAB.EXE
18A8h      554,368    <largest free area>

655,360 bytes (640k) total DOS 5.00 conventional memory.
554,368 bytes (541k) largest executable program.

       0  bytes Extended (AT/286/386) memory, reported by BIOS.
       0  bytes free, reported by XMS driver version 2.0 (2.77).   HMA exists.

C:\>
```

Figure 17.29. Results of running MI

The three columns of information show the address, total bytes, and each program or device driver that has been loaded into your computer's memory. In Figure 17.29, five items have been loaded into my computer's memory: FASTBIOS (a quick BIOS), HIMEM (DOS parking itself in high memory), MOUSE (my mouse driver), SMARTDRV (DOS smart drive), and COMMAND (COMMAND.COM). The rest of my memory is free.

The MI program also shows the amount of memory available, the largest executable program I can run, and the amount of extended memory and extended memory available.

You can also use eight switches that control the way information is displayed when you run MI.

/A   Displays all information.

/F   Hides, or "filters," characters that don't print.

/H   Displays the list of switches you can use, as well as the command syntax. Same as /?.

/N   Does not pause when the screen fills up, but continues to scroll and display more information.

/O   Uses another display format.

/Q   Displays a quick summary only.

/V   Lists the hooked vectors as well.

/?   Displays the list of switches you can use, as well as the command syntax. Same as /H.

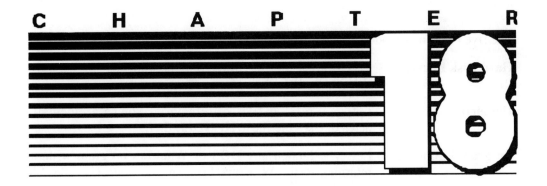

WINDOWS PROGRAMS

V ersion 7 of PC Tools Deluxe provides five programs that run under Microsoft Windows Version 3.0. This chapter is devoted to describing these programs and how they work.

The five PC Tools Windows programs are:

Hard Disk Backup   Lets you backup disk files to archive media. Uses the file WNBACKUP.EXE.

Undelete   Lets you recover files or directories you've accidentally deleted. Uses the file WNUNDEL.EXE.

Program Launcher   Lets you launch any DOS or Windows program without returning to the Windows Program Manager. Uses the file WNLAUNCH.EXE.

TSR Manager   Lets you manage any TSR programs loaded under DOS and still resident in your computer's memory. Uses the file WNTSRMAN.EXE.

Program Scheduler   Lets you select one of the four previous programs to work with. Uses the file WNSCHEDL.EXE.

Before you can use any of these programs, you have to install them on your hard disk using the PC Tools Install program, or by inserting them into your Windows Applications module.

INSTALLING PC TOOLS WINDOWS PROGRAMS

You can install the five PC Tools Windows programs in three different ways:

• Use the PC Tools Install program. This creates a separate group window called PC Tools that will contain PC Tools Windows program icons only.

• Copy the PC Tools Windows programs to your hard disk, then run the Windows Setup program again. This locates the PC Tools Windows programs and installs them in the Windows Applications window of the Program Manager.

• Install each PC Tools Windows program individually while working in the Windows Program Manager. This lets you install them in any Program Manager window that you want to use.

Both the PC Tools Install program and the Windows Setup program run by themselves, so there's not much you need to know about if you want to use either of those methods. If you want to install each program individually, the following information will be helpful.

Installing Windows Programs Individually

First, make sure you're working in the Windows Application module of the Program Manager. Your display screen should look more or less like Figure 18.1, although the icon in your Windows Applications screen might differ slightly.

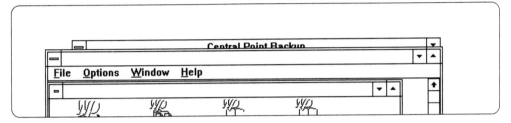

Figure 18.1. The Windows Application screen in Windows 3.0 Program Manager

Next, open the File menu and select the command *New*. This opens the New Program Object window, which asks whether you want to install a New Program Group or a New Program Item. Select *New Program Item* and press [Enter] or click OK. This option should be selected by default. It opens the Program Item Properties window. Now:

Type: WnBackup

This stands for *Windows Backup*, although you can type any text that reminds you of the program attached to the icon.

Press: [Tab]

This moves your cursor to the next field, Command Line. Next:

Type: C:\PCTOOLS\WNBACKUP.EXE

Click: OK

This is the path and name of the file that runs the Backup program. It tells Windows which file to use when you click on the icon for WnBackup. When you click OK, Windows automatically checks to make sure the filename exists in the directory you've specified. It will notify you if you've typed the wrong directory or filename.

When Windows accepts your path and filename, the appropriate icon will appear in your Windows Application window. Once you become familiar with loading programs into Windows Applications, you can load all five PC Tools Windows programs. Figure 18.2 shows the five icons for the PC Tools Windows programs.

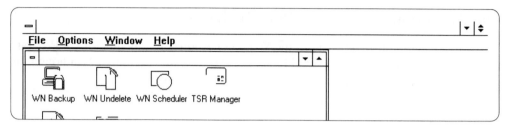

Figure 18.2. The five icons for PC Tools Window programs

When you install them one after the other, the icons will line up automatically on the top row of your screen, as shown above. If you want to place the icons in other positions, you can point and click on the icon, then drag it to a new location, or you can use the *Arrange* command in the Windows pull-down menu. If you use the second method, your screen should change to look like Figure 18.3.

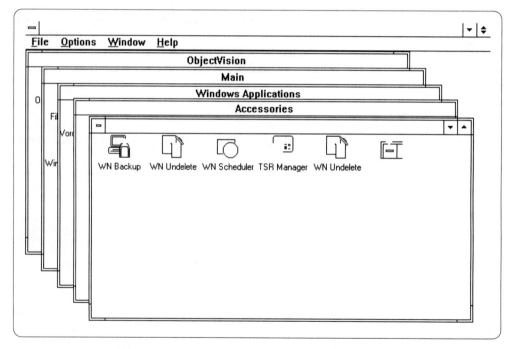

Figure 18.3. Icons rearranged for PC Tools Windows programs

The files that run the PC Tools Windows programs are:

Launcher   WNLAUNCH.EXE

Backup	WNBACKUP.EXE
Scheduler	WNSCHEDL.EXE
TSR Manager	WNTSRMAN.EXE
Undelete	WNUNDEL.EXE

You can find all of these files in the path C:\PCTOOLS, unless you copied them to another directory when you ran the PC Tools Install programs.

Once you have loaded these programs as Windows applications and their icons appear in your Windows Applications Module window, you can click any of them to open the individual application.

Now let's take a look at each of the five PC Tools Windows programs in turn.

> Because Windows programs can be operated with a mouse or with key commands, both will be given in this chapter.

BACKUP FOR WINDOWS

The Backup program lets you backup data on your disk for several purposes:

• You can preserve all files on your disk by running full backups on a routine basis, say, every Friday afternoon.

• You can update your saved files by backing up only those files that have changed since the last time you ran Backup.

• You can backup related groups of files that work together; for instance, program files, configuration files, and text files for Ventura Publisher.

The Windows version of Backup is identical to its counterpart that runs under DOS, which is covered extensively in Chapter 17. The only difference is the way the program looks on screen.

To run Backup for Windows, click twice on the Backup icon. This opens the Central Point Backup main menu, which looks like Figure 18.4.

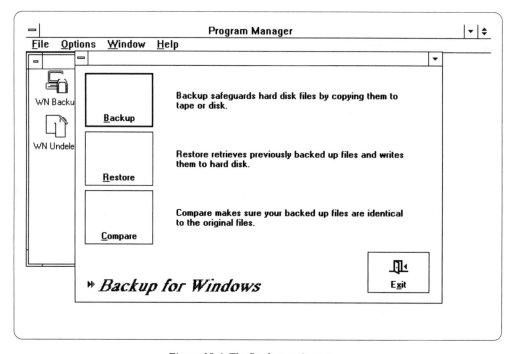

Figure 18.4. The Backup main menu.

The Backup for Windows main menu gives you four options:

Backup   Lets you run a backup according to your specifications or specifications saved in the setup file you want to use. Click on this or press [Alt]-[B] to move into the Central Point Backup screen for Windows, which looks like Figure 18.5.

Restore   Lets you restore one or more files from a backup disk or disks according to your specifications.

Compare   Lets you compare the files on a backup disk to original disk files.

Exit   Lets you exit the Central Point Backup main menu and return to your previous work.

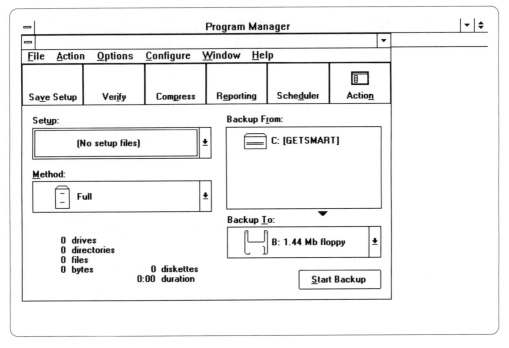

Figure 18.5. Central Point Backup screen for Windows

The six pull-down menus along the top of the window are File, Action, Options, Windows, Configure, and Help. Six function-key commands also appear on the screen—*Save Setup, Verify, Compress, Reporting, Scheduler,* and *Action*—as well as four settings, or fields—Setup, Method, Backup From, and Backup To.

Once you're finished running a backup, you can return to the main menu with four options:

Press: [Alt]-[N]

The Restore and Compare modules of Backup for Windows are similar to their counterparts that run under DOS. To look at the Restore screen:

Press: [Alt]-[R]

Figure 18.6 shows the Central Backup Restore screen for Windows.

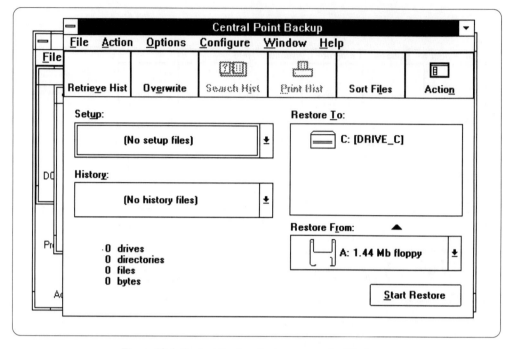

Figure 18.6. Central Backup Restore screen for Windows

Exit the Backup module and return to the Backup main menu:

Press: [Alt]-[F]

Press: [X]

UNDELETE FOR WINDOWS

You use the Undelete program to recover files and directories that have been deleted accidentally. The Windows version of Undelete lets you recover these files while working in Windows, though you aren't limited to recovering files and directories that were deleted while working in Windows.

It is easy to restore files and directories you've deleted accidentally, although there are all sort of peripheral issues that you might want to consider. For example, it is easier to recover some information if you generally run the other PC Tools programs that are described earlier in this book. Using these programs in conjunction with Undelete is described in Chapter 17.

If you accidentally format a disk that contains files you want to keep, try running the PC Tools program Unformat first, as it might restore some or all of the files; if it does not, then run Undelete under DOS or Windows to try to recover the files.

When you use Wipe to erase data on a disk, the data is lost forever. The Wipe program works by substituting repetitive or random characters for data characters on disk. It is designed to destroy data you don't want prying eyes to discover. It would be contradictory for Central Point to design a program that destroys data whose damage can be undone.

Before you start working with the Windows-based version of Undelete, you should understand some of the differences between the program when run under DOS and when run under Windows.

Running Undelete Under Windows versus DOS

While the general appearance of the Undelete program in Windows is similar to that in DOS, there are details on each screen that are quite different. First, the Windows version provides only three pull-down menus, while the DOS version provides an additional menu, Disk, which lets you scan disks for deleted files.

In the other three files—File, Options, and Help—some commands remain the same, but others are unique to the DOS or to the Windows version. Also, the Windows version assigns six buttons, while the DOS version assigns ten function keys. There are other, less significant, differences between the programs, but for most of your undeleting needs, either version will do.

Running Undelete Under Windows

To run the Windows version of Undelete, make sure Windows 3.0 is running, and that you are looking at the Windows Application Module window. Point at the Undelete icon and double click your mouse.

When the Undelete for Windows screen appears, it should look like Figure 18.7.

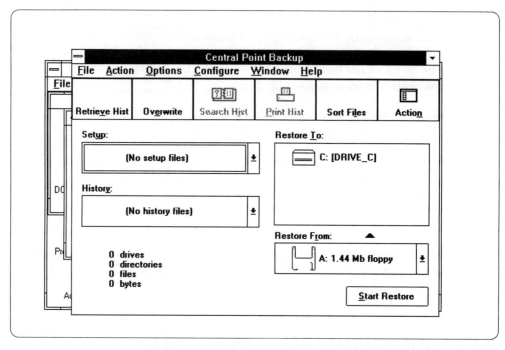

Figure 18.7. The Undelete for Windows screen

Each time you run the program, it scans the current drive for deleted file and directory names. If it finds any, it displays the information it finds about the file. For example, in Figure 18.7, files are marked *destroyed*, *good*, and *excellent*. These labels indicate your chances of recovering these files.

There are five buttons you can select on the Undelete screen:

Drive/Dir   Opens the Change Drive and Directory window, which lets you select another disk drive or directory to work with.

Find   Opens the Find Deleted File window, which lets you specify which deleted files you want to look for—a single file, files with common characteristics in their filenames, or a group of files that can be identified by their type, such as all Windows Write files or all zip files (files archived by the PKZIP archiving program).

Sort by   Lets you sort undeleted file by name, extension, size, deleted date and time, modified date and time, or condition.

Print   Lets you print the contents of a deleted file as long as you have installed a printer for Windows.

Info   Displays information about the currently highlighted file.

To exit the Undelete program for Windows:

   Press: [Alt]-[F4].

This returns you to wherever you were working before, most likely the Windows Applications window.

THE PROGRAM LAUNCHER

The Central Point Program Launcher lets you launch programs in Windows while working in another program.

Before you can use the Launcher, you must first load the program. You do this by pointing to the Launcher icon and double clicking your mouse.There is no Launcher screen, but if you look closely, you'll see the icon in the upper-left corner of your display terminal change in appearance. If you're viewing a color screen, it will change colors (most likely it will turn red). If you're viewing a monochrome screen, it will change shades. This means the Launcher is loaded. If you don't notice this change, and try to load the Launcher a second time, you'll be prompted that the Launcher is up and running.

Once the Launcher is running, you access it from the Windows Control menu. This menu is available in all Windows-based applications. To open the Windows Control menu:

   Press: [Alt]-[Spacebar]

The *Launcher* command is the bottom command on the menu. To open the Launcher menu:

   Press: [L]

 Or highlight the command and press [Enter]. Figure 18.8 shows the Launcher menu.

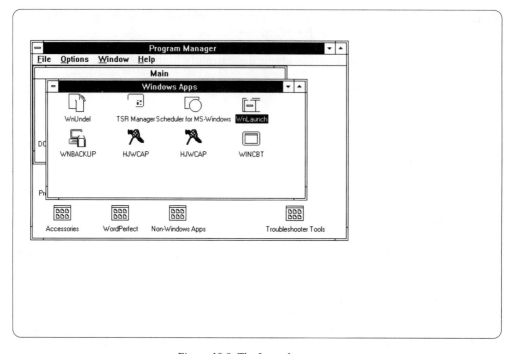

Figure 18.8. The Launcher menu

Once the Program Launcher has been configured, it will appear in any Windows Application Control menu.

To open the Control menu of a current Windows application:

> **Press:** [Alt]-[Spacebar]

Then:

> **Press:** [L]

This opens the Launcher menu, which gives you the following commands:

Undelete	Lets you run Undelete program.
Backup	Lets you run Backup program.
Configure	Lets you configure the Launcher to it can run other programs.
Run	Runs a program from the Launcher.

Remove Launcher   Removes Launcher from active status.

About Launcher   Provides rudimentary information about your version of Launcher.

Exit Windows   Closes Windows down completely.

The top section of the Launcher menu might contain different programs, depending upon how Launcher has been configured.

To go directly to the Undelete for Windows program, when the Launcher menu appears:

   Press: [U]

In a moment, the Undelete for Windows window will appear on your screen, and you can work with the program as you wish. As with all Windows applications, to close Undelete:

   Press: [Alt]-[F4]

Configuring the Launcher

You can configure the Launcher to display the names of other Windows application programs, and launch those programs by configuring the Launcher menu.

First, open the Launcher menu. Next, select the *Configure* command:

   Press: [C]

This opens the Configure Central Point Launcher window, as shown in Figure 18.9.

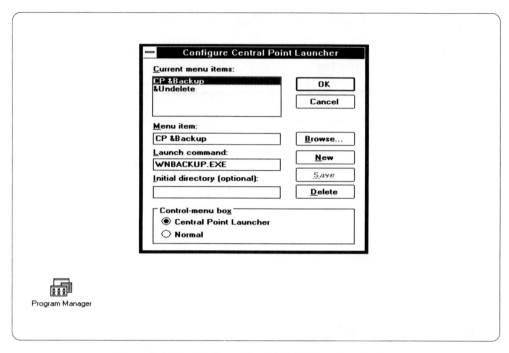

Figure 18.9. The Configure Central Point Launcher window

You use the fields in this window to insert the program name in the Launcher menu, to determine which key will actually launch the program, and to tell Windows where to find the file. Move through the fields by pressing [Tab].

Inserting the Scheduler Program

To insert the PC Tools Windows program Scheduler, first open the Control menu:

Press: [Alt]-[Spacebar]

Now, open the Launcher menu:

Press: [L]

Press [Tab] until the Menu Item field is highlighted, then:

Type: &SCHEDULER

Press: [Tab]

Don't forget to insert an ampersand; it makes *s* the hotkey for this command, which allows you to open the Scheduler program simply by pressing [S].

Highlight the Launch Command field, then:

Press: [Tab] three times

Type: C:\PCTOOLS\WNSCHEDL.EXE

Press [Esc] to close all menus. That's all there is to it. To double-check your work, open the Control menu, the Launcher menu, and the Scheduler program in turn:

Press: [Alt]-[Spacebar]

Press: [L]

Press: [S]

Once the Scheduler main menu appears, you can work with the program or return to your previous work by closing the Scheduler program.

You can use the Scheduler to load Windows programs other than Tools Windows programs. In the Configure Central Point Launcher window, enter the name of the program as you want to see it displayed on the Launcher menu; then select a hotkey. Make sure the path to the program filename is correctly specified.

You can use the *Configure* command to insert new programs, edit existing program information, and delete program entries. Just make sure that any program you want to insert is a Windows program (an appropriate .PIF file is available), and that you use a unique hotkey. For example, if you were to add Collage, the Windows image-capture program, it would be inefficient to use *C* as the hotkey, since this is already taken by the *Configure* command.

Other Launcher Commands

The bottom section of the Launcher menu also contains the commands:

Run   Lets you run a DOS application. Selecting this command opens the Run window, which lists the filenames in the current directory. You can switch directories and drives to list other filenames. When you find the filename you want to run under DOS (it must end in .EXE, .COM, or .BAT), highlight it and press [Enter].

Remove Launcher   Removes Launcher from activity after showing a warning prompt. When Launcher is no longer active, it won't appear as a selection on the Control menu. To reload Launcher, return to your Windows Application and press [Ctrl]-[Esc]. Select *Program Manager* and click on *Launcher*.

About Launcher   Displays information about your version of the Launcher.

Exit Windows   Displays a prompt asking whether you want to exit the current Windows session and return to any previous DOS applications.

You'll find the Launcher a handy tool for switching between Windows applications and DOS.

THE TSR MANAGER

The TSR Manager is a Windows program that lets you communicate with three PC Tools DOS programs:

VDefend   Anti-virus protection.

Commute   The electronic bridge between two computers.

Data Monitor   Six programs that monitor access to your data.

These programs must be loaded in resident mode for the TSR Manager to work. Since these are DOS programs and not Windows programs, and part of their purpose is to flash timely messages on your screen, these programs have to be managed correctly to respond while Windows is running.

When the TSR Manager window appears, it will display the icons of any of the three PC Tools programs that have already been loaded resident into DOS. It also contains one pull-down menu, Options, which contains these three commands:

Show Icon   Shows any icon that isn't yet displayed.

About TSR Manager   Provides more information about the TSR Manager.

Exit   Exits the TSR Manager program and returns you to your previous work.

Icons appear in the TSR Manager screen for the three programs that can be managed: VDefend, Data Monitor, and Commute. If more information on any of these programs is loaded, simply press the associated hot key to access it.

When you select *VDefend* ([V]), you're told that the program is loaded and will display a message about virus infection when any is detected.

When you select *Datamon* ([D]), the Central Point Data Monitor window will appear. This lets you enable or disable Directory lock and Write protection. For more information on these settings, see the section in Chapter 17 describing Data Monitor.

When you select *Commute* ([C]), you're told that the Commute program is loaded and will respond to any calls. You can also work in the Commute program.

When you exit the TSR Manager, you may see a warning that exiting the program could confuse the handling of any of the resident programs. To avoid such trouble, you should probably avoid closing the TSR Manager once you open it.

THE PROGRAM SCHEDULER

The Program Scheduler lets you set starting and stopping times for events for different Central Point programs. The four programs are:

Backup   Lets you schedule backups at preset intervals. You must specify which setup file to use and the day and time to run the backup. At least one setup file must exist in your PC Tools directory before you can schedule any sort of backup. Setup files store settings that control the parameters of the backup. This means you can run partial backups during the day to backup files that have changed since the last backup, and you can run full backups at the end of every day.

Commute   Lets you schedule communications between computers running the PC Tools Commute program. You must specify which script file to use and the day and time to begin the communications. Script files contain commands that control the communication parameters.

E-mail   Lets you set schedulers to automatically send and receive e-mail at scheduled times. Messages parked in your inbox (C:\PCTOOLS\INBOX) will be sent, and all mail received will be parked in your outbox (C:\PCTOOLS\OUTBOX). You can specify the time of day sending and receiving is started and stopped, and how often mail is handled.

DiskFix   Lets you schedule when to run the PC Tools DiskFix program. You can set a regular interval, or you can set a starting and stopping time. You should be careful when you run DiskFix while working in Windows, since Windows needs to know where specific files are on disk. DiskFix needs to move file data from one location to another when a section of disk surface goes bad. If this happens to a file that Windows is using, your computer will probably crash.

You can set start and stop schedules for any of these programs using the Scheduler. To do so, you must first load the Scheduler. Begin by clicking its icon. This opens the Scheduler window, which is shown in Figure 18.10.

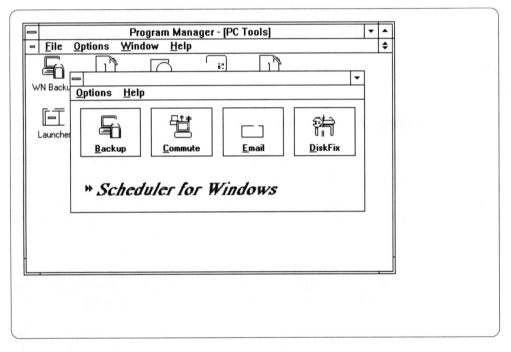

Figure 18.10. The Scheduler window

This shows the four buttons that lead to schedules for each program, as well as two pull-down menus, *Options* and *Help*.

To set a schedule for any of the four programs, press [Alt] and the letter key that begins the program name. For example, to set a set a schedule for Backup, press [Alt]-[B]. This opens the Backup Schedule window, which looks like Figure 18.11.

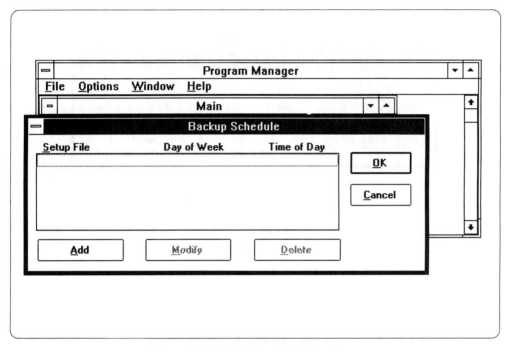

Figure 18.11. The Backup Schedule window

This window lets you specify three things about your schedule:

Setup File   Displays the name of a setup file created in the Backup program that will control the configuration and behavior of the Backup program when it is run by Scheduler.

Day of Week   Displays the days of the week when you want the schedule to be run.

Time of Day   Displays the times of day when you want Scheduler to run the Backup program.

To insert specific entries into these three slots, click the *Add* command, or press [Alt]-[A]. This opens the Add New Backup Schedule Item window, as shown in Figure 18.12.

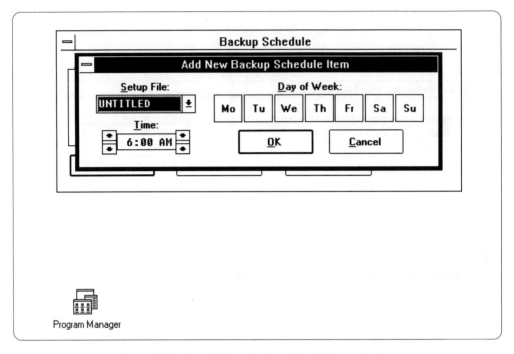

Figure 18.12. The Add New Backup Schedule Item window

The Setup File field displays the names of all the setup files it can find in your PC Tools directory. Next to that, you're given a button for each of the seven days of the week. Below the setup filenames, you're given the Time field, where you select times of the day to run Backup. You can work in increments as small as one minute.

Once you select the setup file to control Backup and the day and time you want it to run, click OK. This returns you to the Backup Schedule window, and inserts the information in the list. Once you've inserted an item into the list, you can modify or cancel it by highlighting the item you want to change, then selecting the *Modify or Delete* command. The Modify window is identical to the Add window.

You can set schedules for the other three programs in the same way, although there are some minor differences between the scheduling windows.

When you schedule *Commute Events*, you'll be asked to name a script file instead of a setup file. You're also given the option of toggling *Events* on or off.

When you schedule e-mail events, you can set schedules for sending and receiving mail. Figure 18.13 shows the Create E-Mail Schedule window.

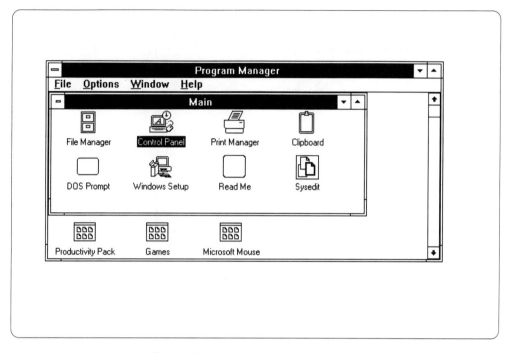

Figure 18.13. The Create E-Mail Schedule

Again, you can set time in one-minute increments. You can also toggle e-mail events off or on.

When you schedule DiskFix events, you can set how often DiskFix is run, starting and ending times, and the drives that will be checked. You can also toggle DiskFix *Events* on or off.

When you're finished with your work in the Scheduler, you can close it. You'll be shown a prompt asking if you want to OK the exit, cancel the exit, or minimize the performance of Scheduler. When you minimize Scheduler, you remove its appearance from your screen. It is still active, however, and stored for use. When the Scheduler has been minimized. you'll see its icon at the bottom of your screen, as shown in Figure 18.14. This reminds you that the Scheduler is working.

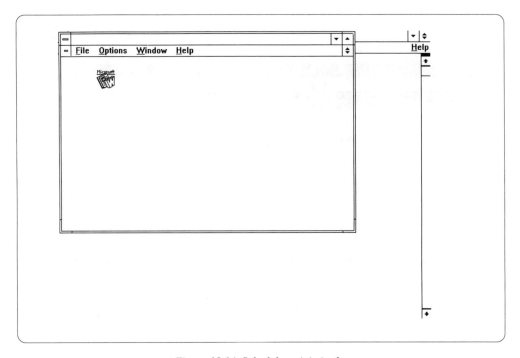

Figure 18.14. Scheduler minimized

Once you've set a schedule, you'll have to make sure the Scheduler is loaded. If you haven't set it to load automatically, you should load it manually each time you boot up. Simply open the program by clicking on the Scheduler icon, then minimize the program and continue with your other work.

Windows will probably become one of the most popular ways to display and manage your IBM PC programs, so even if you are not using it now, you will probably want to switch to it in the future. Therefore, the sooner you learn how to work with Windows programs, the better off you'll be.

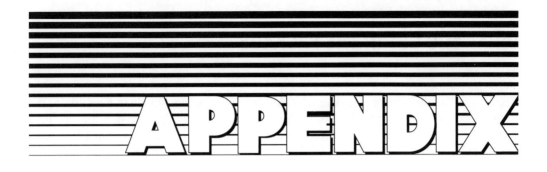

INSTALLING THE PROGRAMS

Installing PC TOOLS is easily done. Before you install the program, however, you should verify that you received everything you paid for. Then you should make back-up, or archival, copies of the disks that came with the package. This is your best protection against accidental damage to files.

WHAT YOU GET IN THE PACKAGE

The PC Tools Deluxe program comes with two sets of disks and three books.

The two sets of disks cover the sizes of disk media you are most likely to need: six 5.25-inch disks and three 3.5-inch disks. The same files are on both disks; they're just grouped differently in archived files, which you de-archive when you run PC Setup. Disk 1 in both sets contains the PCSETUP.EXE file you'll use to install the program.

PROGRAM FILES SUPPLIED ON DISK

Once you've run the PC Tools Install program and installed every PC Tools program, the files will be arranged in at least five directories on your hard disk: PCTOOLS, SYSTEM, DATA, SEND, INBOX, and OUTBOX.

If you already have a version of PC Tools on the same hard disk, you'll also have a sixth directory called OLDPCT. This directory contains all special files that apply to your version of PC Tools, such as your phonebook files (>TEL), script files (>SCR), and configuration files that control the way Desktop, PC Shell, and other PC Tools programs look and behave on your computer.

The SEND, INBOX, and OUTBOX directories will not contain any files until you start using the Notepads and Telecommunications modules to create, send, and receive e-mail.

MAKING ARCHIVAL COPIES

You should make backup copies, also called *archival* copies, of all disks you buy. The software copyright law allows this.

Making Copies on a Two-Floppy System

To make copies of the PC Tools Deluxe program disks on a two-floppy-disk drive, place the first original disk in drive A and a blank formatted disk in drive B. Now log onto the A drive:

Type: A

Press: [Enter]

526

When the A:\> prompt shows on the DOS command line, you can run the DOS program DISKCOPY:

Type: DISKCOPY A: B:

Press: [Enter]

The program will ask you to insert the disk you want to copy *from* into drive A and the disk that will be copied *to* into drive B. You should have already done this, but you might want to double-check now. When the disks are as they should be:

Press: [Enter]

This begins the disk copying process. When the first disk is copied, the program will ask if you want to copy any more:

Press: [Y]

Press: [Enter]

Next, the computer asks you to replace the first original disk with the second original disk in drive A, and insert a new blank formatted disk into drive B to receive the copied files. When you've done this:

Press: [Enter]

Continue this way until all the disks have been copied. You might want to make several sets of copies just for your own protection.

Making Copies on a Hard Disk

To make archival copies on a hard disk, first create a temporary directory that can hold each disk's files. Next copy the original disk files to the directory. Begin in your root directory, which appears each time you boot your computer.

Type: MD TEMP

Press: [Enter]

Next, log into this temporary directory:

Type: CD TEMP

Press: [Enter]

527

You're ready to begin the copying when your DOS prompt says C:\TEMP>. Place the first original disk in your floppy drive, presumably the A drive.

> **Type:** COPY A: *.*

> **Press:** [Enter]

This copies all the disk files to the hard disk. When the copying is complete, remove the original disk and replace it with a blank formatted floppy. To copy the files to a new floppy disk:

> **Type:** COPY *.* A:

> **Press:** [Enter]

When copying is complete, delete the first set of files. Make sure you're still working in the TEMP subdirectory on your hard drive.

> **Type:** DEL *.*

> **Press:** [Enter]

> **Press:** [Y]

Now repeat the procedure for each original disk. If you want to make several copies of disk sets, do so before you delete the hard-disk files.

Remember to mark clearly all disks and the names of the files they contain. Once you've installed the programs, place the original disks and copies in a safe location—preferably in two different locations. Some people put their most important disks in a fire-safe box or in their safety deposit box at the bank.

READING THE READ.ME FILE

You should read the contents of a simple text file called README.TXT for important new information about several aspects of the PC Tools programs. This file contains information that turned up too late to go into the manuals, and recently discovered facts about the program.

You can read the file using the Notepads Editor screen, unless you haven't yet installed Desktop Manager. If you can't wait until it is installed, you can either view the file using another printer or word processor, or print out the file using the DOS redirection command >PRN:

Type: TYPE README.ME>PRN

Press: [Enter]

Make sure your printer is turned on and contains paper.

INSTALLING THE PROGRAM

PC Tools Deluxe provides its own installation program, PCSETUP.EXE. This is a menu-driven full-screen program that requires little work on your part except to answer a series of questions. You run this program to copy and configure the various files you might want to use in your version of the PC Tools Deluxe program.

There are two versions of the Install program. One installs program files for the first time, and the other can be run periodically to fine-tune features of your PC Tools programs.

Installing PC Tools Programs for the First Time

There are several ways to install the program, and the installation of some files is optional. You can install the PC Tools programs using the default option settings, or you can configure them for various modes of operation. If you've never worked with the PC Tools Shell or Desktop utilities, the default configuration is probably best for you.

The installation program will walk you through a series of screens, asking you questions. Don't worry if some of the questions don't seem to make sense the first time you use PCSETUP. You can always go back and reconfigure the program to suit your needs.

To begin the configuration, place Disk 1 of either set of disks into drive A. To load the program PCSETUP.EXE:

Type: INSTALL

Press: [Enter]

If for some reason you want to cancel the installation at any point, press [Esc]. You can always start the program over and run through the steps quickly.

The first screen that appears looks like Figure A.1.

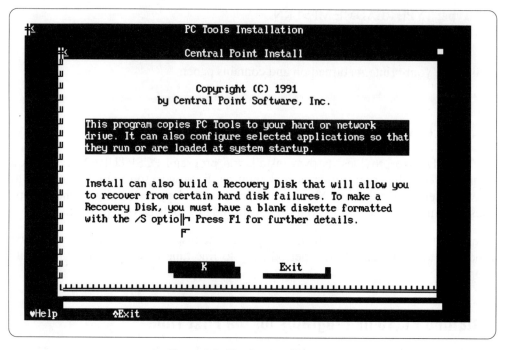

Figure A.1. The first Install screen

This first screen lets you select one of three ways to install the program:

1. Copy the files selectively (the ones you want to use) to a single personal computer and modify commands in your AUTOEXEC.BAT file.

2. Change a previous configuration by modifying your AUTOEXEC.BAT. You can use this feature to reconfigure for new applications you've installed on your hard disk, or you can modify the Applications menu on your own (described in Chapter 4).

3. Copy files to a computer on a network facility.

The rest of the program will walk you through similar screens where you can select your install options.

Fine-Tuning PC Tools Programs

Once you've installed the PC Tools programs onto your hard disk, the Install program is also copied to your hard disk but in a reduced version (the file size shrinks). You can run this program whenever you want to fine-tune aspects of your PC Tools programs.

Type: INSTALL

Press: [Enter]

> If your hard disk has another program called INSTALL (such as INSTALL.EXE, INSTALL.COM, or INSTALL.BAT), you should probably switch to your PCTOOLS directory before trying to run the PC Tools Install program.
>
> **Type:** CD\PCTOOLS
>
> **Press:** [Enter]
>
> Make sure you've logged onto your PCTOOLS directory (the name may appear after your prompt).
>
> As an alternative you could rename the PC Tools INSTALL.EXE program INST.EXE. Then all you have to do is type INST and press [Enter].

When the reduced version of the PC Tools Install program is up and running, your screen will look like Figure A.2.

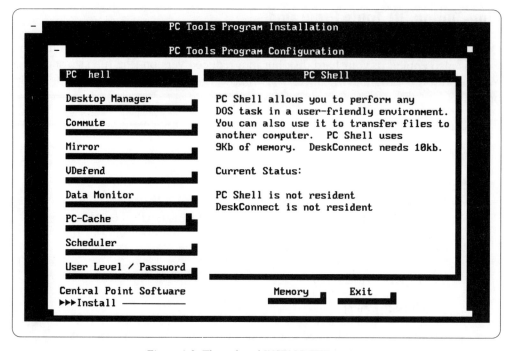

Figure A.2. The reduced INSTALL.EXE screen

Use the menu selections along the left side of the screen to adjust the way the eight PC Tools programs behave, and to set a password to run the programs and select one of three user levels.

The menu selection that's currently highlighted will appear on the right side of your screen:

PC Shell

Lets you determine whether to load PC Shell as a standard or resident program when you boot your computer, and whether to load the DeskConnect program. You can also have PC Shell search your hard disk for any new application programs to insert into your Program List menu.

Desktop Manager

Lets you determine whether to load Desktop Manager as resident when you boot up, whether to load Backtalk, and whether to load Fax Support. These last two programs always remain in the background, ready to serve when called upon.

Commute
Lets you determine whether to load the Commute program, which remains resident, upon boot up, or the COMMSML program, which takes less memory.

Mirror
Lets you determine whether to run the Mirror program upon boot up.

VDefend
Lets you determine whether to load the VDefend program, which remains resident, and if so, whether to load it using a command in your AUTOEXEC.BAT file or your CON-FIG.SYS file.

Data Monitor
Lets you determine whether to load various parts of the Data Monitor program, such as Delete Sentry, Delete Tracker, and so on.

PC-Cache
Lets you determine whether to load the PC Cache program, which is resident, and if so, whether to turn on the Enable Write Delay feature.

Scheduler
Lets you determine whether to load the Schedule program, which is resident.

User Level/Password
Lets you select between Beginner, Intermediate, and Advanced levels of operation for the CP Backup program and the PC Shell. You can also declare a password that controls access to these programs, if you want to use one.

Two commands at the bottom of the reduced Install Program screen lets you look at your potential memory usage and exit the program.

Memory
Displays a graphic chart for how your current memory will be used by the configuration options you've chosen in the Install screen.

Exit
Lets you exit the Install program and save or discard your changes. You can also review any changes that will be made to your CONFIG.SYS and AUTOEXEC.BAT files, and modify them if you want to.

TEST RUN

To make sure that you've installed the major programs correctly, reboot your computer:

> **Press:** [Ctrl]-[Alt]-[Del]

You might notice this time that it takes a bit longer for your computer to boot. This is because two new PC Tools programs are being run, and two others are being loaded into your computer's memory. A screen telling you that PC Shell is installed will appear, followed by a second screen that says PC Tools Desktop has been installed.

To open the Desktop menu:

> **Press:** [Ctrl]-[Spacebar]

If your screen changes to look like Figure A.3, Desktop is loaded properly.

Figure A.3. The Desktop main menu

Don't worry if your screen doesn't look exactly like Figure A.3. To return to the DOS prompt:

Press: [Esc]-[Spacebar]

To open PC Shell:

Press: [Ctrl]-[Esc]

You should see a message saying the system area is being checked. It takes longer than usual to open the PC Shell screen in resident mode the first time you use it, because the system area has to be read and recorded to the disk file PCSHELL.TRE. When it finally appears, your screen should look something like Figure A.4.

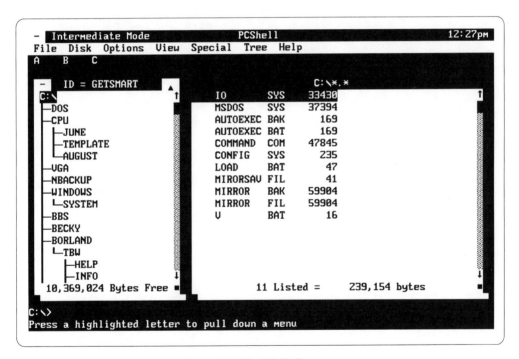

Figure A.4. The PC Shell screen

To close PC Shell:

Press: [Ctrl]-[Esc]

PC Tools Deluxe should now be properly installed.

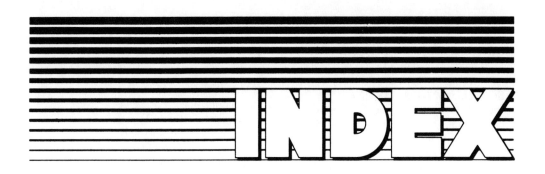

Index

Index

in View program, 478
in Wipe program, 487

G

Go To command, in Notepads, 150
graphical user interfaces (GUIs), 32
groups, in Appointment Scheduler, 283-287

H

hard disks
Compress program for, 461-466
CP Backup program for, 490-496
for Microsoft Windows, 507-510
Directory Maintenance program for, 471-476
DiskFix program for, 447-450
installing PC Tools Deluxe on, 529-530
making archival copies of PC Tools Deluxe disks using, 527-528
PC Format program for, 479-481
System Information module for, 469-471
Unformat program for, 459-451
VDefend program for, 500
hardwire connections between computers, 362
headers, 159-160
headlines, 185, 189-195
Help facilities
in Desktop Manager, 9-12
in PC Shell, 39-40
in System Information module, 94
Help menu, 94-95
Hex Editor, 63-65
hiding database records, 241-242
hotkeys, 7
in Clipboard, 172
conflicts between TSR programs over, 28
resetting, 125-127

I

INKILL.BAT program, 9
inserting
items on To-Do list, 294-295
in Notepads, 150
insert mode, 139
installation of PC Tools Deluxe, 525-535
for Microsoft Windows, 504-507
Install program, 488, 504

K

keyboards, 489
KILL.BAT program, 8, 9, 28, 380

L

labels, printing, 261-263
launching programs, 111-115
in Microsoft Windows, 513-518
learn mode, for macros, 398-403
lists, printing databases as, 258-260
logging onto CPS BBS, 375-376
Lotus 1-2-3, 450-452

M

macros, 383, 392-395
commands for, 397-398
learn mode to build, 398-403
Macros Editor for, 384-386
printer control, 160-161, 403-404
in SAMPLE.PRO file, 387-392
saving and activating, 395-396
used with Appointment Scheduler, 299-300
Macros Editor, 384-386
learn mode in, 398-403
MCI Mail, 165, 166, 299-300, 351-353, 355-356

script files for, 363-365
  CPS.SCR, 366-370
  creating, 374-379
  MCI.SCR, 371-374
Telecommunications module, 301
  CPS.SCR script file used in, 366-370
  for direct telephone links, 360-362
  for electronic mail, 322-325
  for fax transmissions, 325-333
  modems and, 302-306
  On-Line screen in, 313-317
  phonebooks for
    creating, 317-319
    entries in, 306-313
  screen in, 302
TELECOM.DBF file for, 319-322
telephones
  Autodial feature, 268-271
  hotkeys for, 125-127
  with Databases module, 268-271
  direct links using, 360-362
.TEL file extension, 302, 317
Text Viewer, 84-85
time
  changing, 87-88
  macro to insert, 398
.TM file extension, 274
To-Do list, 294-296
TRANSFER.LOG file, 382
transferring database records, 237-239
Tree List window, 32
Tree menu, 94
TSR (terminate-and-stay-resident)
    programs, 4
  BACKTALK.EXE as, 380-381
  PC Shell as, 27-28
  PC Tools Deluxe as, 6-8
  TSR Manager program for, for Windows,
    3, 518-519
  see also resident programs
.TXT file extension, 132

U

Undelete program, 2, 452-459
  for Microsoft Windows, 510-513
undeleting database records, 240
Unformat program, 2, 452-459
uploading files, 346-347
user levels, 77-79
  in CP Backup program, 495-496
Utilities command, 124
utility programs, 445-447
  Commute, 496-499
  Memory Information, 500-502
  for Microsoft Windows, 504
    Backup, 507-510
    installing, 504-507
    Program Launcher, 513-518
    Program Scheduler, 519-524
    TSR Manager, 518-519
    Undelete, 510-513
  recovery tools
    DiskFix, 447-450
    File Fix, 450-452
    Undelete, 452-459
    Unformat, 459-461
  security tools
    Data Monitor, 485-486
    PC Secure, 482-484
    Wipe, 486-487
  setup tools
    CP Backup, 490-496
    Install, 488
    PC Config, 488-490
  system tools
    Compress, 461-466
    Directory Maintenance, 471-476
    File Find, 466-469
    PC Format, 479-481
  System Information, 469-471
  View, 477-478
  VDefend, 500
  Windows tools, 488